GENOCIDE IN IRAQ
Volume II

VOLUME II

GENOCIDE IN IRAQ

THE OBLITERATION
OF A MODERN STATE

BY

ABDUL HAQ AL-ANI
& TARIK AL-ANI

CLARITY PRESS, INC.

Clarity Press, Inc.
Ste. 469, 3277 Roswell Rd. NE
Atlanta, GA. 30305 , USA
http://www.claritypress.com

We dedicate this book to the memory of our parents.

ACKNOWLEDGMENTS

We would like to acknowledge with gratitude the contribution of our editor Diana G. Collier, Joanne Baker and James Thring who provided us with encouragement, editing, correction and proof reading. Any error or failure in presentation is completely ours.

TABLE OF CONTENTS

Chapter 1
The Imperialist Design for Iraq: A New Strategy for the Middle East
    Western Conquests in the Arab World / 10
    Containing Iraq / 12
    Sykes-Picot Agreement / 13
    Successful or Failed Nation-State / 15
    Palestine, The Jewish Problem and Zionism / 16
    Evolution of a New Vision / 17
    New Imperialist Strategy / 19

Chapter 2
Iraq on the Eve of the 2003 Invasion / 24
    Britain's Plans for Iraq / 24
    Qasim's Rule / 26
    The Ba'ath Rule / 29
    Saddam's Rule / 31
    The Imperialists' Manipulation of Iraq and Iran / 33
    Events Leading to the Invasion of Kuwait / 36
    The First Invasion of Iraq in 1991 / 37
    The Genocidal Sanctions / 38

Chapter 3
Preparation for the Invasion / 39
    The Iraq Liberation Act / 39
    The Sanctions Committee / 44
    The Project for the New American Century / 45
    Post 9/11 / 48
    Future of Iraq Project / 52
    Regular Aerial Bombardment / 55
    Dossier of Lies and Fabrications / 56

Chapter 4
The Shock and Awe Invasion / 61
    Preparing for the Invasion / 68
    The Invasion / 71

Chapter 5
The Failure of the Security Council / 82
  Anomalies of the UN Charter / 83
  Security Council Resolutions on Iraq
      Prior to the 2003 Invasion / 85
  Security Council Failing to Act After the 2003 Invasion / 86
  Security Council Facilitating Crime / 90
  Reforming the United Nations / 97

Chapter 6
Bremer Dismantles Iraq / 100
  Invading Iraq / 101
  Summary of International Law Principles on Occupation / 103
  CPA Actions / 104
  Eliminating Iraq's Defense System / 107
  Militia Forces / 109
  Destroying Iraq's Military Industry / 110
  Converting Iraq from Socialism
      to the Neoliberal "Free Market" / 111
  Legal and Judicial Restructuring / 117
  Development Fund for Iraq / 122

Chapter 7
Instituting Federalism:
Planting the Seeds of Ethnic and Sectarian Division / 127
  Enter General Garner / 127
  Appointing Paul Bremer / 128
  De-Ba'athification / 129
  Dissolving the Army / Creating a New Army / 131
  The Transitional Government / 134
  The Governing Council / 135
  The Cabinet / 137
  The Interim Iraqi Constitution / 137
  The Transitional Administrative Law (TAL) / 138
  The Interim Iraqi Government / 142
  The Transitional National Assembly / 144
  Drafting the Permanent Constitution / 145
      1. Abolishing Iraq's Arab Identity / 146
      2. The Federal Nature of the State / 147
      3. The Region of Kurdistan / 150
      4. Oil and Gas / 150
      5. Islam and Democracy / 151
      6. Amending the Constitution / 151

Chapter 8
The Destruction Continues / 153
        The Destruction Was Intended / 153
        Killing, Torture and Displacement / 158
        Cultural Cleansing / 168
        Cultural Genocide / 170
        Health and WMD / 174
        Children and Education / 182
                Psychological Problems / 183
                Malnutrition / 183
                Child Labour / 184
                Drug Abuse / 184
                Education / 184
                Disabilities in Children / 187
                Child Mortality / 188
        Women / 189
        The Grab for Iraq's Oil / 193
        Utilities / 199
        Water / 203

Chapter 9
The Right of Remedy / 208
        The Inviolability of Security Council Resolutions / 208
        The Crime of Aggression / 210
        Crimes in Using WMD / 212
        Crimes Against Humanity / 213
        Crimes That Breach Basic Human Rights / 215

Appendix I / 221

Appendix II / 225

Endnotes / 229

Index / 271

THE IMPERIALIST DESIGN FOR IRAQ

A NEW STRATEGY FOR THE MIDDLE EAST

Western Conquests in the Arab World

No serious work, in our view, has been undertaken to explain the Western European[1] constant determination to conquer and subjugate the Arab World. While we do not claim to address this lacuna, it remains a fact that the West has, over the last millennia, demonstrated that desire in the form of waves of conquests, invasions and occupations. The justifications for such violence were only fabricated later to avoid divulging the ulterior motive.

Long before the concept of the nation-state took hold of European thinking, the crusaders settled the west coast of Greater Syria using the propaganda of religious expeditionary wars and Christian entitlement, due to it being the birthplace of Jesus.[2] The campaign had little if anything to do with Christianity and everything to do with power and conquest. It was no more religious than the attempt by the Ottomans to extend their empire into the Balkans. The crusades were a unique experiment in conquest, the like of which had not been seen before. This assemblage between 1095 and 1291 of armies from so many different countries to invade that part of the Arab world set a precedent. It was repeated in 1991 when almost all the countries of the West took part in the war on Iraq.[3] Between the crusades and the invasion of Iraq in 1991, no other similar Western expedition was carried out with such zealous, destructive and deadly barbarity. This in itself should raise questions!

The creation of the crusaders enclave on the Eastern Mediterranean demonstrated the existence of another phenomenon, namely that of the intention, asserted as a right, of Europeans to settle any part of world and, if necessary, cleanse it of its original inhabitants.[4] After the crusades, Europeans—mainly Anglo-Saxon, French, Spanish and

Portuguese—went on to cleanse the Americas and Australia totally, and New Zealand, South Africa and Palestine partially. This "right" has become so entrenched in the Western psyche that very few Westerners bother even to question it. It is this self-appointed 'right' which lies behind many of the tragedies of the last five centuries and which has baffled many peoples of the world, including the Arabs. Why do Westerners feel such a sense of superiority that permits them to commit all these atrocities against innocent, peaceful people, who have done them no harm, and justify them as civilizing missions?

> The paradox of the West lies in its ability to produce universals, to raise them to the level of absolute, and to violate in an extraordinarily systematic way the principles that it derives from them, while still feeling the need to develop theoretical justifications for those violations.[5]

The Zionists of the twentieth century have gone a step further by labelling anyone 'anti-Semitic' who questions their 'God-given' right to the land of Palestine.

The disintegration of the crusader's settlement in 1291 did not eliminate their will to conquer the Arab World because the knights who returned from Palestine set up their Temple,[6] the Masonic order,[7] and a few other secret organizations whose objective had always been the rebuilding of the Temple in Palestine which could only be done through conquest and settlements. However, for a few centuries, actual implementation was not achieved for several reasons, not least of all the power and ascendancy of the Ottoman Empire, which was not simply securing most of the Arab World but was in fact encroaching on mainland Europe itself.[8]

This dormant will to conquer the Arab World was reactivated slowly when the grip of the Ottomans began to wane. The Portuguese were the first to come to the shore of Southern Arabia and encroached on the rule of Muscat.[9] They were followed by the Dutch[10] and then finally by the British who came at the opportune time as the Ottoman Empire was really in demise.[11]

Arabia has a very special position, in that it hosts the most sacred places for Muslims throughout the world. It is for that reason that it has never been overtly invaded. British Imperialists realized this sensitive nature of Arabia and dealt with it cleverly to ensure that it was subdued without need for actual occupation. Towards the end of the eighteenth century, they managed to form an alliance between Ibn Saud and Ibn Abdul-Wahhab.[12] The former was a simple, but ambitious Bedouin from Najd, but the latter was an astute member of the clergy, who disappeared for some seven years and returned with a new religious message which claimed to revive the Hanbali sect of Islam, which had already been resurrected by Ibn Taimiya some 450 years earlier.[13] This alliance secured a division of power between the families of both men so that political power rested with the descendants of Ibn Saud while religious authority rested with the descendants of Ibn Abdul-Wahhab (Ãl ash-Sheikh as they are called today). The fact that this alliance has survived for over two hundred years only shows how successful the British have been. It guaranteed that Arabia, and all that it represents for Muslims worldwide, remained in the Imperialist camp. We shall show later in the book how Arabia came to play a major role in assisting Imperialism in controlling Iraq.

In 1830 France invaded Algeria, occupied it and started to settle it.[14] The French settlers in Algeria not only treated Algerians as second-class citizens and transformed the whole country into a vineyard producing good French wine, but also insisted that Algeria was an integral part of France. This was not an event of ancient history. The French settlers and part of the French army fought for this up to 1962 when they were forced by the heroic '1 Million Martyrs' Revolution' to relinquish their hold.[15] On the Eastern Mediterranean, France stepped in as the Ottoman rule began to wane and secured a role in running the affairs of the Christians of Greater Syria.[16] This right of action granted to the French led automatically to the division of Greater Syria after WWI and Greater Lebanon was created to be a "safe haven" for the Maronite population of the Mutasarrifia (Ottoman administrative unit) of Mount Lebanon.[17] Even today, the French feel they have a divine right to interfere in Lebanese internal affairs and politics.[18] In the beginning of April 2013, President Francois Hollande hailed the effort by Lebanese President Suleiman to form a new government and prepare for the next elections.[19]

We shall not give more examples of the policy of Western determination to conquer the Arab World, subdue it and subjugate its people to demeaning status, because this is not the intention of this book. We believe that the examples cited above suffice to expose the strategy.

Containing Iraq

The British encroachment on the Eastern coast of Arabia started in the early days of the 18th century in the form of the activities of the East India Company, which was a tool of British colonization.[20] The British were aware of the political and social realities in the area. At no time in history has there been any political entity on the East coast of Arabia between Basrah of Iraq and Muscat. The official administrative records of the Ottoman Empire in 1913 show that the political authority of the *Wali* (Governor) of Basrah extended down the Eastern coast of the Persian Gulf up to the governorate of the Sultan of Muscat whose authority covered the coast of Oman. This corresponds to parts of today's United Arab Emirates (UAE).[21]

But lobbies in the British hierarchy, predicting the fall of the Ottoman Empire as an historical inevitability, were already planning to contain Iraq. They knew that there was little they could do to prevent Iraq becoming a political reality to be reckoned with, but they were determined to strangle it by denying it access to its natural port on the deep waters of the Persian Gulf in today's Kuwait.[22]

There are several examples that prove British awareness of the facts. We shall cite three of them here:

1. *Warba and Bubyan*: As the British wanted to ensure Iraq's strangulation, they needed evidence to put to the Ottomans to justify detaching the two islands of Warba and Bubyan from Basrah and annexing them to the enclave under British authority in Kuwait. They asked the Sheikh to present evidence of any of his people having inhabited these islands. When none was found, the British decided not to raise the matter again with Ottomans.[23]

2. *Qasim's Claim:* When General Qasim of Iraq declared in 1961 that Kuwait was part of Iraq, the British Ambassador in Lebanon wrote to the Foreign Office in London that the danger of Qasim's claim was that he might go on to claim other parts of old Basrah which were then part of new political entities.[24]

3. *Lansdowne Memo:* The best exposure of British policy on Iraq at the beginning of the 20th century is given in the memo written in 1902 by Marquess Lansdowne, the then Foreign Secretary. Its significance is seen from reading it in its entirety. We are thus presenting it in full in Appendix I. Its main admission is that the British did not in reality recognize any authority of the sheikh of Kuwait and were burdened by his never-ending demands. The British were only interested in using him to secure their interests and if these interests meant granting him certain rights, so be it. Equally, if it did not suit them, they denied his requests. There were no questions of rights based on principles as some were arguing some ninety years later.[25]

Sykes-Picot Agreement

On the eve of WWI, British Ambassador McMahon had promised the Sheriff of Mecca that the British would support a united Arab state if the Arabs supported the British attack on the Ottomans. However, the truth of the matter is that Britain and France had quite different plans for the region. British and French diplomats, Sir Mark Sykes and François Georges-Picot, were drafting the agreement that drew up the division of spoils of war between the two colonial powers.[26] The agreement conjured up two new geographical entities on the nation-state model arguing that each of its constituents formed a homogenous mixture of people who could form a state. The agreement between the UK and France was later amended, in that the borders were drawn between the new Lebanon and mandated Palestine to suit the interests of both sides.[27]

This was a deviation from the religious nature of the previous states that had prevailed in the area over some sixteen centuries. The colonialists could not have hoped for a better state of affairs. The area was agonizing under the burden of the corrupt and aging Islamic rule of the Ottomans. Most of the peoples under the Ottoman rule, including the Turkish people themselves, were at that time aspiring to be free of the archaic so-called Sharia law. The only option that seemed possible was a series of nation states. However, behind this façade of civilized state building, the British/French agreement concealed a sinister agenda, which could be concluded from the following facts:

1. Iraq was denied its outlet to the deep water of the Gulf with the separation of Kuwait – even beyond the borders that Lansdowne had been willing to concede in 1902.

2. The islands which controlled Iraq's access to the Gulf and which had no value in themselves were annexed to the protectorate of Kuwait under British control. This was before the discovery of oil, so this annexation was probably not intended to sever this resource from the bulk of the Arab masses.

3. In a calculated attempt to eradicate the concept of Greater Syria, which had existed from the Roman times, the region was divided between British and French control.

4. Palestine was put under British mandate with the intention of creating a homeland for the Jewish people. This was in complete disregard of the Palestinians, but accorded with the Western 'right' to settle any land they chose even if it was to the detriment of its native inhabitants. This design was confirmed a year later in the Balfour Declaration.[28]

5. A new political entity was created on the east side of the river Jordan so that it could become the home of the Palestinians once the Jewish state was formed.[29] It should be remembered that what the Zionists are saying today about Palestine being a fully Jewish state is not a new innovation, but part of the original plan of 1917 as set out by Hertzl in 1894 in *Das Judenstaat*.[30]

6. The French paralleled the British success in Palestine when they extended their control over Lebanon which they had secured from the Ottomans long before the latter's demise and set up the most bizarre republic in the world. Lebanon, which has been hailed as a unique republic in the Middle East, is a sectarian state riddled with corruption. Politics are conducted by deals behind closed doors, with politicians simply agreeing on their share in the proceeds of this corruption, as in so many 'western' democracies. It suffices to say that even today this so-called democracy cannot select its Prime Minister without the consent of the despotic regime in Saudi Arabia![31]

Successful or Failed Nation-State

The nation states created post WWI did not turn out to be quite what the imperialists had hoped for. Despite the divisions and artificial borders, it soon became apparent that the outcome did not look promising for securing the imperialist interests in the Arab world. Between the two World Wars a new generation of aspiring Arabs was born. Many of them acquired education, knowledge and information, which opened their minds and led them to question the status quo. They became disillusioned with the puppet governments installed by the imperialists, which did little more than rubber stamp the orders of their masters and allow their retention of military bases, granting them cheap sources of energy and consumer markets for their products.

This process of awareness among the new generation of military officers and intelligentsia turned into revolutionary actions after the end of WWII. The most significant events may be summarized as follows:

1. The Military coup in Egypt in 1952 ousting King Farouk and the rise of Gemal Abdul-Nassir.[32]

2. The nationalization of the Suez Canal by Nassir.[33]

3. The failure in 1956 of the military invasion of Egypt by Britain, France and Israel.[34]

4. The military coup in Iraq in 1958 ousting the monarchy and dissolving the Baghdad Pact which was created between Iraq, Turkey, Pakistan and Iran under UK/US control.[35]

5. The creation in 1958 of the first United Arab Republic between Syria and Egypt.[36]

6. The first measure towards the nationalization of Iraq oil in

Law no. 80 (1961) taking away 99.5% of the IPC's ownership and establishing an Iraqi national oil company to oversee the export of Iraqi oil.[37]

7. The victory of the Algerian revolution on 5 July 1962 and the end of the French settlements in North Africa.[38]

8. The ascendancy and victory of the Ba'ath Arab nationalist movement in Iraq and Syria.[39]

9. The Libyan People's Revolution in 1969 and the rise of Mua'mmar Al-Ghaddafi.[40]

The Western imperialists did not stand idly by as the plans they had worked on for over a century looked shaky. First, they encouraged more Jews to settle in Palestine and eventually in 1947 handed over the country to the powerful Jewish army to set up the state of Israel to the detriment of the indigenous inhabitants of the land. Second, they invaded Egypt in 1956 following the nationalization of the Suez Canal hoping that such an invasion would bring down the rule of Nassir. Third, in 1961, they conspired to and succeeded in dissolving the United Arab Republic formed by Egypt and Syria. Fourth, they encouraged and assisted the armed rebellion of the Kurds in Iraq which would go on to destabilize Iraq and contribute to many catastrophic actions that ended up in the *de facto* division of Iraq.[41] Fifthly, they set out to create more artificial statelets along the Western coast of the Persian Gulf.[42] The purpose of setting up such entities served the imperialists' interests in securing cheap supplies of oil and gas; controlling its distribution to other parts of the world; maintaining military bases in the Arabian Peninsula; and creating consumer markets for their products, whilst still enabling their claim that these statelets were acting as sovereign states.

Palestine, the Jewish Problem and Zionism

Although the creation of the State of Israel is not the subject of this book, it is relevant to consider what part of the imperialist strategy it served. It is no secret that Europe had had a Jewish problem and many European cities had Jewish ghettos. Why this problem arose and who did what, is not relevant to our argument. It suffices to say that many Europeans were eager to remove the Jewish problem whenever and however possible. The Zionist movement in its early days considered the idea of creating a Jewish home in several parts of the world before opting for Palestine.[43]

While Europeans were considering what avenues were available to solve the Jewish problem in Europe, Britain was pondering the dangerous precedent created by Muhmmad Ali of Egypt by sending his army into Syria. The British expressed their alarm at the possibility of a union being formed between Syria and Egypt.[44] When Palestine was put under mandate it dawned on the British imperialists that it was possible to achieve both objectives of solving the Jewish problem and at the same time creating a physical barrier between Egypt and Syria via the establishment of a Jewish state in Palestine. The efficacy of this was tested in 1961 with the conspiracy in Syria to sever Syria from the United Arab Republic. It was by then physically impossible for Egypt to send army units to put down that rebellion.

Zionism is an active political movement with a clear ideology. Accordingly it has worked hard over the last century to exploit events to its advantage. Its cooperation with Nazism towards that end is very well documented.[45] Although Zionism started with the meagre pretence of being a movement aspiring to protect the Jews and save them from persecution, it has since become the most powerful political player in the world. In short the Zionist movement, which a hundred years ago looked deceptively like a movement subservient to imperialism, has today become the worst manifestation of imperialism. Yesterday's imperialists are themselves subservient to Zionism, and the Zionist-controlled capitalist system works to forward the Zionist political agenda. It is now a declared purpose of Zionism to convert all of Palestine into a purely Jewish state.[46] How many so-called liberals in the West have come out publicly to denounce this strategy as being totally unacceptable for the principles of liberal democracy on which Europe has been lecturing the rest of the world for the last century? The answer is: not many[47]. The reason is that Zionism has become so powerful that even the so-called liberals are too intimidated to come out against it. In short Zionist imperialism has also become the ultimate intellectual dictatorship.

Evolution of New Western Vision

The Western strategy for the Arab world, based on conquest and subjugation, has not changed over the last two hundred years. It was summed up by a British Foreign Secretary in 1949 as follows:

> British interests in the Middle East ... have changed little in the past 200 years and are as valid today as they were in the time of Napoleon. Today they are also, to a very large extent, the interests of the whole western world. The Middle East is a bridge between Asia and Africa and a road between the Mediterranean Sea and the Indian Ocean ... Oil has given the Middle East a new and dangerous value, but geography is still the master.[48]

It has been shown that the Western imperialists (old and new) soon discovered that the nation-state model was not working as hoped and new revolutionary movements were born that challenged the security of their interests in the region. To discredit the new revolutionary regimes in Egypt, Iraq, Syria, Algeria and Libya, the imperialists repeatedly pointed out the lack of democracy in these states. However, the question that they hoped no one would ask and which the Western media makes sure is never asked is about the lack of democracy in the despotic regimes in Arabia, the Gulf and North Africa that the West fully supports.

When the West realized the failure of the plan to set up small nation-states, which were meant initially to block any attempt at Arab unity, it had to come up with a new strategy. One measure alluded to earlier was the setting up of statelets in the Gulf with the objective of having them assume a leading role in the Arab world through their monetary strength.

The second and no less significant measure was the support for the Islamic movements that started with support of the Muslim Brotherhood in Egypt (MBE). The MBE, which was created in Egypt in 1928,[49] did not seriously oppose the monarchy in Egypt but as soon as Nassir took power they not only opposed his nationalist rule but also attempted to assassinate him in 1954.[50]

In Syria the imperialists supported the Muslim Brotherhood of Syria (MBS) against the nationalist Ba'ath regime in its first military uprising of 1982.[51] The crushing of the MBS which followed lost them a generation before they could re-launch a more vicious and better organized second attempt in 2011.[52]

In Libya the nationalist movement of Ghaddafi was causing trouble not only in Libya itself, but also in neighbouring African states. There was little political dissent in Libya, but soon the imperialists with the support of the now powerful Gulf rulers managed to support the weak Islamic movement in an uprising and the West sent in their destruction machine (NATO) to finish off the regime. Libya has been left in ruins and is now in the grip of armed factions and primitive tribal affiliations.[53]

In Iraq very similar tactics were employed. We will discuss how Islam was manipulated both to destroy the Ba'ath rule and then to turn Muslims against each other over sectarian differences. It suffices here to state that the formidable grip the Ba'athists had on Iraq was opposed by the Westerners through the direct support of Islamic movements in Iraq. During the years of sanctions, 1990 to 2003, the imperialists extended their support to religious parties in Iraq and maintained continuous contacts and meetings until the invasion and occupation of Iraq, when the leaders of these religious movements were brought in to rule Iraq. The Shi'ia Da'wa Party (DP) had regular weekly meetings with the Iraq desk at the Foreign Office, which is manned by an MI6 intelligence officer. Ibrahim Al-Ja'fari, who represented the DP in these meetings, later became Iraq's Prime Minster. The Sunni Muslim Brotherhood of Iraq (MBI) was represented in the Governing Council by Mohsen Abdel Hamid, while Hajim al-Hassani, from the same party who came with the Americans from California, later became speaker of Iraq's new parliament.[54] The so-called Prime Minister of the Syrian opposition in exile today is also an American citizen.[55]

New Imperialist Strategy

The Western Imperialists realized that the nation state had resulted in the birth of strong Arab nationalist movements in the form of Nassir and the Ba'ath. Both the Nassirites and the Ba'athists were very nationalistic, socialist and consequently anti-capitalists and anti-Imperialists. Containing them turned out to be very difficult. Their influence soon spread over the rest of the Arab world with reverberations in North Africa (leading to Ghaddafi assuming power in Libya) and uprisings in Southern Arabia to name only a few. The other powerful political movements in these countries were allied with communism but they were no less antagonistic to the imperialists design than the Arab nationalists.

The imperialists had to change strategy and fight Arab Nationalism with new tools. Although very early on they had supported Islamic movements by way of opposing Arab nationalist regimes, they did not consider these movements to be a viable alternative to rule these states. The change in strategy, which came later, was born out of new realizations and appeared to be the only possible means to serve the imperialist design.

Firstly, they came to realize that political Islam was no threat to their interests. They took comfort in observing that all the clergies in the puppet regimes in the Arabian Peninsula were ensuring that the masses would obey their despotic rulers in accordance with religious strictures, despite their waste of national assets, and with the presence of foreign troops in the region. These same clergies were ready to find religious justification for any measures these rulers implemented on behalf of the imperialists, from tacit peace with Israel to attacking and destroying a Muslim state. In this atmosphere, the imperialists did not feel under any pressure to find justifications for their actions. When the Arab Governments were themselves calling for the destruction of Iraq, there was little need for Bush and Blair to explain their actions.[56]

Secondly, the rise of political Islam in Turkey formed the greatest sign of hope for the Western imperialists. When the Muslim Ottoman Empire officially ended in 1924, the West was apprehensive about a revival of Islamic sentiment in the newly formed Turkey and thus went on to support the regime of Atatürk and his followers. But the new political Islamic movement that surfaced in the 1990s appeared to pose no such dangers to Western imperialist interests. It was during the rule of the Islamic leader Erbekan that Turkey, in 1996, entered into a Military Industry Cooperation Agreement with Israel, which was in turn instrumental to the signing of "a secret agreement" with Israel Military Industries to update its tank division and modernize its helicopter fleet and its F-4 and F-5 combat planes. In turn, the two countries entered into negotiations with a view to establishing a Free Trade Agreement, which came into operation in 2000. In 1997, Israel and Turkey launched "A Strategic Dialogue" involving a bi-annual process of high-level military consultations by the respective deputy chiefs of staff.[57] Islamic Turkey has been more attached to NATO and Europe than Atatürk's Turkey, as some of the leaders of the latter had some nationalist sentiments, which were not always in line with the designs of the West.

Thirdly and more importantly it became clear that the West could not argue for the viability of a multi-cultural nation-state in the Middle East while Zionism was declaring its intentions of having a purely Jewish state in Palestine. A purely religious state would be incompatible with the notion of a nation-state based on equality and liberty which the West thought it was going to market in the Middle East. When this stage was reached in Israel, it was time for the new strategy based on a Middle East composed of small statelets on sectarian or ethnic divisions. Each and every one of these newly formed statelets would compete to secure protection from the imperialists by offering more and more cooperation. The winner in all this would be the Jewish state of Israel, enjoying established legitimacy as one among many sectarian entities on the one hand while, on the other hand being the most powerful and only nuclear power among them. That would mark the end of history in the Arab world, owing to the success of Zionism.[58]

The early signs of this new strategy emerged when it was implemented in Iraq in the 1990s when Saddam Hussein, in the midst of his despair, was convinced to use Islam to rally support from people inside and outside Iraq. He initiated the so-called 'Faith Campaign' in which clergy of all sorts, including Wahhabis, were given free hand to advocate a return to Islamic fundamentals.[59] Saddam Hussein's misconceived act failed on three fundamental counts. Firstly, it violated the basic secular Ba'ath doctrines, which Arabs had been taught for five decades. Secondly, it created a backlash in Iraq generally and in the Party particularly among the Shi'ia community because most of the clergies in the 'Faith Campaign" were fundamentalist Sunni and some were even *Salafis*,[60] the ultimate enemy of the Shi'ia. Thirdly it suffered from a lack of credibility. The free hand of Islamic parties in Iraq post invasion and occupation will be discussed in detail later in the book.

Other examples of the implementation of the new strategy in the Arab world are still unfolding. Since the invasion and occupation of Iraq, the imperialists realized how weak and splintered the Arab nationalist movement has become. It is very hard to accept the simple description of the turmoil in the Arab world as being spontaneous dissatisfaction by the underprivileged Arab masses. It is true that the Arab political order has failed and equally true that young Arabs throughout the Arab world have little expectation of any decent future. But these facts have existed for some time. What stands out is the fact that these uprisings came simultaneously as if there was a master plan to instigate them in one major chaotic shuffle of events.

The imperialists were aware of the lack of any serious and organized political movements in the Arab world, except, in part, the Muslim Brotherhood, that could be a challenge to established regimes. The danger of allowing this status to continue was unacceptable for fear of the birth of new revolutionary movements like the creation of the Arab nationalist movement between the two World Wars. We believe, although we have no proof yet, that the imperialists instigated parts of these uprisings and supported others. The objective was to create a new system of states affiliated to the West's ideology which in effect means subjugation of these states. If such an outcome were not secured, then the state would be left in political and social chaos, guaranteeing exploitation by the West and the establishment of their interests.

James Thring believes that it is a plot that was hatched by the International Crisis Group founded by Zbigniew Brzezinski and Rothschild protégé George Soros to sow dissent amongst disaffected youth. They were encouraged by the 'Alliance of Youth Movements' founded by ardent Zionists Jared Cohen and Joe Liebman in New York. This was given a cloak of respectability by instilling calls for 'democracy' and denunciations of current leaders as 'dictators'. This was orchestrated and funded by the 'National Endowment for Democracy' run by ex-Israeli General Carl Gershman, also in New York. An ulterior motive to pay for this intervention was presumed to be to gain access to resources such as oil and gold whilst chaos reigned. It was also likely the view that disrupting Arab nations would take their attention away from supporting an embryonic Palestinian State.[61]

In Tunisia the imperialists sided with the *Nahdha* Islamic Party and its leader Rashid Al-Ghanouchi who, despite his rhetoric about US imperialism during Iraq's destruction, started his reign by declaring his strong ties to the Americans.[62] In Libya there was a weak Islamic movement and a rather strong regime. The West had to fabricate a fictitious story about Gaddafi attacking his civilian population with military aircraft,[63] and ended up destroying Libya from air and sea, thus enabling the small gangs of murderous Islamists and irreligious thugs to put the country to ruin. Libya today is in total chaos but with all its oil in the hands of Western companies[64].

In Egypt the situation was slightly different. We should remember that Egypt was a major base for Arab nationalism during Nassir's rule between 1952 and 1970. However, Arab nationalism in Egypt, as opposed to Iraq and Syria, was mainly centred on Nassir personally. Once he died, it subsided slowly, especially with Sadat and Mubarak both distancing themselves from it. Having said that, it transpired that the concept of Arab nationalism still lingers in people's conscious and subconscious minds. In the last presidential election the candidate who loosely represented the Nassirite ideals managed to secure over 5 million votes.[65] The Muslim Brotherhood of Egypt (MBE) was the only organized political party with some 80 years of political experience and its powerful network of mosques and continuous religious indoctrination. We pointed out earlier that MBE was backed by the British Imperialists against Nassir. It seemed very proper to back them in ousting Mubarak's regime, which had outlived its purpose and become a liability. As soon as the MBE won the elections, they declared their adherence to Camp David, the surrender treaty with Israel; expressed their hate of Nassir and all that he represented, and called for the overthrow of the Ba'ath nationalist regime in Syria.[66]

We believe that what happened in Libya was a prelude to the major attack on Syria, the last bastion of Arab nationalism. Syria is very different from the rest of the Arab world. The Ba'ath Party has ruled it for fifty years and it has a very cohesive army indoctrinated with Arab nationalism. The Imperialists realized that the campaign to obliterate Syria was going to be different from that against Iraq or Libya. However, the plans have so far failed for two main reasons. Firstly, the West miscalculated the international mood with the expectation that a repeat of a massive NATO attack on Syria similar to that carried out on Libya would be accepted. But when both Russia and China, for a multitude of reasons, refused to consent to such an authority for the Security Council, the West was faced with the stark choice of either invading Syria or letting or helping the rebels of Syria fight the toughest Arab army. But the world had changed since the 2003 invasion of Iraq. In addition to the disastrous state of global capitalism, a military attack on Syria threatened uncontrollable consequences, which could involve Iran and Israel in a major war whose outcome could not be predicted.

Secondly, despite the open recruitment of Muslim fanatics from all over the world, the massive Gulf financial and military support, the huge arms shipments to the rebels, the training of these fanatics by US/UK/French personnel in Jordan and Turkey, and the massive unprecedented media war, the political and military resilience of the Syrian regime has shocked its adversaries. As at this writing, the military back of the rebels has been broken and their expectations of a victory over the Ba'ath have all but evaporated. That said, Syria has been put back some twenty years in economic and military strength. As for the social upheaval, one is unable to estimate the scale of damage to not just the material infrastructure but the psychological fabric of society. Thus despite not having been able to obliterate Syria as they hoped, the imperialists have been successful in wounding Syria so badly that Israel can breathe a sigh of relief at the threat from Syria having been neutralized for some time to come without having fired a bullet or lost a soldier, although they have dropped several bombs on Syrian defences, intelligence centers, convoys and the military research facility in Damascus. Syria has also been forced into giving up its chemical weapons and its manufacturing capabilities which were a deterrent to any Israeli possible use of WMDs.

At this writing, it is reasonable to conclude that imperialism has attempted to change its strategy for controlling the Arab world from that of direct military invasion and occupation, to relying on political Islam and the full support from Gulf oil money. This is not simply less costly for the West in personnel and money, but it also appeared to carry the civilized pretence of supporting popular uprisings and good ideals. To what extent this vision has been brought to a crashing halt by the military coup in Egypt against a democratically elected MB government that actually tried to pursue an Islamic rather than Western agenda remains to be seen, as Western governments pursue business as usual with the new-old military regime.

IRAQ ON THE EVE OF THE 2003 INVASION

It would be impossible to comprehend what has happened in Iraq since the 2003 invasion without some basic understanding of the situation of Iraq on the eve of that invasion.

Britain's Plans for Iraq

The previous chapter illustrated how Britain attempted to strangulate the new Iraq even before it was restructured out of the remnants of the Ottoman rule. Following the implementation of the plans in the Sykes-Picot agreement and the subsequent arrangements with France, Britain realized that it was not politically possible to remain as an occupying power in Iraq indefinitely. It had thus to work out an alternative system to ensure long-term subservience. It had to look for Iraqis willing to cooperate with it so that it could set up some form of administration that could claim legitimacy while Britain still kept its grip on Iraq. After centuries of oppressive Ottoman rule, Iraq was in a poor state when it came to education and information. The Turkification of Ottoman rule ensured that few people in Iraq were able to speak Arabic properly. In fact, had it not been for the Qur'an, Arabic would have died as a language of communication in most of the Arab world. Thus apart from the religious clergy, the only educated people in Iraq were those who were educated in Istanbul. Britain could not rely on Muslim clergies for obvious reasons, but it found ready collaborators amongst young ambitious Iraqis who were already working for the Ottoman. Whether people like Nuri As-Saeed, Ja'afar Al-Askari and Yasin Al-Hashimi[1] were real Iraqi nationalists who believed the interests of Iraq lay nonetheless in aligning itself with Britain, or simply opportunists who wanted power and thus switched sides from Ottomans to British, is not significant to our argument. It suffices to say that Britain found that those young educated Iraqis were willing to cooperate.

Britain must have borne in mind that it had double-crossed Hussein, Sheriff of Mecca, when it failed to honour any of the commitments made by McMahon.[2] When the nationalists declared Syria independent and proclaimed Faisal king in March 1920, the French general, Henri Gouraud, captured Damascus and deposed the new king.[3] During the Cairo Conference in March 1921, British Colonial Secretary Winston Churchill and his colleagues decided to compensate Faisal for his loss of the Syrian kingdom by offering him the crown of the new kingdom of Iraq.[4] At the same Cairo conference, British officials decided to bestow the territory of Transjordan on Faisal's brother, Abdullah, as an inducement not to avenge Faisal's defeat in Syria[5] and because they had promised that he, not Faisal, would be king of Iraq. While still partially redressing the personal injustice to Hussein, this also ensured that, as an outsider, the king of Iraq would always be reliant on the British for his survival.

A new administration for Iraq formed by King Faisal I and allied to Britain was put in place. The bickering and infighting between different political factions in Iraq in the 1920s and 1930s was not about independence, sovereignty or economy, but over power. All those in the official political circles were allies of Britain. The situation was very similar to that of post 2003 Iraq with one main striking difference, namely that the politicians of the 1920s were not as corrupt as those of today. While the politicians of the 1920s were fighting over power, the politicians in post 2003 have been fighting for the biggest cut of Iraq's oil money.

The new political order created by Britain in Iraq resulted in the 1922 Anglo-Iraqi Treaty of Alliance, followed by the expanded treaty of 1932 that made foreign, military, financial, and judicial affairs directly subject to British control. Subsidiary agreements authorized the establishment of British troops and bases in the country.[6] Even more significant is the fact that Britain secured a treaty that gave over the whole of Iraq for British exploration of oil for the next 75 years.[7] The Turkish Petroleum Company (later to become the Iraqi Petroleum Company - IPC) and its associated companies became the sole explorers and exporters of Iraq oil out of which Iraq was to receive sums decided by the oil companies themselves. IPC's control of Iraq's oil also meant that it alone decided what strategy it employed for exploitation and production of Iraq's natural resources, which in turn enabled Britain to control Iraq's development for as long as it desired through the control of its meagre oil revenue.[8]

Such denial of national resources, pride and limited sovereignty soon gave rise to discontent in Iraq. While Britain was engaged in fighting on several fronts during WWII, a few Iraqi military officers[9] and some nationalists staged a coup against the King and his government. Swiftly and ruthlessly Britain crushed the rebellion and reinstated the old regime, which executed the plotters. The so-called 1941 revolution became a symbol for nationalist aspiration in Iraq for many decades.[10]

When two powerful movements, the Communists and Arab Nationalists, began to mount a credible political opposition to the pro-British regime, the British responded by creating a new safety system in the form of the Baghdad Pact in 1955. This pact, ostensibly between Iraq, Iran, Turkey and Pakistan, remained under British supervision and control.[11] The declared purpose of the Pact was to protect its members against foreign threat. However, since the only enemy to Iraq at that time was the State of Israel and since the Baghdad Pact was not designed to oppose Israel, which Britain had just helped to create, it is safe to conclude that the purpose of the Pact was to create a unified block of pro-British oppressive regimes which might come to each other's aid, in the event of regime overthrow in any one of them.[12]

Rumour has it that, for two days following the 1958 coup, Nuri As-Saeed[13] was looking at the sky waiting for the landing of troops from the Baghdad Pact to rescue the old regime. When the rescue failed to materialize, he declared that the British had instigated the coup. If Nuri As-Saeed made such a statement, then it must have been made in a moment of despair. General Qasim and his comrades in the Free Officers Movement were genuinely nationalist Iraqis aspiring to liberate Iraq from foreign domination, but it is also conceivable that the British and the Americans were aware of the possibility of a military coup in Iraq and did nothing to prevent it, or alert Nuri to it. With the ascendancy of Nasirist Arab Nationalism, Iraq might have fallen into the hands of the Nationalists, with the possibility of a United Arab Republic comprising Egypt, Syria and Iraq. This was the nightmare which the British had feared way back at the time of Muhammad Ali of Egypt.[14] To avert such a possible scenario, the imperialists likely preferred to allow the 1958 joint military coup to succeed and then consume it in political infighting between the extreme polarities of communism and Arab Nationalism.

Qasim's Rule

The events that followed substantiate the above contention. The naïve and inexperienced leadership of both the communists and Arab Nationalists were manipulated into bloody conflict very shortly after the July 1958 coup. The sad episodes of brutal incidents that took place in Iraq between 1959 and 1963 reveal some aggressive and barbaric streaks in the Iraqi psyche that have not yet been understood or studied. A similar episode of barbarity spread in Iraq post the 2003 invasion. It could easily be noted that similar episodes of barbarity had manifested themselves in history during revolutions and upheavals like the French Revolution of 1789[15] and the Bolshevik Revolution of 1907[16] or indeed, the English Civil War of 1649 or the American Civil War of 1861. Needless to say, the American soldiers took ears of Vietnamese victims as souvenirs.

There was an attempt by the Ba'athists on Qasim's life.[17] He survived it with permanent injury to his arm and the perpetrators who were caught escaped the death sentence. Those who escaped Iraq, like Saddam Hussein, came back to play a major role in Iraq for the next thirty years. The major incident, however, was a military uprising in Mosul, north of Iraq. Many people including communists and nationalists were killed and the uprising was put down.[18] Although Qasim was against bloodshed, so much so that he only consented to the execution of four members of the old regime, he took a very different view after the failure of the Mosul uprising. His decision to approve the execution of some 20 high ranking military officers and civilians, some of whom were prominent members of the Free Officers Movement, went on to contribute to the conspiracy against him and his failure and death in February 1963.[19]

The 1958 coup played a major role in the history and events of the 20th century Arab world. Although it likely took place with the tacit approval of the West, we believe that it was not in any way under their tutelage. Thus Qasim soon came to believe, like many other aspiring leaders in the developing world post WWII, that he was the promised leader who was destined to deliver national independence and salvation, peace, security, development and a decent standard of living. He was assisted in these beliefs by the Communist propaganda, which hailed him as "the Undisputed Leader".

He did indeed change things to such a degree that it took a full invasion of Iraq to reverse them. He severed the dependency of Iraqi currency on the Pound Sterling until the 2003 invasion linked it again to the dollar[20]. He drove the death nail into the Baghdad Pact[21] until the puppet government of Nuri Al-Maliki again tied Iraq to the Imperialist camp. He set up the first unit of the Palestinian Liberation Army which he believed would go on to liberate its usurped land.[22]

Qasim clearly upheld the Iraqi belief that Kuwait had been unlawfully severed from Iraq under British mandate. Thus on 20 June 1961 he sent a latter to the Sheikh of Kuwait in which he indirectly welcomed the Sheikh back to Iraq after the British announced their intention to withdraw.[23] In a press conference on 25 June, Qasim demanded the return of Kuwait to Iraq as a municipality, which was part of Basrah. On 26 June, the Iraqi government distributed a memorandum to the ambassadors of Arab and foreign states in Baghdad explaining the history of Kuwait and declaring that Kuwait was part of Iraq that should return.[24] This declaration brought a swift response from the British in the form of mass British troop deployment in Kuwait, another proof of its strategy to strangulate Iraq.[25]

But we believe that the most significant revolutionary measure taken by Qasim was the promulgation of Law No. 80 (1961), which reclaimed 99% of Iraq from the hands of the oil companies.[26] This subsequently enabled Iraq to nationalize its oil and carry on exploring, producing and exporting it[27] for the benefit of Iraq until the 2003 invasion. Then, once again, Iraq's oil was taken by the imperialist companies with top politicians having a cut in the open theft of Iraq's assets.[28]

Looking back at Iraq over the years between 1959 and 2003, it seems that imperialism's major message to the Iraqi people is that all the struggle and sacrifices of that era were in vain because today they are in a worse position than they were in 1958!

Qasim, similar to most leaders of the developing world of his time, naively believed—partly because of his success—in the power of general public support. The popular demonstrations, which were mostly organized and supported by the communists, strengthened his belief that he was really "the Undisputed Leader" and needed no political organization to underpin his legitimacy and rule. Although he was well read, he missed the great wisdom of Ali Bin Abi Talib who is quoted some thirteen centuries earlier as having said:

> The mob when congregating destroy, but when dispersed they become insignificant.

When all his enemies including the Ba'athists, other Arab Nationalists, Islamists and Imperialist agents ganged up against him on the morning of 8 February 1963, there were no masses to support him save the members of the Communist Party who came out to the streets led by their heroic Secretary General of the Politburo to fight against what they called the imperialist reactionary plot against Iraq. The outcome was swift and savage. Qasim and his closest aides were summarily executed; many communists were either killed or imprisoned. In fact neither Qasim's Iraqi nationalism nor the Iraqi communists ever recovered from the devastation of February 1963.

The Ba'ath Rule

The leadership of the Ba'ath Party in 1963 was going through an adolescent stage of political maturity. It was riddled with personal desires for leadership that enabled its partners in the coup from the other factions of the Arab Nationalist movement to sow discord which eventually enabled them to get rid of the Ba'ath, if only temporarily.[29] The rule of the two Arif brothers, which extended from 1963 to 1968, witnessed more stability than the preceding five years.[30]

The Ba'ath movement as a whole, and not just in Iraq, went through a semi-meltdown with major changes and challenges to the Pan-Arab National leadership of the Party. The vacuum that was created by the failure of the Ba'ath leadership in Iraq in November 1963 enabled Saddam Hussein and Ahmad Hasan Al-Bakr to restructure the Party as they desired. Although the Party was still very weak and undergoing restructuring, both Al-Bakr and Hussein could not resist the temptation of seizing power when it became known to them that a CIA plot to oust President Arif was under way. They forced themselves on the plotters and joined them in sharing power on 17 July 1968, ten years after the ousting of the monarchy, signalling the return of the Ba'ath almost five years after their first failure.[31] Both men had learnt from the mistakes of the Ba'ath of 1963 and ensured they were not repeated. So before their US sponsored conspirators had time to feel their way into the corridors of power, they posted their loyal men in command positions in the army and managed to oust the US allies among their co-conspirators on 30 July 1968.[32] This signalled that the rule of the Ba'ath would last until the US led invasion toppled the party on 9 April 2003.

We believe that the Ba'ath genuinely believed in its mission of building a strong nationalist Iraq which would go on to unify the Arab world, fulfilling the Ba'ath objective of a united Arab nation guided by social justice and full independence. Towards that end, between 1970 and 1980, the Ba'ath managed to put into action an effective development plan the like of which had not been achieved in many countries in the developing world. The results speak for themselves. The Economic, Social and Political policies of the Ba'ath have been analyzed in detail in Volume One of *Genocide in Iraq*,[33] but it may be useful to give some tables to remind the reader.

The following table sums up the allocations of GDP for the period between1970-1990 up to the point of US/UK/Security Council-imposed sanctions on Iraq.

Period	Oil	Agri-culture	Water & Electricity	Manufac-turing	Building
1970-74*	72.3%	9.7%	0.2%	3.1%	1.8%
1975-80**	68.3%	6.3%	0.2%	4%	5.6%
1981-85***	30.3%	7.1%	0.6%	5.3%	7.8%
1986-90****	42.6%	7.1%	0.8%	4.1%	5.8%

* The success of oil nationalization led to oil constituting 70% of the GDP.

** This period witnessed a limitation of growth in manufacturing and agricultural sectors.

*** This period was characterized by a reduction in oil revenue caused by the Iran-Iraq war. Most resources were directed towards the military. The war had one positive aspect. It forced the authorities to pay more attention to agriculture.

**** This period witnessed further deterioration due to the effects of war.

Oil Revenue, Oil Output, Gross Domestic Product and Population 1960-1990[34]

Year	Oil Revenue ($ billion)	Oil Output (million bpd) in 1980 prices)	GDP ($ billion (million)	Population
1960	3	97	8.7	6.9
1970	.6	1.5	16.4	9.4
1980	26.3	2.6	53.9	13.2
1985	10.1	1.4	31.7	15.3
1990	9.5	2.1	16.4	18.1

The Government invested heavily in the public sector industry in an attempt to strengthen it. According to official figures, annual investment in the nonpetroleum industrial sector increased from 39.5 million ID (about $130 million) in 1968 to 752.5 million ID (about $2.5

billion) in 1985. As a consequence of these investments, the industrial output in 1984 was almost 2 billion ID ($6.6 billion), up from about 300 million ID (about $990 million) in 1968, and up more than 50 per cent from the start of the Iran-Iraq War in 1980. But productivity relative to investment remained low.[35]

Selected indicators in Iraq before sanctions, 1988-1989[36]

Health indicators:
- Birth rate 43 per I 000 population - Crude death rate 8.0 per I 000 population - Infant mortality rate 52 per I 000 live births - Under 5 mortality rate 94 per I 000 live births - Maternal mortality rate I60 per I00 000 live births - Low birth weight 5% (below 2.5 kg) - Life expectancy 66 years
Socioeconomic indicators:
- GNP per capita $2 800 - % female literacy 85% - % population with health care 93% - % population with safe water 90% - % pregnant women with maternity care 78% - % pregnant women with trained birth attendant during delivery 86%

Saddam Hussein had always had a grandiose vision of his destined role in the Arab World. But in 1968 he was too young, too inexperienced and there were many elder Party and army members who would have opposed his ascendancy to the leadership which he had always considered to be his right. By 1979, however, he had accomplished his dream, managing to organize the Party and the intelligence service to suit his design and had eliminated all his opponents.

Saddam's Rule

Saddam Hussein's total control of power was achieved at very high cost to the Party when some fifty members of the Party's Congress were either executed or imprisoned in July 1979 in what we call the Party Massacre.[37] We believe that that brutal action was the death knell for the Party from which it never recovered. Despite its expansion in numbers, the party became merely a rubber stamp for Saddam's wishes.

Saddam's ascendancy followed an historic and dramatic event in the Middle East, namely the victory of Ayatollah Khomeini over the Shah of Iran.[38] It may even be argued that Saddam Hussein intensified his grip on power in order to meet the challenge, which Khomeini posed for Iraq in particular and the Ba'ath movement in general. The Islamic revolution in Iran led by Khomeini was fundamentally religious and thus anathema to any nationalist movement like the Ba'ath. It talked of the "*Umma*", meaning the community of Muslims, which cut through borders and rejected the nation-state. The religious fervour caused by Khomeini was already reverberating throughout the Muslim world, and Saddam Hussein believed this was happening and had to be confronted in Iraq as well as in the Gulf.

Saddam Hussein had another grudge against Iran, which he believed the time was right to settle. In 1975 he had to sign a humiliating treaty with the Shah of Iran in which he conceded parts of Iraq's sovereignty over the Shatt Al-Arab waterway to Iran in return for the latter terminating its backing of the Kurdish rebellion in northern Iraq. He thought the Khomeini regime was weak enough to enable him to achieve both objectives of confronting the religious advance into Iraq and the Gulf, and the scrapping of the Algiers Treaty of 1975. In September 1980 he launched an attack on Iran which was to last for eight years, would reshape the Middle East for decades to come, and lead to the invasion and destruction of Iraq only two years after it ended.

Saddam Hussein's greatest shortcoming in politics was his inability to understand imperialism. He had always thought that his comrades in the Ba'ath did not know how to deal with imperialism. He believed that the Ba'ath ideology of confronting imperialism was misguided and it needed a new approach in which the Ba'ath could succeed by demonstrating to the Imperialists that a strong Ba'ath regime was the best guarantor of imperialist interests in the Arab world. Saddam Hussein demonstrated this view when he sided with the Ba'ath faction in Syria which opposed the left faction of Salah Jedid and his comrades in 1966.[39] He, like Hafidh Al-Assad,[40] never really understood what imperialism is about. This strategy surfaced clearly when he was advised by Fahd of Arabia[41] that the US and its allies were ready to assist him in attacking Iran. Saddam readily relied on this and went into Iran believing that after a victory over Iran, the US would come to an understanding with him that would allow him to share control of the Gulf.

Following his entry into Kuwait, several dignitaries from within the Arab world and outside it visited Iraq to warn or explain to him the danger of confronting the US. Rashid Al-Ghanouchi, leader of Tunisian Nahdha Party was one of those visitors. When he tried to explain to Saddam Hussein that the US was bent on destroying Iraq, Saddam is reported to have responded that he was sure the Arab nation would not allow the US to destroy Iraq.[42] More than ten years later when every observer of Iraq and world affairs was absolutely sure that Iraq was going to be invaded,

Saddam Hussein was still hoping that the US would negotiate with him. In an interview with Russia Today TV Arabic Service, Salim Al-Jumaili, the head of the US section at the Iraqi Intelligence Service on the eve of the invasion advised the viewers that Saddam Hussein's response to the intelligence advice that Iraq was going to be invaded was that it would be a limited military action that would lead to negotiation.[43] We were dismayed at such naivety.

Imperialists' Manipulation of Iran and Iraq

The statement by Ernest Bevin on British interests in the Middle East quoted in chapter 1 could be applied to the French at that time, as well as the newly acquired contemporary US interests. One way to secure these interests has been the total and unconditional support of Israel. Many foreign policies of the UK, USA and to some extent France—an equally important player in the territorial demarcation of the Middle East since the end of WWII—have been intended to maintain Israel as the unmatched superpower in the Middle East as well as to deflect any censure of Israel for its barbaric treatment of Palestinians despite the offence this causes to the Islamic world. This fundamental objective of shielding Israel's inhumanity whilst condemning much lesser human rights failings in Arab countries explains most of the anomalies an independent observer could point out regarding events and their interpretation in the Middle East over the last sixty years. In the context of these events, what transpired in Iraq is no exception. It also explains why Iraq, despite being the most secular regime of the region and possibly the most liberal among its neighbours in the Arab world, has been, over the last sixty years, opposed and attacked by the Western Governments and media. Other despotic and totalitarian regimes in the same region, notably Saudi Arabia, have either been met with silence or acquiescence in terms of their governance records and priorities. It also explains the suspect silence in the face of what has befallen the ancient Christian community in Iraq since the 2003 invasion, lest it highlight the good times of equality and tolerance which were enjoyed during the previous generations in Iraq, especially under Ba'ath rule.

The strategy of imperialism in the Arab Middle East post WWII was based on two fundamental principles. The primary strategy remains the total and unconditional support for Israel. Next was to establish client regimes consisting of artificially created states that act as guardians for the flow of oil as demanded by the West, and whose populations are non-productive consumer communities who spend the money they earn on importing goods and services produced by their patrons. The Arab states that fall outside this control are essentially contained within certain limits in development and defence lest they constitute a challenge to this Anglo-American hegemony. Examples of such states are Egypt under Nassir, Syria under the Al-Assads and Iraq under Saddam Hussein. Although the political views of the general public in the USA and the UK appear to count for little in international affairs, it would seem important for so-called liberal democracy to function, that the public is carried along and convinced that such policies are right. Towards that end it seems important to demonize that element of Middle East leadership which can be made to epitomize the evils of the regime. The various perspectives on Nassir, Gaddafi, Khomeini, Saddam Hussein and Ahmadenijad highlight this phenomenon.

When Saddam Hussein ill advisedly sent his troops into Iran, the imperialists had a golden opportunity to weaken both potentially threatening powers. The involvement of Saddam Hussein's Iraq in a long drawn out war led to Iraqi surrender of leadership of the Arab world to other forces. It also depleted Iraq's material, socio-economic and intellectual capital, putting the results of the war in line with the foreign policy objectives of the Neocon Zionists in the USA. It afforded considerable progress towards the consolidation of Israel in the region, by removing Iraq from the Arab-Israeli conflict. Iraq was the only country that took part in the short war against Israel in 1948 but did not sign the Armistice that other Arab states signed with Israel. This meant that Iraq remained in a state of war with Israel when Iraq was fighting Iran in the 1980s.[44] US delight with the war was best expressed by Kissinger, who is stated to have said that he wanted both sides to win.[45] It is no secret that towards that end the US supported both sides in that war, suggesting that as long as there continued to be an upheaval, American interests would be served irrespective of victory or defeat for either Iran or Iraq.[46] Strategically, two of Israel's foes would weaken each other.

The principle of containment, the original US policy at the beginning of the Cold War to check the expansion of the Soviet Union,[47] is embedded in the imperialist strategy. When Arab states appear impossible to contain or control, a second leg of that strategy is often put into action. This involves the fragmentation of the state into statelets based on sectarian lines following time-honoured divide and rule strategies. This process weakens the state and ensures in-fighting between statelets over natural resources or borders, further enhancing the hegemony of the Zionist state and the argument that it is no more than one other sectarian state among many in the Middle East. That is what has happened in Iraq, what has arguably been happening in Lebanon and has begun to unfold in the contemporary Syrian context.

The nature and rules of the game have changed since Iran's success in consolidating the first semi-democratic Islamic state and transforming itself into a regional power. The most significant change in the post Cold War Middle East has been the belief by the regimes opposed to US hegemony that there is no superpower they can rely upon for defence or deterrence in the way that they had relied on the USSR during the Cold War era. This was an early realization by Al-Assad of Syria who saw the wavering of the Soviets even before their demise, and opted for an alliance with Iran. This alliance, which survived three decades of attempts at dismantlement by European and Gulf States, posed a real threat to US policies for the Middle East. If small regional powers could unite and succeed in opposing the US in the Middle East, then the latter would have to revise its strategy and tactics. Both Syria and Iran and their allies, Hizbullah and Hamas, appeal greatly to the Arab and Muslim masses at large. They stand for a simple proposal—namely for the US and its European allies to leave the peoples of the Middle East to decide the nature of the political and economic system they want to live under. This request is widely understood and accepted by the masses in the area. When Syria and Iran are accused by the US of oppressing their people, the reaction of the masses in the street of the Middle East is anti-American ridicule. They respond that the US and its European allies support the most despotic regimes in the world in Arabia, the Holy Land and the Gulf.[48] Both Syria and Iran have agreed that Israel, the USA's forward base in the Middle East, must be challenged, its expansion limited and its superiority matched. Towards that end they adopted a new political and military strategy. Militarily they realized that no technology in the world could match US air superiority, which is instantly and freely available to Israel. However, insofar as rockets are cheaper, easier to manufacture, do not need trained pilots, and may effectively render the whole of the Israeli air force useless, they instead embarked on such a strategy and have since made advances in it. This strategy is suited to the geographical spread, which both Iran and Syria have in comparison to Israel. It leaves Israel seriously considering the unthinkable nuclear option.

Politically Syria and Iran's strategy succeeded on two fronts. First they exposed the US policies of blind and unconditional support for Israel to make the former look like the real enemy of the Arabs and Muslims. This is not the sentiment of the revolutionaries in Damascus and Tehran alone but of ordinary people in the streets of the capitals of Gulf States, which one of these authors has discovered to his great surprise during the last few years. Secondly, the use of Syria and Iran's allies in Iraq, Lebanon and Palestine has turned out to be effective, with little cost to them. They cite among their successes the forced exit of the US from Iraq, although the economic and human cost to the US has been minute compared to the calamity to which Iraq has been subjected. Furthermore, they cite the success of Hizbullah and Hamas in opposing the massive Israeli onslaught in 2006 and 2008 respectively. To the charge by Israel, the USA and some European countries, that Syria and Iran interfere in the national affairs of other states in the Middle East, both have an ideological rebuttal. Syria (on an Arab Nationalist basis) and Iran (on an Islamic religious basis) believe, teach and argue, albeit not in a publically declared policy, that the nation (*Umma*) is one (Arab and/or Islamic) that has been divided by European colonial policy, and its salvation lies in its unity. Acceptance of this hypothesis suggests that any means could be utilized to achieve that unity, be it political interference, corrupt manipulation or even military intervention. Thus Syria/Iran and their allies in the Arab world argue that while Syrian, and to a lesser extent Iranian, interference is legitimate, that of the USA and its allies is fundamentally unacceptable. When the Egyptian writer, Heikel, drew the question of international law to his attention, Ayatollah Khomeini expressed his disregard for this body of law:[49] a sentiment shared by millions of Arabs/Muslims in the world.

When the Iraq war with Iran ended on 8 August 1988 with both sides losing (Henry Kissinger's desired effect), Saddam Hussein genuinely expected that his allies in the Gulf and the West were going to assist in rebuilding bruised Iraq. He was soon confronted with the reality of the Imperialist design for the Arab World. There was going to be no rebuilding of Iraq and its military industry was going to be dismantled unless Saddam Hussein agreed, along with the Gulf States, Egypt and Jordan, to a total surrender to Zionism and acceptance of Israel's hegemony.

Events Leading To the Invasion of Kuwait

The sequence of events between August 1988 and August 1990 is well documented.[50] On 8 August 1988, the Iran-Iraq war came to an end with calamitous results for both countries.[51] As soon as the war ended a concerted campaign started against Iraq. It transpired later that Saddam Hussein had allegedly reneged on an understanding that he would be supported in the war against Iran provided he would enter into a peace agreement with Israel.[52] The campaign started with the release of a book seemingly written by the CIA but attributed to an Iraqi architect, Kanan Makiya, whose office in London was said to have many consultancy works in Iraq.[53]

The campaign took a nasty turn when Kuwait was encouraged to force a reduction in Iraqi oil revenues by syphoning Iraqi oil out of the cross-border fields and demanding that Iraq pay back its alleged debt to Kuwait incurred during the war with Iran. Iraq, however, had understood that debt as Kuwait's contribution to Iraq for defending it against the oncoming flood of the Khomeini revolution.[54]

History has shown us that economic strangulation can result in war, as epitomized by the German experience of the interwar period. In 1990 Iraq felt the effects of the Kuwaiti measures, preventing it from rebuilding its shattered economy. Many attempts by Iraq to persuade the Kuwaitis to change their policies through Arab mediators and the offices of the Arab League failed. Rather, the more Iraq pleaded, the more intransigent the Kuwaitis became. It was baffling to see how Kuwait could feel so confident to follow that route without fearing the consequences, unless it had been assured that whatever happened, it would benefit from the protection of the USA. In view of the extent of available evidence that preceded the entry of Iraqi forces into Kuwait, it sounded odd for such a well-informed academic as Joy Gordon to assert that 'in 1990, Iraq invaded Kuwait without provocation'.[55]

There is evidence to suggest that the US not only encouraged the Kuwaitis to pursue that antagonistic path,[56] it even discouraged mediation by the Arab League and misled Iraq through Ambassador Glaspie's advice to Saddam Hussein before leaving Baghdad, that the dispute with Kuwait was a local matter between neighbours and the US would not get involved.[57]

Whether or not Saddam Hussein had options other than military action against Kuwait to put an end to what he called the 'cutting of Iraqi necks by the Kuwaitis', or whether he chose the worst moment in the second half of the 20th century to do so remains a question for historians to argue. In our opinion, whatever the rights or wrongs of his reclaiming Kuwait for Iraq against the colonialists' rule that their artificial and imposed borders were inviolable, he should have pulled his troops out within a day or two without waiting for negotiations or new Security Council Resolutions. That would have pre-empted attempts at a Security Council Resolution to attack Iraq. It would then have been difficult for the USA to obtain the support it needed from the Arab League. In the worst case, even had a US attack followed, it would not have been as ferocious and would have been considered a breach of international law. In short Saddam Hussein could have saved Iraq the calamities of the last twenty something years had he pulled out of Kuwait a few days or weeks after retaking it. He would have still made his point and achieved some success in reactivating Iraq's rejection of the colonial borders.

The First Invasion of Iraq in 1991

The attack on Iraq in 1991 and the total blockade of the whole country's imports and exports that followed raises many moral and legal questions. Some of the legal questions have been addressed in Volume One of *Genocide in Iraq* but little has been written to address the moral questions. In fact the moral questions have generally been met with indifference in Europe, which has been criticized by some authors as a rejection of common humanity.[58]

First and foremost among the legal questions is the fact that the attack and blockade were contrary to the objectives of the UN. The UN was set up 'to save succeeding generations from the scourge of war' and to that end 'to practice tolerance and live together in peace with one another as good neighbours'.[59] The prohibition of the use of armed force and the corresponding obligation to settle disputes peacefully is a fundamental pillar of these objectives.[60]

Nations that fail to reach a settlement as per Article 35 of the UN Charter are invited to seek Security Council intervention and the latter may make recommendations for a pacific settlement.[61] It would be in accordance with the ethos of the Charter to expect the Security Council not to resort to Chapter VII prior to exhausting the pacific means of settling the dispute even if that is not explicitly so stated in the Charter.[62] In support of this suggestion it is worth noting that the text of Articles 41 and 42 investigates other means, short of the use of force, to settle the dispute even when the Council concludes a threat to the peace exists. The Security Council has followed this practice in its handling of the Palestinian problem. For 65 years the Palestinians have been uprooted and scattered over the Middle East, and despite the fact that their presence in these countries has been a threat to the peace, the Council has constantly insisted that they should resort to peaceful negotiation to settle their demand to return home, rather than demand cessation of unlawful Israeli land grabs and attacks against civilians. No such leniency was allowed in the case of Iraq. In fact events disclose the opposite. The massive build up of forces from the outset indicates that military action was planned long before any of the measures under Article 41 and 42 were even allowed to be tested.

The Genocidal Sanctions

The twelve plus years of sanctions imposed upon Iraq have been extensively covered. In Volume I of *Genocide In Iraq*[63] we discussed these years of genocidal blockade, the like of which had never been witnessed before. We argued the illegality of the total blockade of a country, the criminal collaboration of states and persons in these actions, the cowardice and complicity of the rest of the world by acquiescence, the failure of the Security Council to act in accordance with the principles of the UN Charter and international law, the covert abuse of sanctions control to favour selected interests whilst pretending to be objective, and the moral bankruptcy of Western media and intelligentsia in their handling of the criminality against Iraq. We also contrasted the preceding building of Iraq by the Ba'ath administration with the destruction of Iraq by the West's imposed genocidal blockade. Further, we outlined the criminal proceedings that could and should be brought against anyone who had been involved in committing those heinous crimes against the millions of innocent civilians of Iraq.

After ten years of total blockade which prevented children from having medicines and essential nutrients or even pencils for school, the imperialists discovered that the strategy of destroying Iraq was not going according to plan as it had not achieved the objective of crippling the state and disintegrating it into sectarian statelets. In fact there were signs that Iraq was capable of surviving the sanctions and minimizing their genocidal effects. Iraq managed to set up bilateral exchange treaties with a few states (like Jordan Turkey and Saudi Arabia) in which it was able to exchange goods and secure some basic minimum needs.[64] The international revulsion at the effects of the total blockade was increasing and creating more pressure on the imperialists to ease some of the draconian measures. The Security Council was forced to make new arrangements towards easing the imports of some fundamental items to Iraq without them having to go through the dictatorial Sanctions Committee.[65] It was becoming apparent to the imperialists that soon the total blockade was going to loosen, which meant that the Ba'ath regime was likely to survive it. That was a nightmare scenario for them. Dismantling Iraq was pivotal to the plan of dividing the Arab world into sectarian statelets and obliterating any regime that threatened to come to the aid of Palestine.

The imperialists cruelly decided that improvements in the *status quo* and their possible development should not be allowed to continue. The arrogant decision was made to invade Iraq and occupy it in order to initiate the plan for dismantlement via sowing sectarian division, a plan that has since expressed itself in North Africa and Syria. In the next chapter we shall consider the preparations and fabricated excuses for the invasion.

PREPARATION FOR THE INVASION

We both were born and grew up in post WWII Iraq. We lived through the turmoil and many changes that were experienced by all Iraqis. It is not always possible in life to pinpoint an event or incident that led to the formulation of a particular opinion or conclusion. Our conclusion regarding what had been designed for Iraq has been gathered from experience and has always been that Iraq was targeted to be subjugated and dismantled because the policy of containment envisaged post WWI had failed. Iraq's fragmentation was to be the first stage in the redesigning of a new Arab World (which the West likes to call the Middle East to justify including Israel in it) that the Zionist imperialism post WWII wanted to create. Once this objective was achieved, it was thought Syria would collapse under the pressure imposed by its neighbors, and the total victory of Zionism over the region would be achieved. We appreciate that for an objective observer such a viewpoint will not be easily accepted without some evidence. Towards that end, we will attempt to piece together the story of how such a plan was designed and how it was later implemented.

The Iraq Liberation Act

Neither the British nor the French imperialists, even during their heyday, declared their intention to interfere in the internal affairs of any country even if they planned to invade it. However, the Zionist imperialism of the US changed all this. They had the audacity to make their intention to interfere in the affairs of other states not only public but also mandatory and lawful by legislating for such intervention in breach of principles of international law. Towards that end, the 105th Congress of the US in 1998 enacted The Iraq Liberation Act.[1] This Law is so bizarre that one cannot count its shortcomings. Thus in section 2 under the heading of 'Findings', Congress made the following finding among others:

(2) In February 1988, Iraq forcibly relocated Kurdish civilians from their home villages in the Anfal campaign, killing an estimated 50,000 to 180,000 Kurds.

We are not going to talk about the so-called 'Anfal Campaign'[2] which has become, like the 'Holocaust', a taboo not even to be discussed. But it seems to be ludicrous for the legislative body in the most powerful country in the world to use a headline from a report by a US NGO, unknown for its impartiality when it comes to US policies, and adopt it as a finding in one of its legislations. How could any reasonable person believe that any regime could kill some 100,000 of its own people in one month without there being significant resistance and press coverage? Indeed, how to believe an estimate varying in its numbers by some 130,000 persons? This is not like estimating crowds in the streets where later they melt away; this entailed corpses, massive numbers of which would have had to have been disposed of. It seems that Congress was not interested in the truth, but rather in hyping matters to justify its intervention in Iraq under the guise of humanitarian intervention.

In section 3 Congress declared:

It should be the policy of the United States to support efforts to remove the regime headed by Saddam Hussein from power in Iraq and to promote the emergence of a democratic government to replace that regime.

We hold that this policy, declared in 1998, had always been the intended policy of the US for regime change in Iraq and the excuses made up later about the alleged dangers of Iraq's WMD were fiction.

Among the actions authorized against Iraq in section 4 Congress legislated that:

(2) MILITARY ASSISTANCE- (A) The President is authorized to direct the drawdown of defense articles from the stocks of the Department of Defense, defense services of the Department of Defense, and military education and training for such organizations.

One need not be a military expert to understand that such an authorization by Congress makes it lawful for the President of the US to intervene in the internal affairs of a sovereign state by arming an insurrection inside it or an aggression from outside it.

It is worth remembering here that Congress passed a similar legislation regarding Syria in the form of the Syria Accountability and Lebanese Sovereignty Restoration Act (SALSRA). It was passed into law on December 12, 2003[3] following the invasion and occupation of Iraq. Several other legislations on Syria have since been adopted.[4] These legislations make the US the only state in history to legalize in advance its criminal intentions towards the government of another sovereign state.

The story of luring Saddam Hussein into Kuwait has been covered in Chapter 2.[5] The scale of the assemblage of armies that formed the alliance surpassed that of any previous alliance even during WWII and the ferocious attack on Iraq in 1991 was unprecedented. We would like to emphasize here that that attack was part of the design to strangulate Iraq and work towards its dismemberment. One pentagon planner commented on the scale and purpose of the attack as follows:

> People say: You didn't recognize that it was going to have an effect on water and sewage. Well, what were we trying to do with sanctions – help the Iraqi people? No. What we were doing with the attacks on the infrastructure was to accelerate the effect of sanctions.[6]

Needless to say, accelerating the effect of sanctions means accelerating the destruction of Iraq.

However, despite the scale of destruction of Iraq's infrastructure, medical facilities and food storage which had been documented earlier, it seems that imperialism was not satisfied because these measures did not lead to the desired disintegration of Iraq. Thus we read the accounts of several US officials voicing concern at not having been able to eliminate Iraq's brains and know-how.

The imposition for twelve years of the unprecedented genocidal blockade on Iraq was designed to cause the disintegration of the state. However, the resilience of the Iraqi people meant that Nationalist Arab Iraq was likely to remain intact. This was a nightmare for the imperialists because it meant the failure of their plans and a need for new tactics to create the new Arab World. We believe that the decision to invade Iraq was taken sometime half way through the sanctions period. We do not believe that a document exists showing when this decision was made, but the piecing together of events will give credence to such a conclusion.

This is what James Woolsey, the Director of the CIA 1993-95, said in a typically arrogant speech, which was applauded by his gullible but no less imperialist American audience:

> The problem is not Islam. The problem is tyranny. And if we convince the decent Muslims of the world, the

decent people in the world, the people who are in slavery essentially including in many of these states the women, that we are on their side we will ultimately prevail just we did in World Wars one, two and three, the Cold War. As we do this we will make people nervous. We will make the Saudi Royal family nervous. We will make the Mubarak regime in Egypt nervous. And if we succeed in freeing Iraq and begin to turn our attention to the Syrias and the Libyas and the other rogue states and exert pressure for them to change the Saudi Royal family and the Mubarak regime will come to us and say we are very, very nervous and our response should be good. We want you're nervous. We want you to realize that now for the fourth time in a hundred years this country and its allies, its democratic allies, are on the march and we are going to win because we are on the side of those whom these regimes most fear, their own people.[7]

Such a statement ought to be taken to represent the policy of US imperialism. The Director of the CIA is not just an ordinary man — he heads the organization whose duty it is to spy on others; secure the implementation of state policy; and carry out all illegal activities required for such implementation, which the US prefers not to do overtly. In short his statement reflected the true official policy of the US in regard to Iraq, which may be summarized as follows:

1.   Zionist imperialism was determined to dismantle Iraq as a country.

2.   After Iraq, this strategy was going to be extended to cover Libya and Syria—precisely what has since happened for the former and is being attempted for the latter.

3.   Imperialism sees its attack on Arab nationalism as its *fourth* war in a hundred years following, WWI, WWII and the Cold War. An independent observer may see some justification for the US in being involved in the three wars Woolsey referred to. But it would be difficult for such an objective observer to understand the reason for equating the situation in the Middle East with the three global wars, considering that Arab Nationalism had not attacked or threatened the US. We believe that it supports our early contention that this is due to the ascendancy of Zionism to rank as the dominant force directing imperialism today.

4. Zionist imperialism reveals its high moral ground in describing the Saudi Royal family, the world's most corrupt and despotic family, which rules a country without a constitution, laws, human rights and treats its women and immigrant work force as slaves, as being decent Muslims, whilst labeling the two most secular regimes in the region, Iraq and Syria, that had achieved social justice, economic development, fair treatment of minorities and better treatment of women than some European states, as rogue states!

The Sanctions Committee

The evidence keeps accumulating. The imperialists managed in 1990, at the time when the Soviet Union was at its weakest since its establishment, to secure any resolution they desired from the Security Council. Among the articles of one of those resolutions on Iraq was the setting up of the Sanctions Committee, the like of which had never been seen before, to monitor the strict application of sanctions against Iraq.[8] The Committee enabled the imperialists to carry out their agenda for the destruction in Iraq behind closed doors with little attention and away from the media. They achieved that through two sinister mechanisms. Firstly, the Committee met *in camera* and kept few records of its meetings if any. Secondly, any member of the Committee had a right to prevent the import to Iraq of any item without having to give a reason for that veto. The scale of killing and destruction caused by the actions of the Sanctions Committee, we believe, was greater than the direct effect of the 1991 attack, as detailed in *Genocide in Iraq*.[9] If there had been a true nationalist government in Iraq since 2003, it would have been able and begun to gather evidence to show the scale of the criminality of the Sanctions Committee.

The sinister actions of the Committee can be exemplified by a practice which was calculated to give the impression that the Committee was being lenient in allowing some items into Iraq, when in fact the intention was to ensure they could not be used. Thus a stand-by generator would be allowed in but the cables needed to connect it to its switchgear and the circuit, and vital for its operation, were not. Such examples occurred repeatedly over the twelve years of sanctions.

Another measure employed by the Committee was the treatment of so-called items of 'dual use'. Under this category, items which were deemed necessary for civilian use were stopped on the ground that they could also have a military use. But in reality there is hardly an item that could not be used by the military. This rule was used to deny Iraqis many essential goods including X-ray films for hospitals and even pencils for schools because the US representative in the Committee claimed that graphite in pencils could be used to fabricate the rods needed for a nuclear reactor. Could the Committee have seriously believed that Iraq was going to import hundreds of millions of pencils to make reactor rods which it did not need because it did not have a reactor in the first place? The reason for the ban could only have been to cause maximum damage to Iraq by denying its children the wherewithal for a basic education.

The Project for the New American Century

In the spring of 1997, a group of Neocons set up 'The Project for the New American Century (PNAC)'. This was no ordinary think tank amid the plethora of such organizations. Some of its founding members, who served or were affiliated to former President Reagan, became the core of the establishment during the Bush era and determined US policy for eight years. This indicates how important it is to consider what PNAC advocated between 1997 and 2003.

In its Statement of Principles published on 3 June 1997, PNAC had this to say:

> America has a vital role in maintaining peace and security in Europe, Asia, and the Middle East. If we shirk our responsibilities, we invite challenges to our fundamental interests. The history of the 20th century should have taught us that it is important to shape circumstances before crises emerge, and to meet threats before they become dire. The history of this century should have taught us to embrace the cause of American leadership...
>
> .. a Reaganite policy of military strength and moral clarity may not be fashionable today. But it is necessary if the United States is to build on the successes of this past century and to ensure our security and our greatness in the next.[10]

Reading the literature on the Iraq war written by PNAC proponents and published on their website, one comes across a campaign of disinformation and hate, calling for the overthrow of the Ba'ath regime in Iraq, in line with its declared principle of total Zionist hegemony in the Middle East. There is no limit to the evil oozing out of their publications. Not once during the five-year campaign, which culminated with the invasion and destruction of Iraq, did PNAC mention the plight of the hapless Iraqi civilians. PNAC even opposed the 'smart sanctions'[11] which were adopted by the Security Council in May 2002 to ease some of the suffering of the Iraqis. All that PNAC was interested in was the invasion and destruction of Iraq. We will cite a few examples of that campaign to show the sinister intentions behind it.

On 15 December 1997, PNAC published an article by John Bolton in which he claimed that "the U.N. Security Council last week effectively rewarded [Saddam Hussein]. Not only did the council extend the misnamed 'oil for food' program at current levels – a loophole in the sanctions that lets Iraq export roughly $2 billion worth of oil every six months..."[12] What Bolton purposely neglected to state is that the proceeds from the sale of oil were in the hands of the UN and were going to be used to buy food for the people of Iraq, rather than rewarding Saddam.

On 26 January 1998 and eight years into the genocidal sanctions, the Neocons wrote a letter to President Clinton in which they expressed their imperialistic indifference to international law and the world community, saying:

> ... American policy cannot continue to be crippled by a misguided insistence on unanimity in the UN Security Council.[13]

On 2 February 1998, PNAC published an article by one of its prominent members, Robert Kagan, which gave a clear description of how it saw the Middle East under Zionist hegemony:

> A successful intervention in Iraq would revolutionize the strategic situation in the Middle East, in ways both tangible and intangible, and all to the benefit of American interests. Continued failure to take such action against Saddam will progressively erode our strategic position and will put the world on notice as the 21st century begins that the Americans, like the French and British of the 1930s, have lost their nerve.[14]

Arrogantly demonstrating how the imperialists have constantly treated and considered the UN as an extension of the State Department, PNAC published another article on 9 March 1998 by John Bolton, stating: "The reason U.N. Secretary General Kofi Annan went to Baghdad is not hard to understand.... What is harder to understand is why the Clinton administration allowed him to go at all, or permitted him any negotiating flexibility.[15]

On 16 November 1998, PNAC reproduced an editorial by Robert Kagan in the *Weekly Standard* titled 'How to Attack Iraq'. He wrote: "CIA director George Tenet said last January that Iraq already had the 'technological expertise' to produce biological weapons 'in a matter of weeks.'" And according to former U.N. weapons inspector Scott Ritter,

Saddam needs only six months without inspectors looking over his shoulder to build those weapons and deploy them on missiles capable of reaching Israel and other targets in the Middle East."[16] It is clear from the article that Kagan was advocating two objectives of the campaign to invade Iraq; one was to protect Israel and the other to remove Iraqi technological skills. The latter was later achieved when hundreds of Iraqi scientists were assassinated after the 2003 invasion, as we shall show later.

On 4-11 January 1999, as part of the campaign of lies following four days of air bombardment of Iraq, Kagan made the following incredible statement on behalf of PNAC under the title *"Saddam Wins–Again"*:

> When the strikes began Secretary Cohen declared that the "objective of the attack is to go after those chemical, biological or weapons of mass destruction sites to the extent that we can." This proved to be an artful and misleading claim. When the strikes ended, we learned that military planners had decided not to target weapons-production facilities after all because they were concerned about exposing innocent civilians to chemical and biological agents.[17]

By 1999 Kagan, like everyone else, already knew full well that there were no weapons manufacturing facilities in Iraq after the UN inspectors had searched every part of the country for eight years. If there were indeed such sites in January 1999, Scott Ritter and his fellow UN inspectors on the ground would have verified them without the need to strike them from the air. But Kagan intended full well to mislead people.

There was a lull in PNAC posting between March 1999 and July 2002 with only seven publications appearing on their website. PNAC became active again in July 2002 and intensified that activity as the invasion got closer. We conclude that this happened when PNAC knew that the final timetable to invade Iraq had been set and that it was necessary to prepare the American public.[18]

The first clear indication from PNAC that a concrete decision had been taken to invade Iraq came in its publication of an article by Kagan in July 2002 in which he confirmed our contention that the invasion of Iraq was pivotal in the Zionist strategy to subjugate the Arab World:

> But Iraq is no "window." It is a historical pivot. Whether a post-Hussein Iraq succeeds or fails will shape the course of Middle Eastern politics, and therefore world politics, both now and for the remainder of this century.

Europeans worry about that, and they're right to do so. If it's true that an invasion may be only six months off, this would be a good time to start thinking about D-Day plus 1. ....

Iraq may not be that different. Surrounded as it is by vulnerable friends such as Turkey, by Arab states of tenuous legitimacy, such as Jordan and Saudi Arabia, and by such worrisome nations as Iran and Syria, Iraq's success after Hussein's fall will be a vital American interest if ever there was one. If the United States goes into Iraq, it better be ready to stay there for as long as it takes. When President Bush makes it clear to our European allies that he understands this, at least some of them may breathe a little easier. And so should we.[19]

The above sample of writings propagated by the PNAC and the fact that the Bush administration had decided on 12 September 2001 that Iraq should be targeted, demonstrate how the preparation to invade Iraq was being planned independently and irrespective of any later claims about a fictitious threat of WMD. Iraq had to be invaded because it constituted the pivotal point in dominating and reshaping the Arab World for the 21st century.

Post 9/11

Anyone who reads *Zionism in the Age of the Dictators*[20] would not find it difficult to accept as possible the theories about the collusion of some US official circles in the 9/11 attack.[21] It is not inconceivable that some circles in the US needed to speed up the implementation of the strategy for Iraq and the rest of the Arab World through the attack on the New York towers. The mood of the public after the attack was not dissimilar to that following the attack on Pearl Harbor. The imperialists were granted free hand to make war with impunity and free from public scrutiny, arguing that they were acting in defence of the nation.

9/11 was the gift Bush and his group of Neocons were waiting for. They got their *casus belli*. What is relevant here is how the US wanted to use the attack as an excuse to invade Iraq. The following events will show clearly that the US was not interested in who really carried out the attack of 9/11 but was more interested in how to use the event as a cover to implicate Iraq. A few hours after the 9/11 attack, US Defence Secretary Donald Rumsfeld held several meetings within his Department. Contemporaneous notes of the meeting, which were taken by Stephen Cambone, Principal Deputy Undersecretary of Defense for Policy, and leaked to CBS News, were later declassified in February 2006 in response to a request by a law student and blogger, Thad Anderson, under the US Freedom of Information Act. Here are some of the notes as reported by History Commons:

> 12:05 p.m. September 11, 2001: Rumsfeld Finds Evidence of Al-Qaeda Role Not Good Enough
> CIA Director Tenet tells Defense Secretary Rumsfeld about an intercepted phone call from earlier in the day at 9:53 a.m. An al-Qaeda operative talked of a fourth target just before Flight 93 crashed. Rumsfeld's assistant Stephen Cambone dictates Rumsfeld's thoughts at the time, and the notes taken will later be leaked to CBS News. According to CBS, "Rumsfeld felt it was 'vague,' that it 'might not mean something,' and that there was 'no good basis for hanging hat.' In other words, the evidence was not clear-cut enough to justify military action against bin Laden." [CBS News, 9/4/2002]

> (2:40 p.m.) September 11, 2001: Rumsfeld Wants to Blame Iraq
> Defense Secretary Rumsfeld aide Stephen Cambone is taking notes on behalf of Rumsfeld in the National Military Command Centre. These notes will be leaked to the media nearly a year later. According to the notes, although Rumsfeld has already been given information indicating the 9/11 attacks were done by al-Qaeda (see 12:05 p.m. September 11, 2001) and he has been given no evidence so far indicating any Iraqi involvement, he is more interested in blaming the attacks on Iraq. According to his aide's notes, Rumsfeld wants the "best info fast. Judge whether good enough hit S.H. [Saddam Hussein] at same time. Not only UBL [Osama bin Laden]. ... Need to move swiftly. ... Go massive. Sweep it all up. Things related and not."[22]

We believe that the above notes are sufficient evidence to prove that US imperialism was bent on destroying Iraq irrespective of cause. Commenting on the above events James Moore wrote:

> Unless Rumsfeld had an inspired moment while the rest of the nation was in shock, the notes are irrefutable proof that the Bush administration had designs on Iraq and Hussein well before the president raised his hand to take the oath of office.[23]

The London *Guardian* commented on revelation of the notes as follows:

> .. these notes confirm that Baghdad was in the Pentagon's sights almost as soon as the hijackers struck.[24]

In reality, the plans for Iraq were underway already in the 1990s even before George W. Bush became President. A few examples of statements, interviews and actions that go to support this contention follow.

According to former White House insider Richard Clarke: "So what was urgent for them [the Bush administration] was Iraq. Al-Qaida was not important to them."[25]

Micky Herskowitz, who was a Texas writer hired to help President Bush construct his candidate autobiography, told freelance journalist and blogger Russ Baker in a taped conversation:

> He [Bush] was thinking about invading Iraq in 1999.... It was on his mind. He said to me: 'One of the keys to being seen as a great leader is to be seen as a commander-in-chief.... My father had all this political capital built up when he drove the Iraqis out of Kuwait and he wasted it..... If I have a chance to invade....if I had that much capital, I'm not going to waste it. I'm going to get everything passed that I want to get passed and I'm going to have a successful presidency.[26]

When Bush was asked by Fox News reporter Brit Hume, during the New Hampshire Republican Primary debate on 2 December 1999, what he would do differently from Clinton regarding Saddam Hussein, Bush replied: "I wouldn't ease the sanctions, and I wouldn't try to negotiate with him. I'd make darn sure that he lived up to the agreements that he signed back in the early '90s. I'd be helping the opposition groups. And if I found in any way, shape or form that he was developing weapons of mass destruction, I'd take 'em out. I'm surprised he's still there. I think a lot of other people are as well".[27] Because Hume seemingly thought Bush was referring to Saddam, he asked: "Take him out?", to which Bush replied: "To out [*sic*] the weapons of mass destruction."[28] This certainly doesn't explain the previous statement of "I'm surprised he's still there."

During the 2nd Presidential debate on 11 October 2000, Bush said: "....we don't know whether he's developing weapons of mass destruction. He better not be or there's going to be a consequence should I be the president.... I would hope to be able to convince people I could handle the Iraqi situation better. I mean, we don't –". When Jim

Lehrer, the moderator, asked: "Saddam Hussein, you mean, get him out of there?" Bush answered: "I would like to, of course, and I presume this administration would as well."[29]

General Wesley Clark, Retired 4-star US Army general, Supreme Allied Commander of NATO during the Kosovo War said the following in an interview with Democracy Now:

> ... What I did warn about when I testified in front of Congress in 2002, I said if you want to worry about a state, it shouldn't be Iraq, it should be Iran. But this government, our administration, wanted to worry about Iraq, not Iran....I knew why, because I had been through the Pentagon right after 9/11. About ten days after 9/11, I went through the Pentagon and I saw Secretary Rumsfeld and Deputy Secretary Wolfowitz. I went downstairs just to say hello to some of the people on the Joint Staff who used to work for me, and one of the generals called me in. He said, "Sir, you've got to come in and talk to me a second." I said, "Well, you're too busy." He said, "No, no." He says, "We've made the decision we're going to war with Iraq." This was on or about the 20th of September. I said, "We're going to war with Iraq? Why?" He said, "I don't know." He said, "I guess they don't know what else to do." So I said, "Well, did they find some information connecting Saddam to al-Qaeda?" He said, "No, no." He says, "There's nothing new that way. They just made the decision to go to war with Iraq." He said, "I guess it's like we don't know what to do about terrorists, but we've got a good military and we can take down governments." And he said, "I guess if the only tool you have is a hammer, every problem has to look like a nail.[30]

In September 2002 Secretary of State Colin Powell, speaking on "Fox News Sunday", said:

> And that's why it's been the policy of this government to insist that Iraq be disarmed in accordance with the terms of the relevant U.N. resolutions. And we believe the best way to do that is with a regime change, and that's why that has been U.S. policy, even though it's not United Nations policy....
>
> ... And the United States, often accused of being unilateral, is now bringing the problem back to its

original source, the United Nations, and saying here is the case. They have violated all of these resolutions, all of these conditions within the resolutions. And we can no longer turn away, it is no longer an option, as the president has said and as Prime Minister Blair said, it is no longer an option to simply ignore this and do nothing.[31]

On 19 September 2002, in a photo opportunity with Secretary of State Colin Powell at the Oval Office, President Bush was asked about the Resolution he was sending that day to the Congress: "how important is it that that resolution give you an authorization of the use of force?" to which he replied: "That will be part of the resolution, the authorization to use force. If you want to keep the peace, you've got to have the authorization to use force."[32]

This resulted in a joint resolution by the Senate and House of Representatives of the United States of America in Congress on 2 October 2002 for the "Authorization for the Use of Military Force against Iraq".[33]

In October 2002 at the Cincinnati Museum Center, President Bush hinted strongly at nuclear weapons stating:

We've experienced the horror of September the 11th. We have seen that those who hate America are willing to crash airplanes into buildings full of innocent people. Our enemies would be no less willing, in fact, they would be eager, to use biological or chemical, or a nuclear weapon. ...

Knowing these realities, America must not ignore the threat gathering against us. Facing clear evidence of peril, we cannot wait for the final proof—the smoking gun—that could come in the form of a mushroom cloud.[34]

We should emphasize here that all of the above was happening when there were no indications or revelations on WMD. Nor indeed was there any evidence of Iraq having the capability of delivering any weapon, assuming that it did have it. The US was thus preparing the world for its coming aggression.

Future of Iraq Project

Attempts to justify Rumsfeld's instruction to find a link between the 9/11 attack and Saddam Hussein as being anything but US official policy[35] soon evaporated when the Future of Iraq Project (FIP) was initiated.[36] The purpose of the project as revealed from the available unclassified document was to prepare and build Iraq, post Saddam Hussein. Considering that Iraq in 2001 was in a better position than it was in the mid-1990s and the Iraqi Government was beginning to overcome the burden of the sanctions through bilateral agreements with different countries and some easing of the control by the Security Council, then it could not be argued that the US expected the inevitable collapse of the Ba'ath regime. The only logical explanation for the setting up of the FIP must have been that the decision to invade Iraq was finally taken in 2001, relying on the mood of the US public and world sympathy post 9/11. This is how the unclassified documents on the National Security Archives described the FIP:

> Less than one month after the September 11 attacks, the State Department in October 2001 began planning the post-Saddam Hussein transition in Iraq. Under the direction of former State official Thomas S. Warrick, the Department organized over 200 Iraqi engineers, lawyers, businesspeople, doctors and other experts into 17 working groups to strategize on topics including the following: public health and humanitarian needs, transparency and anti-corruption, oil and energy, defense policy and institutions, transitional justice, democratic principles and procedures, local government, civil society capacity building, education, free media, water, agriculture and environment and economy and infrastructure...
>
> The result of the project was a 1,200-page 13-volume report that contains a multitude of facts, strategies, predictions and warnings about a diverse range of complex and potentially explosive issues, some of which have since developed as the report's authors anticipated, and have contributed to miring the U.S.-led nation-building experiment in disaster... [37]

The imperialists gathered some two hundred Iraqis, some of whom were known and some unheard of, mainly residents of the US or holding US nationality, and divided them into different groups to study Iraq's position during the Ba'ath rule and prepare the plans for a post Ba'ath regime. Looking at the released names of the Iraqis involved, we doubt very much if many of them took part in the actual preparation of the project or its findings. We personally know a few of them and know about a few others, and would conclude that if the rest were of the same caliber then there was very little chance of any serious constructive contribution coming from those chosen. The Iraqis, we believe, were chosen to give some legitimacy to the plan and convince the gullible American intelligentsia that it was a real Iraqi effort for a regime change. Needless to say, even if those two hundred Iraqis were genuinely looking for a regime change, what right did they have to model future Iraq on their ideals without a prior consent from the Iraqi public for such a change?

We doubt very much if many people have actually read the full 1200-page report. The accuracy of some material calls into question the claim that it contained multitudes of facts. But when the US considered the information of one Iraqi in a café in Amman, without corroboration, as factual it becomes secondary whether or not some material in such a report is accurate. [38]

Let us take a couple examples from that report that show inaccuracies or falsifications of facts. On page 1 of the report of the Education Working Group the following is stated:

> It must be recognized that before the advent of the Ba'athist regime of Saddam Hussein, Iraq had what is generally regarded as a high-quality education system at all levels....
>
> Now all that has been undermined by the Ba'athist approach to education. There is therefore a dual challenge for a renewed Education system in Iraq [39].

Only two paragraphs after that, the report states:

> ...the technical institutes and the universities of Iraq are for the most part still accepted internationally for the quality and rigour of their academic and technical training standards.

Anyone can see the contradiction between those two statements, which goes to show that the issue was not the realities of the matter, but the attempt to undermine any achievements of the Ba'ath, in this case in the field of education.[40]

On the issue of Agriculture, the report states:

> Iraq has considerable potential to increase cereal production. The present low productivity is due to several factors: lack of improved seeds, fertilizers, and pesticides; drought; deficient irrigation facilities; insufficient and old equipment; obsolete technology; and inadequate personnel.[41]

The report does not mention the role the US played in imposing the sanctions regime, the detrimental impact of same, and the steering of the activities of the sanctions committee, which prevented Iraq from purchasing pesticides and fertilizers or modernizing its equipment or even receiving books or journals related to the field. Examples of similar inaccuracies and/or deliberate misrepresentations occur in abundance throughout the report.

An analysis of these documents allowed us to conclude three points. First, the decision to invade Iraq in the revealed documents so far seems to have been made immediately after the September 11 attacks, using 9/11 as an excuse to justify action by the USA. Second, the documents refer to a post-Saddam transition, which could only signify prior knowledge about an impending occurrence. It indicates a process of planning within one sovereign state involving the deposition of the government of another, in clear violation of the principle of non-interference in sovereign State's internal affairs as guaranteed by article 2(7) of the UN Charter and as established in the context of the definition of aggression in General Assembly Resolution 3314 (XXIX) in 1974. Third, it strongly suggests that the US government planned to be the architect of change in the post-Saddam transition. After briefly considering some of the fallacies and misrepresentations on Iraq which appear in the released documents, we reached the conclusion that 'The Future of Iraq Project' is evidence that the US was planning to *reshape Iraq completely* after its occupation, despite the fact that this had nothing to do with its *casus belli*, the WMDs or purported presence of Al-Qaeda.

Regular Aerial Bombardment

Between the years 1991 and 2003 the US, UK and France set up what they unilaterally and illegitimately called "no-fly zones" in Northern and Sothern Iraq, contrary to many principles under international law. According to the imperialists, Iraq was not allowed to fly any military or civilian aircraft over 80% of its airspace, which in actuality meant that no domestic flights were allowed in Iraq for over twelve years. The imposition of these zones was designed to enable them to free Iraq's air space so that they might monitor and destroy any target they selected as part of the continuous degradation process.

During the twelve years of blockade, the imperialists carried out numerous aerial bombardments on military and civilian targets in Iraq without any provocation. The targets included anti-aircraft guns, roads, food warehouses, stocks of harvested wheat and sheep.[42] If the reports of these attacks came from Iraq, some might claim reasons to doubt their accuracy. But since such reports were made by sources that could not be labeled as Saddam Hussein's friends, there is no reason to doubt their authenticity. In his address to the Security Council the representative of the Russian Federation had this to say:

> Today we cannot fail to react to another problem that has been pointed out. The socio-economic and humanitarian situation in Iraq is worsening because civilian facilities in Iraq are constantly the targets of air strikes by the United States and Great Britain. This is happening in the so-called no-flight zones established unilaterally, without the United Nations taking any decision, and which encompass almost 65 per cent of Iraq's territory.
>
> Our data show that United States and United Kingdom aircraft invaded Iraqi airspace nearly 20,000 times between December 1998 and mid-March 2000. We are particularly concerned about reports of strikes against facilities that are being used in the United Nations humanitarian operation, in particular against food distribution warehouses and against metering stations along oil pipelines.
>
> According to these analyses, 42 per cent of these air strikes have resulted in human casualties. Over the past year, 144 innocent civilians have died and 466 people have been wounded as a result of these air strikes. Our data show that 57 people have been killed and 133 wounded in southern Iraq, and that 87 people have been killed and 313 wounded in the north. Claims that these strikes were not directed against civilian targets do not hold water. Facts—including facts from international experts—attest to the contrary. Nor does the notion that these air strikes were in retaliation for actions by Iraqi anti-aircraft defenses hold water: our data show that facilities unrelated to anti-aircraft defense systems are being hit.[43]

The regular aerial attacks on Iraq during the sanctions period were clearly designed to weaken Iraq to the stage where its invasion would become an easy undertaking with less cost to the imperialists irrespective of how much suffering, destruction and killing this caused the civilians.[44]

Dossier of Lies and Fabrications

Although it has been revealed that the decision to invade Iraq was finalized between George Bush and Tony Blair at the beginning of 2002, there is a still a concerted effort in some circles to present the invasion of Iraq as having been made to remove WMDs.[45] For more than twelve years UN inspectors had covered every inch of Iraq looking for alleged WMDs and their delivery means but found nothing. The inspection operation was best described by Major General Michael Laurie in his secret evidence to the Chilcot inquiry.[46] In a written submission to the Inquiry, he stated: "There has probably never been a greater detailed scrutiny of every piece of ground in any country."[47]

Yet British PM Tony Blair needed to convince a few skeptics in his party and the general public at large that there was a real danger from an imminent attack from Iraq against Britain.

Thus on 24 September 2002, Prime Minister Tony Blair published his dossier on Iraq's WMDs, the dossier which has since become known as the Downing Street's "dodgy dossier".[48] The dossier claimed that Iraq possessed weapons of mass destruction, including biological and chemical weapons. It claimed that the evidence was based on work of the Joint Intelligence Committee, but whose origins were kept secret.

In his Foreword to the dossier, Blair wrote how it indicated that:

> .... Saddam has continued to produce chemical and biological weapons, that he continues in his efforts to develop nuclear weapons, and that he has been able to extend the range of his ballistic missile programme.[49]

Blair went on to say:

> ...the document discloses that his military planning allows for some of the WMD to be ready within 45 minutes of an order to use them.[50]

The normal practice in any state is that the Government relies on its intelligence services when it comes to information and advice before it formulates its foreign policy or military strategy. But for Blair it was done in reverse. He told the intelligence services what he wanted the intelligence dossier to include, and had it resent to them more than once so that its final draft met his wishes. In plain and simple English, it was 'sexed-up'. Laurie, who was director general in the Defence Intelligence Staff, responsible for commanding and delivering raw and analysed intelligence, wrote to the Chilcot inquiry:

> We knew at the time that the purpose of the dossier was precisely to make a case for war, rather than setting out the available intelligence, and that to make the best

out of sparse and inconclusive intelligence the wording was developed with care...

... I am writing to comment on the position taken by Alastair Campbell during his evidence to you ... when he stated that the purpose of the dossier was not to make a case for war; I and those involved in its production saw it exactly as that, and that was the direction we were given.[51]

The final Intelligence Dossier claimed to have been based on solid intelligence when in fact "Much of the key intelligence used by Downing Street and the White House was based on fabrication, wishful thinking and lies."[52]

By September 2002 all the Western intelligence services were satisfied that Iraq could not have had any WMDs. Muhammad ElBaradei, the head of IAEA, knew that Iraq could not have any nuclear program. Hans Blix, head of UNMOVIC, although equivocating, knew that Iraq could not have any chemical or biological weapons especially since it had uncovered many dumping sites of its stocks of WMD to the UN inspectors.[53]

It is misleading for anyone to write that there was "an intelligence failure".[54] There was no such failure and both the political leadership and the intelligence services knew that. There was an effort to have the services reproduce discredited reports from a few dissatisfied Iraqis,[55] together with articles published on the web, with a view to producing the pack of lies which led to the invasion and destruction of Iraq. It transpired soon after its publication that "whole swathes were lifted word for word–grammatical slips and all–from a student thesis (Ibrahim al-Marashi, an American postgraduate student of Iraqi descent who works at the Monterey Institute of International Studies in California)... " Glen Rangwala, an Iraq specialist at Cambridge University who analyzed the Downing Street dossier, told Reuters that 11 of its 19 pages were "taken wholesale from academic papers."[56]

Thus when Blair's dossier talked about Iraq having WMDs with the ability to deliver them within 45 minutes, which the next day became the headlines of the *Sun* and *Star* inviting the British public to believe that a serious threat existed, it was simply lying. Incredibly, not one single Member of Parliament raised the logical question of how, even if it had some WMDs hidden underground, Iraq could have delivered any of these WMD to Cyprus or anywhere outside its borders, since every missile with a range beyond 150 km had been accounted for and destroyed by the UN inspectors?

The buildup in the US was no less theatrical although the President was not under the same pressure as that faced by Blair.

One year and one day after the 9/11 attacks, President Bush addressed the UN General Assembly telling the world states to confront "grave and gathering danger" from Iraq, and indicating that the US will act:

> The Security Council resolutions will be enforced–the just demands of peace and security will be met–or action will be unavoidable.[57]

Bush had few skeptics and the public in the US at that time was ready to go to war anywhere. But the US needed to appear to the rest of the world to be acting as a responsible international player. Towards that end, on 5 February 2003, the then Secretary of State Colin Powell, staged a rather comical presentation to the Security Council. In addition to basing his assertions about Iraq possessing WMD "on numerous human sources",[58] he presented to the Security Council with what he claimed were mobile production facilities for biological agents in Iraq. Any university graduate in biology would find such a claim to be preposterous. In the absence of any credible US scientist challenging the possibility of the existence of such facilities in Iraq, it would not really matter whether Powell or his aide, Col. Lawrence Wilkerson, who prepared the UN speech, had any scientific skills to assess the plausibility of what was being presented. The whole story was completely invented.[59]

Despite the fact that on 27 May 2003, US and UK experts examined the trailers and declared they had nothing to do with biological weapons,[60] "as late as February 2004, then-CIA Director George J. Tenet continued to assert that the mobile-labs theory remained plausible. Although there was "no consensus" among intelligence officials, the trailers "could be made to work" as weapons labs, he said in a speech delivered on Feb 5." [61]

A decade later, with over one million Iraqis dead, over four million displaced and unprecedented corruption in a divided country that now lacks in every basic amenity, Col. Lawrence Wilkerson had this to say on the trailers claim:

> I don't believe the hype about that presentation having been the ultimate presentation ... that led us to war with Iraq ... George W. Bush, Dick Cheney and others had decided to go to war with Iraq long before Colin Powell gave that presentation. ... It added to the momentum of the war. ... Frankly, we were all wrong. Was the intelligence politicized in addition to being wrong at its roots? Absolutely.

... it wasn't the seminal moment that sent us into war; it was just one of those moments. And as one of those moments, as I've said before and as you quoted me, I feel like it was the lowest point in my professional and personal life that I had a hand in managing it.[62]

4

THE
SHOCK AND AWE
INVASION

In preparation to invade Iraq and overthrow its regime, the US, with Britain by its side, embarked on a campaign of lies, fabrications and falsifications to set the ground for its invasion. There is no doubt anymore, with the amount of information revealed in the past ten years, that the final decision to attack Iraq was made on 12 September 2001 following the 9/11 attacks.

What remained for the imperialists was to find a way to make it look like an act of self-defence or a claim to uphold international law, rather than the illegal act of aggression that it clearly was.

The US and Britain were thus telling the world that they were seeking to overthrow the Iraqi regime because of its alleged non-compliance with Security Council (SC) resolutions imposed on it. Powell had specifically denied accusations that the US was acting unilaterally, saying that the US was "bringing the problem back to its original source, the United Nations."[1]

On 19 September 2002, one week after the address of President Bush, Iraq's President Saddam Hussein addressed the UN General Assembly in a speech read by Foreign Minister Naji Sabri.[2] The speech responded to UN Secretary General Annan's statement to the UN General Assembly on 12 September that readmitting inspectors was "the indispensable first step towards assuring the world that all Iraq's weapons of mass destruction have indeed been eliminated, and—let me stress—towards the suspension and eventual ending of the sanctions that are causing so many hardships for the Iraqi people".[3] Quoting the Iraqi president, Sabri said:

> Our country is ready to receive any scientific experts, accompanied by politicians you choose to represent any one of your countries, to tell us which places and scientific installations they would wish to see, particularly those about which the American officials have been fabricating false stories, alleging that they contain prohibited materials or activities... I hereby declare before you that Iraq is clear of all nuclear, chemical and biological weapons.

But Iraq's offer to admit the inspectors met with deaf ears in the United States and Britain, who had begun drafting a resolution that would tighten the timetable for Iraq to comply with previous resolutions and authorize force if it failed to do so. On the same day, Bush asked Congress through Secretary of State Colin Powell for authority to use military force to overthrow the Iraqi government.[4] The US failure to respond to the Iraqi offer to admit the inspectors exposed the fact that the persistent allegations by the US and UK that Iraq was continuing to develop biological, chemical and nuclear weapons were nothing other than cynical propaganda for war.[5]

On 8 November 2002, the SC unanimously adopted Resolution 1441 calling for new inspections to find and eliminate Iraq's WMD, establishing revised or additional authorities, binding upon Iraq, to facilitate their work in Iraq.[6] Under the terms of the resolution, which Iraq accepted,[7] the chief inspectors were to report promptly back to the Security Council if Iraq obstructed their work, after which the SC would "convene immediately" to consider the situation and "the need for full compliance." The resolution also threatened "serious consequences" if Iraq failed to comply.

At this stage, the United States, backed by Britain and Spain, began to seek a new SC resolution declaring Iraq in material breach of its obligation to disarm in order to carry out the attack and impose regime change. But permanent members France, Russia and China, as well as a number of other members, opposed the resolution. France, for example, was worried then that the US would take "unilateral action" against Iraq with British support. France also believed that the declared attempt to secure a new SC Resolution authorizing an attack on Iraq was in reality a "trap", insofar as existing SC resolutions did not justify war. Foreign Minister Dominique de Villepin stated that France remained opposed to a new resolution because it believed UN weapons inspectors still needed time to do their work in Iraq.[8] Paris was further afraid that the US and the UK would use negotiations at the UN as "cover for a better basis for war" and not to prevent military action.[9]

On 24 February 2003, the US, UK and Spain tabled a draft resolution, which British Ambassador Jeremy Greenstock said would set a deadline for Iraq's compliance, "implicitly or explicitly," to force the Security Council to limit how much longer inspections would continue without Baghdad's full cooperation.[10] Despite significant diplomatic efforts, the sponsors soon concluded that they were not going to be able to secure a consensus within the Security Council on this new resolution.[11]

Colin Powell's appearance at the Security Council on 5 February 2003 will remain as one of the most ignominious fabrications in the history of the orchestrated campaign against Iraq. He went to the SC prepared to deceive the United Nations, the American public, and the soldiers his country was about to send to kill and die in Iraq. It is now clear that the "evidence" presented by Powell was fabricated and that he had ignored repeated warnings that what he was going to say was false. What Powell said will be remembered by Iraqis, and he will certainly carry the shame of that appearance for the rest of his life. Even though he later apologized for spreading these falsifications, it does not change the fact that he was an active tool in the attempts to overthrow the Iraqi government.[12]

Colin Powell assured the Security Council that "every statement I make today is backed up by sources, solid sources. These are not assertions. What we're giving you are facts and conclusions based on solid intelligence."[13]

Powell claimed that Iraq was cooperating with and harbouring Al-Qaeda and providing training to its members. He showed photos of what he claimed was a poison and explosives training camp in northeast Iraq, operated by Al-Qaeda. Powell alleged that these training camps had been operating with help from Iraqi agents, in spite of the fact that the Kurdish northern Iraq, where these alleged camps were, fell outside the *de facto* Iraqi Government control. That same morning, the BBC reported that an official British intelligence report submitted to PM Tony Blair had stated that there were no current links between the Iraqi regime and the Al-Qaeda network.[14] The Top Secret report said that Al-Qaeda leader Osama Bin Laden viewed Iraq's ruling Ba'ath party as running contrary to his religion, calling it an "apostate regime", and that "his aims are in ideological conflict with present day Iraq."

This was one week after Bush claimed to have evidence of links between Iraq and Al-Qaeda in his state of the union address:

> Evidence from intelligence sources, secret communications, and statements by people now in custody reveal that Saddam Hussein aids and protects terrorists, including members of al Qaeda. Secretly, and without fingerprints, he could provide one of his

hidden weapons to terrorists, or help them develop their own.[15]

Bush also said:

> From three Iraqi defectors we know that Iraq, in the late 1990s, had several mobile biological weapons labs. These are designed to produce germ warfare agents, and can be moved from place to place to evade inspectors. Saddam Hussein has not disclosed these facilities. He's given no evidence that he has destroyed them.
>
> The United States will ask the U.N. Security Council to convene on February the 5th to consider the facts of Iraq's ongoing defiance of the world. Secretary of State Powell will present information and intelligence about Iraqi's legal–Iraq's illegal weapons programs, its attempt to hide those weapons from inspectors, and its links to terrorist groups.[16]

Powell played what he said were intercepted conversations between Iraqi officers who were discussing ways to conceal prohibited materials from UN inspectors. It is interesting to see how Powell and his aids had falsified the translation and added their own interpretation to the Arabic language conversation. Here is what Powell presented:

> And we sent you a message yesterday to clean out all of the areas, the scrap areas, the abandoned areas. Make sure there is nothing there.

But the correct interpretation, posted by the US Department of State in the full transcript of conversation, is:

> And we sent you a message to inspect the scrap areas and the abandoned areas.[17]

Powell referred to Iraq having produced four tons of the deadly nerve agent, VX, asserting that the evidence was acquired after the defection of Hussein Kamel, Saddam Hussein's late son-in-law. But Powell omitted the most important part of the story: that Iraq had produced the VX before the Gulf War of 1991, and that Hussein Kamel had told the Americans and UN officials that all such weapons were destroyed under his order.[18]

Assuring the members of the SC that his conclusions were the result of "painstaking work of photo analysis" which had taken experts "hours and hours over light tables", Powell used satellite images to support the allegations that Iraq was still producing and hiding chemical weapons. Powell claimed that these images show Iraqis "sanitizing" bunkers used for storing chemical munitions. Again Powell left out the fact that days before Powell's presentation UNMOVIC's chief, Hans Blix, had already refuted these allegations in an interview with *The New York Times*.[19] Blix "challenged several of the Bush administration's assertions about Iraqi cheating and the notion that time was running out for disarming Iraq through peaceful means". Here is how *The New York Times* reported the interview:[20]

> Mr. Blix took issue with what he said were Secretary of State Colin L. Powell's claims that the inspectors had found that Iraqi officials were hiding and moving illicit materials within and outside of Iraq to prevent their discovery. He said that the inspectors had reported no such incidents.
>
> Similarly, he said, he had not seen convincing evidence that Iraq was sending weapons scientists to Syria, Jordan or any other country to prevent them from being interviewed. Nor had he any reason to believe, as President Bush charged in his State of the Union speech, that Iraqi agents were posing as scientists.
>
> He further disputed the Bush administration's allegations that his inspection agency might have been penetrated by Iraqi agents, and that sensitive information might have been leaked to Baghdad, compromising the inspections.

Relying on unnamed "eyewitnesses" (which brings to mind the infamous "eyewitness" in the incubator case in Kuwait in 1990), and testimonies from unknown "defectors", Powell's claim that Iraq had mobile production facilities used to make biological agents lacked any hard evidence. In a desperate attempt to explain what these laboratories were supposed to look like, Powell used "diagrams" based on the alleged description given by those "unknown" sources, stating: "....we know what the fermenters look like, we know what the tanks, pumps, compressors and other parts look like. We know how they fit together. We know how they work. And we know a great deal about the platforms on which they are mounted." In a ridiculous act of theatrics for which American politicians are known, Powell then produced a vial containing a white substance, to emphasize the threat of Iraq allegedly still having Anthrax.[21].

What Powell intentionally left out of his presentation was that the US itself had been the provider of WMD to Iraq. He chose not to tell his listeners that the biological material to make anthrax, E. coli, botulism and other biological diseases were supplied to Iraq by an American company, the American Type Culture Collection, under contracts approved by the US Commerce Department[22] probably intended for use against Iran.

The "evidence" presented by Powell did not convince Russia, China, France and Germany. He failed to change their opinions on authorizing an attack on Iraq. They seemingly knew, from their own intelligence, what the US knew: that these were fabrications. If such "evidence" were to be presented in a US court, it would be thrown out because it would never have satisfied the basic requirement of "beyond a reasonable doubt". What Powell presented amounted to nothing more than shameful old allegations, hearsay and inventions.

When the Americans and British became aware that their resolution would not be adopted, they resorted to another escalating tactic: that of the need to act in self-defence. But putting forward the notion of their being under imminent threat generated a new inconsistency which those parties glossed over; that of fusing different categories of weapons into one word: WMD. The Carnegie Report explains the issue in the following way:

> ...nuclear, chemical, and biological weapons were routinely conflated: that is, treated as a single WMD threat. This made it technically accurate to say that Iraq had, or might still, possess weapons of mass destruction. However, such statements were seriously misleading in that they lumped together the high likelihood that Iraq possessed chemical weapons, which themselves constitute only a minor threat, with the complete lack of evidence that it possessed nuclear weapons, which would be a huge threat. Talk of "mushroom clouds" certainly led Americans to believe that the latter were in the picture.[23]

As further evidence that the US and UK were manufacturing a 'Cause for War' rather than reacting to genuine threats of attack, they embarked on dishonourable espionage against fellow Members of the UN Security Council. Ms Katharine Gun, a GCHQ employee, was charged under the Official Secrets Act for revealing a secret e-mail from US spies asking British officers to tap phones of nations voting on war against Iraq.[24] Cabinet Minister Clare Short confirmed that Britain spied on UN secretary

General Kofi Annan ahead of the Iraq war.[25] When it was clear they would not support such a resolution, UK Attorney General Lord Goldsmith was pressured by his US counterparts to revise his early Opinion that an attack without specific UN approval would be unlawful, to say that an attack had already been authorized by an earlier Resolution (1441).

With the threat of war looming, huge protests and demonstrations were held in many cities around the world, some coordinated to occur simultaneously. The biggest of those demonstrations took place on 15 February 2003, according to Guinness World Records, with

> [the] largest occurring in Rome, Italy, where a crowd of 3 million gathered to protest against the USA's threat to invade Iraq. Police figures report that millions more demonstrated in nearly 600 cities worldwide: on the same day, 1.3 million rallied in Barcelona, Spain, 1 million participated in a peace march through the streets of London, UK, and 500,000 people in Melbourne and Sydney, Australia, joined the biggest marches since the Vietnam War peace protests.[26]

It is estimated that "between 3 January and 12 April 2003, some 36 million people took part in nearly 3,000 protests around the world against the Iraq war."[27] But that did not dissuade Bush or his supporters. The plans for the attack were proceeding.

On 17 March 2003 President Bush addressed the American people with these words:

> Intelligence gathered by this and other governments leaves no doubt that the Iraq regime continues to possess and conceal some of the most lethal weapons ever devised. This regime has already used weapons of mass destruction against Iraq's neighbours and against Iraq's people.
>
> The regime has a history of reckless aggression in the Middle East. It has a deep hatred of America and our friends. And it has aided, trained and harboured terrorists, including operatives of al Qaeda.
>
> The danger is clear: using chemical, biological or, one day, nuclear weapons, obtained with the help of Iraq, the terrorists could fulfil their stated ambitions and kill thousands or hundreds of thousands of innocent people in our country, or any other.
>
> The United States and other nations did nothing to deserve or invite this threat. But we will do everything

to defeat it. Instead of drifting along toward tragedy, we will set a course toward safety. Before the day of horror can come, before it is too late to act, this danger will be removed.

The United States of America has the sovereign authority to use force in assuring its own national security. That duty falls to me, as Commander-in-Chief, by the oath I have sworn, by the oath I will keep.

Recognizing the threat to our country, the United States Congress voted overwhelmingly last year to support the use of force against Iraq.[28]

He also gave an ultimatum to Saddam Hussein:

Saddam Hussein and his sons must leave Iraq within 48 hours. Their refusal to do so will result in military conflict, commenced at a time of our choosing. For their own safety, all foreign nationals—including journalists and inspectors—should leave Iraq immediately.

Preparing for the invasion

Before embarking on any military action, the US wanted the support of the regional countries and took measures to ensure the open support of Saudi Arabia, Kuwait, Bahrain, Oman, Qatar, and the United Arab Emirates and the "quiet" support of Jordan.[29] The aim was to give the impression that there was a large "coalition" facing Iraq, especially from among Arab states. The US had already gained the full backing of the UK and Australia whose prime ministers took their decisions in spite of strong opposition in their parliaments and respective publics.

Over a period extending from June 2002 to February 2003, those Arab "allies" assisted the US and UK in their build-up and delivery of their supplies and major land combat equipment by sea.[30] This took place much earlier than any talk of the need for a new SC resolution! These Arab countries gave the two major coalition partners access to the Gulf bases they needed for the planned invasion. When Turkey refused to allow the US to openly use its land or air, the plans were modified to allow for simultaneous attacks from north and south. Special Operations forces from the CIA and US Army managed to build and lead the Kurdish Peshmerge from the KDP into an effective force and assault from the North,[31] with the primary bases for the invasion being in the Gulf States and Jordan.

The CIA had been working hard before the war started to bribe, persuade or coerce Iraqi officers not to fight. More than 50 Special Forces teams with British and Australian Special Forces had entered the Iraqi desert with the purpose of taking out Iraqi observation posts along Iraq's borders with Jordan, Kuwait, and Saudi Arabia. They are reported to have succeeded in taking out 50 such posts on the first night of the war and 50 more on the second. Other Special Forces teams were tasked with preventing the deployment of Scud missiles, even though details of these operations are still classified.[32]

During the preceding decade, the coalition had established a complete set of military bases in several of the Gulf States to which it had moved equipment and supplies nearly a year earlier, while also improving its forward facilities in Qatar and Kuwait. But the build-up in Saudi Arabia had started some three decades earlier, with Jimmy Carter's strategy of rapid deployment forces and the building of bases and airports in Arabia for which there was no need.[33]

In reality, the war on Iraq had started in September 1990 and never stopped, as the patrols of the unilaterally imposed no-fly zones concentrated, throughout the whole 1990s and especially starting 2002, on destroying Iraqi air defence systems with precision-guided weapons.[34]

At the outset of the war in March 2003, some 10,000 soldiers from the US army with 200 fighters, tankers and surveillance aircraft were based at Prince Sultan Base in Saudi. The ruling family had already agreed in February 2003 to every US request for military and logistical support.[35] Saudi Arabia "granted" overflight rights to US planes and missiles, and further provided the US Special Operations forces with staging grounds into Iraq.[36] Saudi airbases were extensively used for "no-fly-zone" missions that had been going on since 1991 and thus helped weaken Iraq's air defenses before and during the war.[37] The Saudi regime provided AWACS and E-8C missions on Saudi soil with fuel at minimal cost. In addition to allowing the use of the Combined Air Operations Center (CAOC) to manage coalition air operations, the Saudis put facilities at Ar'ar at the disposal of Special Forces search and rescue missions. But perhaps the most important step taken by the Saudis was ensuring the steady flow of oil exports to compensate for the loss of Iraqi and Venezuelan exports.[38]

In addition to the use of bases and facilities in the Gulf States, Egypt gave free passage through the Suez Canal and opened its airspace for Coalition flights. Jordan not only allowed the use of its airspace for overflights and permitted Patriot units and missile warning systems to operate from its soil, but it also allowed the US Special Forces to operate from bases in East Jordan whose main aim was to prevent Iraqi Scud missiles from being launched at targets in Israel. F-16s carrying laser-guided bombs flew over 700 sorties into Iraq from Jordan.[39]

The British contribution to the coalition is detailed by the MOD's report, Operations in Iraq: First Reflections:

Our maritime contribution to the coalition was the first to be announced, on 7 January 2003, and built on the standing Royal Navy presence in the Gulf. Naval Task Group 2003... was expanded to a much larger force totaling some 9000 personnel.

... On 20 January, the Defence Secretary announced the deployment of a major ground force ... which eventually totaled some 28,000.

... The Royal Air Force already maintained a presence of some 25 aircraft and 1000 personnel in the Gulf, flying sorties over Iraq to enforce the No-Fly Zones and to restrict the regeneration of Iraqi air and Integrated Air Defence capabilities. On 6 February the Defence Secretary announced that the RAF contribution would be increased to around 100 fixed wing aircraft manned and supported by a further 7000 personnel.

... Overall, the UK contribution amounted to some 46,000 personnel out of a total of some 467,000 coalition forces.

... Many others provided crucial assistance with intelligence, logistics and the deployment of combat units. President Bush confirmed on 18 March that over 40 countries were supporting the coalition.[40]

Added to the superiority of the striking power of the coalition armies, the advanced technology of its weaponry and Iraq's practically non-existent defence, the total forces committed by the coalition outnumbered Iraq's forces. The overall number of US personnel deployed at different stages in "Operation Iraqi Freedom" amounted to 466,985. Other active coalition personnel were: 40,906 from Britain, 2,050 from Australia, 31 from Canada and 180 from Poland.[41]

We should recall that the British Ministry of Defence clearly stated in its report of 18 March 2003 that the aim of the campaign against Iraq was "to rid Iraq of its weapons of mass destruction and their associated programmes and means of delivery, including prohibited ballistic missiles, as set out in relevant United Nations Security Council Resolutions (UNSCRs)."[42] The report went on, to state that:

The main tasks of the coalition are to:

a. overcome the resistance of Iraqi security forces;
b. deny the Iraqi regime the use of weapons of mass destruction now and in the future;

c. remove the Iraqi regime, given its clear and unyielding refusal to comply with the UN Security Council's demands;

d. identify and secure the sites where weapons of mass destruction and their means of delivery are located;

e. secure essential economic infrastructure, including for utilities and transport, from sabotage and wilful destruction by Iraq; and

f. deter wider conflict both inside Iraq and in the region.[43]

It is thus irrefutable that the aim of the force was not to destroy Iraq's alleged WMDs, but rather a full invasion of Iraq, the destruction of any force it had left, and the overthrow of the regime. The size of the armies and the kinds of weapons they were employing leaves no doubt about these aims. The alleged existence of WMD was only an excuse, as it was later proved.

The Invasion

One day before the lapse of the deadline, two US stealth planes dropped four satellite-guided 2,000-pound bunker busters on a bunker in a little-used residential palace in Dora Farms, a neighbourhood in the south of Baghdad, where an intelligence report had said Saddam Hussein and his sons Uday and Qusai were.[44] That intelligence proved to be wrong as Saddam and his sons were nowhere near that compound. The Imperialists have been so successful in conditioning our thinking that we have come to accept acts of assassinations as commonly accepted actions by states. Attempts at the lives of state leaders like Saddam Hussein are crimes under international law, irrespective of whether or not war is legitimate. We must bear in mind: these are the principles of law and order that have permeated international relations for a century.

The actual invasion began in the early hours of 20 March 2003, a bit over an hour after the lapse of the deadline. "Shock and Awe" began with "50 strikes in a 10-minute volley of almost biblical power that followed the opening blast."[45]

"Shock and Awe" is a military term that explains the doctrine of the use of overwhelming power and extreme display of force to destroy the adversary's will to fight and thus paralyze him. The doctrine was coined by Harlan K. Ullman and James P. Wade in 1996 and is a product of the National Defense University of the United States. It should remain synonymous in the public mind with an earlier term of similar portent: *blitzkrieg*. The US and its allies had therefore planned from the beginning to use the most horrifying forms of terror on the Iraqi people to force them to submit to their will. The variable that the "shock and awe" campaign was designed to destroy was the will to fight.

But "Shock and awe" is nothing more than state terrorism. [46]

George Bush announced the beginning of the war on Iraq in an address to the nation on 20 March 2003 [10 PM on the evening of 19 March EST] in which he outlined the alleged objective of the war as "to disarm Iraq, to free its people and to defend the world from grave danger".[47] Bush explained that "coalition forces" from 35 countries were on his orders opening stages of what would be a broad and concerted campaign, striking selected targets of military importance to undermine Saddam Hussein's ability to wage war.[48] Bush went to great length to assure his listeners that the attacking forces will show an "honorable and decent spirit", that they "will make every effort to spare innocent civilians from harm" and that his forces had come to Iraq "with respect for its citizens, for their great civilization and for the religious faiths they practice" without any ulterior motives, only "to remove a threat and restore control of that country to its own people."[49] It did not take long for the world to see how false those words were. It is rather comical to listen to the US President telling the world that Iraq in 2003, after 13 years of genocidal sanctions and years of weapons inspections, could have constituted a threat to the US. Bush was doing no more than what he told Micky Herskowitz he wanted: to enter history as a victor of a main war![50] It should have been clear from the first day of the invasion when Iraq failed to retaliate, that it had not done so because it had no means to do so, and that the whole campaign was based on falsehood and ought to have stopped after the first day. If Iraq had had any WMD it would have used them against the invader.

However, the syndicated 'western' media conspired to ignore this odd failure to retaliate, and its corroboration of the fact that UNSCOM had destroyed all Iraq's WMD in the early 1990s. It also ignored the 'collateral damage' i.e. the murder of innocents and the disproportionate destruction of essential civilian infrastructure. And it persisted in what is becoming the time-worn demonization of every leader who opposes its policies—that Saddam was 'an evil dictator' and 'a threat to the region' to justify all human suffering due to coalition forces.

On the same day, Australian PM John Howard addressed his nation, repeating the same lies about the dual threat of WMD and terrorism—a ludicrous attempt to justify the invasion on the grounds of an alleged right to self-defence of his distant country:

> We believe that so far from our action in Iraq increasing the terrorist threat it will, by stopping the spread of chemical and biological weapons, make it less likely

that a devastating terrorist attack will be carried out against Australia.[51]

Details of the military actions have been collected from numerous printed and published sources, personal follow-ups and media reports. We have put them as a summary of events, and it would therefore not always be possible to refer each incident to a single source.[52]

The "coalition" launched more than 1100 cruise missiles aimed at some 1,000 targets throughout Iraq, including command and control installations, structures, and buildings. The other targets were the northern towns of Kirkuk, Mosul, and Tikrit. The "coalition" used its most sophisticated planes in these attacks including B-52 bombers, B-2 stealth bombers, and F-117 stealth fighter-bombers, while F-15s were used for the suppression of Iraqi air defense systems.

The planes also struck "communication sites near Ash-Shuaybah, Mudaysis, and Ruwayshid; long-range artillery near Az-Zubayr; a mobile early-warning radar and an air defense command center in western Iraq; long-range artillery on the Al-Faw peninsula; a surface-to-surface missile system and an air traffic control radar near Al Basra."[53] The airstrikes in early March 2003 also targeted Iraq's secure optical fiber communications network, which was vital for its communications, forcing the authorities to use easily tracked high frequency radio communication systems.[54] Coalition airstrikes had been covertly destroying Iraq's air defences and Early Warning Systems in the North and South No-Fly Zones since 1991, under the false guise of preventing Saddam Hussein from attacking his own people. The aim was clearly to weaken Iraq to the extent that an attack would not have to endure any response from Iraq's defences.

Tomahawk missiles were also launched from 30 U.S. Navy and coalition warships, as well the RAF's new Storm Shadow missiles which were successfully used for the first time in operations. It is estimated that 2,500 missiles and bombs were dropped in the first 72 hours. Based on available information from the Pentagon and UN, experts have estimated that US-led military forces used between 1,100 and 2,200 tonnes of depleted uranium during the invasion of Iraq,[55] much of which appears to have been in or near urban areas, where the Iraqi people live, work, draw water, and grow and sell food.

The American forces were soon to realize how false a picture they had been given of the level of Iraqi support for their attack. Lt. General William Wallace, the commander of the 5th Corps, later explained the situation as follows:

> ...we had to adjust to his paramilitary (forces), which were more fanatical and more aggressive than we expected (them) to be. The adjustment that we made was to

actually fight and have a presence in some of these urban areas that we had not really planned to do. We planned to bypass them. But we found it necessary to establish a presence to stop these paramilitaries from influencing our operations.

The Iraqis had devised a strategy based on luring the attackers deep into cities then entrapping and ambushing them, where they could then use massed RPG, rifle, mortar, and small arms fire to destroy enemy units. The defending units could thus remain small and almost independent of each other, operating in populated areas where the need for communications would be greatly reduced because they would be informed in advance to defend from a particular area.[56]

The US had either relied on falsified information supplied by members of the Iraqi opposition, most of whom had no real knowledge of the Iraqi people, no respect for Iraqi patriotism and nationalist cohesion, or it had again relied on its own "experts" who lacked the understanding of the Arab mentality. The US had not understood that Iraqis blamed Capitol Hill for their suffering under the sanctions it had imposed and maintained; for the US unconditional support for Israel; for the fact that the US was coming to seize their oil and knew that America had scant regard for human lives as it had shown during the preceding decade of starvation and suffering under its totalitarian embargo.

Members of Coalition special operations had crossed the Jordanian border into Iraq some time before the beginning of the official attacks, entrusted with attacking isolated Iraqi units and monitoring stations in the western border areas.[57]

A few battles stand out as extremely fierce and a surprise to the attacking forces. These were in Basrah, Nasiriyah, Najaf and Baghdad.

The first air and amphibious assault was carried out in the south of Iraq by a joint operation of commandos from the British Army and Royal Marines with the support of warships of the Royal Navy, Polish Navy, and Royal Australian Navy, taking Al-Faw peninsula.

The second day saw an escalation of the attacks, especially the air campaign where Coalition aircraft flew some 3,000 sorties. The targets of these attacks and cruise missiles were military command and control installations, structures and buildings in different parts of Iraq. The Iraqi port city of Um Qasr was the first obstacle in the face of the attacking forces. A British Armed Division entered Iraq from Kuwait moving towards Basrah. British, American and Polish units attacked Um Qasr port, but were surprised by the stiff resistance they faced. After days of fierce battles in which the attacking forces suffered heavy casualties, they secured the port and nearby oil wells. This took place at the same time as US warships and British navy submarines launched missiles at targets throughout Iraq.

On the same day, a joint force of US Marine and British forces succeeded in securing the Rumaylah oil fields with their gas oil separation plants, crude oil export facilities, and oil wells. Lt. Gen. James Conway, commanding general of the 1st Marine Expeditionary Force described this important oil facility: "Over half of the Iraqi oil production, approximately 1.6 million barrels per day produced by 1,074 Rumaylah oil wells, has been secured for the Iraqi people."[58] We know that in truth they were not 'secured for the Iraqi people' but exactly the opposite: for the invaders. The Iraqi people had already benefitted from the proceeds of this oil, until the sanctions imposed in the 1990s. The Mina' al-Bakr export facility, as well as the pumping station at Az Zubayr, a metering station on the Al Faw peninsula, and the offshore crude oil export facilities were also captured. One cannot escape noticing that the first installations secured in south Iraq were the oil facilities, which goes to further strengthen views that securing Iraq's oil was a major objective of the attacking forces.

The air bombing campaign continued on the following days with more thousands of strike sorties and cruise missiles targeting hundreds of different targets all over Iraq, concentrating on communication nodes. By March 24th, there were more than 170,000 US Army, US Marine, and allied ground forces in Iraq.

A US marine division advancing from the south fought through the Rumaylah oil fields while moving northwards towards the city of Nasiriyah, a city on an important road junction with strategically important bridges over the Euphrates River, also housing Ali bin Abi Talib major Air Base. They were met with fierce resistance from Iraqi forces—a mixture of regular army units, Ba'ath loyalists and *Fedayeen*—losing 26 soldiers in one day, forcing the advance to halt. Coalition planes were also facing heavy anti-aircraft fire.

US army units bypassed the city of Nasiriyah to the west, moving northwards to avoid being drawn into a confrontation with the Iraqi units. But that did not prevent US army units from being ambushed when they entered the city mistakenly on 23 March, resulting in twelve soldiers dead and six taken prisoner, including the soldier, Jessica Lynch, who later became famous to her own disgust through a propaganda campaign alleging her heroism and mistreatment.[59] On the same day, US marines suffered heavy losses when they tried to enter the city by force in the face of determined resistance from *fedayeen*. This must have come as a surprise to the Americans who believed that the Iraqis would receive them as liberators with "roses".

The Americans finally succeeded on 24 March to push through Nasiriyah and establish a 15-kilometer perimeter north of the city. The Iraqis made several counterattacks, with reinforcements from Kut, but the Americans repelled them with the help of superior air power. The city was finally taken and two major bridges vital for the movement of troops were secured. Nasiriyah was declared secure, even though uncoordinated attacks by Iraqi *fedayeen* continued. The Americans established their important logistics center and first forward operations base in the south of Iraq outside of Nasiriyah.

The land forces advancing towards Baghdad at the end of March avoided major Iraqi cities and military formations succeeded in gaining ground, but then faced fierce resistance near As Samawah and Al Faysaliah[60] from Iraqi forces using whatever small and inferior weapons were available to them to heroically try to hinder the US advance. The US relied on air support to destroy Iraqi resistance which continued near Nasiriyah and An Najaf, causing countless civilian deaths and casualties. Even when hunting by helicopter gunships the US forces killed innocent people at close range, as shown by footage of one incident released by Bradley Manning.[61]At the same time, the Americans and British continued to face attacks from Iraqi paramilitary units in the Al Faw and Basrah areas. All Coalition claims of securing Um Qasr[62] and Basrah on the first days of the attacks seem to have been false propaganda because resistance continued until early April, and Abu al Khasib[63] was only secured on 31 March after a heavy offensive according to Coalition claims.

Coalition land forces that were trying to advance northwards continued to face stiff resistance in Nasiriyah and Basrah areas sustaining casualties. British troops still faced resistance from paramilitary forces in the Basrah area. They managed to enter the city of Basrah on 6 April, after two weeks of fierce fighting, which included what the British considered to be their biggest tank battle since World War II.

Another fierce battle took place at Najaf,[64] where U.S. airborne and armored units with British air support fought an intense battle with Iraqi army units, Republican Guard units, and *fedayeen* forces. The battle started when several US helicopters were severely damaged and shot down by Iraqi heavy anti-aircraft, small arms, and RPG fire. Iraq managed to damage helicopters with personnel weapons even though Iraqi forces, because of lack of sophisticated guided weaponry, were unable to shoot down aircrafts. The US retaliated on 26 March with a barrage of artillery fire and bombardment by F18s, but was again faced with fierce counterattacks by Iraqi forces and *fedayeen* engaging them in heavy fighting over a strategic bridge in Najaf. The Iraqis were defeated after 36 hours of fighting and the US succeeded in isolating Najaf from the north.

On 29 March, US airborne and armored divisions attacked Iraqi forces in the southern part of the city, near the Imam Ali Mosque and captured Najaf's airfield. Najaf was not captured by the Americans until 4 April after several days of heavy fighting and massive air support.

By 25 March, Iraqis noted a military force composed of approximately sixty tanks and armored vehicles advancing about

20 kilometers southwest of the Ar-Rutbah region, in what the Iraqis considered an attempt by the Americans to open a new front from Jordan. This was a successful ploy to mislead the Iraqi military into deploying major forces in Northern and Western Iraq in anticipation of major thrusts from Turkey or Jordan, which never took place. Iraq thus mistakenly concentrated on these fronts, greatly reducing its defensive capacity in the rest of the country and especially against attacks from Kuwait and the Gulf in the southeast.[65] Because of lack of advanced weapons to fight the invaders, and the heavy losses it had sustained, the Iraqi army was forced by late March to try to block the main thrusts of the coalition advance by committing its Republican Guards in a series of unsuccessful engagements which left them exposed to the coalition superior airpower. The Iraqi leadership had withdrawn elements of the Special Republican Guards (SRG) away from Baghdad and Tikrit and deployed them in those battles, but the result was that these SRG units were outgunned and bombed from the air, suffering huge losses.

In late March, the tower housing the main Communication centre in downtown Baghdad was destroyed with two precision-guided bombs with DU shells, cutting all communications links.

The air dominance of the "coalition" forces, facing no Iraqi air force and no significant air defences and with new technologies, made the advance quicker than the Iraqi defending forces were able to resist. Because of this, Iraq's army was forced to close on advancing coalition forces in what became a series of engagements in which coalition airpower could attack them as they closed in, leaving them outgunned and out-targeted by the attacking units.

Karbala[66] was considered by Iraqi commanders as of high strategic importance to the defence of Baghdad and was therefore defended by two divisions of the best units of the Republican Guards which were heavily targeted by air attacks.

However, whether due to miscalculations, lack of intelligence or complicity of some officers, Qusay Saddam, who was in charge of commanding units in the middle sector of Iraq, ordered Iraqi troops on 2 April to be re-deployed from the Karbala front to the north of Baghdad, believing that the invasion from the south was a trick and that the main thrust was coming from the north. Even though Lt. Gen. Raad al-Hamdani, who was in charge of Iraq's Republican Guard south of Baghdad, down to Najaf, protested this and argued that US forces would reach Baghdad within 48 hours unless reinforcements were rushed to the Karbala area immediately, his assessment and request were not heeded.[67] This enabled American troops to advance to the Euphrates River at the town of Al-Musayib, from where they managed to boat-cross the Euphrates and capture the vital Al-Qaed Bridge which Iraqi demolitions teams had failed to destroy in time in accordance with the military plan.[68]

The Iraqis launched night counterattacks, but were repulsed with tank fire, artillery rockets and aircraft and helicopter fire. The Republican Guard units broke down under the massed firepower, enabling the US forces to advance towards Baghdad.

Even though Turkey had officially prohibited the US from using its airspace or land to attack Iraq's territory, it did allow its airspace to be used by American planes to attack bases of the Kurdish Ansar-ul-Islam, near Halabjah, which the US and Turkey considered a terrorist organization with links to Al-Qaeda. Air missions also included attacking Iraqi units in the north to prevent them from giving assistance to other units in the center and south. American units also assisted the Kurdish parties, PUK and KDP, in attacking the Iraqi divisions near Mosul and Kirkuk.

The occupation of Kirkuk on 10 April came after two weeks of battles which involved US Special Forces, paratroops, CIA Paramilitary Teams and Kurdish Peshmerge. After Kirkuk, further units were deployed in Erbil and subsequently Mosul, allowing the British Parachute Regiment, the US Special Forces, CIA Paramilitary officers along with Kurdish Peshmerge to advance south towards Tikrit, destroying a full Iraqi division. This was the largest deployment of the US Special Forces since Vietnam.[69]

American forces with their allies advanced towards Baghdad after three weeks of operations. The city was defended by units of the Iraqi Republican Guards assisted by a mixture of regular army units, *fedayeen Saddam*, and non-Iraqi Arab volunteers. The attacking forces succeeded in destroying defending units in the southern outskirts of the city, opening the way for the attackers to enter the city. On 5 April, 29 tanks and 14 Bradley armored vehicles from the US army advanced towards Saddam International Airport. They were met with very strong resistance and sustained huge losses. Iraq's information minister, Mohammad Sa'eed as-Sahhaf, warned of a surprise awaiting invading U.S. troops if they attacked Saddam International Airport. Later, as-Sahhaf claimed, the Iraqi Republican Guard had slaughtered U.S. troops, and was in control of the entire facility. It seems that his claims were true, even though the US countered this with a campaign of evasions and distortions while ridiculing as-Sahhaf as *Baghdad Bob*.[70]

This is a part of the war that the Americans and their allies have kept a secret. Perhaps the Iraqis were not lying or exaggerating when they said that the whole advancing unit was destroyed. This caused the Americans to use what the Iraqis described as a "horrible weapon" which killed soldiers without damaging anything else. There has been speculation that a Neutron bomb was used, and increasing evidence that the Americans want to cover up that issue.

The former commander of Iraq's Republican Guard Saifeddin Fulayh Hassan Taha ar-Rawi has said that US forces used neutron and phosphorus bombs during their assault on Baghdad airport before the April 9 capture of the Iraqi capital. He has explained that "... there were bodies burnt to their bones" and that bombs annihilated soldiers but left the buildings and infrastructure at the airport intact.[71]

Captain Eric H. May, a former intelligence and public affairs officer in the military had this to say about it:

> The truth is that the battle started April 5, the night that Baghdad Bob said that they had counterattacked us at the Baghdad Airport and there was a sustained fight that went on for several hours. The best evidence that I have from international sources, scientific sources, is that our position was becoming untenable at the Baghdad Airport and we used a neutron warhead, at least one. That is the big secret of Baghdad Airport.
>
> If one looks into international data, there are reportings of enhanced radiation of some livestock, and of human metabolic effects—death and disease. It explains why, after the Battle of Baghdad, we got fragmentary stories of things like truckloads of dirt being moved out and moved in. It made no particular sense at the time, until one puts it into perspective, as a decontamination operation. Again, that part of the Battle of Baghdad, the fact that we went nuclear, explains a lot of things that came out afterwards and also explains why it is that it had to be covered up. You can't go to a country to try to make sure that nobody tries to start a war with WMD against you and WMD 'em. It's a highly embarrassing position to be in.
>
> *I think Baghdad laid bare that we really weren't going into a limited war at all, we were going into a world war, and were prepared to use nukes.*[italics added] Incidentally, since the nuking of Baghdad Airport, the Bush Administration has retrofitted our military doctrine to allow for the use of tactical nukes in that sort of situation."[72]

There are grounds to suspect that the US used 'battlefield' nuclear weapons on Iraq. The international community needs to take some action against such covert, lawless tactics defying conventions of war.

On 6 April, an American infantry unit attacked one of the Presidential palaces inside Baghdad and occupied it after fierce fighting.

On 7 April, two tanks crossed the Jumhuriya Bridge over the Tigris River in central Baghdad, shelling the Ministry of Planning and the building housing Al Jazeera Satellite Channel, killing one of its reporters. The lack of any opposition to such a feeble attack indicates that the resistance had evaporated for whatever reason. The absence of Ba'athists, fighting for their city, needs some addressing from the Party. There have been rumors that the Pentagon and the Ba'ath Party leadership made a "secret deal" for the fall of Baghdad, which may have included a package of American green cards for top Republican and Special Republican Guard commanders and their families.[73] In May 2003, General Tommy Franks, who assumed control of Iraq as the supreme commander of the coalition occupation forces, said in an interview with *Defense Week* that the US had paid Iraqi military leaders to defect.[74]

Also on 7 April, Ahmad Chalabi, founder of the Iraqi National Congress opposition group and favorite of the Dick Cheney clique and the Pentagon, was airlifted with a group of 700 of his supporters and soldiers from the north of Iraq to Nasiriyah in the south of Iraq. A high-ranking Pentagon officer said these would form the basis of a new Iraqi army, and an INC news release on the deployment said the contingent has been designated the 1st Battalion of Free Iraqi Forces.[75]

US forces issued an ultimatum to Iraqi forces either to surrender or Baghdad would face a full-scale assault. But Iraqi officials had disappeared and the army was in disarray, with a large number of its members leaving their posts and weapons, and going home.

Baghdad was formally occupied by the US and its allies on 9 April.

Between 20 March and 1 May, the day Bush announced the end of war, the US claims to have lost a total of 138 dead.[76]

During the whole of 2003, the British lost 53 dead, 32 very seriously injured and 14 seriously injured.[77]

An animated map of Iraq showing the dates and locations of coalition fatalities is available and serves to give an idea of Iraq's geography and place names.[78]

When it comes to Iraqi military casualties, there is no available record of the number of dead or wounded. All is speculation and guess work. However, US General Tommy Franks had reportedly estimated soon after the invasion that as of 9 April 2003, there had been 30,000 Iraqi casualties.[79] This is of course the same Tommy Franks who is known for his infamous statement "We don't do body counts".[80]

The Iraqi Air force suffered from lack of maintenance and spare parts and thus never flew in action. The Iraqi land-based out-dated air defenses failed to protect Iraqi forces in the field against the advanced technology and could not even defend Baghdad against air strikes by coalition forces.[81]

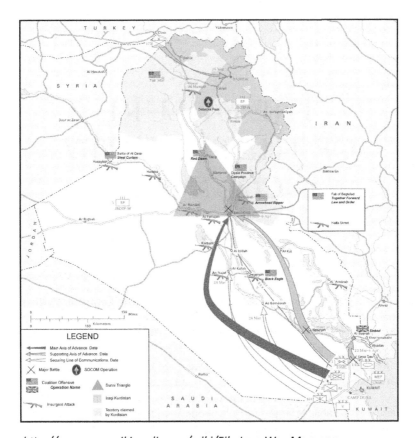

http://commons.wikimedia.org/wiki/File:Iraq-War-Map.png

According to documents of Coalition losses, up until 18 April 2003 the coalition forces lost 16 aircraft and 16 helicopters. In addition to that almost 30 tanks were destroyed and 7 Abrams tanks were captured by the Iraqis. Twenty trucks of different kinds, some 30 Humvee jeeps and one Patriot fire-control radar were destroyed.[82]

The Iraqi army was ill-equipped, with out of date Soviet equipment that was no match for the sophisticated weaponry of the American and British armies. Iraq had not been able to maintain its military equipment because of the sanctions regime, and its air force was largely destroyed in the First Gulf War of 1991. Its air defenses had already been destroyed by the bombing attacks by the US and British in the no-fly zones. The U.S. Air Force, Marine Corps and Naval Aviation, and British Royal Air Force operated with impunity throughout the country, declaring air supremacy over all of Iraq. But the Iraqis fought even though they lacked the equipment and the means. Baghdad was left in ruins and ten years after the occupation its infrastructure has not been rebuilt.

THE FAILURE OF THE SECURITY COUNCIL

The Security Council (SC) was created by the victors of WWII as part of the restructuring of the United Nations (UN) following the failure of the League of Nations to prevent the war. The structure of the SC and its authority was outlined in the Charter of the United Nations. Before we attend to the failure of the SC in Iraq we need to shed some light on the anomalies in the UN charter and in the practice adopted by the SC itself.

The reason for this is that there is a general misconception among the public at large—not just people in the Middle East—concerning the authority and power of the SC. This misconception has been enhanced by politicians, some of whom use it to push through their policies and some who simply feign ignorance and indifference. However, some, even in the western world, are truly ignorant. *This misconception revolves around the belief that the SC can pass any resolution it likes to the extent that it can set itself above the law.* That is why few people stop to argue the morality or legality of some of its resolutions. The ordinary citizens in the Anglo-American world may be excused for being indifferent to their leaders exploiting the SC to push through their aggressive imperialist policies. However, no such excuse could be made for the legal profession, philosophers, moralists, socialists and so-called liberals in general. The SC should at all times operate within its remit as set out in the UN Charter and as bound by the principles of international law. If that is not the case, then it assumes to itself a position of legal authority that is arbitrary, indeed dictatorial, and not contracted to by the member states of the UN. Part of the misconception is caused by the anomalies in the UN Charter and part by the SC illegally assuming the right to a practice that is outside its remit. We shall briefly attend to this.

Anomalies of the UN Charter

It is important to focus on the analysis and appraisal of the United Nations, its Charter and the Security Council, because all that has happened to Iraq has been facilitated by these organs and instruments. The questions that arise from Iraq have applied to similar conflicts in the world, such as Libya, Syria and the Ukraine. There are several issues worthy of consideration in view of the matters discussed in this project and summarized in preceding paragraphs of this statement. We shall look at this matter from two angles although they are inseparable and interdependent—that of the Charter and the functioning of the Security Council.

The UN Charter is an odd treaty/agreement. A careful reading reveals that it is not an agreement between members of the General Assembly which form the world community but a document written by the Permanent Members of the SC (as victors of WWII) who created the General Assembly subservient to the Council so that they could control world affairs. The most significant Article in the Charter and consequently the authority it grants is Article (27).[1] Paragraph 3 of that Article reads:

> Decisions of the Security Council on all other matters shall be made by an affirmative vote of nine members including the concurring votes of the permanent members; provided that, in decisions under Chapter VI, and under paragraph 3 of Article 52, a party to a dispute shall abstain from voting.

This carefully drafted Article ensured that any of the five permanent members of the SC retains the right to 'veto' any resolution it objects to which in reality means that none of the five could ever be found at fault for any wrongdoing.

Thus one year before Iraq's incursion into Kuwait, the US invaded Panama, killed a few thousand of its people, kidnapped its legitimate President and unlawfully transferred him to the USA where he languished in jail until September 2011, and installed a puppet regime in Panama.[2] The Security Council made no move to criticize the unprovoked US aggression on the tiny defenseless state of Panama. When, in 1982, Israeli tanks marched across the Lebanese border, killing hundreds and destroying property before reaching Beirut, the SC met on 6 June but its resolution contained no condemnation of the aggression.[3] In addition to the killing and destruction on the way to Beirut, it is important to note that in the context of that invasion there is clear evidence of genocide at *Sabra* and *Shatila* Palestinian refugee camps undertaken at the behest of the invading army.[4]

The balance of power during the so-called Cold War gave the SC some semblance of functionality. The balance of power between the capitalist camp led by the US and the socialist camp led by the then Soviet Union resulted in some sort of a working mechanism with a mutual recognition of where the lines were drawn. Most of the states of the world allied themselves directly or indirectly to one of the camps and thus were partially protected from blatant aggression. However, since the ending of the Cold War—which has been a calamity for the Third World—the SC has become a tool of US imperialism. Iraq has been the test case for that.

The problem with Article (27) does not end there. The SC has adopted a practice which blatantly breaches the Article. Although it calls for a *'concurring'* vote of all permanent members, the SC has come to accept an abstention as amounting to concurring. We do not know of a single logical or legal argument that could sustain such an interpretation of Article (27). It is unlikely that a judge ruling the refusal of an accused to respond to a charge would mean an admission of guilt. It has been suggested that an abstention is not a 'veto' but that is putting the argument on its head. The premise is that for a resolution to pass there should be a majority in favour including the permanent members. If one permanent member refuses to concur then the resolution should not be passed. In fact there is no mention of the word 'veto' in the Charter. All that Article 27 requires is a concurring vote of the permanent members. The logical conclusion from this is that if one permanent member does not give "the concurring vote" then the resolution has failed to pass and should not be adopted. Many vital and critical SC resolutions were passed with one or more members abstaining as in resolution 678 (1990) which enabled the first invasion of Iraq in 1991. We contend that all resolutions passed without the concurring votes of the five members are null and void and the members that abided by them should bear the full responsibility under international law.

Another example of the anomalies of the UN charter is Article (25).[5] According to this article, all UN members accept to be bound by decisions of the SC. Furthermore, in Article (108) members of the UN agree to restrain their power to amend the Charter so long as one permanent member of the SC declines to do so.[6] It is a rare incident in law for parties to a contract in domestic law to accept signing off their authority to a subsidiary organ without retaining the right to overrule that organ. We would suggest that such articles in an ordinary domestic contract could be construed by a court of law as rendering the contract voidable. If we consider that Article (103) of the Charter[7] states that states' obligations under the Charter supersede any other obligation, be that regional agreement, bilateral agreement, judicial judgment, it becomes apparent that the Charter grants the SC the position of the supreme political, military and economic council which is subject to the veto of any of the five permanent members. But more alarming, in our opinion, is the fact that by disarming the International Court of Justice (ICJ), and subjecting the ad hoc tribunals and access to the International Criminal Court (ICC) to the control of the SC, the Charter has turned the political organ of the SC, which does not necessarily have much legal expertise, effectively into the World's Supreme Court from whose decisions no appeal is available. It is in the light of these facts that what happened to Iraq has to be seen.

Security Council Resolutions on Iraq Prior to the 2003 Invasion

There are three main features that distinguish the Security Council resolutions following the Iraqi incursion into Kuwait from any others. Firstly, they were passed with speed and swiftness without attempting to reach a peaceful settlement. Secondly, the Security Council applied different standards to Iraq as compared to other recent invasions. Thirdly, and more importantly, these resolutions breached the fundamental principles the Security Council was created to uphold. Resolution 678 (1990) to attack Iraq was also adopted by means of a campaign of bribery, coercion, blackmail and threats. Opposition among Middle East governments to the use of force was wiped out through certain 'incentives'. Egypt was bribed with 14 billion dollars in 'debt forgiveness'. Syria was given a free hand in Lebanon. Iran was bribed by allowing the World Bank to approve a loan of 250 million dollars. Bribing the Soviet Union was of utmost importance, and achieved through Saudi Arabia whose foreign minister offered Gorbachev a billion dollars in aid, followed by 3 billion dollars once he agreed to the resolution.[8] China's incentive was ending its international boycott following its crushing of the Tiananmen Square protests.

The Finnish President, Mauno Koivisto, had already promised President Bush during the OECD summit in Paris in November 1990 that Finland would vote for the resolution[9] without even knowing its wording. In Yemen, US Secretary of State James Baker warned Yemen's President Ali Abdullah Saleh that he was risking $70 million in annual US aid by refusing to cooperate with the USA in the SC. Nonetheless, in a press conference after the meeting, Saleh delivered a resounding no to the resolution.[10] Baker toured seven countries in November 1990 to acquire support for the US plan, and on November 28 he met with representatives of China, Cuba and the Soviet Union at the UN. UK Premier Margaret Thatcher also played a part in persuading 16 nations to join the Gulf Cooperation Council to give the attack an appearance of international weight of approval.

The votes of the non-permanent members of the Security Council were crucial for unanimity. Zaire was offered undisclosed 'debt forgiveness' and military equipment in return for controlling the SC when the attack was under way. Thus it refused, as the rotating president of the Council, requests from Cuba, Yemen and India to convene an emergency meeting of the Council, even though it had no authority to refuse them under the UN Charter.[11]

When Yemen voted against resolution 678, a senior American diplomat told the Yemeni ambassador: 'That was the most expensive 'no' vote you ever cast.' Within three days, a US aid program of 70 million dollars was stopped. Yemen suddenly had problems with the World Bank and the IMF, and 800,000 Yemeni workers were expelled from Saudi Arabia.[12]

Iraqi troops marched into Kuwait on 2 August 1990. Within hours the Security Council met and adopted resolution 660 condemning the invasion. Later it imposed total sanctions on Iraq with Resolution 661 on 6 August. No diplomatic attempt was made by the Security Council to find a peaceful settlement in accordance with the letter and spirit of the UN Charter.[13] The length, speed and detail of the resolution give the appearance that it had already been written and prepared, waiting for the action. The harshness of measures and language give the impression that it was intended to pressure Saddam Hussein into refusing to withdraw, as it would sound like capitulation to the *diktat* of the US. Between 2 August and 29 November no less than 12 resolutions were adopted on Iraq. All were designed in such a way that their acceptance would have been impossible for someone like Saddam Hussein, thus effectively ensuring that military action was inevitable. There was a gradual ramping up of the demands on Iraq: first that it should withdraw from Kuwait or face sanctions, then when it agreed as long as Israel withdrew from Occupied Palestine, the agreement was ignored and the sanctions were nevertheless continued.

It is worth pointing out here that not one single resolution was adopted by the Security Council in the invasion by the US of Granada[14] and Panama[15] despite the fact that neither of them had WMD or was even alleged to have constituted a threat to the US. It seems clear that the Security Council was created to protect the victors of WWII in their pursuit of controlling the world.

Security Council Failing to Act after the 2003 Invasion

Although the imperialists had decided to invade Iraq irrespective of what the SC was going to do, they still wished that the SC could be persuaded to allow them to act under some pretext and thus to appear on the surface not to have committed an aggression. Similar coercive measures to those adopted in the period 1990-2003 were again used in order to force hesitant states to change their stand on the inevitable invasion. One such state, which is reported to have changed its view and moved towards the US, is Mexico. *USA Today* reported that US officials visited Mexico to put pressure on its government to change its stand and support the US at the SC. One Mexican diplomat is quoted as having said that the US officials told them that 'any country that doesn't go along with us will be paying a heavy price'.[16]

SC resolution 1454 (2002) adopted on 30 December 2002 under the heading 'Situation between Iraq and Kuwait' was the last resolution prior to the invasion.[17] But it only dealt with adjustments to the Goods Review List and its review.

Despite the fact that the SC held itself to be still seized of the matter and not having made any decision that related to legitimizing an attack on Iraq, it did not react in any way when missiles hit Iraq on 20 March 2003 and troops crossed into it from three countries in one of the largest invasions since WWII. We need to remind ourselves that the Security Council met within hours of Iraqi troops entering Kuwait on 2 August 1990 and adopted Resolution 660 as follows:

> The Security Council,
>
> Alarmed by the invasion of Kuwait on 2 August 1990 by the military forces of Iraq,
>
> Determining that there exists a breach of international peace and security as regards the Iraqi invasion of Kuwait,
>
> Acting under Articles 39 and 40 of the Charter of the United Nations,
>
> 1. Condemns the Iraqi invasion of Kuwait;
> 2. Demands that Iraq withdraw immediately and unconditionally all s its forces to the positions in which they were located on 1 August 1990;r
> 3. Calls upon Iraq and Kuwait to begin immediately intensive negotiations for the resolution of their differences and supports all efforts in this regard, and especially those of the League of Arab States;
> 4. Decides to meet again as necessary to consider further steps to ensure compliance with the present resolution.

The SC action on Kuwait was based on Articles 39 of the Charter which reads:

> The Security Council shall determine the existence of any threat to the peace, breach of the peace, or act of aggression and shall make recommendations, or decide

what measures shall be taken in accordance with
Articles 41 and 42, to maintain or restore international
peace and security.

The SC concluded that Iraq's incursion and occupation of Kuwait constituted such aggression and threat to peace. It is inconceivable that the SC or any of its members did not consider that the invasion of Iraq in 2003 was any less an act of aggression and threat to peace than the invasion of Kuwait in 1990, especially in the light of the declared objective of such invasion which was the overthrow of the Iraqi government.

The first question which any defender of the impartiality or independence of the SC needs to address is why the SC failed to act in March 2003. The most likely objective explanation is that most states believed that it would have been futile to meet and discuss the invasion because the US would have prevented any such meeting taking place. And in the odd case of a successful meeting despite the US objection, a resolution could not have been taken on the matter because the US/UK would have vetoed it, as has been shown in the cases of Grenada and Panama. It is also indicative of the ruthless contempt in which the US holds the other SC Members that the US and UK invaded without any authorization from the SC. The aggressors did not want to await the final report from the UN's own UNSCOM inspection team into Iraq's alleged WMD program which did not exist, perhaps because they knew that UNSCOM would declare Iraq's compliance. And we now know that the perpetrators of that war knew it did not exist. Andrew Gilligan quotes Major General Michael Laurie, Head of the UK Defence Intelligence Staff in 2003: "we could find no evidence of planes, missiles or equipment that related to weapons of mass destruction (WMD)".[18] This whole scenario goes to prove our earlier argument regarding the anomaly with the UN Charter. Had the Charter been justly enforced, then it would stand to reason that a member of the UN, the US in this case, should not be allowed to prevent the SC sitting in judgment on its action. Even if given the right of 'veto', which is not fair, then such member should not be allowed to vote on any matter to which it was a party, as stipulated in Article 27 (3).

When the SC met on 28 March 2003, it adopted resolution 1472 (2003).[19] This was eight days after the beginning of the invasion, while Iraq was being destroyed from air, sea and land. The resolution lacked any reference to any threat to peace or act of aggression. Although defining what constitutes a threat to peace may be debatable, defining aggression is not. Both the amended statute of the International Criminal Court[20] and the UN General Assembly have defined aggression as:

Considering also that, since aggression is the most

serious and dangerous form of the illegal use of force......

Aggression is the use of armed force by a State against the sovereignty, territorial integrity or political independence of another State, or in any other manner inconsistent with the Charter of the United Nations, as set out in this Definition.[21]

We doubt that anyone with the slightest of common sense would disagree that what the US and its allies did in 2003 falls within the above definition. Consequently the action of the US and its allies (UK, Poland, and Australia) was an act of aggression contrary to international law and justiciable before the ICC.

In the case of an argument being made in favor of US actions on the grounds that the US does not recognize the ICC or the Rome Statute and thus does not find itself bound by its decisions being criminalized, we would respond that the Nuremberg Tribunal established aggression as the most heinous crime, described by the chief American prosecutor, Robert H. Jackson in saying:

To initiate a war of aggression, therefore, is not only an international crime; it is the supreme international crime differing only from other war crimes in that it contains within itself the accumulated evil of the whole.[22]

But despite the clarity of the fact that it was addressing an act of aggression, SC Resolution 1472 instead noted Art. 55 of the IV Geneva Convention on the protection of civilians at time of war and called on all parties to respect the Geneva Conventions and maintain the aid program. It also maintained the authority of the infamous Sanctions Committee. However, the irony in the resolution comes in the following statement:

Reaffirming the respect for the right of the people of Iraq to determine their own political future and to control their own natural resources[23]

It is difficult to see how the SC was able to reconcile such a principle with the fact that Iraq was being invaded at the time the resolution was being adopted. One explanation could be that the SC was echoing US/UK propaganda that their invasion intended the removal of a tyrant and the installation of democracy. And we now know that the invasion was undertaken partly to grab those very resources and deprive the people of self-determination by imposing a Constitution written by foreigners for their own benefit[24].

Security Council Facilitating Crime

Following the adoption of resolution 1472, the SC entered a new era in which it became a facilitator of crime by adopting resolutions that tried to legitimize the crime of aggression against Iraq.

Thus when the invaders completed the first leg of destruction after they fully occupied Iraq, both the US and the UK sent a letter to the Security Council in which they effectively summoned the SC to meet and grant them the free mandate to rule Iraq contrary to principles of international law. The letter of 8 May 2003,[25] which is reproduced in Appendix II, is a very important letter because it is the most blatant example since WWII where a member state has tested international law, seeking to legitimize an act of aggression against another member state. Thus although the letter started by claiming that the US, UK and their allies were acting to disarm Iraq—which they had no authority to do in any case—the letter soon expressed the real object of the invasion, namely regime change, when it stated:

> The United States, the United Kingdom and Coalition partners recognize the urgent need to create an environment in which the Iraqi people may freely determine their own political future. To this end, the United States, the United Kingdom and Coalition partners are facilitating the efforts of the Iraqi people to take the first steps towards forming a representative government, based on the rule of law, that affords fundamental freedoms and equal protection and justice under law to the people of Iraq without regard to ethnicity, religion or gender.

The SC met on 22 May 2003, some thirteen days after it was summoned by the US/UK, and adopted the very significant Resolution 1483.[26] The SC not only failed in its duty to address the aggression against and occupation of a sovereign member state, but went on to grant legitimacy to such a crime. Thus when it stated that it was:

> *Reaffirming* the sovereignty and territorial integrity of Iraq

while knowing that occupation is a negation of sovereignty, the SC was attempting to redefine terms under international law which were evidently self-contradictory. The resolution deviated from the norm of resolutions adopted by such an important organ of international order, when it used a language more suited to deceptive political propaganda than a responsible legal forum when it stated:

> *Encouraging* efforts by the people of Iraq to form a representative government based on the rule of law that affords equal rights and justice to all Iraqi citizens without regard to ethnicity, religion, or gender, and, in this connection, *recalls* resolution 1325 (2000) of 31 October 2000,
>
> *Welcoming* the first steps of the Iraqi people in this regard, and *noting* in this connection the 15 April 2003 Nasiriyah statement and the 28 April 2003 Baghdad statement...

Firstly, the SC overlooked the basic principle that it has no right to interfere in the internal affairs of states as it was created to deal with inter-nation problems. Secondly, it would have been impossible for the SC to verify whether or not Iraqis had taken steps to form a representative government only two weeks after being occupied. It is more likely that the SC was relying on the preparations in the US/UK for some of their agents to take over. Thirdly, and in support of the previous observation, the Resolution made a reference to insignificant and contrived incidents as if they were an historical event of moment. An ordinary reader assuming some respect for the SC would not question such a statement. However, on closer look, the whole question of the integrity of the SC becomes suspect.

The truth about the statements referred to in the SC resolution as pieced from CENTCOM press releases is as follows. On 15 April, a C130 took off from Al Udeid Air Force Base towards south Iraq. On board were the US National Security Council's Zalmay Khalilzad, the State Department's Ryan Crocker, the Defense Department's Larry Dirita, Admiral Jim Robb, the J5 from CENTCOM, Jim Wilkinson, director of strategic communications for CENTCOM, Ambassador David Litt, the political adviser to General Tommy Franks, and the former ambassador to the UAE and several other staff from the State Department and CENTCOM. On board were also three diplomats from the three countries which contributed troops to the invasion of Iraq and two Iraqis. They were the Polish Ambassador Ryszard Krystosik, who ran the US interest section in Baghdad for six years until 2001, the Australian Peter Varghese, the Briton Edward Chaplin, and Emad Dhia, an Iraqi American living in Detroit and Entifad Qanbar, the DC representative of the Iraqi National Congress (INC) and its rep at CENTCOM. After arriving at Nasiriyah they held a meeting which was addressed by a few of them and four Iraqis who lived outside Iraq. The statement in the SC resolution was referring to this meeting.[27]

However, despite the contemporaneous press releases, the State Department made the following claim:

On April 15 near the town of Nasiriyah, up to a hundred Iraqis representing every part of Iraq came together to discuss the visions they have for their own future and how best to chart a course toward a democratic representative government. Also at the meeting were the President's Special Envoy Ambassador Khalilzad, Deputy Assistant Secretary of State Ryan Crocker, other Department officials and coalition representatives. At the end of the session, the Iraqi participants voted and approved a final statement proposing 13 principles for a future Iraqi government.[28]

There is no evidence of the existence of the 100 Iraqis representing every part of Iraq who are alleged to have attended. The CENTOCOM press release reported Iraqis who came from abroad, who could not be considered genuinely to represent Iraq. In view of the above facts the SC reference to the statement supports our contention that the SC had been for a long time a rubber stamp of resolutions drafted by the US/UK without even attempting to verify their contents.

The SC Resolution goes on in its observations to state it was:

Affirming the need for accountability for crimes and atrocities committed by the previous Iraqi regime,

The SC thus endorses regime change by acknowledging that the political regime in the State of Iraq ceased to exist. In doing so the SC not only acts against the principles it called on all parties to respect, but itself breaches international law as established under customary international law and the Geneva Conventions which prohibit regime change after occupation.[29] Furthermore, the SC confirmed its bias by presuming the accuracy of reports received from imperial sources when it commented on atrocities committed by the previous regime without having undertaken any independent investigation of its own.

The resolution noted the 8 May letter and accepted the Coalition Provisional Authority that the occupiers had put in place to rule Iraq. But it failed to question the legality of such an Authority. If we were to assume that the SC was convinced that a valid purpose of the invasion was to disarm Iraq (which is itself questionable both in the given Iraqi context of years of weapons inspections, and in general as it relates to the right of sovereign states to self defense), then the proper way for the SC to handle the matter would have been to accept the invasion and call on the invaders to withdraw after having disarmed Iraq, leaving the legitimate Government of Iraq to run the country without any need for the Authority. The legitimate government of Iraq was in hiding following the invasion just as much as the legitimate government in France went into hiding after Hitler invaded France. In which case the SC ought to have declared its recognition of the legitimate government of Iraq and its right to fight the invader.

Paragraph 12 of the Resolution consolidated the occupation of Iraq and legitimized the first step in the total control of Iraq through the control of its oil revenue. Thus:

> 12. *Notes* the establishment of a Development Fund for Iraq to be held by the Central Bank of Iraq and to be audited by independent public accountants approved by the International Advisory and Monitoring Board of the Development Fund for Iraq...

The resolution neglected to indicate who had established the Development Fund for Iraq (DFI) or indeed what authority established it. Later in the paragraph the picture became clearer when it is stated that the International Advisory and Monitoring Board (IAMB), which fully controlled Iraq's finances, would be composed of representatives of the President of the World Bank, of the MD of the IMF, of the Secretary General and of the Director of the Arab Fund.

Here we have the SC, which was created to maintain peace and order, acting as an agent of aggression, assisting invaders and occupiers to change the political regime in one sovereign state and to shape the economic system as the invaders and occupiers saw fit, to ensure their own benefit.

The SC resolutions from May 2003 were all drafted in the form of putting Iraq under the mandate of the US/UK. Although the word mandate had never been used in any resolution, effectively all the resolutions were drafted on this ground. The SC breached the UN Charter and acted unlawfully when it collaborated with the invaders to breach the sovereignty of a member state, however abhorrent some members of the UN thought that state's leader was. The SC should not function outside the Charter or principles of international law. In short it should not be allowed to rewrite international law. But this was precisely what the SC did in Iraq and in doing so it facilitated the crimes committed by the invaders. Iraq was not only a sovereign state whose sovereignty should not be any less protected than any other member state, but also it was a founding member of the UN and one of the 50 states which signed the original UN Charter on 26 June 1945 before Poland and Spain, both of which invaded Iraq in 2003![30]

Thus when, on 14 August 2003, the SC adopted resolution 1500, it acted on the presumption that Iraq was under benevolent US/UK mandate and that measures taken by these two states needed ratification.[31] In it the SC welcomes the setting up of the Governing Council, on 13 July 2003, by Paul Bremer, the actual new ruler of Iraq. The Governing Council was made up of 26 people, most of whom carried British or US passports, who had not lived in Iraq for some time and thus had little or no knowledge or connection to Iraq. The only thing the members of the Governing Council had in common was their allegiance to US imperialist policies. Yet the SC found it proper to welcome this Council as a first step towards a "representative government that will exercise the sovereignty of Iraq".

The conspiracy against Iraq, in which the SC was a full partner, progressed from describing the Governing Council as 'a first step towards representative government' to resolution 1511 in which the SC welcomed the process started by the Governing Council leading to the drafting of a "constitution to embody the aspirations of the Iraqi people," adopted on 16 October 2003.[32] To us, this sounds worse than the League of Nations adopting the resolution in which it welcomed the steps taken by the pro-Nazi Vichy Government of Marshal Philippe Pétain to draft a new constitution for France—a government which could easily be argued to have had more popular support in France than the Governing Council did in Iraq[33].

But paragraph 1 of resolution 1511 is more baffling. It stated that it:

> 1. *Reaffirms* the sovereignty and territorial integrity of Iraq, and *underscores*, in that context, the temporary nature of the exercise by the Coalition Provisional Authority (Authority) of the specific responsibilities, authorities, and obligations under applicable international law recognized and set forth in resolution 1483 (2003).

In view of the fact that by the time resolution 1511 was adopted the CPA had made changes in Iraq in the form of new legislation, dissolving fundamental state establishments, economic and financial measures and other changes that could not be reversed, then it is proper to ask how could the SC have been so oblivious of the actual situation as to talk about the temporary nature of the measures taken by the CPA? Perhaps because the SC did not bother to verify any statement that appeared in a resolution as it was purely a rubber stamp to the US policies and these supporting resolutions were actually drafted by the US/UK?

Resolution 1551 reemphasized the setting up of the International Advisory and Monitoring Board (IAMB) as decided in resolution 1483 of 22 May 2003. But considering that the SC believed that it was imperative to set up the IAMB to monitor the way Iraqi assets were being used, one is forced to ask who had been monitoring Iraq's assets over the previous five months and why had the IAMB not already been set up?

The SC attempted to sanitize occupation by accepting the setting up of a Multi-National Force (MNF) under US command to secure stability and order in Iraq.

The next important SC resolution on Iraq was resolution 1546 adopted on 8 June 2004[34]. Its importance arises from the fact that it was adopted at the time it was supposed to transfer some nominal authority from the occupiers to their Iraqi puppets in Baghdad. The resolution endorsed the formation of the 'Sovereign Interim Government of Iraq', which was chosen by the Governing Council, which was itself chosen by Paul Bremer. It also welcomed the request of the appointed PM from the SC to retain the presence of the US forces in Iraq. The annexed letter from the appointed PM started with:

> On my appointment as Prime Minister of the Interim Government of Iraq

The SC omitted to address the fundamental legal problem of the lack of authority to appoint a Government for Iraq, which had a legitimate Government when it was invaded, and which under international law should have remained the legitimate authority.

It is worth noting that this resolution was the first since the invasion in which the SC referred to the independence of Iraq, stating that it was:

> *Reaffirming* the independence, sovereignty, unity, and territorial integrity of Iraq

The SC's lack of legal knowledge or concern as to the legality of its own actions became increasingly apparent as the US duped it to rubber-stamp US actions. This is exemplified in paragraph 2 when the SC:

> 2. *Welcomes* that, also by 30 June 2004, the occupation will end and the Coalition Provisional Authority will cease to exist, and that Iraq will reassert its full sovereignty

This exposes a total ignorance of the meaning of occupation under international law. Occupation under international law ends in one of two ways: either the invading army pulls out willingly or it is thrown out by force.[35] There is simply no middle way; occupation cannot be said to have ended when the occupier still maintains a presence that then purports to be legitimized by a government which it puts in place. The SC was wrong to welcome the end of occupation of Iraq when it knew that the US forces were going to stay in Iraq. It is comical to attempt to explain that the US occupying forces were staying in Iraq upon the request of a legitimate Government. The Government of Iyad (Ayad) Allawi in 2004 was no more legitimate than that of Marshal Philippe Pétain was in 1940.

The setting up of a client government in Iraq gave the SC a breathing space as it was relieved from having to adopt more illegal resolutions once it had bestowed, without authority, legitimacy on an illegal administration to rule an occupied formerly sovereign member state. Thus between June 2004 and December 2010, and with one noticeable exception, the SC adopted an average of two resolutions each year in which it extended the mandate of Multi National Force, the euphemism for the US occupying forces; extended the mandate of UNAMI (United Nations Assistance Mission for Iraq) and extended the deposit of funds from Iraq's sale of oil to the DFI under the monitoring of the IAMB – all measures indicating that the country is under occupation or under mandate.

The only noticeable exception was resolution 1762 adopted on 29 June 2007.[36] The resolution terminated the mandate in Iraq of both UNMOVIC and the IAEA as it became clear that Iraq had been telling the truth about its having disarmed itself of all WMDs, an excuse used by the US/UK for the invasion. It is hard not to put the following question to the SC: In view of the fact that both the US and UK claimed in their letter of 8 May 2003 that they invaded Iraq in order to disarm it of WMDs, and in view of the fact that it transpired that Iraq did not have any WMDs, what remaining justification was there for their continued presence in Iraq as invited by the government they had imposed, and who is responsible for all the killing and destruction caused by the invasion? Is it not part of the SC's remit to ensure peace and order in the world to require that when one state breaches this it should redress the damage caused?

On 15 December 2010, the SC adopted three important resolutions on Iraq. In Resolution 1956 the SC decided that Iraq was not obliged after 30 June 2011 to deposit its revenue from oil and gas into the DFI.[37] Although this sounds like easing the mandate over Iraq, it was not totally so. In fact the resolution went on to put Iraq under the supervision of the IMF but more seriously it decided that 5% of Iraq's revenue should continue to be paid into the Compensation Fund for Kuwait created by resolution 687 (1991). As the resolution put no limit on payment of compensation and left that to the United Nations Compensation Commission, then it is likely that such open-ended payment can go on indefinitely or until the US decides otherwise. If Iraq is still paying compensation to Kuwait some twenty years after its very brief occupation, would it not be proper to raise the question we posed earlier: who is going to pay compensation to Iraq for the calamity that has followed its illegal invasion and occupation under pretexts which proved to be untrue, and should the SC not address this?

In Resolution 1957 (2010)[38] the SC decided: "to terminate the weapons of mass destruction, missile, and civil nuclear-related measures imposed" by previous resolutions after having realized that Iraq had indeed complied with its obligation under the treaties it had ratified.

Resolution 1958 of the same date[39] started with:

> *Recognizing* the importance of Iraq achieving
> international standing equal to that which it held prior
> to the adoption of resolution 661

and went on to terminate the Oil for Food Program and enable the people of Iraq to live like normal human beings with some of their basic human rights restored. However, still flying in the face of the illegality of the invasion, the occupation, the discredited pretexts and the imposed proxy government, the SC carried on its old practice of assuming its right to dispose of Iraqi wealth (helping itself to any sum of money) and decided to authorize the General Secretary to set up an escrow account and retain sums of Iraqi money to cover expenses and indemnities without Iraq having any say in it. Beyond blaming the victim, it was making the victim pay.

In 2011 and 2012 the SC resolutions dealt with extending the mandate of UNAMI.[40]

It should be emphasized that in all the SC resolutions from 1990 until 2012, the SC ensured that it decided "to remain seized of the matter". But in view of the fact that Iraq was invaded and occupied and a new 'democratic' regime was created under SC supervision, it remains difficult to see why Iraq remained under ChapterVII until 2013 and even since has not in fact been out of it, and why the SC should remain seized of the matter. Either the invasion, occupation and regime change have failed to solve the problem of the potential resurgent power of Iraq and/or the perpetrators want to keep Iraq on a leash for their own nefarious purposes and the SC is facilitating this. In either case the SC discredited itself, and cast the entire UN system into disrepute and functional lawlessness.[41]

Reforming the United Nations

Between August 1990 and March 2003 the SC adopted some 55 resolutions on Iraq, most of which were under the heading of 'Situation between Iraq and Kuwait' despite the fact that Kuwait had been re-occupied by the imperialists in January 1991, and presumably removed from any sort of "crisis". It has been reported that all these resolutions were in fact written by the US and adopted with little or no discussion by the SC which effectively meant that the SC was being abused to rubber stamp US policy.[42]

Between March 2003 and July 2012, the SC adopted 27 resolutions on Iraq. Resolutions between March 2003 and August 2004 were still adopted under the heading of the 'Situation between Iraq and Kuwait'. We are not able to find the relation between invading and occupying Iraq in 2003, with the situation between Iraq and Kuwait. It seems that the SC was not competent or perhaps not permitted to question the headings of its resolutions and how relevant they were to their adoption. However, the SC decided in August 2005 to begin adopting resolutions on Iraq under the heading of 'Iraq'.

During that period the SC breached international law in many ways. The following is a summary of these breaches where the SC either initiated the breach, was complicit in it, or omitted to act when it ought to have acted.

The Security Council:

1.   Imposed total sanctions on Iraq four days after it entered Kuwait without enabling any means of peaceful settlement as clearly required by the spirit if not the letter of the Charter. Article 33 for example, calls on 'Parties to a dispute...to seek a resolution by negotiation, enquiry, mediation, conciliation, arbitration, judicial settlement...or other peaceful means of their own choice.' [43]

2.   Converted the objective of forcing the Iraqi army out of Kuwait into a campaign of destruction of Iraq through the application of total sanctions against it based on the alleged claim of eradicating Iraq's WMDs;

3.   Accepted that the imposition of sanctions was perpetual, requiring a new vote to remove them rather than a new vote to renew them, which meant again that removal was held to ransom by one vote in the SC;

4.   Transformed a requirement for the removal of alleged WMDs to a requirement for the total disarmament of Iraq in breach of the right of every sovereign state to defend itself;

5.   Set up the Sanctions Committee which awarded itself unprecedented powers in international relations and which exceeded the statutory powers of the SC;[44]

6.   Kept silent on the clear breach of Iraq's sovereignty in the

illegal imposition of no-fly zones by the USA and UK;[45]

7. Kept silent on the regular destructive air raids on Iraqi civilian targets by US/UK between 1991 and 2003 despite Iraq having surrendered after the ceasefire and despite the SC being seized of the situation in Iraq;[46]

8. Kept silent following the 2003 invasion and dismantling of the sovereign state of Iraq;

9. Subsequently bestowed legitimacy for the aggression, invasion and occupation of Iraq;[47]

10. Bestowed false legitimacy, in the series of resolutions between May 2003 and June 2004, on the CPA while the latter was acting in breach of international law in dismantling Iraq,[48] so deceptively and effectively that Lord Hope ruled that he could not judge a case of possible breach of law because he believed the authorities in Iraq were acting under the authority of the SC.[49]

The above observations raise a fundamental question that has been omitted from the Charter. *What happens when the SC breaches international law, especially if it is a peremptive norm and, more seriously, what happens when a permanent member commits an international crime?*

There is no simple answer to the above question because the world order in existence today is still a prisoner of the powers which created it, post WWII, where the victors ensured they remained beyond accountability. The system worked moderately well between 1945 and 1990 due to checks and balances between the two superpowers. This equilibrium ensured that certain lines were not crossed by either party and gave some stability in the rest of the world.

6

BREMER
DISMANTLES
IRAQ

The fall of Baghdad into the hands of the imperialist invaders on 9 April 2003 meant that all of Iraq became occupied. A new era began, similar to the one that had been initiated in 1918. But this time there was one specific feature which distinguished it. When the British imperialists invaded Iraq in 1916, they were hoping to set up a nation state consisting of most of political Iraq (except Kuwait) as it had been under the Ottoman rule. Their reneging on the promise they made to the Kurdish leader, Mahmood Al-Hafid, to set up a Kurdish state in Iraq verifies this intent.[1] But as we have already argued, the imperialists concluded post WWII that the nation state in the Arab world was not a reliable ally. In fact in most cases the liberated nation state was antagonistic to the Western imperialists. A new Arab world had to be conditioned or created. Such a world had to be based on a different concept from that of the nation state. Two examples in the Arab world lent credence to the alternative sought. First there was Lebanon where the constitutional framework of the state was designed to facilitate sectarian and religious differences, so much so that all its affairs since WWII have been conducted behind closed doors between the main sectarian players. The second example is the State of Israel, which was built on religious basis to be a home for the Jewish people of the world.

Thus the decision was reached that the alternative to the secular universalist nation state in the Arab World should be a sectarian state. This is not done because the Arab World consists of different sects and different ethnicities. There are many parts of the world, like the US, which have an even broader mixture. The reason was to maintain full control of the Arab World by dividing every Arab state along sectarian and ethnic lines with power sharing in some proportion, affording an opportunity to play groups against each other. There were two conditions for such states to receive imperialist approval. Firstly, they should accept Israel's supremacy in the region. Secondly, they should adopt capitalist economic principles. Beyond that the state could do what it liked. However, if such a plan failed to create the desired result, then its fragmentation into sectarian and ethnic statelets would be an even more preferable outcome, and not difficult to achieve. When a small country like Iraq or Syria is divided into three statelets then every small and weak state will endeavour to find patronage outside its borders in order to survive. Such a patron would be the familiar old colonialist/new imperialist. This plan served another no less important purpose of making the Jewish state of Israel look no different than the surrounding states since all are equally sectarian.

We believe that such a plan was a recipe for anything but a viable state. It was precisely what was implemented from the first day of the occupation of Iraq, signalling the end of the Iraqi state.

Invading Iraq

Evidence of the decision to invade Iraq, irrespective of the outcome of UN investigation of WMD, is shown in President Bush's issuing, on 20 January 2003, National Security Presidential Directive 24 (NSPD-24) titled "Post-War Iraq Reconstruction". The pre-war date of issue of the Directive itself indicates that not only had the decision to invade Iraq already been taken, but a decision had also been made to overhaul its governmental structure under the guise of reconstruction. The Directive set up, within the Department of Defence, the Office of Reconstruction and Humanitarian Assistance (ORHA) for Iraq.[2]

On 11 February 2003, Douglas J. Feith, Under Secretary of Defense for Policy, made the following statement on ORHA to the Senate Committee on Foreign Relations.

> To prepare for all this [the coordinated, balanced progress of economic and security reconstruction in a post-conflict Iraq], the President [George Walker Bush] directed on January 20 the creation of a post-war planning office. Although located within the Policy organization in the Department of Defense, this office is staffed by officials detailed from departments and agencies throughout the government. Its job is detailed planning and implementation. The intention is not to theorize but to do practical work—to prepare for action on the ground, if and when the time comes for such

work. In the event of war, most of the people in the office will deploy to Iraq. We have named it the Office of Reconstruction and Humanitarian Assistance and we describe it as an 'expeditionary' office.

The Office of Reconstruction and Humanitarian Assistance is charged with establishing links with the United Nations specialized agencies and with non-governmental organizations that will play a role in post-war Iraq. It will reach out also to the counterpart offices in the governments of coalition countries, and, in coordination with the President's Special Envoy to the Free Iraqis, to the various Free Iraqi groups.

The immediate responsibility for administering post-war Iraq will fall upon the Commander of the U.S. Central Command, as the commander of the U.S. and coalition forces in the field. The purpose of the Office of Reconstruction and Humanitarian Assistance is to develop the detailed plans that he and his subordinates will draw on in meeting these responsibilities.

There are three substantive operations within the Office, each under a civilian coordinator: Humanitarian Relief, Reconstruction, and Civil Administration. A fourth coordinator is responsible for communications, logistics and budgetary support. These operations are under the overall leadership of Jay Garner, a retired Lieutenant General who held a senior military position in the 1991 humanitarian relief operation in northern Iraq. He is responsible for organizing and integrating the work of the three substantive operations and ensuring that the office can travel to the region when necessary and plug in smoothly to CENTCOM's operations. His staff consists of representatives from the Departments of State, Defense, Justice, Treasury, Energy, and Agriculture, the U.S. Agency for International Development and the Office of Management and Budget.[3]

General Jay Garner, who was called from retirement to head OHRA, had strong Zionist credentials. He was the former President of the California based defense contractor SY Technology, which worked on the development of US-Israeli Arrow missile defense system. He also signed onto a 12 October 2000 statement by the arch-conservative Jewish Institute for National Security Affairs (JINSA) which praised the Israeli army for having exercised 'remarkable restraint in the face of lethal violence orchestrated by the leadership of a Palestinian Authority.'[4]

However, Garner carried out little work in the period between 21 April and 6 May before he was suddenly replaced. He is reported to have told BBC Newsnight, on 18 March 2004 that his ousting was due to his desire to hold free elections in Iraq which did not suit the mainstream US administration which was more interested in the de-Ba'athification of Iraq.[5]

US Ambassador Paul Bremer, whose previous job was ambassador to the Netherlands, arrived in Iraq on 12 May 2003 to replace Garner. Bremer was not chosen at random for such a role. He was a protégé of Henry Kissinger, the committed Zionist who has spent his life, both within the US administration and outside it, in the service of Israel. Bremer became the US Presidential Envoy and Administrator in Iraq and the chief executive of the Coalition Provisional Authority (CPA) with Jeremy Greenstock as his British deputy. As part of the misinformation put out by the US, Bremer was referred to in US circles, including the White House, as Ambassador Bremer when in fact there was no US diplomatic mission in Iraq and Bremer was no ambassador but the absolute ruler of Iraq, as we shall show later.

Another indication of the misinformation on Iraq which lasted over twenty years is shown in the reference in Security Council resolution 1483 (22 May 2003) to the CPA which failed to state who had set it up. The CPA was neither an international body nor an offshoot of the UN. It was created and funded by the US as a division of the Department of Defense. This meant that Bremer as Administrator reported directly to the Secretary of Defense.[6]

The US Central Command (USCENTCOM), which is under the command of Secretary of Defense, provided the military personnel and equipment needed to enforce the occupation and CPA authority in Iraq.

Summary of International Law Principles on Occupation

The invasion of Iraq was an act of blatant aggression which is the most heinous of international crimes, a view held by the Nuremberg Tribunal[7] and since incorporated in the Statute of the ICC.[8] But as Iraq was invaded and occupied, we need to look at international law as it applies to occupation. The main instruments, but by no means the only ones, germane to the occupation of Iraq are: The Hague Regulations 1907, the Geneva Conventions 1949 and the International Criminal Court Statute 2000. Here are the violations of the main principles enshrined in these instruments which occurred during the occupation of Iraq:

- *Prisoners of war taken by the US were not subjected to the laws in force in the army of the US* contrary to Article 6 of The Hague Regulations 1907[9] and Article 82 of the Third Geneva Conventions.[10]

- *The US altered the status of public officials and judges* contrary to article 54 of the Fourth Geneva Conventions.[11]

- *The penal laws of Iraq were altered by the CPA even though these laws as they existed did not constitute a threat to the security of the CPA or an obstacle to the application of the Fourth Geneva Convention,* contrary to Article 64 of the Convention which would have entitled to modify the code.[12]

- *Iraqis were arrested for acts committed or opinions expressed prior to the occupation* contrary to Article 70 of the Fourth Geneva Convention.[13]

- *Members of the Ba'ath Party which ruled Iraq for thirty five years were persecuted for their political belief* contrary to Article 7 (1.h) of the ICC Statute which held that such act to be a crime against humanity.[14]

CPA Actions

Bremer ruled Iraq through Regulations, Orders and Memoranda issued in the name of the CPA. Regulations were the instruments defining the institutions and authorities of the CPA. Orders were binding legal instructions and Memoranda were interpretations of legal instruments. In addition to that Bremer chose also to rule by issuing Public Notifications whenever he felt like doing so.[15]

On 16 May 2003 Bremer promulgated Regulation 1, the significance of which can be seen from the following. In the preamble to the regulation Bremer states:[16]

> Pursuant to my authority as Administrator of the CPA, relevant UN Security Council resolutions, including Resolution 1483(2003), and the laws and usages of war, I hereby promulgate the following.

Considering that Resolution 1483(2003)[17] was only adopted on 22 May 2003, which was *six days* after Bremer relied on it, it can only be concluded that all Security Council Resolutions were in fact drafted by the US and their adoption was assumed as a formality. How else did Bremer rely on a Resolution which the SC had not adopted and which could have been amended at any stage before its adoption?

Section 1 paragraph 2 reads:

The CPA is vested with all executive, legislative and judicial authority necessary to achieve its objectives to be exercised under relevant U.N. Security Council resolutions, including Resolution 1483(2003), and the laws and usages of war. This authority shall be exercised by the CPA Administrator.

In the above paragraph Bremer granted himself absolute power which no previous ruler of Iraq had ever claimed for himself. In short Bremer, contrary to principles of international law and laws of war, made himself a dictator par excellence.

Following from Regulation 1 Bremer went on to make 12 Regulations, 100 Orders and 16 Memoranda which dismantled the state and created a void that has not been filled since.

The first law passed by Bremer after assuming absolute power in Iraq reveals the purpose of the invasion, namely regime change, which extended far beyond the mere toppling of Saddam Hussein. Order 1 of 16 May 2003 titled "De-Ba'athification of Iraqi Society" reflects the desire of the Zionists to eradicate Arab Nationalism from Iraq. It is needless to analyze what has happened in Iraq in the eleven plus years since the invasion to affirm that this objective has been achieved. Not one single political party or campaign in Iraq in over a decade has even hinted at the Arab Nationalist character of Iraq or the Arab Zionist conflict. It could be safely concluded that the main objective of Zionism has been achieved: the Iraq that was once its formidable enemy has been ground into the dust. It also makes all talk about the US having been defeated in Iraq empty rhetoric, since its primary goal was so clearly achieved.

In the preamble, Bremer again claimed an authority under international law and Security Council Resolution 1483 which had not yet been adopted. The Order[18] stipulated that:

- The Ba'ath Party of Iraq be disestablished.

- Senior party members be removed from their positions and be banned from future employment in the public sector.

- Officials at the top three management layers in Government be interviewed to discern any affiliation with the Party.

- Any person detained and found to be an ordinary member of the Party would be removed from employment.

- Any person providing information leading to the capture of senior members of the Party would be financially rewarded.

Order 1 first and foremost is a crime against humanity as it contravenes a fundamental principle of international law which has since been incorporated into the ICC Statute. ICC Article 7 reads as follows:[19]

> 1. For the purpose of this Statute, "crime against humanity" means any of the following acts when committed as part of a widespread or systematic attack directed against any civilian population, with knowledge of the attack:
>
> ....
>
> (h) Persecution against any identifiable group or collectivity on political, racial, national, ethnic, cultural, religious, gender as defined in paragraph 3, or other grounds that are universally recognized as impermissible under international law, in connection with any act referred to in this paragraph or any crime within the jurisdiction of the Court;

It is clear from Article 7 that De-Ba'athification is a crime against humanity. The fact that the US does not recognize the ICC does not make it less of a crime under international law. Furthermore, while the US may rely on its not recognizing the ICC as its defense, no such defense is available to the UK which jointly controlled the CPA and had ratified the ICC Statute.

The scope of the crime is obvious when we consider the following facts. The Ba'ath Party was set up in the early 1950s and took control of Iraq fully in 1968. Throughout its 50 years of appeal and recruitment it managed to claim over three million members or affiliates. It is destabilizing for any society to remove hundreds of thousands from employment and deprive millions of any income with a stroke of a pen.

Bremer enhanced Order 1 with further legislation when he passed Order 5 of 25 May setting up the De-Ba'athification Council.[20] The Council, serving at the discretion of Bremer, was entrusted with the task of investigating the Ba'ath Party and identifying the whereabouts of its members and officials. It went on to act with such dictatorial authority as a court of law with no appeal, enabling people to settle old personal disputes with Ba'athists. It became a tool of intimidation as it was possible to silence anybody with the threat of investigation.

Two further pieces of legislation were needed to seal the process of irreversible political change. The first was Memorandum 1 of 3 June 2003[21] which called on the US commander of the Coalition

Forces to provide the military investigative resources required to receive and compile information concerning the affiliations of Party members in all ministries. The De-Ba'athification Council was further entrusted with the task of advising the CPA on de-Ba'athification policies and procedures. A group of people who were chosen to sit on the Council and whose only credentials were being anti-Ba'athists ended up deciding who should and should not be employed. In Iraq of 2003, after over 12 years of total sanctions, there were few possibilities of employment outside Government. Giving the Council the authority to determine the employment of Iraqis meant that those few anti-Ba'athists were given the control of right to life.

Towards the end of his tenure Bremer issued Order 62 of 28 February 2004 on Disqualification from Public Office.[22] That order enabled members of the Council to determine who was a senior member of the Party. Once such a determination was made then Bremer would rule that such person be disqualified from participating in an election as a candidate, or accepting a nomination to, or holding public office, at any level.

The above sequence of legislation ensured that Iraq's political system was irreversibly changed. As the Ba'ath Party was disbanded and Arab Nationalism was effectively criminalized, the stage was ready for any group of people to set up so-called political parties whose only objective was to take part in the forthcoming administration set up by Bremer.

In addition to the crimes of invasion and crimes against humanity, the invaders revealed their hypocrisy by their alleged campaign to bring democracy to Iraq while preventing thousands of people, who had not been found guilty of any wrongdoing, from participating in the electoral process.

Eliminating Iraq's Defense System

Bremer promulagted several laws that eliminated Iraq's military and destroyed all its weaponry, leaving Iraq, for the first time in 80 years, reliant on an outside force to defend it and protect it.

The following is a summary of these legislations:

- Order 2 of 23 May 2003 for the Dissolution of Entities[23]

- Order 22 of 7 August 2003 for the Creation of a New Iraqi Army[24]

- Order 23 of 7 August 2003 for the Creation of a Code of Military Discipline for the New Iraqi Army[25]

- Order 26 of 24 August 2003 for the Creation of Department of Border Enforcement[26]

- Order 27 of 4 September 2003 for the Establishment of the Facilities Protecting Service[27]

- Order 28 of 3 September 2003 for the Establishment of the Iraqi Civil Defence Corps[28]

- Order 42 of 19 September 2003 for the Creation of the Defense Support Agency[29]

- Order 75 of 15 April 2004 for Realignment of Military Industrial Companies[30]

- Order 91 of 2 June 2004 for Regulation of Armed Forces and Militias within Iraq[31]

Among the many dissolved entities in Order 2 were: The Ministry of Defence, The Ministry of Information, The Ministry of State for Military Affairs, The Iraqi Intelligence Service, The National Security Bureau, The Directorate of National Security (Amn al-'Am), and The Special Security Organization.

The following military organizations were dissolved:

- The Army, Air Force, Navy, the Air Defence Force, and other regular military services

- The Republican Guard

- The Special Republican Guard

- The Directorate of Military Intelligence

- The Al Quds Force

- Emergency Forces (Quwat al Tawari)

In short the occupiers, contrary to principles of international law, dissolved all military and security forces in Iraq.

Order 22, which set out to establish a new Iraqi army under Bremer's control, revealed another sinister element in the objectives of the invasion and occupation of Iraq. Section 2 of Order 22 reads:

> The Iraqi Military Law Code Number 13 of 1940, the
> Iraqi Military Procedures Code Number 44 of 1941, the
> Code of Legal Notification of Military Personnel Number
> 106 of 1960, Punishment of Military Deserters law
> Number 28 of 1972 and the Penal Code of the Popular
> Army Number 32 of 1984 are hereby suspended.

The above section calls for two observations. Firstly, it shows that the Ba'ath Government had not intervened, as its enemies tried repeatedly to convince international opinion, in legislations passed before it in order to suit partisan objectives. The military legislations passed between 1940 and 1960, prior to the Ba'ath assuming power were still in force. Secondly and more importantly, it showed that the real objective of the invasion went far beyond searching for WMDs and regime change to a fundamental attack on Iraqi society and culture in general. How could the US feel it necessary for Iraq to annul legislations that were developed over decades of different regimes in Iraq and were part of the cultural development and fabric of Iraqi society, especially since none of these legislations created any barrier to the CPA's rule?

Militia Forces

Any observer of Iraq during the years following the invasion could not have missed the proliferation of militia forces across the country. The cause and roots of this is to be found in Bremer's legislation. The preamble to order 91 setting out to regulate Armed Forces and Militias within Iraq stated that it was:[32]

> Acknowledging that those who fought against the
> Ba'athist regime in resistance forces should receive
> recognition and benefits as military veterans for their
> service to their people.

> In section 1 on definitions it gives the following:

> 2) "Armed Force" means an organized group of
> individuals bearing firearms or weapons. The term
> "Armed Force" includes government forces and Militias.

> 3) "Militia" means a military or paramilitary force that is
> not part of the Iraqi Armed Forces or other Iraqi security
> forces established pursuant to CPA Orders, Regulations
> and Memoranda, or pursuant to Iraqi federal law and
> the Law of Administration for the State of Iraq for the
> Transitional Period.

4) "Private Security Company" means a private business, properly registered with the Ministry of Interior and Ministry of Trade that seeks to gain commercial benefits and financial profit by providing security services to individuals, businesses and organizations, governmental or otherwise. Private Security Companies are subject to, and must comply with all applicable criminal, administrative, commercial and civil laws and regulations unless exempted by CPA Order Number 17, Status of Coalition, Foreign Liaison Missions, their Personnel and Contractors.

The above Order led to two outcomes both of which had serious consequences for Iraq. The first was the proliferation of militia forces and their integration into the new Iraqi military and security forces. The second was the creation of a new army whose number reached a magnitude of 190 000 in the service of Private Security Companies by 2008.[33] As most of these mercenaries were ex-soldiers from the US, UK, South Africa and Australia, it needs no excessive intelligence to realize what dangers such a military force could pose to a country with a small, if any, army. In revised Order 17 Bremer ensured that all members of the Private Security Companies were immune from the 'Iraqi legal process' thus permitting them to operate with impunity beyond the law and answerable to nobody.[34] The incident of the massacre by Blackwater is but one example of such a situation created by Bremer.[35]

It is in the light of Bremer's legacy that one can understand what happened in Iraq regarding the sectarian massacres which were committed by the armed militias commended by Bremer and allowed to operate on the grounds that they opposed the Ba'ath.

Destroying Iraq's Military Industry

In the preamble to Order 75 for the Realignment of Military Industrial Companies, Bremer decided the following:[36]

Recognizing that many state-owned enterprises previously engaged in military industrial production (heretofore "military industrial companies") sit idle and largely abandoned throughout Iraq,

Concerned that buildings and factories of companies formerly assigned to the military industrial commission (or "military industrial companies") often contain stockpiles of hardware and materials that remain deployable for violent uses against Coalition

Forces and the people of Iraq, and that employees of these companies remain needlessly underemployed and unable to utilize their skills to promote the welfare of Iraq.

Bremer went on to decide:

This Order promotes public order and safety for the Iraqi people by providing for the security and destruction of materials abandoned after the closure of military industrial companies throughout Iraq.

Bremer used the unsustainable argument of alleged danger to Coalition Forces from materials existing at military industrial sites to order the destruction of Iraq's entire military industry. It is clear that Bremer made sure that no military industry remained in Iraq regardless of when that industry was established.

Following the destruction of Iraq's military industry and armaments, all the steel resulting from the conversion of thousands of tons of industrial machines, tanks, troop carriers, artillery etc. into scrap metal was shipped to Jordan. All the equipment and armaments, which cost Iraq billions of dollars to purchase, were sold off as scrap metal. We do not know who in fact sold the scrap metal or who received money for it. Bremer gave one indication of what was happening when in Memorandum 8 of 25 January 2004 he advised that as of 1 February anyone intending to export scrap metal needed to acquire an export license.[37]

Iraq was the only Arab country which had taken part in the short skirmishes in 1948 with the State of Israel and did not sign the armistice with it. Iraq supported Egypt and Syria in the 1967 war and took part in the 1973 war fighting alongside the Syrians on the Golan Heights. Last but not least Iraq was the first Arab country that dared to attack Tel Aviv when it fired some 39 missiles into it in 1991. It was quite an achievement for Israel to have rid itself of any threat not only from an Iraqi army but also from a potential Iraqi military industry without having had to fire a shot or lose a soldier. This, we believe, was at the heart of the invasion of Iraq. This was Bremer's mission and he achieved it for Israel.

Converting Iraq from Socialism to the Neoliberal "Free Market"

Imperialism seeks to achieve two objectives in the Arab World. The first is to ensure that Israel remains supreme and that all states around it accept this and acquiesce to it. The second is that all states in the Arab

World should adopt the neoliberal capitalist principles of a globalized economy, ensuring that each state ends up with an enslaved economy fully dependent on the neoliberalized capitalist system under the control of Western banking. Such enslavement of states rich in energy sources but with primitive economies results in their progressive underdevelopment, led by governments unable to exercise any policies in their peoples' interests in any aspect of life, be that political, military, cultural or social.

Parallel with the dismantling of Iraq's army and military industry, Bremer passed sufficient legislation to ensure the complete privatization of Iraq's economy, and the undoing of its socialist orientation, institutions and programs. Bremer promulgated four Regulations and twenty Orders to achieve this. The intention of the legislation was repeated clearly in all of them. Thus in the preamble to Order 64 Bremer stated it to be:

> ... for the development of Iraq and its transition from a non-transparent centrally planned economy to a free market economy characterized by sustainable economic growth through the establishment of a dynamic private sector, and the need to enact institutional and legal reforms to give it effect.[38]

Bremer never cited any legal basis for his assumption of the right to convert Iraq's economy, which had been based on socialist principles long before the Ba'athists came to power, without seeking the will of the Iraqi people. Perhaps because there was none. In fact it is an offence under international law to change the economy of countries under occupation. This is how Julius Stone summed it up:

> Most Western writers would argue that the occupant could not transform a liberal economy into a communist one; and Soviet writers would no doubt be concerned about the reverse transformation.[39]

We shall review some of the main features of the legislation in the fields of economy and finance that were passed in order to achieve this transformation. The legislation centred on three different aspects of the transformation: Banking, foreign investment and the liberalization of trade. Western finance capital has been trying for decades to transfer the control of central banks from Governments to private enterprise, leading to the worlds' central banks being controlled by the Rothschilds and their ilk. In order 56 of 1 March 2004 titled 'Central Bank Law' Bremer made the purpose of the new legislation, which repealed Central Bank of Iraq Law, Law No. 64 of 1976, clear:

> This Order establishes a safe, sound, and independent Central Bank for the purposes of achieving and maintaining domestic price stability, fostering and maintaining a stable and competitive market-based financial system, and promoting sustainable growth, employment, and prosperity in Iraq.[40]

It is worth pointing out that in the above stated purpose of setting up the new Central Bank is to make it 'independent' (of government and thereby of popular control) and based on 'market economy' principles (in which local needs and rights have no play). This was a fundamental departure from the basis by which central banks have been established in developing nations, placing the 'independent' central banks under the control of global finance capital through its capacity to manipulate and control the flows and values of money, and the rules by which this is governed.

In Banking Law Order 94 of 6 June 2004 promulgated just before the alleged handover of power to an interim Iraqi Government, Bremer ensured that the grounds were set for opening Iraq to foreign banks in what became the most detailed and the longest legislation of his reign, running to 70 pages.[41] The purpose was spelt out in glowing terms which obfuscated its intended outcome.: "[T]he need for the development of Iraq and its transition from a non-transparent centrally planned economy to a market economy characterized by sustainable economic growth through the establishment of a dynamic private sector, and the need to enact institutional and legal reforms to give it effect" meant, in plain language the opening Iraqi banks to be swallowed by the well-organized international sharks.

Bremer had already used Order 76 of 22 May 2004 for the 'Consolidation of State-Owned Enterprises' to effectively liquidate the following four state owned banks:[42]

The Real-Estate Bank
The Agricultural Bank
The Industrial Bank
The Socialist Bank

As some of these banks were not created during the period of the Ba'ath assuming power, it becomes clear that the measure had nothing to do with de-Ba'athification but struck deeper, transforming Iraq into the kind of vulnerable and permeable state desired by Western capitalism. These banks had originally been created under different Iraqi Governments to provide almost interest free loans for building houses, industry and agriculture. Most Iraqis had benefitted from these banks especially through the provision of houses to millions of Iraqis over the previous fifty years. But the principles favored by finance capital and fronted by the IMF demanded that the state subsidy be eliminated (enabling state revenues "saved" from expenditures on local needs to be flushed to western banks). Bremer was acting in line with these principles.

Parallel to banking transformation legislation, Bremer enacted foreign investment laws that opened Iraq's markets to foreign domination after fifty years of a state-controlled socialist economy. In Foreign Investment Order 39 of 19 September 2003, amended in Order 46,[43] Bremer allowed foreign individuals and entities to own up to 100% of the equity in an Iraqi business. Bremer stated that despite the legal framework that already existed in Iraq which favored and protected domestic development by preventing foreign investment, his intention was to develop Iraq's infrastructure, foster the growth of Iraqi business, create jobs and raise capital. The falsity of all this is transparent. The Ba'ath regime in Iraq had achieved remarkable growth and full employment without ever getting into national debt. Is it logical to think that the very parties who had been instrumental in the rollback of all of this via sanctions and destruction of infrastructure now had a sincere interest in the development of the country *in its own interest*?

No less significant was Order 64 of 29 February 2004[44] which effectively repealed Company Law No 21 of 1997. Among the main changes to the Company law introduced by Bremer were:

1.   Enabling foreign companies to become shareholders in Iraqi companies;

2.   Eliminating the need to conform with the state planning goals as a condition of approval for the company to be set up;

3.   Eliminating the requirement to have trade union representatives on the board of private of companies.

Prior to his departure Bremer passed the following legislations to consolidate the creation of Iraq as a US colony:

1.   Order 80 of 26 April 2004 on Amendment to the Trademarks and Descriptions law no. 21 of 1957;[45]

2.   Order 81 of 26 April 2004 on Patent, Industrial Design, Undisclosed Information, Integrated Circuits and Plant Variety Law;[46]

3.   Order 83 of 29 April 2004 on Amendment to The Copyright Law.[47]

Although Order 80 amended a law which was passed long before the Ba'ath came to power and although we do not believe in Copyright Law in principle, we believe the most sinister element in the above three Orders appears in Order 81 under the title 'Plant Variety'. Here is how Jeremy Smith put it:[48]

> Under the guise of helping get Iraq back on its feet, the US is setting out to totally re-engineer the country's traditional farming systems into a US-style corporate agribusiness. They've even created a new law–Order 81–to make sure it happens.

He went on to reveal the sinister plan the US had for agriculture in Iraq:

> The most significant part of Order 81 is a new chapter that it inserts on 'Plant Variety Protection' (PVP). This concerns itself not with the protection of biodiversity, but rather with the protection of the commercial interests of large seed corporations.
>   To qualify for PVP, seeds have to meet the following criteria: they must be 'new, distinct, uniform and stable'. Under the new regulations imposed by Order 81, therefore, the sort of seeds Iraqi farmers are now being encouraged to grow by corporations such as WWWC will be those registered under PVP.
>   On the other hand, it is impossible for the seeds developed by the people of Iraq to meet these criteria. Their seeds are not 'new' as they are the product of millennia of development. Nor are they 'distinct'. The free exchange of seeds practiced for centuries ensures that characteristics are spread and shared across local varieties. And they are the opposite of 'uniform' and 'stable' by the very nature of their biodiversity. They cross-pollinate with other nearby varieties, ensuring they are always changing and always adapting.
>   Cross-pollination is an important issue for another reason. In recent years several farmers have been taken to court for illegally growing a corporation's GM seeds. The farmers have argued they were doing so unknowingly, that the seeds must have carried on the

wind from a neighbouring farm, for example. They have still been taken to court. This will now apply in Iraq. Under the new rules, if a farmer's seed can be shown to have been contaminated with one of the PVP registered seeds, he could be fined. He may have been saving his seed for years, maybe even generations, but if it mixes with a seed owned by a corporation and maybe creates a new hybrid, he may face a day in court.

Remember that 97 per cent of Iraqi farmers save their seeds. Order 81 also puts paid to that. A new line has been added to the law which reads: 'Farmers shall be prohibited from re-using seeds of protected varieties or any variety mentioned in items 1 and 2 of paragraph (C) of Article 14 of this Chapter.'

The other varieties referred to are those that show similar characteristics to the PVP varieties. If a corporation develops a variety resistant to a particular Iraqi pest, and somewhere in Iraq a farmer is growing another variety that does the same, it's now illegal for him/her to save that seed. It sounds mad, but it's happened before. A few years back a corporation called SunGene patented a sunflower variety with avery high oleic acid content. It didn't just patent the genetic structure though, it patented the characteristic. Subsequently SunGene notified other sunflower breeders that should they develop a variety high in oleic acid that would be considered an infringement of the patent.

So the Iraqi farmer may have been wowed with the promise of a bumper yield at the end of this year. But unlike before he can't save his seed for the next. A 10,000-year old tradition has been replaced at a stroke with a contract for hire.

Iraqi farmers have been made vassals to American corporations. That they were baking bread for 9,500 years before America existed has no weight when it comes to deciding who owns Iraq's wheat. Yet for every farmer that stops growing his unique strain of saved seed the world loses another variety, one that might have been useful in times of disease or drought.

In short, what America has done is not restructure Iraq's agriculture, but dismantle it. [italics added] The people whose forefathers first mastered the domestication of wheat will now have to pay for the privilege of growing it for someone else. And with that the world's oldest farming heritage will become just another subsidiary link in the vast American supply chain.

Legal and Judicial Restructuring

When the laws of war were being formulated, it did not escape the attention of their drafters that one of the most powerful tools in the hands of an occupier would always be controlling the laws and the judiciary in the occupied land. It was thus established from the outset that the interference by an occupying power should be as limited as necessary and only when the security and protection of the occupying power necessitated it.

The importance of these facts is obvious because once the occupying power is allowed to change the laws and judges in the occupied land, it could rule the land under the guise of the rule of law and get away with anything and thus possibly legalize the illegal. That was precisely what Bremer did in Iraq. His action regarding the changes to Iraq's law and judges did not arise spontaneously but has its roots in the report of the Working Group on Transitional Justice which was part of the Future of Iraq Project.[49]

We shall firstly consider the major changes made to Iraqi criminal code and procedure and then consider the more serious changes in the structuring of courts and the appointment of judges.

In Order 7 of 9 June 2003 on Penal Code, Bremer made the following illegal statement:

> All judges, police and prosecutors shall perform their duties in accordance with CPA Regulation No.1 (CPA/REG/23 May 2003/01) and in accordance with any other Regulations, Orders, Memoranda or instructions issued by the CPA.[50]

Here, as in Regulation 1, Bremer made himself the absolute ruler of Iraq with absolute power; Order 7 breached international law by subjecting Iraq's judges to his power.

Bremer went on to repeal some 26 amendments to Iraq's Penal Code of 1969 without indicating which section was a 'threat to the security of the occupying power' such that it was lawful for him to repeal.

In order 31 of 19 September 2003 on 'Modification of Penal Code and Criminal Proceedings Law',[51] Bremer imposed harsher sentences in some crimes and denied bail in others. It is significant here to remember that Bremer, who has no legal authority to modify Iraq's laws as a matter of principle, had criticised the Iraqi Government for having imposed harsh sentences for some crimes to suit the Ba'ath regime policies.

The action on judges is more serious and lasting than amendments to laws because those could be amended at any time. However, removing judges and appointing new ones carries a heavier effect on the legal and judicial process. It should be remembered here that the Ba'ath ruled Iraq between 1968 and 2003 and during those 35 years most of Iraq judges grew up within the ideology of the Ba'ath. Some of them came to believe in it and some simply pretended to do so. But invariably all judges in Iraq in 2003 were affiliated to the Ba'ath Party in one way or another. Thus when all judges who were affiliated to the Ba'ath were removed, it was inevitable that the new judiciary in Iraq was composed of inexperienced people, some of whom had never been on a bench before nor undergone the mandatory judicial institute course training. The posts were filled with graduates of law schools whose only credentials were being anti-Ba'athist.

Bremer, having accused the Ba'ath of having 'stacked the courts' by appointing people who were either Ba'athists or affiliated to the Party, proceeded to take identical measures by stacking the courts with anti-Ba'athists. Thus in section 5 of Order 13 as revised on 22 April 2004 in which he set up the Central Criminal Court of Iraq, Bremer stated among the conditions for appointing judges that they must:

> have a background of either opposition to the Ba'ath Party, non-membership of the Ba'ath Party or membership that does not fall within the leadership tiers described in CPA/ORD/16 May 2003/01 and entailed no involvement in Ba'ath Party activity.[52]

In order to implement the policy of creating a new judiciary subservient to US policies Bremer promulgated Order 15 on 23 June 2003 to set up the Judicial Review Committee. In the preamble to the order Bremer stated among the reasons for setting up the Committee:

> that the Iraqi justice system has been subjected to political interference and corruption over the years of Iraqi Ba'ath Party rule[53].

Order 15 suspended, among its provisions, the Iraqi Organization of the Judiciary Act of 1979. The members of the Committee, which consisted of three Iraqi members and three international members, were chosen by Bremer to act under his discretion in accordance with the principle of de-Ba'athification. The powers and functions of the Committee were given in section 4 as:

The Committee shall investigate and gather information on the suitability of Judges and Prosecutors to hold office. It shall have the power to remove judges and prosecutors from office, confirm their continued holding of office, appoint replacements for judges and prosecutors removed from office and resolve the claims of judges and prosecutors who assert that they were improperly removed from office.

It is important to note that according to Article 54 of the Fourth Geneva Convention the measures taken by Bremer in Order 15 above are illegal.

To further consolidate the restructuring of Iraq's judiciary, Bremer passed Order 35 of 13 September 2003 for the Re-Establishment of Council of Judges.[54] The new Council, which consisted of seven members chosen by Bremer, set out, without even an attempted justification, to replace the Council of Justice that was previously established by the Judicial Organization Law (Law No. 160/1979). The Council was entrusted with overseeing the functioning of the judiciary in Iraq from appointing judges and prosecutors to disciplining them.

Thus Bremer ensured that before his departure the judiciary in Iraq was set in the proper context with its structure and personnel chosen by US officials. That was significant in that up until today the laws in Iraq are being applied and interpreted by the same men chosen or appointed by Bremer or those who were later appointed by these appointees.

To conclude his unique contribution to judicial imperialism, Bremer undertook two measures, both illegal, with one attempting to assume compliance with international law.

In Order 17 which was revised on 27 June 2004 on the 'Status of The Coalition Provisional Authority, MNF- Iraq, Certain Missions and Personnel in Iraq',[55] Bremer ensured a few days before his departure, the granting of immunity from Iraqi legal process for the CPA, the so-called MNF, Foreign Liaison Personnel, International Consultants, contractors, Private Security Companies and many others that could be interpreted to fall with the definitions in the Order. As the puppet Government in Iraq later adopted all the legislations passed by Bremer, thousands of people operating in Iraq were put beyond the rule of law, all contrary to Iraqi and international law. The case of Blackwater and its crimes in Iraq is just one example of the consequences of such measures.

Memorandum 3 on 'Criminal Procedures', which Bremer revised on 27 June 2004,[56] was a serious breach and muddle. It was a breach because it amended Iraq Criminal Proceedings Act 1971 arguing that it was inadequate on human rights. It was a complete muddle because in trying to enable MNF to act within the rule of law, Bremer assumed that the Fourth Geneva Convention applied in Iraq after June 2004. Thus in the preamble he stated:

> *Determining,* that the relevant and appropriate provisions of the Fourth Geneva Convention of 1949 Relative to the Treatment of Civilians in Time of War (hereinafter "the Fourth Geneva Convention") constitute an appropriate framework consistent with its mandate in continuance of measures previously adopted.

And in section 1 of the Memo he stated among its purposes:

> ...the ongoing process of security internee management in accordance with the relevant and appropriate standards set out in the Fourth Geneva Convention which shall be applied by the MNF as a matter of policy in accordance with its mandate.

But the Fourth Geneva Convention only applies to people under occupation. So while the Security Council and the US were hailing the end of occupation by the transfer of sovereignty at the end of June 2004, Bremer was telling us that Iraq was indeed to remain under occupation with the MNF acting under the Geneva Conventions. Another problem with Memo 3 is that it refers to people detained after 30 June 2004 but makes no mention of people who were detained prior to that date. Most Ba'athists in Iraq had been arrested prior to 30 June 2004. Bremer's legal drafters avoided referring to those detained prior to June 2004 because they would have been unable to rely on the Geneva Conventions whose Article 70 states:

> Protected persons shall not be arrested, prosecuted or convicted by the Occupying Power for acts committed or opinions expressed before the occupation.

But all the Ba'athists were arrested for alleged acts or opinions expressed prior to occupation!

In his casual way of throwing whatever he liked into his orders and Regulations, assuming nobody would ever seek to verify, Bremer repeated that practice again in Section 6 of Memo 3 which stated:

> Any person who is detained by a national contingent of the MNF for imperative reasons of security in

accordance with the mandate set out in UNSCR 1546
(hereinafter "security internee") shall, if he is held for
a period longer than 72 hours, be entitled to have a
review of the decision to intern him."

But there is no such mandate in UNSCR 1546. Furthermore, it
is incredible that Bremer refers to reviewing people's detention some 72
hours after their detention. There are people, like Tariq Aziz,[57] who have
been in detention since 2003 with no review, trial or charge!

Despite Bremer's calculated deception in assuming legitimacy
for his measure, he was supported by legal men/women who knew all
aspects of international law and guided him whenever it was necessary
to adjust things so as not to appear as being in blatant breach of the law.
They did not always succeed as we have seen.

Before his departure from Iraq, Bremer enacted several Orders
to lay down the grounds for Iraq's political system. Among those were:

- Order 92 of 31 May 2004 setting up 'The Independent
Electoral Commission of Iraq';[58]

- Order 96 of 15 June for 'The Electoral Law';[59]

- Order 97 of 15 June 2004 for the 'Political Parties and Entities
Law'.[60]

Apart from the fact that Bremer had no authority under Law
to enact any of the above legislations insofar as occupying powers have
no right to plan the political future of occupied territory, there is a much
more profound problem with the above legislations: Bremer set out, in
principle, to deceive people.

The preamble of the three Orders/ 92, 96 and 97 noted:

that the Law of Administration for the State of Iraq
for the Transitional Period (the "TAL") provides for
the Iraqi people to choose their government through
genuine and credible elections to be held no later than
31 January 2005

and went on to base the purpose of each on them on the terms of (TAL).
But what was TAL?

The Law of Administration for The State of Iraq for the Transitional
Period (TAL) of March 2004 consisted of 62 Articles and defined itself as
an effective interim constitution when in Article 62 it stated: [61]

> This law shall remain in effect until the permanent
> constitution is issued and the new Iraqi government is
> formed in accordance with it.

However, this interim constitution, which later became the basis
of Iraq's so-called permanent constitution even though it was adopted
while still under occupation, was not even enacted according to Bremer's
laws. His Regulation 1 of 16 May 2003 granted Bremer supreme power
and became the source of all legislation in Iraq. But when we looked for
a Regulation or Order that enacted TAL we found none. In fact TAL simply
appeared on the CPA website without any reference to the method by
which it was promulgated or adopted. We believe that Bremer was
advised by his legal team that he had no authority to promulgate a
constitution for Iraq because Iraq Constitution 1970 was still the legal
constitution under Iraqi and international law. So in order to avoid being
accused later of having breached this rule, he simply put it on the website
and everyone took it to be effective and all the legislation that followed
depended on its validity.

We suggest that TAL was and remains invalid and legislations
and measures relying on it were and remain equally invalid.

Development Fund for Iraq

In May 2003 the US set up the Development Fund for Iraq (DFI) as
an account at US Federal Reserve Bank of New York to act as Iraq's Central
Bank. The Security Council, acting as it had done throughout the years of
sanctions and invasion as a rubber stamp for the US, called in its Resolution
1483 of 22 May 2003 for the setting up of the DFI, making it sound like its
own creation and not one that had already been created by the US. The
DFI, which was put under the control of the CPA, was entrusted with the
administration of proceeds from the export sales of Iraq's oil, as well as
funds remaining from the UN Oil for Food Program and all other Iraqi assets.
The Resolution called for the creation of the International Advisory and
Monitoring Board (IAMB) whose task was to be an independent oversight
body for DFI and to ensure transparency and financial accountability of
the DFI.[62]

However, despite the fact that the IAMB was set up to monitor
Iraq's Central Bank it had very little Iraqi participation. The IAMB website
indicates its membership:

> shall consist of duly qualified representatives of each
> of the Secretary-General of the United Nations, the
> Managing Director of the International Monetary
> Fund, the Director-General of the Arab Fund for

Economic and Social Development and the President of the International Bank for Reconstruction and Development and a duly qualified individual designated by the Government of Iraq.[63]

It also advises us that:

The principal role of the IAMB is to help ensure that:

- The DFI is used in a transparent manner for the benefit of the people of Iraq, and
- Export sales of petroleum, petroleum products, and natural gas from Iraq are made consistent with prevailing international market best practices.

However six months passed after Resolution 1483 was adopted, and the IAMB effectively was not born until 24 October 2003. We shall see later who was monitoring Iraq assets and revenue in the interim period and whether or not it mattered anyway.

According to the IAMB website, it held thirteen meetings between December 2003 and January 2011. These meetings were held in many cities but not a single one was held in Baghdad. So much for transparency! No less significant is the fact that an Iraqi representative wasn't selected to sit on the IMAB until June 2004, and attended the 14-15 July 2004 meeting for the first time i.e. there was no Iraqi representative on the IAMB during the rule of Bremer.

Making a decision on whether or not a law should be repealed or amended can generally be argued either way. However, when funds go missing with no accounting, this is another matter. The manner of functioning of the IAMB reveals part of the major crime of the disappearance of Iraq's assets and revenue during the occupation. Global Policy Forum shed some light on this, stating:

Though the US and the UK had promised Council members that the IAMB would be "the eyes and ears of the international community", procedural wrangling and US manipulation delayed the oversight process for many months. Meanwhile, billions flowed into the DFI, and some Council members grew irate at what they called a "black hole" of unaccountability.[64]

In fairness to the IAMB it should be pointed out that when it discovered the failure of the CPA to cooperate, it negotiated with the latter to select an international auditor, choosing KPMG international auditors in April 2004 to audit the CPA's expenditures from Iraq's oil revenue in 2003.

On 15 July 2004, KPMG released audit documents that highlighted several failures by the CPA and serious accounting discrepancies. Among the failures of CPA as found by the auditors were: [65]

> 1.   Refusal of Bremer to hold one single meeting with the auditors.

> 2.   The failure of Bremer to appoint an independent auditor despite having stated in Regulation 2 that: "The Fund and the export sales of petroleum, petroleum products, and natural gas from Iraq, shall be audited by independent public accountants nominated by the Administrator and approved by the IAMB."

> 3.   The failure to employ proper bookkeeping thus ended up with a single entry, cash-based, transaction list which disposed of $20 billion of petty cash.

> 4.   The failure of the CPA to repair Iraq's oil metering resulted in over $4 billion worth of oil being siphoned off during the year of the CPA's administration. [66]

> 5.   The failure of the Program Review Board, [67] which was appointed by Bremer under Regulation 2, to keep records of its activity or have recorded minutes of its meetings, attendances and discussions despite having awarded over 800 contracts out of the DFI.

In its report covering the Period from the Establishment of the DFI on 22 May 2003 until the Dissolution of the CPA on 28 June 2004, the IAMB :

- expressed concern at an early stage about inadequate controls over Iraq's oil resources and other aspects of DFI operations;

- noted that the absence of metering for crude oil production precluded a reconciliation of all crude oil extracted with its eventual utilization;

- was also informed by the CPA that some of Iraq's

oil resources were not accounted for and had been smuggled;

- noted, at its meeting in March 2004, that some contracts using DFI funds had been awarded to a Halliburton subsidiary without competitive bidding;

- was informed of the bartering of residual fuel and crude oil for electricity and other products with neighboring countries. In March 2004, the IAMB raised concerns that such barter transactions are not reflected in the DFI as required by UNSCR 1483. The use of barter transactions makes it difficult to determine whether fair value has been received for Iraq's oil revenues. These barter transactions are not recorded in the DFI statement of cash receipts and payments, and the commodities bartered are not considered assets or liabilities, as these transactions will not materialize into cash at any time.[68]

The US was forced partly due to IAMB request to set up its own auditing of the DFI. The Minority Report of June 2005 submitted to the first hearing of the Committee on Government Report investigating the DFI made the following findings:

- The Federal Reserve Shipped Nearly $12 Billion in U.S. Currency to Iraq

- The CPA Failed to Provide Adequate Financial or Physical Controls.

- There is Mounting Evidence of Extensive Waste, Fraud, and Abuse.
    1. Overcharges by Halliburton.
    2. Fraud by Custer Battles.
    3. Irregularities and Fraud in the Commanders' Funds.
    4. Irregularities and Corruption in Disbursements to Iraqi Ministries.
    5. Irregularities in Disbursements to Provincial Governments.

The Report made the following stark conclusion:

After the invasion of Iraq, the U.S.-run Coalition Provisional Authority took control of more than $22.4 billion in Iraqi resources and spent or disbursed $19.6 billion. While these Iraqi assets were under U.S. control, unprecedented sums were withdrawn in cash from the Federal Reserve and shipped to Iraq, where they were spent or disbursed by the CPA with virtually no financial controls. Partial audits of these expenditures have disclosed evidence of substantial waste, fraud, and abuse.[69]

In his statement to the Committee, Representative Henry Waxman said that since the DFI was the successor to the Oil for Food Program:

...there has been a stark—and telling—contrast between Congress' approach to the Oil for Food Program and the DFI. Five separate congressional committees have been investigating U.N. mismanagement of the Oil for Food Program, and more than a dozen hearings have been held. But before today, there was not a single hearing in Congress on U.S. mismanagement of the Development Fund for Iraq.[70]

On 7 July 2005 the London *Guardian* published an article titled: "So, Mr. Bremer, where did all the money go?" [71]

More than eleven years after the squandering of $20 billion of Iraqi assets, there is still no answer. Nor has the squandering stopped!

INSTITUTING FEDERALISM
PLANTING THE SEEDS OF ETHNIC AND SECTARIAN DIVISION

In addition to planning the dismantling of Iraq and all its institutions including the army and its military industry, as we explained in Chapter 6, and shackling Iraq with laws whose purpose was to subjugate it completely, the Americans, and seemingly the British too, had also made plans for setting up a new state in order to secure a total and indefinite grip on Iraq and its future.

Here are the main steps taken by the US leading to the setting up of a new state.

Enter General Garner

Retired Army Lieutenant General Jay Garner was appointed on 9 January 2003, before the start of the invasion, to run the office set up by the Department of Defence to plan for the post-war administration of Iraq. This office, created by a 20 January 2003 executive order, became known as the Office of Reconstruction and Humanitarian Assistance (ORHA).[1]

OHRA deployed 151 staff members from Washington to Kuwait on 16 March 2003.[2] OHRA assumed that Iraqi ministries would function normally after the war, with slight changes at the top requiring the replacement of ministers and senior officials, while the ministries' civil servants would run affairs under a new leadership.[3] OHRA also assumed that this would require a Ministerial Advisory Team consisting of "a senior US or coalition partner government official to guide ministry decisions and retain veto authority during the transition period; expatriate Iraqi technocrats to provide technical expertise in each ministry's issues, and the most senior technocrat remaining in each ministry after the top-level Ba'athists were removed, to oversee the rest of the ministry's personnel."[4]

It seems that Garner had not been given any information regarding the war plans. He was soon to discover that his plans for OHRA to go to Basrah and start reconstruction efforts immediately after the military had secured the city, were not what the military had in mind.[5] OHRA had no idea what the realities of the situation were in Iraq, nor was Garner privy to the discussions of the National Security Council (NSC). In fact Garner claimed that he never received any of the plans prepared by the Office of Special Plans (OSP), which took over planning by the DOD to develop policy recommendations which contradicted those of the State Department as it related to postwar government reorganization, the future of the Iraqi army, and de-Ba'athification.[6] Nor did he know that Douglas Feith, who ran OSP, had been involved in any post-war planning before coming to Iraq.[7] There is no way of verifying these claims.

Garner arrived in Baghdad on 21 April 2003 followed on 24 April by most of OHRA's staff.[8] Garner declared that his priority was to restore basic services such as water and electricity "as soon as possible".[9] He was only publicly stating the concepts developed by the DOD, which are explained in some detail by Under Secretary of Defence Douglas Feith's book. *War and Decision*. Feith's concept, which he presented to the Senate Foreign Relations Committee on 11 February 2003, was that Iraqis "might play a progressively greater role in administering the country", listing key elements towards that objective which included forming the Iraqi Consultative Council (ICC), the judicial council, a constitutional committee to draft a constitution followed by a referendum on it, with government institutions to remain in place after vetting top officials, and then early town and district elections.[10]

In March 2003 Feith's office developed a concept which called for the formation of an Iraqi Interim Authority (IIA) that would include internals, Kurds, and exiles and would share leadership responsibilities with the coalition (more like a consultative body). The IIA would serve only in the interim, until a more fully representative government could be established through elections. At a session of the National Security Council on 10 March 2003, President Bush approved the IIA concept which Feith presented.[11] The IIA never materialized.

Appointing Paul Bremer

In May 2003, former Ambassador L. Paul Bremer, who was chosen by Rumsfeld, was appointed President Bush's special envoy to Iraq, reportedly to be in charge of rebuilding the country's government and infrastructure.[12] Rumsfeld "had long envisioned that Mr. Bremer would ultimately fill the role of overall civilian administrator for Iraq,"[13] heading a "Coalition Provisional Authority" (CPA), into which ORHA was subsumed. The authority's mission was officially stated as being "to restore conditions of security and stability, to create conditions in which the Iraqi people can freely determine their own political future, (including by advancing efforts to restore and establish national and local institutions for representative governance) and facilitating economic recovery, sustainable reconstruction and development."[14]

In Chapter 6 we discussed how, contrary to the official intent, during Bremer's year of absolute rule in Iraq, the laws he changed and those he imposed, were all in contradiction to international law. Bremer's job was not only to issue orders and laws to strengthen the US grip on Iraq. His mission was far more sinister, and is described by the White House as follows:

> In his capacity as Presidential Envoy, he will oversee Coalition reconstruction efforts and the process by which the Iraqi people build the institutions and governing structures that will guide their future. General Tommy Franks will maintain command over Coalition military personnel in the theater. Ambassador Bremer will report to Secretary of Defence Rumsfeld and will advise the President, through the Secretary, *on policies designed to achieve American and Coalition goals for Iraq* [emphasis added].[15]

One passage from Bremer's book, which is otherwise a concoction of bluster, half-truths and falsifications, exposes his true role. He narrates that when he asked the UN official in Baghdad, Ambassador Ramiro da Silva, for money to buy grain, da Silva refused on the grounds that the Oil for Food money belonged to the Iraqi government, to which Bremer had replied: "I *am* the Iraqi government for now..."[16] He compared himself to General Douglas MacArthur, de facto ruler of Imperial Japan after World War II, and General Lucius Clay, who led the American occupation of defeated Nazi Germany.[17]

De-Ba'athification

On 16 May 2003 Bremer issued the first CPA order that called for "De-Ba'athification of Iraqi Society."[18] De-Ba'athification meant that anyone who had become a member of the Ba'ath party, regardless of intent in joining or actions after joining, was henceforth expelled from his/her Government job; and banned from participating in Iraqi politics or public office.

The decision to dissolve and prohibit the Ba'ath Party in Iraq had been long in the making and had its roots in the 1990s. The policy of dissolving the Ba'ath Party was a major objective of the US supported opposition groups,[19] even though the term "de-Ba'athification" itself is reported to have been first used by Ahmad al-Chalabi in an article in the *Times* of London in the summer of 2002 where he is reported to have said "What we need is a de-Ba'athification programme like a de-Nazification programme."[20] Ahmad al-Chalabi also told *The New York Times*: "If the U.S. wants to do it, who are we to say no? We can't stop them. They are talking about demilitarization, and de-Ba'athification, which is very good, what we want."[21] A month before the invasion, Ahmad al-Chalabi wrote in the *Wall Street Journal* the following:

> For Iraq to rejoin the international community under a democratic system, it is essential to end the Ba'athist control over all aspects of politics and civil society. Iraq needs a comprehensive program of de-Ba'athification even more extensive than the de-Nazification effort in Germany after World War II. You cannot cut off the viper's head and leave the body festering. Unfortunately, the proposed U.S. plan will do just that if it does not dismantle the Ba'athist structures.[22]

The NSC had proposed that only those in the highest ranks of the Ba'ath Party—about one percent of the membership—would be fired from government jobs. Others would be subjected to a South Africa–style "truth and reconciliation process."[23] But Feith's office extended the NSC recommendation by including a clause in the policy that prevented regular Ba'ath party members from holding positions in the top three layers of management in every governmental office.

Bremer told Feith on 9 May that he wanted his arrival in Baghdad to "have a theme". He decided that his first priority would be to implement the policy of "de-Ba'athification", to offer assurance that "the Ba'athists are not coming back."[24]

Bremer wrote:

> Here's how the decisions were made. Gen. Tommy R. Franks, the head of the military's U.S. Central Command, outlawed the Ba'ath Party on April 16, 2003. The day before I left for Iraq in May, Undersecretary of Defense Douglas J. Feith presented me with a draft law that would purge top Ba'athists from the Iraqi government and told me that he planned to issue it immediately. Recognizing how important this step

was, I asked Feith to hold off, among other reasons, so
I could discuss it with Iraqi leaders and CPA advisers. A
week later, after careful consultation, I issued this "de-
Ba'athification" decree, as drafted by the Pentagon.[25]

*Thus, with one stroke of a pen, Bremer removed a few hundred
thousand Iraqis from their jobs.*

Order 1 was followed on 25 May 2003 with Order 5 setting up
the De-Ba'athification Council, whose job was to investigate and identify
members of the Party.[26] The Council was headed by none other than
Ahmad al-Chalabi and staffed by members whose only credential was that
they were anti-Ba'athists, enabling people to settle old personal disputes
with Ba'athists. Now Al-Chalabi had the extraordinary power to end
anyone's employment, strip away his pension, and leave him destitute. In
Bremer's Order 62 of 28 February 2004,[27] the De-Ba'athification Council
was given further authority to determine who was a senior member of
the Party, leading to the disqualification of such person from participating
in an election as a candidate, or accepting a nomination, or holding
public office, at any level. De-Ba'athification appears to have gone some
way towards "dismantling a state that had been left largely intact by the
unexpectedly swift war," as the *Economist* put it.[28]

It should be emphasized here that De-Ba'athification, which
has been in force to this writing, is a crime against humanity under
international law. It was incorporated into the Statute of the International
Criminal Court.[29] It is not a defense for Bremer or the US Government
that the latter had not specifically ratified the ICC Statute, insofar as the
principle has become part of customary international law binding on all
states.

Dissolving the Army/ Creating a New Army

As part of the US plan for Iraq, Rumsfeld directed General
Franks on 19 December 2002 to "conduct planning for the transition
of operations in Iraq from decisive combat through the post-hostilities
restoration of Iraq." He also instructed him to plan for "the disarming,
demobilizing, and re-shaping of the Iraqi military to a force capable of
defending Iraq, accountable to civilian authority and not a threat to Iraqi
citizens or regional states," and to identify forces required to provide
security throughout Iraq and defend against external threats, including
"the threat of internal groups hostile to US and coalition forces."[30] All
such objectives sound noble on paper but as we shall show later none
of them was achieved.

Bremer then issued CPA order No. 2 on 23 May 2003 by which
he dissolved not just the Army, but also the Air Force, Navy, Air Defence

Force, and other regular military services, the Republican Guard, the Special Republican Guard, the Directorate of Military Intelligence, the Al-Quds Force, the Quwat al Tawari', Saddam Fedayeen, Ba'ath Party Militia, Friends of Saddam and Saddam's Lions Cubs (Ashbal Saddam).[31] In short he dissolved all the Iraqi State defences.

The dissolution of the Iraqi armed forces put roughly 350,000 Iraqi men out of work, subjecting their families to financial suffering. The International Crisis Group criticized the decision stating:

> Disbanding the former army was almost certainly the most controversial and arguably the most ill-advised CPA decision. The 23 May 2003 decree, one of the first promulgated by the new civil administrator, Paul Bremer, in one fell swoop reversed prior U.S. policy and put an end to an institution whose origins predated Saddam Hussein's rule, whose identity was distinct from that of his Ba'athist regime, and which has been intimately linked to the history of the Iraqi nation-state since the 1920s.[32]

And equally significantly, it left Iraq with no defence or security forces.

However, the plan for creating a new army was put forward on 21 January 2003 by head of the Office of Special Plans William Luti,[33] billed in Feith's book as deputy Assistant Secretary of Defence for International Security Affairs for Near East and South Asia Affairs.[34] Bremer's decision followed this plan and the CPA was charged with building from scratch a full complement of security services.[35] Bremer believed that the Iraqis were not ready to assume independent responsibility for their own affairs and that the new army would be concerned chiefly with external security.[36]

The presumed New Iraqi Army was created by Bremer's order 22 of 7 August 2003.[37] What is of importance in the mission and command structure of this army is that "Supreme command, control and administrative authority over the New Iraqi Army and of additional units of the national Defence forces of Iraq and all authority formerly vested in the Ministry of Defence will reside on an interim basis with the Administrator of the CPA as the civilian Commander-in-Chief..."[38] Bremer thus authorized himself to appoint officers to command positions and in the national Defence force as a whole. Iraqi forces operating with Coalition forces will be under the command of an officer of the Coalition forces. The Order also integrated militia forces into the New Iraqi Army on the grounds that they "fought against the Ba'athist regime". Bremer's Order No. 91 of 2 June 2004 allowed Private Security Companies to operate in Iraq in exemption of the prohibition of private armies and militias as stated in Section 2 of the Order.[39]

The first recruits reflected the coalition's aims of creating a new army along the lines of ethnic and sectarian division: 60% Shi'ia, 25% Sunni, 10% ethnic Kurd and 5% from other minority groups.[40]

It should be mentioned here that the majority of the personnel of the Iraqi army during the Ba'ath rule were Shi'ia Muslims. This is because military service in Iraq was by conscription, which meant that the different ethnicities and sects were relatively represented in the army. The Ba'ath regime did not practice sectarian policies because it had no reason to do so, being a nationalist movement. When Iraq went to war with Iran the composition of the Iraqi army was of a Shi'ia majority! It seems that Saddam Hussein had no problem with it nor indeed did he have any problem in having a Shi'ia as a Chief of Staff of his army! While some may contest this on the grounds that the dissolution of the army by Bremer impacted primarily on Sunnis, creating massive unemployment there, it should be noted that the new army created by Bremer's order 22 of 7 August 2003, absorbed the Shi'ia to the exclusion of the Sunnis. This was all part of the US policy to fragment Iraq and create divisions amongst its people.

Today with Government supporting militia being 100% Shi'ia and with armed forces of over 90% Shi'ia after most of the Sunnis who enlisted in the new Iraqi army having left it since, it is fair to say that the new democratic federal Iraq has, for the first time in its history, a sectarian army.

The successive Iraqi Governments since Bremer's departure inherited the presumed new Iraqi army which was created and trained by the CPA. Yet eleven years later and with tens of billions of dollars having been spent on it, it took only five hundred Islamic fundamentalists in 2014 to route three of its divisions in Mosul leading to a full melt down of the whole Iraqi army. Further evidence of the failure of the US plan to build an Iraqi army was demonstrated recently when the US announced in November 2014, that it is planning on arming Sunni tribesmen in Iraq to help in fighting ISIL. The document prepared by the Pentagon to the Congress stated that "Engagement from Sunni tribes is critical to the long-term defeat of ISIL. If these fighters do not receive the support they need to counter-ISIL, in conjunction with the GOI tribal outreach, they will not be effective in combating ISIL in their areas." [41] How is it possible to build a united nation when the occupiers discover eleven years after occupation that the only way for the state to survive is to arm its tribes on sectarian bases?

It would be natural to question the sincerity or otherwise of Rumsfeld's intention to form a new Iraqi army. Why is it that the Americans failed to form an army in Iraq which had managed under the Ba'ath rule to maintain one of the strongest armies in the Middle East and fought three wars in two decades?

The Transitional Government

Next on Bremer's agenda was the important political issue which the US had been working towards since the 1990s, that of transforming Iraq's governing institutions into ones reflecting and vulnerable to American interests.

In 1998, Clinton had signed the Iraq Liberation Act and allocated $98 million for the training of Iraqi exiles. In October 2002, President Bush approved the expenditure of $92 million in Defence Department funds for the training of Iraqi exile militias, estimated at as many as 5,000 recruits for an initial training phase, to aid in the overthrow of the Iraqi Government.[42] The US also sought to reward the two main Kurdish parties, the Patriotic Union of Kurdistan (PUK) and the Kurdistan Democratic Party (KDP) in return for their participation in its operation in Iraq. The US is reported to have assumed that the Iraqis "would accept exiles as legitimate leaders," that "Iraq's governmental infrastructure would be easily transferred to new leadership, and overall political transformation would be rapid and relatively easy."[43]

Two days after the fall of Baghdad, Deputy Defense Secretary Paul D. Wolfowitz told the Senate Armed Services Committee that the US and its partners would appoint Iraqis to civilian leadership posts.[44] US officials had already clearly stated that the US and UK armies would "play the leading role" in appointing an Iraqi Government, giving the UN an advisory role.[45]

On 5 May, General Garner said that an interim Iraqi government would emerge by the end of May and it was expected to have "eight or nine Iraqi leaders, who would effectively become the heads of a committee that would govern Iraq under US tutelage for a number of months until a new political system and government can be organized to replace the Ba'ath Party rule of fallen president Saddam Hussein." He specifically named the five leaders most likely to be selected: Ahmad al-Chalabi of the INC, Massoud Barzani of the KDP, Jalal Talabani of the PUK, Abdul-Aziz al-Hakim of SCIRI, and Iyad Allawi of the INA.[46]

However, when Bremer arrived, everything changed. The plan to set up an interim government by June 3, agreed by Garner and the Iraqi Leadership Council (ILC), was not acceptable to Bremer who decided he needed more time to form a more representative government.

Bremer summarized to his staff how the President had insisted that "since the interim Iraqi government will have to write a new constitution, a legal code, and oversee Iraq's economic reform, that governing body has to be fully representative of all Iraqis, north and south, Sunni, Shia, Kurd, Turkmen, and Christian. And it's not going to happen overnight, despite what the exile leaders hope or even believe."[47]

On 22 May 2003, the Security Council adopted Resolution 1483 in which it recognized the US and UK as occupying powers, and requested the UN Secretary General to appoint a Special Representative for Iraq to work with the Coalition Authority and the people of Iraq to "facilitate a process leading to an internationally recognized, representative government of Iraq" and the formation of "an Iraqi interim administration as a transitional administration run by Iraqis, until an internationally recognized, representative government is established by the people of Iraq and assumes the responsibilities of the Authority".[48] UN Secretary General Kofi Annan appointed Ambassador Sergio Vieira de Mello (a Brazilian) as the UN Special Representative. In a joint press conference with Annan on 27 May 2003, de Mello said: "...as I hit the ground, priority number one will be to establish contacts with the representative Iraqi leaders, representatives of the media, of civil society – and there are many".[49] De Mello went further than his mandate, conveying the impression of UN legitimization of the occupation by stating that "Iraqi society is rich and that richness has been suppressed brutally for the last 24 years".[50]

Bremer's plan was for the CPA to appoint an interim government of around thirty members chosen by him, allegedly representative of all major strands of Iraqi society, and at the same time to launch a constitutional process, with national elections to be held by the summer of 2004. He assumed that the Iraqis could write a new constitution in six months, which could then be ratified.[51]

Bremer's staff had compiled a list of more than eighty Iraqis from all over the country whom they regarded as qualified candidates for the intended Governing Council.[52] It included tribal chiefs, women, Kurds and other minorities. From these candidates, the names of 25 to 30 men and women were to be selected for the Governing Council which was to be established by 15 July.[53] During these weeks, Bremer held discussions with many Iraqis to set out the US views on the GC, assuring them all that the Iraqis would themselves draft the Constitution.[54] Needless to say that such a promise was never kept. Both the interim and final constitutions of Iraq were drafted by the US. By Saturday 12 July, Bremer had a list of the 25 members of the Governing Council.

The Governing Council

The announcement of the establishment of the Governing Council did not go without the typical American theatrics. The 25 members selected by Bremer met on Sunday 13 July 2003 and constituted themselves as the "Governing Council," after which they duly informed the UN, US and UK, that they had formed the Governing Council.[55]Bremer, his British colleague Ambassador John Sawers and Ambassador de Mello met with the GC and its newly elected spokesman, Sayyid Muhammad Bahr al-Uloum, who gave a speech announcing the first two decisions taken by the Council: the repeal of all Ba'ath Party holidays, including the upcoming July 17 revolution anniversary and the declaration that April 9, "Liberation Day," was a national holiday.[56] This is akin to the Vichy Government having declared the day on which Paris fell to Hitler as a French national holiday!

The major figures on the GC included the leaders of several of the major anti-Saddam factions including SCIRI's leader Abdul-Aziz al-Hakim; Da'wa leader Ibrahim al-Ja'afari; INC leader Ahmad al-Chalabi; Iyad Allawi; and Kurdish leaders Talabani and Barzani. The GC also included some obscure figures including Ghazi al-Yawer, a senior member of the Shammar tribe and president of Saudi-based Hicap Technology; Iraqi Communist Party head Hamid Majid Musa, and others.[57] The inability to agree on main issues caused the Council to settle on a rotating presidency, which worsened its already obvious inefficiency.[58] But the GC members had no problem agreeing on paying themselves very well: a salary of $50,000 a year, handsome in local terms.[59] On 14 August 2003, the UN Security Council adopted Resolution 1500 at 14-0 votes, with Syria abstaining, welcoming the formation of the Governing Council as an important step towards the formation of a representative and widely recognized government.[60] The Security Council did not discuss the composition of, or the method in which the GC was created. It acted as it had done for twelve years as a rubber stamp for US decisions.

In Resolution 1511,[61] the Security Council determined that the Governing Council and its ministers "are the principal bodies of the Iraqi interim administration embodying the sovereignty of the State of Iraq during the transitional period," while at the same time it reaffirmed the CPA as the real Authority in Iraq until "an internationally recognized, government established by the people of Iraq is sworn in and assumes the responsibilities of the Authority." The resolution also asked the Governing Council to cooperate with the CPA and the UN representative to provide the Security Council by 15 December 2003 with "a timetable and a program for the drafting of a new constitution for Iraq and for the holding of democratic elections under that constitution."

Regardless of all these resolutions and nice words, the Governing Council's authority was non-existent as it was not able to make decisions or appoint cabinet ministers without approval of the CPA. The Governing Council was formed by the US to give a façade of legitimacy in Iraq and abroad to its occupation, appease the population and deflect criticism of the occupation forces. Many Iraqis did not believe that the Council would succeed in performing its tasks because it lacked democratic legitimacy, both because of the way it was created and because of its non-representative nature, due to the division also between exile and indigenous political groups; its lack of authority, due the occupying forces making the final decisions; the fact that it was formed without consultation with the technically skilled, scientific, and academic sectors of Iraqi society; and because the difficulties created by the war and occupation were too big for such a petty governing body to succeed.[62]

The Cabinet

The Governing Council started immediately to form a Cabinet to run the government. This task naturally faced the same kinds of conflicts that existed within the Governing Council: conflicts related to representation percentages and the division of major ministries, determining the share of each political group in the 'loot' of Iraq. The solution achieved in the end was that each member of the GC would nominate one representative to be chosen, barring objections from other groups, to form a Cabinet. This way the same ethnic, religious and sectarian divisions were maintained in this Cabinet.[63] The result was a Cabinet comprised of people who lacked the competence to serve as ministers, and which had no guidelines as to whom it should report: the Governing Council, the CPA or Bremer.[64]

The Interim Iraqi Constitution

Bremer claimed that he had planned to form a council and give it the task of creating a preparatory committee to write the new constitution and appoint members to it in consultation with political and social groups. The results of that constitution would then be presented for approval by a referendum.

Since the occupation, the Shia' Cleric, Grand Ayatollah Ali As-Sistani had become the preeminent grand ayatollah in all Iraq. Prior to 2003, Sistani was virtually unknown to the non-Shi'ia world. He was considered a "quietist," meaning he was neither interested nor involved in politics. But Sistani entered Iraq's political arena very strongly on 26 June 2003 when he issued a *fatwa* (religious edict) challenging the primary mandate of the CPA, which was to form an interim government for the transfer of sovereignty to the Iraqi government. The irony was that an unelected religious leader was telling the US, which was allegedly bringing democracy to Iraq, that its plans for Iraq's constitutional process were undemocratic.

Because of the large following he has had in Iraq, As-Sistani has come to wield so much political power that transcends politics without having to be politically accountable as is expected. He chose to be selective in interfering in or keeping out of politics in Iraq. Thus he chose not to call for jihad against the infidel's invasion and occupation of Iraq in 2003, but called for jihad against the advances of the Islamic State in 2014. He chose in 2004 to oppose the imposition of TAL, drafted by the US, but called on his followers in 2005 to support the permanent constitution drafted by the same Americans. We have been consistent in criticizing political Islam, Sunni or Shi'ia alike, when we believed that it was party to the Zionist plan for Iraq and the Arab World. When the Kurdish Sunni President of Iraq and the Arab Sunni Speaker of Parliament visit As-Sistani before embarking on serious actions or visits abroad, they are not doing so because they are his devotees but because they believe he plays a major political role in Iraq. So long as he receives them; acquiesce in their actions and does not dissociate himself, then he is implicated in the political jungle called Iraq and cannot be exonerated from any mistake. He is acting by choice and should bear the responsibility of such action. We do not believe that when we point out the political failures of As-Sistani we are doing more than pointing out what other Shi'ia religious leaders have been saying for ten years. Not least among them is the widely circulated statement of Ali Khamenei, for whom we hold great respect and admiration, when he said:

> They say that Ali is their Imam but they refrain from saying one word against the US.

Everybody who reads the statement knew to whom Khamenei, whose political and religious credentials are not in doubt, was referring. The strong opposition to the US decision to make the end of its occupation contingent on having a new constitution in place and holding national elections for a new government, forced it to change its plans: On 17 November 2003, the CPA and GC announced a plan to dissolve both bodies and draft an interim constitution to be adopted by an elected constituent assembly.

The Transitional Administrative Law (TAL)

The first deadline was set for 25 February 2004, with the creation of the interim constitution. This interim constitution would allegedly guarantee freedom of religion, speech and legislature, and equal rights to all Iraqis, regardless of gender, sect, and ethnicity.[65]

During that time, the country would be governed, starting on 30 June 2004, by a Transitional National Assembly selected by caucuses rather than direct elections, leading to national elections for a permanent government by 31 December 2005 under a provisional constitution.[66]

But the constitution was not drafted before going through a complicated process of wrangling and disagreements. The UN wanted to be more involved in Iraq than simply being used "to help choose and sell the GC,"[67] something the US was loathe to accept. UN officials thought that timetables set by the CPA were not realistic and further that the plan of choosing members of the transitional national assembly through caucuses would not appeal to the Iraqis.[68] Though the US wanted total control and to establish the process while letting the UN tinker around the edge and support it, it eventually caved in and agreed with recommendations by its advisers that it needed the UN to aid in the transition process. Thus on 19 January 2004, a meeting was held at the UN in New York, attended by the UN Secretary General and his senior staff, eight members of the GC (led by Adnan al-Pachachi), Bremer and his British deputy Jeremy Greenstock, Meghan O'Sullivan from the Governance Office, US ambassador to the UN John Negroponte, and other US officials.[69] The meeting discussed the desire of the CPA and GC for UN assistance.

As a result of the meeting, UN Secretary General Kofi Annan dispatched a fact finding mission to Iraq from 6 to 13 February 2004 led by Annan's special adviser, Lakhdar Brahimi. The findings of the mission were contained in a report submitted by Kofi Annan to the Security Council on 23 February 2004.[70] Brahimi had mediated a compromise between As-Sistani and Bremer, both being committed to the 30 June date for the transfer of sovereignty, yet leaving two major issues unresolved: the details of the Transitional Administrative Law; and the composition of the interim government that would rule Iraq for the six or seven months between the 30 June handover and the January 2005 elections. As-Sistani welcomed the report in a statement issued on 24 February 2004.[71]

Order 92 of 31 May 2004 setting up the 'Independent Electoral Commission of Iraq' notes 'that the Law of Administration for the State of Iraq for the Transitional Period (the TAL) provided for the Iraqi people to choose their government through genuine and credible elections to be held no later than 31 January 2005'.[72]

Paradoxically, the problem with the TAL is not simply that the CPA had no authority to promulgate a constitution for occupied Iraq, but that it was never promulgated. The following facts may go towards explaining this statement.

> 1. On 16 May 2003, Bremer promulgated Regulation 1 assuming full executive, legislative and judicial authority of Iraq and declared the laws of Iraq will remain in force unless suspended, repealed or superseded by legislation passed by the CPA in the form of Regulations, Orders, or Memoranda.

2.   The Iraqi Constitution 1970 remained in force as it was not affected in accordance with Regulation 1.

3.   No Regulation, Order or Memorandum between 16 May 2003 and 31 May 2004 promulgated a document titled TAL or the Law of Administration for the State of Iraq.

4.   The sudden appearance of the TAL on the CPA website (<http://www.cpa-iraq.org> which has since been removed!) did not bestow legitimacy on it insofar as there was no reference to the authority under which it was promulgated or indeed as to who promulgated it if these are different..

5.   The Governing Council of Iraq which was created by Regulation 6 on 13 July 2003 was not given any legislative power yet was acknowledged in the preamble of the TAL to have 'certain authorities and responsibilities'. Some authorities were granted by the CPA to the Governing Council over the eleven months of its life. However, the Council's authority was so limited in scope that even when it appointed Deputy Ministers, Bremer stepped in and removed that function from the Governing Council, retaining it exclusively for himself. To demean the Governing Council, this measure was issued in Memorandum 9 and not even in an Order. It is safe to conclude, lest anyone attempts to argue, that the Governing Council, which could not appoint Deputy Ministers, could not seriously have assumed the authority to promulgate a constitution.

It follows that TAL, the interim Iraqi Constitution, was never enacted and thus its publication is another constitutional muddle added to that already created by Bremer's legislation. What happened to all the measures that were purported to be based on TAL—The Electoral Law (Order 96), and Political Parties and Entities Law (Order 97 of 7 June 2004) through which Bremer tried to lay down the political future for Iraq—is left for constitutional lawyers to figure out.[73]
TAL's main provisions:

- The laws, regulations, orders, and directives issued by the CPA shall remain in force until rescinded or amended by legislation duly enacted and having the force of law.

- While Islam was the official religion of Iraq, the freedom to practice other faiths was guaranteed.

- The Kurdish issue was deferred until consideration of a permanent constitution.

- The Kurdish region will continue to govern itself, and the Kurdish judiciary and legislature will continue to have relative independence.

- Kurdish was made an official language of Iraq, along with Arabic.

- The interim constitution was vague on the issue of federalism, but the federal government was given exclusive control over foreign policy, national security matters, fiscal and monetary policy, and management of Iraq's oil and other natural resources.

- It established a "Presidency Council", consisting of a president and two deputies appointed by the National Assembly, with decisions to be made unanimously among them.

- It stated that 25 percent of the seats in the transitional national assembly should go to women and guaranteed equal protection under the law for all citizens, regardless of gender. [74]

The Transitional Period referred to in the TAL was to start on 30 June 2004, at which time the CPA would decide whom to appoint to run Iraq's government, and would end on 31 January 2005 when an election for a Transitional National Assembly would be held, even though the TAL did not directly address the formation of the government thereafter.

The majority of Iraqis, including As-Sistani, expressed objections to the way the TAL was drafted. Their objections centered on two major points: firstly that the GC was not representative of the people of Iraq, and secondly that the people had not been given an opportunity to debate, amend, and approve the provisions of their interim constitution. There was also objection to the provision that made amending the TAL impossible. But there was nothing anyone could do.

In a reply to a question from Brahimi requesting clarification on the opinion of the religious *Marji'yah* of the coming role of the UN in Iraq, the office of As-Sistani informed Brahimi that the Grand Ayatollah would not consent to any meetings with him unless the Security Council agreed not to impose the TAL on a newly elected transitional assembly. Sistani's demand came in response to seemingly accurate information that the US planned to seek formal recognition of the TAL in the next Security Council Resolution on Iraq, which would also endorse the interim government and the transition process. According to Sistani, a UN endorsement of the TAL "would not be accepted by the general public of Iraq, and it would have serious consequences in the future."[75]

Article 61 of the TAL was of great importance. It stipulated that TAL would remain the governing law of Iraq if the Transitional National Assembly did not complete drafting a permanent constitution by 15 August 2005 and did not request an extension of the deadline. And if the Transitional National Assembly failed to draft a permanent constitution by 15 August 2005 or if the referendum rejected the draft permanent constitution, the National Assembly would be dissolved and new elections called.[76]

The Interim Iraqi Government

UN special envoy Lakhdar Brahimi returned to Iraq on 4 April 2004 to begin the task of constructing the Interim Government whose structure and authority were defined in the TAL.

In his written report of his fact-finding mission in February, Lakhdar Brahimi outlined his view on the composition of the interim government. He wanted "a provisional, caretaker government, with clear and limited powers to prepare the country for free and fair elections and manage the country during the transitional period and the process that establishes it ... a broad-based government that is not based on quotas, one that ideally would be primarily composed of competent technocrats".[77]

In testimony before the Senate and the House Armed Services Committees, Deputy Defense Secretary Paul D. Wolfowitz and Undersecretary of State Marc Grossman said the Iraqi interim government scheduled to take control on 1 July would have only "limited sovereignty" over the country and no authority over US and coalition military forces already there.[78] So much for sovereignty!

On 28 April 2004, the GC was informed by Bremer of the selection of Allawi as interim prime minister. The decision was announced by Bremer, and later accepted by Brahimi. One source at the UN said that Allawi was not Brahimi's choice, but that Allawi had generated enough support within the GC that compelled Brahimi to accept him.[79] Brahimi told the *The New York Times* in a telephone interview: "You know, sometimes people think I am a free agent out here, that I have a free hand to do whatever I want."[80] At a news conference wrapping up his work in Iraq, Brahimi suggested that he would have done things differently had he been given a freer hand. Asked about the selection of the prime minister, he alluded to the role of Bremer saying: "— I'm sure he doesn't mind my saying it — Mr. Bremer is the dictator of Iraq.... He has the money. He has the signature. Nothing happens without his agreement in this country."[81]

Also appointed were two deputy presidents (the Da'wa's Ja'afari and the KDP's Dr. Rozh Shawys). The cabinet included a deputy prime minister, 26 ministers, two ministers of state with portfolio, and three ministers of state without portfolio. Six ministers were women, and the ethnic mix was roughly the same as in the GC. The key defense and interior ministries were headed by Sunni Arabs, and the oil minister was a technocrat, Thamir Ghadban.[82]

On 1 June the thirty-six-member interim government was officially introduced and was empowered to "issue orders with the force of law," if they received the unanimous approval of the presidency; it was also temporarily assigned the powers of the national assembly to make appointments and approve international agreements, but not to conclude a formal treaty. The annex to TAL provided for the holding of a conference of over 1,000 Iraqis (chosen from all around Iraq by a 60-member commission of Iraqis) to choose a 100-seat Interim National Council. This council, which was *selected* under tight security during 13-18 August 2004, had the power to veto, by a two-thirds vote, laws adopted by the interim government. This goes to show that the whole process was a sham as the whole selection claiming to represent a wide consensus among Iraqis was nothing less than appointment by the occupiers.

The interim government was forbidden "from taking any actions affecting Iraq's destiny beyond the limited interim period."[83]

With the completion of the last major steps on the path to the alleged transfer of sovereignty, the Governing Council officially was dissolved by the same authority that created it:

> On 8 June 2004, the Security Council unanimously adopted Resolution 1546 which endorsed the formation of a sovereign interim government in Iraq, reaffirmed responsibilities of the interim government, and spelled out the duration and legal status of US-led forces in Iraq.[84]

Before his departure on 28 June 2004, Bremer issued many vitally important orders. In addition to the decree to establish the "Independent Electoral Commission of Iraq", he issued Order Number 91 (7 June 2004) on the Regulation of Armed Forces and Militias Within Iraq, and Order Number 100 (28 June 2004); the final and perhaps the most important and sinister of all his orders. It was an omnibus measure, amending many of the previous orders, allegedly to make them consistent with the TAL and "to properly reflect the transfer of full governing authority and the dissolution of the Coalition Provisional Authority on 30 June 2004". In reality it was to make all laws compatible with the US plans for Iraq. With this order, Bremer extended Order 17, giving US and other international forces immunity from "any form of arrest or detention other than by persons acting on behalf of their parent states." [85]

The occupation was complete. A puppet state was created. The mission was accomplished.

The Transitional National Assembly

Bremer issued Order 92 (31 May 2004) establishing the Independent Electoral Commission (IEC.)[86]. The Commission was composed of a nine-member Board of Commissioners, of which seven citizens were voting members and two were non-voting members.

Order 96 issued by Bremer on 15 June 2004, [87] stipulated that Iraq would be a single electoral constituency for the election of 275 members to the Transitional National Assembly, where the seats would be allocated among Political Entities through a system of proportional representation. This way the different political parties and groups were forced to form alliances to produce viable electoral lists.[88]

The vicious attack on Fallujah in November 2004 was so grave that the Islamic Party of Iraq withdrew from Allawi's government demanding a postponement of the elections for six months, so that they could be held under more auspicious conditions, while the Association of Muslim Scholars in Iraq announced its boycott of the coming elections.[89] Altogether, some forty-seven Sunni, Shi'ia, Turkoman and Christian bodies declared their boycott of the general elections.[90]Nevertheless, the elections for the Transitional National Assembly 18 provincial councils and the Kurdish regional assembly were held on 30 January 2005 with an announced participation of over 8 million out of 14 million eligible voters. The United Iraqi Alliance (UIA) received a slim majority: 148 seats of the 275; the two Kurdish parties won 75 seats; Interim PM Allawi's bloc, the Iraqi National Accord (INA), won 40 seats and Interim President Ghazi Al-Yawer's group won 5 seats, with the remaining seats going to several other parties.[91].

The 275-seat Assembly convened for the first time on 16 March 2005 and on 29 March selected Hajim Al-Hassani, a Sunni Turkoman Iraqi-American businessman, as its speaker.

In keeping with the agreement between the UIA and the Kurdish parties, PUK leader Jalal Talabani was on 6 April selected as President of the Republic of Iraq. SCIRI official Adel Abdul Mahdi and Interim President Ghazi al-Yawer became Vice Presidents. The three men then nominated Da'wa leader Ibrahim Al-Ja'fari as Prime Minister who was confirmed the next day.[92]Al-Ja'fari formed his cabinet of 32 ministerial posts by 28 April and received Assembly approval for it. UIA's nominee Ahmad Chalabi and KDP's Rozh Shawys became deputy prime ministers.[93]The UIA and Kurdish parties opposed appointing Sunnis who had been in the Ba'ath Party.

Drafting the Permanent Constitution

In 1921 the British occupiers of Iraq post WWI set up a committee of British citizens to draft a new constitution for modern Iraq. In 1923 the committee put forward a draft constitution which was put to an Iraqi committee to study. The Iraqi committee took two years before the 'Basic law of the Iraqi State' was finally adopted in 1925.

However, the American occupiers of Iraq did not extend anywhere near that amount of time to the process. In 2005 they forced Iraq into drafting a constitution in a very short time and by October 2005 Iraqis went to vote on a permanent constitution they had not seen, read, studied, debated or drafted.[94] The reason why Iraqis voted for a constitution they never read or discussed may not be easy to understand but factors such as the state of shock after the invasion, the high expectation of tranquility after thirty years of wars, and the misleading promises of religious leaders and Iraqi exiles may partly explain it. The haste in drafting and imposing the constitution which one Iraqi professor described as 'having been 'dropped from a helicopter onto Baghdad'[95] was not caused as some had suggested because the heavy US losses suffered in Iraq 'pushed US policymakers to adopt an early exit strategy'.[96] The invasion and occupation of Iraq was no historical accident nor an event imposed by necessity. It was a very well calculated and planned series of actions designed to dismantle the Iraqi state, keep Iraq fragmented for as long as possible which serves the interests of Zionist Imperialism plans for the Arab World. Most of the destruction that had befallen the Arab World and improperly labelled the 'Arab Spring' would not have happened had it not been for the fall of Baghdad to the Zionists.

We do not intend here to analyze the failures of the 2005 constitution because such treatment needs a full book. We will identify the main failings which have contributed to the continuous destruction of Iraq and whose effects are visible in what is currently happening in Iraq.

The drafting the 2005 constitution was not very different to that of TAL which, as we had already established, suddenly appeared on the CPA site without any indication of the process of its drafting or adoption. We would not be surprised if it transpires later that both were drafted by the same group of US experts. It is rather misleading to suggest that Iraqis in fact drafted the constitution with US support.[97] It is not sufficient to point out that a 55-member Constitution Drafting Committee was entrusted with the task of drafting the constitution. [98] They lacked the expertise in constitutional matters; were biased according to the ethnic and sectarian basis on which they were selected and were continuously instructed by the US Ambassador on what the US would and would not accept.[99]

The most striking feature about the 2005 constitution is its language. Anyone who knows basic Arabic would conclude after reading it that it could not have been drafted in Arabic which suggests that it was originally written in English and translated to Arabic.[100] This becomes apparent from Article 1 where the Republic of Iraq is defined in Arabic as being *'dawla ittihaddiya wahida'* which translates into English as 'a federal unitary state'. It needs no great political philosopher to realize that the translator had no idea what he/she was translating because a state could not by definition, be both 'federal' and 'unitary'.

The 2005 constitution created more problems than it solved. We identify the main failings of the constitution as follows:

1. *Abolishing Iraq's Arab Identity*

We believe that the most significant change in Iraq's political reality, which the new constitution introduced, is the negation of the Arab identity of Iraq. This is significant not simply because Iraq is 80% Arab but because it is a shift from Iraq's prior constitutions which have stated the Arab identity of Iraq. Large states like China, Russia and USA have very diverse ethnicities but such a fact did not bar any of these states from assuming the identity of its major ethnic element. It could not be argued that, because the Kurds of Iraq constitute some 15% of its population, that should suffice to strip Iraq of its Arab nationality.

The Kurds have one of two options: they either accept the reality of Iraq's Arab identity and stay in a unitary Iraq, or choose to secede and set up their independent Kurdish state. In other words, the Kurds should not expect to have it both ways. On one hand they insist on having the position of the President of the Republic while at the same time demand their right to act as they please inside the Kurdish Region. We have always held that the Kurds are entitled to self-determination in the area they live in, in Turkey, Iran, Iraq and Syria just like any other nation has been granted such a right since WWI. Arab Nationalism cannot express itself justly without recognizing the right of other people to choose to live independently of it.

General Abdul-Karim Qasim, who led the 1958 revolution setting up Iraq's republic, promulgated a short constitution of some 30 Articles. Qasim was neither a Ba'athist nor an Arab Nationalist, both of which conspired to topple and kill him in 1963. Yet in his 1959 constitution, Qasim asserted that Iraq was part of what he viewed as a wider Arab Nation. The Ba'athists who ruled Iraq from 1968 to 2003 put this identity into action by making the battle of Iraq against forces inimical to Arab Nationalism represented by International Zionism.

However, the 2005 Constitution drafted by the Zionists for new 'democratic' Iraq, which was supported by the Kurds with the intention of eliminating Iraq's centuries-old identity, and the Islamic forces loathe to nationalism, set out to strip Iraq off its Arab identity; keep it busy with in-fighting and take it completely out of the Arab Israeli conflict for which Iraq had been the backbone for fifty years. Thus Article 3 of the 2005 Constitution makes Iraq no more part of the Arab Nation as it had been for a millennium but 'a founding and active member of the Arab League and is committed to its charter'. Needless to say, it is quite different to be part of a whole and aspire to unite with the whole and be a member of an organization that was set up by the colonialists post WWII to prevent Arab unity from ever materializing.

2. *The Federal Nature of the State*

Iraq had been a unitary state in one form or another since the Babylonian times despite its diverse ethnicities, religions and sects. This political reality has been part of Iraq's political history and culture. It can only be changed by the free will of the Iraqi people. However, the US politicians decided that Iraq should instead become a 'federal state' and made that part of Article 1 of the constitution. There is no exact translation in Arabic for the English word 'federal'. The choice in Arabic has been '*ittihaddiya*'. But this word in Arabic means uniting together divided entities which is alien to Iraq's political history and culture. Even if one were assuming that the US politicians, who made the decision of making Iraq a 'federal state', had good intentions, their choice of federalism remains short-sighted because Iraq was not formed like the USA by uniting states that were born out of different historic events culminating in its bloody civil war.

All the other Articles in the constitution that followed to elaborate the relationship between the federal authority and the authority of the regions added further to the ambiguity of the constitution and the cause of discourse. We shall attend to the Kurdish issue that may be used as the reason for constitutionally establishing Iraq as a 'federal state' later, but shall deal with the problem of creation of regions in Iraq post 2005. Section five of the constitution deals with the formation and powers of the regions. Article 115 defines the Republic of Iraq as being formed of 'decentralized capital, regions and governorates as well as local administrations'.[101] In Article 117 the constitution recognizes on its adoption the region of Kurdistan as one such federal region. However, if it could be understood that the Iraqis in general have come by 2003 to accept the existence of the semi-autonomous region of Kurdistan it is not possible to understand the reason for Articles 119 and 121. Article 119 states that 'One or more governorates shall have the right to organize into a region....'[102] Article 121 (Second) deals with the case of conflict between the regional legislation which Article 120 enabled each region to adopt and the national legislation as follows:

> Article 121 (Second)
> In case of a contradiction between regional and national legislation in respect to a matter outside the exclusive authorities of the federal government, the regional power shall have the right to amend the application of the national legislation within that region.

It is impossible to see how the US can argue that it intended Iraq to have a united federal state when the constitution it drafted for it enables each Governorate to make laws that supersede national legislation.

It is not difficult to see how such Articles could lead to demands for regional authorities that defy the central government and lead to an even more fragmented 'democratic' Iraq. A few attempts were made for the creation of such regions and the current turmoil indicate the likelihood of further and even successful attempts at setting up such regions of sectarian bases.

The problem with the alleged claim of the US that there should rightfully be a federal Iraq is that it has not been based on any politically viable argument. Federalism cannot be based on ethnic and sectarian grounds and still claim to represent the interest of the nation. Ethnicity divides Iraq between Arabs and Kurds while sectarianism divides it between Sunni and Shi'ia. But these two divisions are incompatible because the sectarian divide transcends ethnicity. Once a state in Iraq is based on sectarian bases as opposed to the secular bases on which Iraq has been institutionalized since WWI, then the argument of nationalism disappears and that of sectarianism takes over, which in turn means that every Sunni and every Shi'ia in the world becomes involved in the State of Iraq. The few hundred million Shi'ia of the world will be supporting the new Shi'ia state in Iraq representing the 'House of Ali' whose rights were usurped 13 centuries ago—whether they like it or not, as we now see with Iran defending the Shi'ia in Iraq under attack by ISIS, irrespective of Khamanei's negative views of the role played by Sistani, indicated above. On the other hand, the one billion Sunnis of the world can be up in arms, as Saudi Arabia has done in complicity with the Americans, against usurping the right of the 'House of Aisha' which had ruled Iraq by virtue of having its theology develop in it. The argument about a majority Shi'ia population being suppressed by a minority Sunnis that demanded such a change will not hold among the billion Sunnis from among whom Sunni fundamentalists will be able to recruit endlessly. It is not possible to build a state on religious or sectarian grounds and then argue that it is proper to do so relying on the right of the people to choose within the confines of that nation-state.

It is misguided to talk about majority Shi'ia and minority Sunnis, which seems to be the naïve approach of some of the so-called Arab World specialists in the US and the UK. Iraq could not be ruled on a sectarian bases by Sunnis to the exclusion of the Shi'ia whatever the number of these Shi'ia may be. Equally it could not be ruled by Shi'ia on a sectarian bases to the exclusion of the Sunnis however small a minority the Sunnis are. Iraqi is equally Shi'ia and Sunni irrespective of the percentage of each sect. The only way the state of Iraq can survive is if it is institutionalized as a secular state, in which both Shi'ia and Sunni have absolute freedom to claim it as their own. The fear among members of both sects since the invasion, occupation and the void created by them, that the other sect is out to secure hegemony, has led to the polarization and bloody strife. This mad spiral and the likely disintegration of Iraq could only be stopped when the above fact is acknowledged and acted upon.

The US intent to produce a fragmented rather than federal Iraq can be adduced by the following. In September 2007, the US senate passed a resolution introduced by Senators Joseph R. Biden Jr. (D-DE) and Sam Brownback, (R-KS), which advocated a relatively weak central government with strong Sunni, Shi'ite, and Kurdish regional administrations and called for a decentralized Iraqi government "based upon the principles of federalism".[103] Biden tried to justify the bill by stating "The idea is to maintain a unified Iraq by federalizing it and giving Kurds, Shiites, and Sunnis control over their daily lives in their own regions".[104] Many inside Iraq and outside it saw this as amounting to partitioning Iraq. Middle East expert Joost Hiltermann, of the International Crisis Group, says regardless of what the resolution aims to do, "It has been interpreted to say (in the region) that the Senate wants to carve up Iraq (in the worst imperial tradition)."[105]

The US was not trying through Federalism to address the inequality in the representation of Iraq's components, but in fact used this state of religious hallucination among both Sunni and Shia' to exploit the situation to its limits and keep Iraq fragmented for as long as possible. Thus in 2003 the US again agitated the Shi'ia to rise up against the Ba'ath, this time they were rewarded with the rule of Iraq, and then the Sunnis were armed under the name of 'Sahwa' to defend themselves. The game of shifting support to alternate sides went on, culminating in the support of the US to both Shi'ia militia and the Sunni tribes against the IS which was first a creation of US and its allies in Arabia! The fact remains today that during some seventy years of modern Iraq there was never a bloody sectarian strife. But the fact that the last ten years have seen more blood spilled over this divide that goes to prove that an Iraq based on sectarian grounds will never work as we have argued before.

3. *The Region of Kurdistan*

At the heart of Iraq's politics since the 1958 revolution has been the Kurdish problem which started, contrary to the prevailing understanding, long before the Ba'ath assumed power as the Kurds' aspiration for recognition of a separate national identity. It would have been natural since the semi-independent status which Kurdistan acquired after the 1991 invasion of Iraq that Kurdistan plays a major role in new 'democratic' Iraq both to serve their aspiration and as a reward for their support of the Zionist plan for the area. However, the 2005 constitution is so ambiguous about the position of the Kurdish Region and its relationship to the central government that more problems have since been created than resolved. Two Articles in the constitution stand out as significant in demonstrating this. Article 140 stipulates that Article 58 of TAL[106] be retained and implemented leading to a referendum on the choice of the people living in Kirkuk and other 'disputed territories'. [107]

It is clear from the above article that some among the Kurdish politicians in agreement with the Zionist plan for Iraq had in mind other parts of Iraq to be annexed to the Region of Kurdistan in addition to disputed Kirkuk. Such ambitions have come to the surface since the recent advances of the Islamic State, the collapse of the Iraqi army and the advances of the Peshmerge into Mosul, Diyala and their occupation of Kirkuk. There have been reports from Kurdistan that some believe that now is the time to discuss the 'disputed territories' in Mosul and Diyala.[108]

Article 141 stipulates that all legislative decisions by the Kurdish authority, as well as court judgments and contracts made in Kurdistan since 1992, are valid and binding. But this raises more questions than it resolves. It declares that Kurdistan had been independent since 1992, which is a misrepresentation of its de jure standing under both international and domestic law. It also shackles the central Government in Baghdad with an obligation it may find deleterious to the national interests and thus leading to further discord and conflict.[109]

4. *Oil and Gas*

Natural resources in Iraq have always been owned and controlled by the central Government in Baghdad. The allegations that some administrations in Iraq had favored parts of the country in expenditure of its oil revenue to the detriment of other parts has not been supported by any hard evidence. In fact the development plans of Iraq since the mid-1960s to 1980s show otherwise. The new constitution which claimed to set up a plan for better distribution of Iraq's oil and gas revenue has since created ambiguity, chaos and opened the gates to further division on selfish and sectarian bases between the Governorates all of which been fuelled by the false allegation of neglect of previous administrations.

Since Article 121 granted each region and Governorate the authority to legislate independently from the central Government it is not difficult to see the potential of each Governorate going its own way in deciding to control its natural resources to the exclusion of others, leading to the disintegration of the State.

5. *Islam and Democracy*

While appearing to satisfy both their religious and secular allies, the US drafters of the constitution sowed the seeds of discord and conflict in Article 2. It stipulates that no law may be enacted if it 'contradicts the established provisions of Islam' and if it 'contradicts the principles of democracy'. But that is a contradiction in terms. Islam is not democratic and no one has ever suggested that Islamic Shari'a upholds democratic principles. So what would happen if liberals seek to legalize gambling or homosexuality and the religious members of Parliament object to it on constitutional bases as contradicting Islamic provisions?

The constitution covers civil rights in section two. Yet despite upholding the 'right to participate in public affairs and to enjoy political rights', [110] 'the freedom to form and join political association and political parties'[111] and 'the freedom of thought, conscience and belief',[112] the constitution denied these rights and freedoms to a sizeable proportion of Iraqi society in adopting the de-Ba'athification policy promulgated by Paul Bremer in 2003. Thus in Article 7 it stipulates that Iraq should be cleansed of the Saddamist Ba'ath and its symbols,[113] while Article 135 outlines the procedure for carrying out this policy.[114] How can a constitution written for a modern 'democratic' state alienate a proportion of Iraqi society considering that the Ba'ath Party had been a powerful ideology in the Arab World and had ruled Iraq for some 35 years, making it evident and inevitable that millions may have truly believed in its ideals?

6. *Amending the Constitution*

The US drafters planned to make the concept of 'creative chaos' in Iraq real by making it impossible to amend the constitution in order to rectify the problems created by an impasse resulting from the conflict and ambiguity of its articles. Article 26 outlines the procedure for amending the constitution. Article 26(4) stands out, as of particular importance. It reads as follows:

> Articles of the Constitution may not be amended if such amendments takes from the powers of the regions that are not within the executive powers of the federal authorities, except by the approval of the legislative

authority of the concerned region and the approval of the majority of its citizens in a general referendum.[115]

However, since the powers of the federal authorities are not clearly defined in the constitution and since any one or more Governorate can set up a region, then it is clear that not only the Region of Kurdistan alone but any single Governorate will be able to prevent any amendment to the Constitution.. It is a recipe for continuous division, chaos and disintegration consciously and deliberately incorporated by the US drafters for the ongoing destruction of Iraq.

THE
DESTRUCTION
CONTINUES

The Destruction Was Intended

History tends not to record what really happened—assuming that there is one who knows what really happened —but rather what people perceived to have happened, be that true or false. Human history is littered with instances, and much of this perspective can be summarized in the axiom that he who writes the history has won the wars. But there is also the history that survives in the popular understanding of the vanquished, passed down even through generations. Thus Iraqis by and large, excluding the few thousands who came with the 2003 invaders and became the benefactors of the new Iraqi 'Loot', believe that the destruction of Iraq was intended in the 2003 invasion. We understand how difficult it is for a Westerner to accept that so many people had taken part in a campaign whose purpose from the outset was to destroy another nation. That is precisely what Professor Thomas J. Nagy expressed when he wrote:

> Many, including the author recoil from contemplating the possibility that a Western democracy, particularly the USA, could commit genocide. However, it is precisely this painful and even taboo possibility which needs to be examined.[1]

Professor Nagy touched on a taboo which not many want to touch, namely that those growing up in the West unavoidably develop certain concepts of superiority that make it impossible to think that they are likely to be criminals. When a number of MPs in London were approached regarding the possible indictment of Tony Blair on war crimes in Iraq, a prominent Labourite Member of Parliament responded that in spite of how much he agreed with the idea, he could not sign a petition which stated that the leader of his party could have been a war criminal. It is in that vein that we find it rare that a Westerner can accept the notion that Iraq was *intentionally* destroyed let alone write on that theme. We believe that Iraq was intentionally destroyed with the objective of rebuilding Iraq anew, insofar as it would be easier to build and mould a state from scratch after having erased not only its existing status but its history, heritage and even its memory.

The invasion of Iraq was not intended simply as regime change because, had it been so, then only a few of the measures taken would have been necessary. In other regime changes, none of the measures taken in Iraq were implemented. It is inconceivable that the US, which took the decision to put into action the plan to invade Iraq soon after 9/11 and set up the massive Future for Iraq Project,[2] had not worked out several scenarios of what could happen once Iraq was invaded. Destroying Iraq would give the Neocons the opportunity to build a state in the American image. But in case that desire became impossible to fulfil, then leaving Iraq destroyed, lost, fragmented, and in amnesia would be the ideal alternative. In fact the second alternative would secure an even easier control of oil. There is ample evidence from public statements that support our contention that destruction was intended from the outset, whatever might occur thereafter.[3] Just calling the operation 'Shock and Awe' is in indication of its intended destructive nature.

Any colonel planning a coup in a developing country knows that in order to control the country a curfew needs to be imposed once the coup is mounted. The need for such a curfew would be more imperative in the case of an invasion and occupation of a vast and complex country like Iraq. It could not have escaped the attention of the planners of the invasion that once Iraq's military and security disappeared from the streets of Baghdad, there was a multitude of reasons for the impoverished and criminal elements to be on the streets helping themselves to whatever they could grab. This is not a feature peculiar to developing countries like Iraq. Even a developed country, like the US, has experienced such a state upon the breakdown of law and order in its poor communities.[4] With this foreknowledge, why didn't the invaders declare a 48-hour curfew until they managed to have their forces protectively displayed in accordance with their obligation as an occupying power?

John Agresto, who was the de facto Minister of Higher Education and Scientific Research during the Bremer rule of 2003–04, believed that the looting of Iraq's universities was a desirable act in that it would allow such institutions to start again with a clean slate, with new equipment, naturally bought from the US, as well as with new curricula.[5] The thoughts of Agresto may be understandable considering his prior background as responsible for a minor liberal arts college in the US,[6] But the question is: why was such a person put in charge of the entire Iraqi Higher Education system with some 400,000 students and tasked with running Iraqi Universities of which he admitted knowing next to nothing, having the temerity to accept the post because "this is what Americans do: they go and help."[7]

The Iraqi National Museum which, as opposed to the British Museum and the Louvre, houses mainly an indigenous collection of artefacts, consists of a modern building built in the heart of Karkh, the western side of Baghdad and within a short distance from the Presidential Palace. It would have been expected that US army units would have been in the vicinity on the day Baghdad fell to the invaders. The invasion of the Museum did not come as a surprise, catching the invaders unaware. A few months before the invasion several universities and interested parties made a presentation to the US Government, urging it to preserve and protect Iraq's heritage in the invasion. Their fears were well-founded. Between 10 and 12 April, Iraqis and foreigners invaded the Iraqi Museum, each looking for something – the Israelis looking for an old copy of the Torah, European art dealers looking for what is light and expensive, and ordinary Iraqis looking for anything they can lay their hands on. One of the Museum curators walked over to the US soldiers nearby and asked them to intervene.[8] The officer in charge, after making the proper contact for authorization, advised the curator that he had orders not to intervene. In 2007 this was accepted by a US official as having been the policy of the US. "Barbara Bodine, the US Ambassador at the time, revealed to Charles Ferguson in his documentary film *No End in Sight* that direct orders had come from Washington stating that no one was to interfere with the looting."[9] Donald Rumsfeld, US Secretary of Defense, when asked about the looting and chaos in Iraq responded that these events were positive signs of the liberation of an oppressed people.[10]

Nonetheless, the imperialist intelligentsia and media persist in dismissing any notion that the US was either bent on destroying Iraq, or had recklessly allowed it to happen.

Peter McPherson, a senior economic adviser to Paul Bremer, had been quoted by Naomi Kline to the effect that the atmosphere of chaos was part of the process of change: "I thought the privatization that occurs sort of naturally [*sic*] when somebody took over their state vehicle, or began to drive a truck that the state used to own, was just fine"[11] It is within the context of this mind-set of the people who were responsible for Iraq after the invasion that the project of rebuilding Iraq must be seen.

We do not believe that the looting of Iraq, which McPherson saw as the beginning of privatization, was purely spontaneous and individual. We have reasons to believe that it was organized and planned ahead by a certain group or groups. The stripping of Ministries, educational institutes, hospitals, vital industries needed more planning than a spontaneous eruption of simple greed or need of some impoverished Iraqis. One eyewitness account supports this belief. On the day following the fall of Baghdad to the invaders, on 9 April 2003, two converted coaches whose seats were removed rammed the gate of Baghdad's main Mental Hospital where our in-law was a Director. Men speaking Arabic with a strange accent jumped out of the coaches. Over the next couple of hours they had stripped the whole hospital of everything including the curtains; loaded them into the two coaches and then they drove away. That could not have been done by ordinary people without prior planning. Who was behind these acts? Iraq is awash with similar stories told by real people, who have lived through this chaos.

No sooner had the looting subsided than Bremer set out to reward the Shi'ia militias for having fought Saddam Hussein. Then the notorious Special Police Commandos (SPC) were formed as we show later in this chapter. The policy of ensuring the fragmentation of Iraq on sectarian and ethnic bases began with the appointment of the Governing Council which was set up according to two criteria by which candidates were measured: 1) allegiance to the US and 2) whether they were either a Sunni, a Shi'ia, a Kurd or representative of another ethnic or religious minority. This gave rise to the sectarian violence of two years later and the current sectarian bombing and the recognized division of the top positions in the state on those sectarian and ethnic bases—the President to be a Kurd, the PM to be a Shi'ia Arab, the Speaker of Parliament to be a Sunni Arab—creating the recipe for disaster. New language was beginning to circulate addressing such entities as the 'Federal Court', or the 'Federal Police' instilling in the minds of people the idea of Iraq as a Federal State.

As soon as the Shi'ia militia finished their job of killing as many Sunni insurgents as they could find, the US decided it was time to arm the Sunnis and created the so-called Awakening (*Sahwa*) force. A new army of some 100 thousand was set up with people being paid to do nothing except serve the US interests and to spy on their fellow Sunnis. No one really knows how many of the members of the *Sahwa* converted to Al-Qaeda in the following years.

It is not easy to conclude whether Bremer was forced to leave Iraq because his policies did not work as planned or it was planned that he should do what he did and leave the matters hanging as they were when he left. But wherever the truth lies, when Bremer left, Iraq was a lawless country with no government, police, security forces, or army but with different militias, each fighting for a larger turf.

During the 35 years of single party rule by the Ba'ath in Iraq, there was little other political activity. The so-called National Progressive Front, consisting of a few small parties of communists and Arab Nationalists, was nothing more than window dressing for the single party rule. Thus on the eve of the invasion, there were only a few organized political forces in Iraq. In the north, the two main Kurdish Parties, the Kurdistan Democratic Party and the Patriotic Union of Kurdistan, who had enjoyed full autonomy since 1991 and the imposition of a no-fly zone by the US/UK, had agreed to share power equally, so much so that even the Parliament in Kurdistan was split equally between both parties. In Arab Iraq, the Ba'ath Party, which had been artificially inflated to millions of members, was undisciplined, disorganized and demoralized.

Thus when Iraq was invaded and the Ba'ath removed from power, a political vacuum was created. Political groups that attempted to fill this vacuum all came from the same political affiliation, namely a pro-imperialist inclination. Almost all of them came from abroad— from Iran, Syria, England, and US. The Islamic Party, Iraq's Muslim Brotherhood, was set up from remnants of the old party with new blood coming to it from the UK, US and the Arabian Peninsula. The Shi'ia became represented by three main political groups. The first group, the Supreme Council for the Islamic Revolution in Iraq, which later dropped the word Revolution as it upset the Americans, was formed in Iran and supported and financed by the Iranians. The second, the Da'wa Party, was originally created by the Shah of Iran in 1959, but changed its allegiance to Khomeini in 1979, which action led to the massive onslaught by the Ba'ath in the 1980s that obliterated the Da'wa Party in Iraq. On the eve of the invasion there were only a few members of the party living in London, Damascus and Tehran. The third Shi'ia grouping consists of the so-called Sadrists following Muqtada As-Sadr. Outside these groups there were other Iraqis equally loyal to the US, keen on having a share in Iraq's wealth, but unwilling to be part of either side of the sectarian divide. They chose to form a loose union called the 'Iraqi National Accord'. All these political groups have many things in common—they are all allies of the US; they have no political programs at all and they fight for bigger share of Iraq's wealth.

During the 35 years of the Ba'ath rule Iraq was almost free of corruption. Today Iraq is rife with corruption. The new class of Iraqi politicians, the majority of whom were penniless abroad, have come to Iraq with one objective: to make as much wealth in the shortest time and deposit it abroad in fear that their rule was not going to last. The following evidence substantiates our claim.

1) The ranking of Iraq by Transparency International, the global coalition against corruption. In its 2014 assessment Iraq ranked 170 out of 175, ahead of only Sudan and Somalia in the Arab world.[12]

2) The following statement by Haider Al-Mulla, an Iraqi National Dialogue Council Member of Parliament in an interview on As-Sumariya TV Channel broadcast on 16 January 2013:

> ...Let me tell you this...all the political class in Iraq and
> I repeat all the political class in Iraq and I head the list,
> have arranged their finances and those of their families
> so that if there is blood on the street they would not
> have to suffer but the hapless Iraqi will.... [13]

Needless to say, the interviewer smiled and did not pursue that line as it is so well known in Iraq that all the politicians are corrupt. This may explain what happens to the $100 billion Iraq makes every year from oil without any development or improvement in the services provided to the Iraqi people. In 2006 the Iraqi Ministry of Planning reported that 40% of Iraqis were living in absolute poverty, making the standard of living worse than it was on the eve of the invasion, which followed upon 12 years of total blockade. The UN Development Program (UNDP) reported in 2006 that 54% of Iraqis were living on less than $1 a day while The World Food Program (WFP) found in the same year four million Iraqis were food-insecure and more than eight million were fully dependent for their survival on daily rations provided by the Public Distribution System.[14]

Corruption is bad in any society but when it reaches the judiciary it becomes a disaster. In implementing US plans for rebuilding Iraq, Bremer dismissed all Ba'athist judges. This meant that almost all of Iraq's qualified judges lost their jobs. To fill those posts Bremer appointed unqualified law graduates to sit as judges, their only qualification being that they were anti-Ba'athists. They were more political appointees than legal experts. It would not be surprising that they slowly sank into the corrupt political environment where it was more important to look for the sectarian or political affiliation of the litigants and their financial capacities rather than the justice of their cases. There is nothing more frustrating for the citizen to realize that he/she has no recourse to justice when injustice is done. Human Rights Watch (HRW) summed up this reality when it quoted an official of the Ministry of Human Rights (MHR) explaining why the authorities failed to stop trafficking in Iraqi women, to which we shall attend later in this chapter—because trafficking is big business and traffickers have the influence, the political connections and the means to bribe those in power who matter. The official of the MHR concluded by saying that: "Corruption in Iraq is very big, including members of the judiciary and lawyers."[15]

Here is a sample of the continuous destruction of Iraq that has since followed from the invasion and the planting in Iraq of the corrupt Iraqis brought from abroad to implement US policies for the New Middle East.

Killing, Torture and Displacement

From the last decade of the 20th century until today, Iraq has been the new killing fields. It has been the ground in which evil has manifested itself in a multitude of forms —deception, siege, aggression, random air raids, invasion, occupation, displacement, clandestine militias, and religious fantasists. There seems to be no end to the on-going calamity, which started with the massive attack on Iraq in 1991, ostensibly to remove the Iraqi army from Kuwait but in fact destroyed all of Iraq and was then followed by the genocidal blockade, which had nothing to do with the declared purpose of the attack. It is as if the US-led 1991 international attack harnessed the entire world's evil which had been waiting to be unleashed. How else could an objective observer describe what has been happening in Iraq since 1991? How else could anyone describe the degrading inhumane treatment of Iraqis at the hands of US interrogators in Abu Ghraib?

In Volume I of *Genocide in Iraq* we tangentially treated the destruction and killing that took place in the blockade years between 1991 and 2003.[16] We have been so numbed by the scale of the killings that we hardly question the moral or legal grounds of such carnage but rather argue whether those killed so far were only half a million or passed the million. While other commentators usually refer to "deaths," we call them "killings," for that is what they were, wilfully and knowingly caused and overseen by state and intergovernmental officials who implemented the so-called "sanctions" against Iraq—another word which we do not use due to its aura of righteous action. Paradoxically, the enormities should surely warrant a different extent of attention. We shall review what is available of the figures of human loss, not in order to question the truth or otherwise of the figures, but in order to understand what it means and what message it carries.

The Iraqi Government, under pressure from the US, has not yet published even approximate figures of those killed since 2003. By compiling figures from the register of the Ministry of Health and the Civil Register in every town it would have been easy for the Iraqi Government to come up with an approximate figure. The London *Guardian* is reported to have written in 2008 that there is no shortage of estimates on casualties which vary enormously. It went on to state that although the Iraqi Ministry of Health tried to keep a count relying on figures from Baghdad morgue, the main recipient of bodies, they stopped releasing figures under pressure from the US-supported Government in the Green Zone.[18]

The estimation was left to a few unofficial parties and a number of surveys. The organization that has been cited by those trying to minimize the scale of killing has been 'Iraq Body Count' (IBC), which seems to rely on media reports in calculating its figures of casualties in Iraq. Their current figure of Iraqis killed as of 22 July 2013 stood at 115,503 – 126,796.[19] The figures of IBC have been criticized as being inaccurate because the organization relied on Iraqi media reports which are either indifferent to such matters as numbers of casualties and/or are mainly pro-government, having no interest in admitting to the alarming scale of the killing. In many cases the deaths are not even reported to the authorities by the families.

The BRussell Tribunal, which has been in the foreground of the campaign for investigating and exposing crimes committed in Iraq since the invasion, has come up with different figures. Dirk Andriaensens of the Russell Tribunal had studied in depth reports on casualties and compiled his figures of the true numbers of those killed, displaced and orphaned since 2003. He relied on an estimate by a survey conducted by *The Lancet* which concluded that up until July 2006 an estimated 600,000 had been killed, and updated that figure to reach the new figure up to 2010. Here are his figures:

> 1,450,000 killed, 7,700,000 refugees, 5,000,000 orphans, 3,000,000 widows, 1,000,000 missing... all in a country of nearly 30 million![20]

We shall now look at figures presented by a few surveys. The first survey was conducted by *The Lancet*. The method used in the survey, which is of great importance for the credibility of any survey, was given by the report as follows: "Between May and July, 2006, we did a national cross-sectional cluster sample survey of mortality in Iraq. 50 clusters were randomly selected from 16 Governorates, with every cluster consisting of 40 households. Information on deaths from these households was gathered."[21] The researchers concluded that the number of Iraqis killed between March 20003 and July 2006, and mainly by gunfire, was 601,027. It is worth remembering that the *Lancet* report was concerned with the period preceding that of the intensification of the sectarian violence.

The US, which has refused to publish any figures of civilian casualties in Iraq despite its claim that it accounts for every screw that goes into war efforts, criticised the *Lancet* report as being 'deeply flawed'. However, Sir Roy Anderson, the UK's Chief Scientific Adviser to the Ministry of Defence (MOD), gave the *Lancet* report the scientific backing when he stated that "The [*Lancet*] study design is robust and employs methods that are regarded as close to "best practice" in this area, given the difficulties of data collection and verification in the present circumstances in Iraq."[22]

Another survey was conducted in August 2007 by Opinion Research Business (ORB), a member of the British Polling Council. The methodology employed in the survey was described as using a "multi-stage random probability sampling and covers fifteen of the eighteen governorates within Iraq. For security reasons Karbala and Al Anbar were not included. Erbil was excluded as the authorities refused our field team a permit."[23] After gathering the results of face-to-face interviews, which showed that 22% of households had lost a member to violence, the researchers projected those results on an estimated 4 million households in Iraq and concluded that the number of Iraqis killed as a result of the invasion and following conflict was, by August 2007, some *1,220,580.*

The latest survey published on 15 October 2013 was conducted by a collaboration of US and Canadian researchers and the Iraqi Ministry of Health. The researchers argued the reasons for the survey as follows:

> A number of earlier studies have estimated the death toll in Iraq since the beginning of the war in March 2003. The previous studies covered different periods from 2003 to 2006 and derived different rates of overall deaths and excess deaths attributable to the war and conflict. All of them have been controversial, and their methodologies have been criticized. For this study, based on a population-based mortality survey, the researchers modified and improved their methodology in response to critiques of earlier surveys. The study covers the period from the beginning of the war in March 2003 until June 2011, including a period of high violence from 2006 to 2008. It provides population-based estimates for excess deaths in the years after 2006 and covers most of the period of the war and subsequent occupation.[24]

The research concluded that approximately *half a million* deaths in Iraq could be attributable to the war.

Global Research reported in 2011 that "The Ministry of Labour and Social Affairs (MLSA) estimates that around 4.5 million children are orphans. Nearly 70 percent of them lost their parents since the invasion and the ensuing violence. From the total number, around 600,000 children are living in the streets without a house or food to survive. Only 700 children are living in the 18 orphanages existing in the country, lacking their most essential needs."[25] But with simple arithmetic we can estimate a new figure for those killed according to the (MLSA). If an average family in Iraq consists of 3 children then the number of those killed since the invasion would be around *one million!*

The killing has not slowed down since 2011. If anything it intensified in 2013 and all indications are that it is on the way up as more men, money and equipment poured in from Saudi Arabia in punishment for the majority of Iraqis (and not the Government) siding with the Syrian regime against the Islamists. The latest figures released in November 2013 by All Iraq News and based on casualties reported monthly by the United

Nations Assistant Mission in Iraq (UNAMI) show that in the previous four months 12,210 had been killed or wounded in Iraq through violence, being 3,819 killed and 8,391 wounded.[26] This means that an average of 100 people had been unjustifiably killed or wounded every day in Iraq during the previous four months. This alarming trend shows the scale of the calamity that has befallen Iraq because of the invasion and occupation and their consequences. But that was only 2013. Now in 2014, we witness an international coalition being formed with a mission to bomb Iraq in order to stop what is now known as the Islamic State, evolved from the very insurgency which once had enjoyed Saudi funding.

It is not possible to talk of the numbers killed without commenting on the wounded. But the Iraqi Government has not published figures of those wounded in the last ten years of violence and it is possible that no such records have even been compiled, as the Iraqi officials are indifferent to the sufferings of Iraqis. It has been suggested that the ratio of wounded-to-killed has been 4:1 or 6:1 or even 7:1.[27] If we settle for the middle figure and assume that the number killed is halfway between the half a million and the million reported above, then we are talking about approximately *four million* Iraqis wounded so far. Most of them would have been wounded by high density explosives carried by suicide bombers, car bombs or roadside bombs. Wounds resulting from such explosions are more likely to lead to amputations or impairment of some bodily senses like hearing or vision. In short, Iraq today has a few millions who have been incapacitated one way or another because of the violence unleashed since the invasion. In a country whose social services were already limited before the invasion and were obliterated since, those millions of wounded Iraqis have no one to look after them or provide them with the medical and the social care they need.

We believe that it would be fitting to close this section on killing with the words of Professor Raymond Baker in his address to the International Seminar in Defence of Iraqi Academia in Ghent on 9-11 March 2011 as quoted by Dirk Adriaensens:[28]

> There is something blinding about destruction on so terrible a scale. There is something just too painful about debating methods for calculating the number of slaughtered innocents when the figures almost immediately take us well beyond hundreds and hundreds of thousands of human souls. How many pages and pages of WikiLeaks reports of killings at checkpoints, unspeakable torture, random murders by unchecked contractors can one read with the revulsion for the occupiers and compassion for the victims they deserve. The mind closes down, or so it

seems. That may be one of God's mercies but it is one
that should be resisted.

Torture is no less painful to write about. While there has
always been torture in the world, we would like to think that humanity
is progressively reducing the inhumane treatment of human beings. But
are we? Was there torture during Saddam Hussein's rule? The answer
would undoubtedly be yes though more in the early decades than the later
ones. The US promise of democracy in Iraq gave people hope that such
practices were behind them. But no such destiny was awaiting the people
of Iraq. Torture continued after the Ba'ath rule, first at the hands of US
personnel with the disgrace of Abu Ghraib exposed for everyone to see.
It continued during the horrible black years that followed. The primary
difference in the practice of torture in Iraq between pre-invasion and
post-invasion has been the fact that while in the former it was practised
by specifically appointed instruments of the State with certain channels to
follow in accountability, in the post-invasion period it has been practiced
by militias in secret dungeons with no system, judicial sanction, records,
channels to question, or accountability.

The Western claim about being actively engaged in eradicating
torture smacks of hypocrisy. The US was caught red-handed in Abu
Ghraib.It had hoped that such practices were not going to be exposed
and if they were, they could brush them aside as propaganda by the
ousted Ba'athists. But what happened in Abu Ghraib were not isolated
incidents carried out by rogue elements in the army or the CIA but rather
practices sanctioned by the highest authority in the US administration,
army and intelligence.[29]

Since domestic legislation prevents torture stateside, US
ingenuity devised a new technique called 'Extraordinary Rendition' (ER)—
the transfer of a detainee, without due legal process, to the custody of a
foreign country, paradoxically one which is likely to be classified as a rogue
state by the US itself, in order for that country to detain and interrogate the
detainee in line with US desires. Several people are known to have been
sent through this route where they were tortured by the recipient state
and the extradited confessions were then passed on to the US.[30] This way
the US avoided being accused of torture while still achieving its objective
of securing confessions. However, US complicity in each crime by ER is
beyond doubt, as well as the complicity of a surprisingly large number
of states such as Albania, Australia, Austria, Azerbaijan, Belgium, Bosnia-
Herzegovina, Canada, Croatia, Cyprus, Czech Republic, Denmark, Egypt,
Finland, Georgia, Germany, Greece, Iceland, Ireland, Italy, Macedonia,
Lithuania, Poland, Portugal, Romania, Spain, Sweden, Syria and the UK.[31]

But in Iraq they did not need ER because they were able to
act with impunity, as there was no supervision or accountably required

from the invader. Bremer was imposed as ruler of Iraq and held absolute authority. Members of the military, intelligence and private security companies found themselves free to do whatever they liked in Iraq. There are many video clips released by US soldiers and available on the Internet in which they appear target shooting at cars behind them on the roads in Iraq. Despite the scandal of Abu Ghraib and the fact that "several homicide cases, involving detainees who died while being interrogated by the CIA, were referred to the Department of Justice for prosecution in 2004 and 2005; yet to date not one CIA agent has been charged."[32]

In addition to the free hand of US personnel in Iraq, the US utilized Iraqi murderous militias to do its dirty work. The US was not new to this practice, as it had done so before in Central America. But it was easier in Iraq because of the lack of independent observers and the absence of any organized opposition to US policies. Two men—John Negroponte and James Steel—played similar roles in Iraq to those which they played earlier in Central America. Negroponte was US Ambassador to Iraq for the period between June 2004 and April 2005. James Steel was a retired Colonel who fought in Vietnam and served as a military adviser in El Salvador "where he guided ruthless Salvadorian death squads in the 1980s."[33] Negroponte started his career in the CIA involvement in Vietnam and later in 1980s became US Ambassador to Honduras where he took part in setting up what became known as the 'death squads' responsible for torture and murder of thousands of Hondurans. At the same time James Steel "was commander of the US Military Adviser Group in El Salvador. He also smuggled weapons to the Contra insurgents in Nicaragua."[34] Post invasion Steel surfaced in Iraq as counsel for Iraqi security forces. The presence of both men in Baghdad was not accidental and their joined activity, apparently, made *Newsweek* in January 2005 name it the "Salvador Option" in Iraq.[35] It is unfortunate but true that the resistance to the invasion and occupation of Iraq was mainly from among the Sunnis of Iraq. It seems that most of the Shi'ia of Iraq were happy with the invasion which enabled them for the first time in their history to assume superficial power. Such a realization made the Americans depend on Shi'ia to oppose the Sunni insurrection. To that end, the Negroponte-Steel effort was to train members of the Badr Brigade, which was originally formed and armed by Iran, and the Mehdi Army, the two largest Shi'ite militias in Iraq, to target the leadership and support networks of a primarily Sunni resistance.[36]

The London *Guardian* and the BBC Arabic carried out a 15-month investigation after the former received thousands of classified US military logs from Wikileaks. The documentary titled 'James Steele: America's Mystery Man in Iraq' was released on 6 March 2013.[37] The classified US military documents detailed thousands of incidents where US soldiers came across tortured detainees in a network of detention centres run by police commandos across Iraq.[38] According to the findings, the Pentagon initially had reservations about adopting the insurgents of Badr, perhaps because they were created and trained in Iran, but decided to lift the ban on these Shi'ia militias joining the security forces in Iraq, presumably after being assured by militia leaders of their allegiance to the invaders. Accordingly, the Pentagon sent a US veteran of the "dirty wars" in Central America (James Steel) to oversee sectarian police commando units in Iraq that set up secret detention and torture centres to get information from insurgents. These units were called Special Police Commandos (SPC) and by April 2005 there were six battalions of them with a Battalion in Baghdad of 5000 men[39].

Steel was supported in his work by Colonel James Coffman, who reported to General David Petraeus, who himself was implicated by the documentary as having knowledge of all of the abuses committed in the centers. Coffman boasted of this relationship, describing himself as Petraeus' 'eyes and ears on the ground' in Iraq. One Iraqi General who worked with both Steel and Coffman is reported to have said:

> I never saw them apart in the 40 or 50 times I saw them inside the detention centres. They knew everything that was going on there ... the torture, the most horrible kinds of torture.[40]

It may be true that Steel and Coffman never tortured people themselves but to suggest that they did not know of the abuses taking place is thus untenable. It would make a mockery of the US intelligence services to claim that anything relating to security could have taken place in Iraq without US high command being directly involved in, acquiescing to or at least knowing about it. In response to the suggestion that the Americans were unaware of what was happening in the detention centres, General Adnan Thabit, head of special commandoes, had this to say:

> Until I left, the Americans knew about everything I did; they knew what was going on in the interrogations and they knew the detainees. Even some of the intelligence about the detainees came to us from them—they are lying.[41]

According to the investigation for the documentary, it seems that the training of the SPC unleashed deadly sectarian militia which went on later to kill hundreds of Sunnis in Iraq. People used to wake up and see their roads littered with bodies, so much so that at the height of it some 3000 bodies a month were strewn on the streets of Baghdad—as our own relatives have experienced.

The *Guardian* made the following observation worthy of mention to sum up the whole matter and show clearly that the US had been directly responsible for torture and killing in Iraq, as it was in Central America:

> The pattern in Iraq provides an eerie parallel to the well-documented human rights abuses committed by US-advised and funded paramilitary squads in Central America in the 1980s. Steele was head of a US team of special military advisers that trained units of El Salvador's security forces in counterinsurgency. Petraeus visited El Salvador in 1986 while Steele was there and became a major advocate of counterinsurgency methods.[42]

In an exchange between Gen. Peter Pace[43] and Secretary of Defense Donald Rumsfeld, the latter indicated his ignorance of the responsibility of the occupier under international humanitarian law to intervene and prevent inhumane treatment of prisoners or civilians alike. One commentator referred to this as an illustration of "the moral vacuity of the American leadership during the Iraq war."[44] We believe it goes beyond that to show the moral vacuity of the world at large as represented by the Security Council, which not only refrained from condemning the invasion of a sovereign member of the UN, but rewarded the aggression by granting the invaders a mandate to rule Iraq as they pleased, which has led to the on-going calamity.

Throughout their presence in Iraq, the US had insisted that only US citizens were allowed to interrogate prisoners in Abu Ghraib and other detention centres. However, Robert Fisk pointed out that the report of US General Antonio Taguba on torture in Abu Ghraib referred to third country nationals being involved in the mistreatment of prisoners in Iraq.[45] Given the Israeli fear of the Ba'athists who vowed to recover Palestine from Zionist occupation, an unavoidable question that springs to mind after this revelation is: was any member of Israeli Mossad holding dual US citizenship involved in these interrogations?

The spiral of killing started with the *'Shock and Awe'* invasion and the expulsion of tens of thousands of Ba'athists from their jobs and the sectarian violence that followed the planned US arming of militias, both Shi'ia and Sunni. This created the greatest displacement of people in the Middle East since the expulsion of the Palestinians in 1948. As the Iraqi Government has no records and, if it had, may not publish them, then most figures are estimates using whatever indications available. The Iraqi Red Crescent estimated in 2007 that in Baghdad, a city of some 6 million people, one out of every four residents, has been displaced from their homes.[46] Another estimate put the number of Iraqis displaced inside Iraq at 2.7 million with some two million forced to move to Syria or Jordan.[47] HRW put it as follows:

> Iraq is home to about two million internally displaced
> persons, about 1.5 million of whom were displaced
> since 2006..... About 500,000 of these 1.5 million live
> as squatters in slum areas, without basic services,
> including garbage collection, water, and electricity.[48]

But whether the figure of internally displaced Iraqis is 2 million or 2.7 million, we are still talking of an equivalent to 50 million being internally displaced in the US! The problem with those forced to seek refuge outside Iraq is even more serious both for them and for Iraq's future. They have had to suffer enormous hardship and Iraq has lost a generation of highly qualified professionals due to their departure.

But the displacement of Iraqis goes beyond the misery it has caused those millions. It is about the irreversible damage to society that resulted. Baghdad has had about 200 districts of communities mixed in sects and religions. We grew up in one district where Jews, Christians and Muslims of both sects lived harmoniously for centuries. But during 2007 only 25 districts in Baghdad escaped becoming homogeneous. All other districts suffered the cleansing which resulted in the majority of Baghdad's districts today being of one sect.[49] This is an irreversible process which has damaged the fabric of Baghdad which had existed for a millennium.

The conspiracy of silence which we identified in our book, *Volume I, Genocide in Iraq*, which ensured that Western media covered Iraq in the bare minimum, has continued after the invasion and since. There is so much evidence yet little coverage of the untold misery of displacement. Let the UN tell the story in the words of John Holmes, UN Undersecretary of Humanitarian Affairs and Relief Coordinator:

> What may surprise some of you is that the number
> of displaced in Darfur is comparable to the number
> of internally displaced people in Iraq. While many are
> aware of the suffering of civilians in Darfur, it saddens
> me to see that the daily threats faced by Iraqis,
> exacerbated, of course, by the ongoing violence, are
> still under-reported and under-estimated.[50]

Cultural Cleansing

We are amazed at the inability of US politicians and planners to understand or appreciate history. The fact that the US as a relatively new settler state has had little time to develop a sense of history, is no excuse. Iraq, on the other hand, is a country that has had a continuum of history for millennia. Things that happen in nations' lives are not necessarily recorded but they are still absorbed by people and passed on from generation to generation. There may have been many calamities, crimes, failures and successes but they all subconsciously form the psyche of the nation. To think that Iraq could be erased and recreated from scratch, as it seems the US planned to do in Iraq in 2003, demonstrates the US failure to comprehend history. Whether the politicians believing in that were evil, mendacious men like Dick Cheney, or naïve men like Paul Bremer, makes no difference as both appear equally oblivious.

Had this failure rested at the politicians' doors it would have been easier to explain. But when the academic world and responsible people exhibit the same sense of cultural superiority, it indicates a failure of integrity or worse, a colonial plot.

Kanan Makiya, a half-Iraqi half-British architect,[51] arrived in Iraq with the invaders and was given a secure free home in the Green Zone. One of his early tasks, which arose from his collaboration with the CIA in writing the *Republic of Fear*, was to get hold of the Ba'ath Party archives. He removed tens of millions of records of the Ba'ath Party Archives from the Iraqi Ba'ath Party Headquarters in 2003, stored them at his abode within the Green Zone for some years. Later he transported the collection to California with US government logistical assistance. He set up the 'Iraq Memory Foundation' (IMF) which has since claimed stewardship over the cache, and has turned it over to Stanford University's Hoover Institute,[52] reminiscent of the old imperialist British and French practices during the 19th century of helping themselves to Egyptian and Iraqi artefacts to decorate the British Museum and the Louvre. We hasten to add that the documents removed by Makiya are not the only documents removed from Iraq. In fact no one really knows the extent of what has been removed from Iraq because no records appear to have been kept and no government since 2003 really cares about Iraq. But there has, however, been an admission that at least seven million documents were removed to Qatar immediately after the invasion and then moved to the US and not been returned.[53]

The first measures taken to eradicate Iraq's heritage in the hope of erasing its memory and thereby its identity were taken by the military. It is true that Iraq has too many historic sites that need protection and keeping predators away from all of them may be difficult for a military strategist, but prior to the invasion, the Iraqi Government did not need to place its army in some of those legendary sites. Evidence seems to point to the fact that the US decided to use the main cultural heritage sites in Iraq as US and coalition military bases. Thus the legendary city of Babylon was turned into the headquarters of South Central Command of the Multi-National Forces.[54] Other sites included Ur, the legendary birthplace of Abraham, Kish, Isin, abu-Hatab, Bezikh, Adab, Larsa, Shmet, Umma, Umm Al-Hafriyat, Tulul al-Dhaher, az-Zebleiat, Tell al Wilaya, Uruk, Nippur, al-Kefel, Ctesiphon, Aqerquf, Assur, Nimrud, Nineveh, Hatra,

Kirkuk citadel, Arbil citadel, the old town of Basrah, the Islamic capital Wasit, the Islamic capitals of Kufa, and Samarra, the Abbasid Islamic imperial city.[55] It was also reported that satellite images show that one ancient site dating to the early second millennium BC was totally levelled in order to accommodate the expansion of the US base nearby.[56] This is how one scholar explained what happened:

> The digging, bulldozing, filling of sand bags and blast-barricade containers, the building of barracks and digging of trenches into the ancient sites have destroyed thousands of years of archaeological material, stratigraphy and historical data. Walls and standing structures have collapsed as a result of shootings, bombings and helicopter landings. The idea that there was no preplanning or high-level military decision making in choosing these ancient sites as major camp installations is difficult to believe.[57]

We had earlier reported how US army personnel were instructed not to intervene when the Iraqi Museum was being looted by Iraqis and foreigners alike. Further evidence is provided in the information reported by the Iraqi scholar who was in charge of Iraq's Antiquity and Heritage who advised us that even the offices of the antiquities departments were seized and occupied for military purposes.[58] He recounted another disturbing element of the campaign to erase Iraq's heritage – the dismissal of the voices of Iraqi archaeologists expressing their concern about the ransacking of Iraq's heritage as politically motivated in order to intimidate them into silence.[59]

In 2007 *The New York Times* summed up the results of the campaign, stating that on America's watch thousands of cultural artefacts disappeared and hundreds of Iraq's sites were looted during "Operation Iraqi Freedom", after its reporter visited the Iraqi Museum. Regarding the Museum it wrote that "looters stripped the galleries of some 15,000 Mesopotamian artefacts and the Museum became a wrenching symbol of the losses of the war." On the theft from some 12,000 of Iraq's archaeological sites, left unguarded or purposely neglected by the US/UK, the *NYT* quoted Abdul Zahra al-Taliqani, a spokesman for the Ministry of Culture, Tourism and Antiquities, saying "that thieves have stolen and likely trafficked 17,000 pieces from these sites so far."[60]

Indeed no one really knows how many artifacts have been removed from Iraq during the years of chaos that had followed the invasion. While it has been argued that a concerted international campaign was undertaken to return the missing artefacts, what percent of the 17,000 have since been returned?

Cultural Genocide

In an earlier section of this chapter we reviewed the scale of killing that has been going on since the invasion. However, here we would like to point out something distinctively different. The killings of Iraqi academics, professionals and intelligentsia portends cultural genocide.

In January 2005, Charles Crain remarked in *USA Today* that in a country with distinct political, ethnic and religious fault lines, the university killings seem to follow no pattern. Reporting on the killing of some 300 Iraqi academics and the fleeing of some 2000 up until 2005, Crain commented: "The dead have been Shi'ites and Sunnis, Kurds and Arabs, and supporters of various political parties. .... They have a common thing: they are Iraqis."[61] And, we should point out, they are academics! There is no dispute that there has been a campaign to deplete Iraq of its professionals in particular and its intelligentsia in general. We shall first review the reports on the scale of the campaign before we try to look at what is behind it.

- Human Rights Watch is reported to have estimated that 331 schoolteachers were slain in the first four months of 2006.[62]

- The *Independent* reported in 2006 that at least 2,000 Iraqi doctors have been killed and 250 kidnapped since the 2003 US invasion.[63]

- The Iraqi Minister of Education is reported to have announced in 2006 that 296 members of the education staff were killed in 2005 alone.[64]
- Medact's report of 16 January 2008 stated that up to 75 percent of Iraq's doctors, pharmacists and nurses have left their jobs since the US-led invasion in 2003 and more than half of those have emigrated.[65]

- According to Andrew Rubin, a surprisingly large number of the 1,000 lecturers and professors[66] who lost their jobs through de-Ba'athification, fell victim to assassination.[67]

- By the end of 2006 the UK's *Independent* reported that over 470 academics had been killed.[68]

- By the end of 2006 the *Guardian* stated that the

figure of academics killed since the invasion stood at around 500 from Baghdad and Basrah Universities alone.[69]

• According to an article in *The Christian Science Monitor*, the figure shared among academics is that 2,500 university professors have been killed, kidnapped, assassinated, or told to leave the country by June 2006.[70]

• By April 2007 the International Committee of Solidarity with Iraqi Professors stated that 232 university professors were killed and 56 were reported missing in Iraq, while more than 3,000 others had left the country after the 2003 invasion.[71]

• Up to 20 August 2012, the BRussell Tribunal's list of murdered Iraqi academics contained 472 names.[72]

• One UNHCR official noted, those who have left Iraq are its 2 million best and brightest.[73]

Wherever the true number of those killed or forced to flee lies, there is no dispute that evidence indicates a campaign to deprive Iraq of its intelligentsia without whom it would be impossible to re-build it. It is part of the plan to recreate Iraq from scratch which requires, inter alia, a need to cleanse Iraq of the influence of the Ba'ath ideology. As most of Iraq's intelligentsia was assumed to be part of that ideology, then it became imperative for the success of the plan to eradicate or remove this intelligentsia from all positions of influence. Indeed many Iraqis believe that there was "a plan to drain Iraq of its intellectuals and experts and dismantle its infrastructure along a pattern known as the 'El-Salvador Option' used in that country by the Pentagon." [74]

So who has been behind that campaign?

The list of suspected assassins that have been suggested is long, extending from the Ba'athists, Islamists and "insurgents," the Badr Brigade, Mahdi Army and other groups linked to political parties, through the Mossad, CIA and the intelligence apparatuses of every surrounding state, as well as private security companies.[75]

But it seems that a few of the elements in that list (like the

Mahdi Army) are unlikely candidates in the killing of academics and intelligentsia. The killing has neither been random nor sectarian which might have indicated that it had been planned, organized and executed by one group. The killing of academics would not have been possible or desired by the various sects and militias in Iraq under the Pre-Invasion Iraqi Government. This puts the blame on the US State Department and its advisers and agents on the ground, and leaves the CIA, Mossad and Private Security Companies as the most likely suspects. We believe that the CIA and the Mossad are as one in objectives, planning and execution when it comes to Iraq. Their common objective is to defeat Ba'athism and eliminate not only Arab nationalism, but any subsequent collective entity from acting as a political force in Iraq. Depleting Iraq of its intelligentsia would achieve that. Who might serve as the instruments of such a policy? Members of the Private Security Companies are mercenaries who had served in armies and are almost automatically willing to work for the CIA and Mossad in their campaign. This is supported by evidence of the money allocated for CIA operations in Iraq. "According to Robert Dreyfuss, writing in the *American Prospect*, $3bn of the $87bn going to Iraq has been allotted to fund covert CIA paramilitary operations there, which, if the CIA's historical record is to be consulted, are likely to include extrajudicial killings and assassinations."[76] And these killings and assassinations would not be—have not been—random, we would add.

The selection of targets and the method used to kill them or force them to flee supports this view. It seems that people were selected on certain criteria; for some only killing them would ensure that they were neutralized, while for others a lesser measure such as demanding their departure from Iraq was sufficient. Whether any of the mostly illiterate militia would have had the intelligence to identify whom to eliminate is doubtful. But most importantly the names of such persons and their locations were not in the public domain. Such information was, however, available to the CIA through its control of Iraq's official records and archives. We are not excluding the possibility of a few killings for revenge because of old feuds or kidnapping for money. But those, we believe, constitute only a small portion of the total crime of cultural degradation and cleansing that has been taking place in Iraq since the 2003 invasion

Before leaving this section we would like to reflect on one idea suggested by one US official as reflective of the deeply supremacist orientation of the US imperialist mind. Soon after the 2003 invasion, Jon B. Wolfsthal, a former non-proliferation policy adviser to the U.S. Department of Energy, wrote an article titled 'Stop Hunting Iraqi Scientists and Start Recruiting Them,'[77] noting how "the U.S. continues to pursue the many weapons experts as war criminals, and even those not emblazoned in a deck of cards fear prosecution for their roles in Hussein's weapons programs." But why should Iraqis working on a weapon program in their country be more criminal than those working in on similar programs in the US? His reference to the people sought in the so-called 'deck of cards' displays complete ignorance of the universal application of the basic principles of international law and justice. Equally significantly, it reveals a lack of understanding by Mr. Wolfsthal of the US plans for the Arab World. He reminded us that following the fall of the Soviet Union, the US, Europe and Japan worked hard to engage Soviet weapons scientists in order to secure that their skills are not sold to rogue states or terrorist organizations. The result was that over 50,000 scientists from Russia and Ukraine were employed by 'western' science research centers. He went on to suggest that a similar approach could be used in Iraq where instead of hunting Iraqi scientists the US could make use of them in civilian science centers. Indeed, one might ask, why not? But to ask such a question would indicate that we, like Mr. Wolfsthal, have not really understood the purpose of the invasion of Iraq. The illegal aggression committed against Iraq was not really about the alleged WMDs, which, even if Iraq had any left, would not pose any threat to the US or Europe. It was about rebuilding the Middle East according to the Neocons' vision of the US's role in the 21st century. Having Iraqi scientists working in civilian research centres would not only have enhanced their skills, but also possibly enabled them one day to go back and work for Iraq or another Arab state to the detriment of the US plans.

In addition to all the slaughter and destruction which the US brought to Iraq, they pursued a unique attempt at cultural genocide which sought to erase even the memory of a nation that is entrenched deep in history. Since 1258, when Hulago ransacked Baghdad and destroyed its culture, nothing similar has happened until George Bush came as a 21st Century 'hooligan'.

In the words of Venezuelan writer Fernando Baez: "It is a paradox: the inventors of the electronic book returned to Mesopotamia, where books, history and civilization were born, to destroy it."[78]

It should be remembered that when the Genocide Convention was being negotiated, the first draft included three groups of acts that could be classified as genocide. One of the groups was labelled 'Cultural Genocide' which means the destruction of the specific characteristics of the persecuted group by various means including forced exile, prohibition of the use of national language, destruction of books and similar acts.[79] The above analysis shows that some of the acts committed in Iraq fall within the definition of 'Cultural Genocide'. Although the final draft of the Convention on the Prevention and Punishment of Genocide adopted on 9 December 1948 did not include the category of Cultural Genocide, we believe that such a crime exists under customary international law and an international court of law would hold the perpetrators of cultural cleansing in Iraq guilty of the crime of 'Cultural Genocide'.

Health and WMD

The state of health services in Iraq has been affected by two factors. Firstly, the availability of doctors and facilities to deliver the service, and secondly the effects of WMD used by the US/UK during the 14 years of attacks starting with the first 1991 attack and up to the attack on Fallujah in 2004.

The report of the Special Inspector General for Iraq Reconstruction (SIGIR) advised Congress that:

> "In the 1970s, Iraq had one of the better healthcare systems in the Middle East, with access available to 97% of urban and 79% of rural populations."[80]

The significance of this statement is that firstly it contradicts all the media hype about the failures of the Ba'ath rule; in fact it was the Ba'ath two five-year development plans that resulted in this kind of good delivery of health services relative to the richest states in the area, and secondly it forces the question as to why has the service deteriorated so badly since the demise of the Ba'ath. We have already addressed the achievements of the Ba'ath rule in providing health services among other aspects of developing in Iraq in Volume I of *Genocide in Iraq*.[81] We will now look at what happened to the excellent medical service of the 1970s.

Between 1980 and 1991 Iraq's budget for health care averaged $450 million annually.[82] Five years after the genocidal blockade of Iraq, a team of international researchers reported that one third of Iraq's hospitals had closed and one third of diagnostic and therapeutic equipment was not functioning for lack of spare parts and maintenance which were all blocked by the total embargo.[83] By 2002 the health care budget had dropped to a mere $22 million or 5% of what it was in 1980s, and 2.7% of the 2003 GDP, when in normal circumstances and without the blockade it would have risen as had been the case since the 1960s.[84].

Has the health care in Iraq improved since the invasion, which was supposed to bring peace, freedom, democracy and social improvements or did the destruction continue?

It is undeniable that some doctors left Iraq during the blockade years as their income deteriorated so much that a doctor who did not have a private practice had to survive on a salary equivalent to $2 per month. But the number who left is nothing compared to the mass exodus which followed the 2003 invasion and occupation of Iraq, as we shall see.

In the 1990s, the country had 34,000 physicians registered with the Iraqi Medical Association. By 2008, this number dropped by over half to around 16,000.[85] However, an even more descriptive number revealing the true effect of the invasion is shown in a recent Oxfam/NCCI report which "estimates that 40 percent of the country's professional class has left the country since 2003."[86] The ICRC has relied on Iraqi Government statistics to report that since the 2003 invasion "more than 2,200 doctors and nurses have been killed and more than 250 kidnapped."[87] We know that in our immediate family covering only siblings, sons, nephews and nieces, at least eleven doctors have left Iraq, five of whom are consultants. If we include relatives, the list will be longer. It may be argued that this is not typical of all families, but it still indicates what has happened in Iraq since the sanctions and invasion. In 2008 the Iraqi Government appealed to medical staff to return but to no avail. Firstly, those who left only did so because they were forced into it and their reasons for fleeing have not been eliminated. Secondly, it is difficult for a highly qualified professional to keep moving around the world with his/her family. Once settled, he/she would hesitate to move again.

Thus Iraq, which was the pride of the Arab World in the 1970s— and people from as far as Yemen came to be treated there—has sunk to the bottom of the whole Muslim world in its medical services and health care. Twenty years after the imposition of total blockade and eight years after the invasion and occupation the WHO reported that:

> Iraq had 7.8 doctors per 10,000 people—a rate two, if not three or four times lower, than its neighbours Jordan, Lebanon, Syria and even the Occupied Palestinian Territory. In the Muslim world, Iraq's doctor-patient ratio is higher only than Afghanistan, Djibouti, Morocco, Somalia, South Sudan and Yemen.[88]

The building and rehabilitation of hospitals and clinics has not fared any better despite the availability of funds and contractors. The record of the occupier in this field is demonstrated in the 2013 SIGIR report to Congress.

In 2004, Bechtel was awarded a contract to build Basrah Children's Hospital for $50 million, envisaged to be a 'state-of-the-art' paediatric oncology unit to serve all southern Iraq. In 2008 the contract was terminated and new money was poured in so that only the building was completed in 2010 but at a cost of $165 million as opposed to its initial cost of $50 million. Where all the money went, why it took so long and why the contract was terminated, indicate the kind of corruption that is to be found in the most corrupt developing states. Despite the claim that the hospital was opened in 2012, it is still partly unfurnished, unequipped and no training of staff has yet taken place.[89] Is it indifference, carelessness and corruption, or a mixture of all that gave rise to such bizarre state of affairs that could not have happened in Iraq in its worst days?

The second example of failure as reported by the SIGIR is that of building Primary Care Centers. In 2004 the Coalition Provisional Authority (CPA) awarded a contract for $243 million to build and equip 150 Primary Health Centers (PHC) across Iraq to be completed by end of 2005. A catalogue of failures and disappearance of funds followed. In 2006 the SIGIR reported that despite having spent $186 million, only *six* PHCs (out of the 150) were considered as having been completed. In 2006, similar to the Basrah Hospital, the contract was terminated and the number of PHCs reduced to 142. Another $57 million was added to the PHC program. But still nothing happened. A further $102 million was added to the cost and the number of PHCs reduced to 133. But still by 2013 the SIGIR advises us that:

> Tens of millions more were spent, but SIGIR's reviews indicated that the construction, installation of equipment, and necessary training were not adequately completed for a significant number of PHCs.

The SIGIR gives some reasons for such a failure, stating "poor performance by follow-on contractors, along with weak U.S. government program oversight."[90]

But whatever the reasons given by the SIGIR, it is fair to conclude that after nearly ten years of awarding the contract for the PHCs and after having spent hundreds of millions, no one really knows what has been completed or where the money went. In short, this episode goes to show that, ten years after the invasion, and the "redesign" has not emerged from the chaos following the destruction.

The World Bank advises that Iraq was spending 8.4% of its GDP on health care by 2010 as opposed to 2.7% of its GDP spent in 2003 which means that Iraq was spending some $6 billion a year in 2010 compared to the $30 million it spent in 2003.[91] But there is little to show in terms of results for such spending when we remember that Iraq managed prior to the invasion and despite the genocidal blockade to maintain reasonable service with a mere $22 million or so (still significant if adjusted for inflation). Thus a survey carried out by the Iraqi Knowledge Network (IKN) in 2011 found that: "40 percent of the population deems the quality of healthcare services in their area to be bad or very bad."[92] It is so bad that people seek medical treatment abroad, selling their homes, cars and other precious possessions to pay for it.

Another indication of the failure of post invasion health care worthy of mention is the scale of immunization. By the end of the 1970s, almost all Iraqi children were immunized. As a result of the blockade and deterioration of all services, immunization dropped to 60.7% by 2000. However, since the post-invasion removal of sanctions, which caused the drop, it would have been natural to expect a rise in the number of immunized children to bring it back to the golden days of the 1970s. But that did not happen as the destruction of Iraq continues. According to the Multiple Indicator Cluster Surveys (MICS)[93] conducted by the Iraqi Government and the UN Children's Fund (UNICEF), immunization dropped to 39 percent in 2006, then rose to 45.4 percent by 2011; nine years after the invasion the immunization is still less than pre-invasion levels which the Ba'ath regime managed despite the hardship of sanctions.[94]

The second element of direct and indirect impact on health is that of weapons of mass destruction (WMD). As there is no single accepted definition of WMDs, we choose our definition to mean a weapon which can kill a large number of people indiscriminately. This means that a WMD may be a conventional weapon like a cluster bomb which can kill a large number of innocent people over a large area, or it may be an unconventional weapon like depleted uranium emitting low energy radiation over billions of years. The process of killing when a WMD is used need not be instantaneous as is the case with a bullet. It may take time and manifest itself in different forms from birth deformities to serious degenerative diseases.

Whenever WMD is mentioned with reference to use in Iraq, people immediately assume it refers to the use of depleted uranium (DU) by the US/UK which has been accepted to have been used both in 1991 in the battlefield and on a wider area and in larger quantity in 2003, with intermediate use during the sorties of US warplanes in the period in between. A book by co-authors Abdul Haq al-Ani and Joanne Baker addressed the use of uranium in Iraq which covered the limited research carried out by Iraqis following 1991 and the actual measurement of radiation conducted on the field in Iraq by the authors in 2004-2005.[95] We are not going to reproduce the material of that book here. But we intend to address a few other issues relating to WMDs.

Four to five years after the 1991 attack, the hospitals in Basrah noticed a sudden rise in children's cancer and horrific and unusual birth deformities. It has been reported that:

> Official Iraqi government statistics show that, prior to the outbreak of the First Gulf War in 1991, the rate of cancer cases in Iraq was 40 out of 100,000 people. By 1995, it had increased to 800 out of 100,000 people, and, by 2005, it had doubled to at least 1,600 out of 100,000 people. Current estimates show the increasing trend continuing.[96]

Once such a reality is faced, people will become concerned. Such a sharp rise of cancer incidence does not occur randomly in the universe. It was quite natural for Iraqi and non-Iraqi doctors and scientists to speculate on the cause of such a rise. As the sharp rise in 1995 in the Basrah District followed the 1991 attack and the sharp rise in 2008 in Fallujah followed the 2004 attack on it, then it is only natural to link the rise of diseases and deformities to the use of DU in both cases. Iraq post 1991 was under total blockade and had little resources to carry out serious research because even medical and scientific journals were not allowed into the country let alone the importation of special equipment and expertise to study the issue. The only piece of research, which Iraqi scientists did, was to carry out measurements in contaminated areas of the scale of radiation pollution. These were reproduced in the uranium book referred to, above.[97]

There was another reason for the Ba'ath Government not to emphasize the danger that the use of DU or other chemicals in Iraq might portend. The Government did not want to add any further panic to the already exhausted and traumatized public by advising them that it was possible that some areas of Iraq were contaminated and that living near them could cause birth deformities or cancers, when the Government could do very little to alleviate the situation. Perhaps it was felt that the prudent measure was to play it low and keep the public misinformed.

Another explanation for the lack of acknowledgement and warning about the effects on human beings of this insidious weapon is that the Iraqi government was under pressure not to criticize its oppressors for fear of further defamation, destabilization, reprisal and hardship.

During the 2003 invasion and the doubly massive attacks on Fallujah in 2004, more DU and chemicals were used. A new surge of cancers or birth deformities surfaced in Fallujah. There are numerous reports on these incidences. We shall look in detail at two such reports.

Mozhgan Savabieasfahani, a reproductive toxicologist who used to work at the University of Michigan School Of Public Health, led a team of researchers who studied birth defects cases in Fallujah General Hospital in 2010 and co-authored studies[98] in 2010 and 2012. She collected samples from 56 families in Fallujah while her co-author collected samples from 28 families at Basrah Maternity Hospital. When these samples were tested they concluded that parents of children with birth defects had higher levels of lead, mercury and uranium than parents of normal children.[99] She told ABCNews.com: "They [parents] feel desperate, ...One major problem we had was that there weren't enough families who had normal children, and therefore we ended up with fewer normal family studies."[100]

The second report was published in the *International Journal of*

Environmental Research and Public Health (IJERPH) in September 2010. It reported the results of a population-based epidemiological survey in Jan/Feb 2010 of 711 houses and more than 4000 individuals in Fallujah organized by Malak Hamdan and Chris Busby. The researchers concluded that Fallujah had, in the five years following the 2004 attacks by USA-led forces, a 4-fold increase in all cancer cases as well as infant mortality. This and perturbations of the normal human population birth sex ratio were significantly greater than those reported for the survivors of the A-Bombs at Hiroshima and Nagasaki in 1945.[101]

The significance of the sex ratio result is given as follows:

> Birth sex ratio is a well-known indicator of genetic damage, the reduction in boy births being due to the fact that girls have a redundant X-chromosome and can therefore afford to lose one through genetic damage; boys do not. Sex ratio was similarly reduced in the Hiroshima survivors' children. "This is an extraordinary and alarming result" said Dr Busby.[102] He added: "To produce an effect like this, some very major mutagenic exposure must have occurred in 2004 when the attacks happened. We need urgently to find out what the agent was. Although many suspect Uranium, we cannot be certain without further research and independent analysis of samples from the area." Malak Hamdan, who organized the project said: "I am so glad that we have been able to obtain proper scientific confirmation of all the anecdotal evidence of cancer and congenital birth defects. Maybe now the international community will wake up."[103]

While the school of thought led by Dr Chris Busby, relying on the epidemiological studies, has been insisting on the existence of a link between the rise of birth defects and cancer and the use of uranium in Iraq, there is a persistent refusal by the US/UK authorities to accept any such link. It is unfortunate that they have received some support from certain scientific circles, perhaps reflecting the fact that scientific integrity has been compromised since the privatization of research. Scientists today look to multinational conglomerates for support, and in order to get financial support for research they need to please these corporations. Thus both the WHO and the Royal Society have lent some support to the counter-intuitive US/UK claim that there is no link between the radiation of DU and the rise in cancer and birth defects.[104] The reason for the WHO support is more obvious than that of the Royal Society.

More significant than the fact that the WHO is the least independent of the UN bodies, there is the link between the WHO and the IAEA which is not in public knowledge. On 28 May 1959, the WHO signed an agreement with the IAEA to keep away from any research that has a connection with radiation or radioactivity.[105] The Royal Society report on the link between DU and cancer has not been a straight rebuttal as the US/UK claim.[106] But as any observer can see, both states have passed a plethora of legislation regarding the handling, storing, transport and disposal of DU. As there are no such legislation for handling steel, for example, then the question must be: why is there a need for such legislation if the dispersion of DU is as safe as alleged?

The Royal Society report, which was not based on scientific research into DU, its effects or its specific use in Iraq but rather based on secondary scientific articles, reported the following:

> DU is radioactive and poisonous. Exposure to sufficiently high levels might be expected to increase the incidence of some cancers, notably lung cancer, and possibly leukemia, and may damage the kidneys. The key question is whether exposures to DU on the battlefield are such that the increased incidence of cancer or the likelihood of kidney damage are significant or are high enough to cause concern.[107]

We believe that despite this clear hazard indication in the Royal Society's report, the US/UK have been very successful in diverting attention from the toxic effects of DU and concentrating the argument on the effect of its radiation. As it has been difficult to prove a link between the low-energy radiation of DU and cancer, because proving such link requires quite intensive scientific research, the effects of the toxicity of DU have been overlooked. In fact, even if it is later proved that DU radiation causes no damage to tissue (which we do not believe), then it suffices to accept that using poisonous material is a war crime. The Royal Society confirms what is scientifically accepted: that DU is toxic. Thus when the US/UK argue that there is no link between DU and illnesses, they are intimating that the radiation link is not proven. But there is no way they can argue that the toxic effect is not proved.

We had already explained the reason why during the blockade period Iraq acted as it did regarding the use of DU and other chemicals. But since the new Governments came to power, there has been public disquiet about the rise of cancer and birth defects which Iraqi doctors had never seen before. It would be expected that great pressure has been put by the US/UK on the Iraqi authority not to investigate the use of DU or other chemicals in Iraq. A direct ban was placed on reports by Dr Doug Rokke, and American serviceman who suffered as a result of recovering DU munitions in Iraq. The reason for the fear in the US/UK is that any such research could find an obvious link. It is not only that they do not care about Iraq and its contamination. The issue is also financial and political. If it were established that US/UK soldiers were exposed to abnormally high levels of DU, heavy metals, dioxins and white phosphorous[108] then settlements resulting from the lawsuits likely to be brought by these soldiers against their Governments, especially the US, would be astronomical.

The Iraqi Government gave in to popular pressure and decided to undertake a study of child cancer and birth defects. Unsurprisingly, the Iraqi Ministry of Health resorted to the WHO to carry out the study. The study began in May 2012 and was completed in October 2012 but only published in late 2013. Chris Busby described the report as 'nothing short of a disgrace.'[109] He went on to condemn those responsible for the politicization of science, writing:

> I have written and given presentations on scientific dishonesty. The truth can be established by science, but not if it is dishonest and political. And it seems that this report, and the events and decisions that preceded it, and particularly the London School of Hygiene and Tropical Medicine peer review meeting, are a classical example of scientific dishonesty. The use of the London School of Hygiene and Tropical Medicine reminds me of the use of the Royal Society to produce a disgraceful report on depleted uranium in 2001. Since the outcome is intended to exonerate the US and UK military from what are effectively war crimes, and since the result will be employed to defend the continued use of uranium weapons, all concerned in this chicanery should be put before a criminal court and tried for what they have done. Their actions are responsible for human suffering and death and cannot be forgiven. This is a human rights issue.[110]

In the midst of the deception of the US/UK in using radiological and chemical weapons in Iraq one legal issue was missed or purposely set aside. A vital element of liability, as enshrined in Protocol 1 to the Geneva Conventions, must be pointed out. Article 36 of the Protocol 1 reads as follows:

> In the study, development, acquisition or adoption of

a new weapon, means or method of warfare, a High Contracting Party is under an obligation to determine whether its employment would, in some or all circumstances, be prohibited by this Protocol or by any other rule of international law applicable to the High Contracting Party.[111]

The obligation of both US/UK to show that the use of DU weapons is safe under international law is beyond dispute. It is thus not open for the US/UK to argue that there is no evidence to link its use with death or diseases without their having to publish the results of their research that will show such a conclusion. It is quite evident how prudent the drafters of the Protocol have been. They realized two fundamental reasons why this Article was necessary to protect civilians. Firstly, it is beyond the capacity of any individual to prove that his ailment or death of a relative was caused by a new weapon. Secondly, it would be too late to reverse the damage or rectify the situation once damage is done and thus proof needs to be given of the safety of such new weapons on civilians before they are accepted for use.

Both US/UK have so far failed to come up with proof that satisfies their obligation under Article 36. The destruction continues.

Children and Education

For two decades, Iraqi children have been subjected to grave violations of human rights. Due to decades of war, foreign occupation and international sanctions, Iraq has turned into one of the worst places for children in the Middle East and North Africa with around 3.5 million living in poverty, 1.5 million under the age of five undernourished and 100 infants dying every day.[112]

Although Iraq fought Iran for eight years, the economy was not affected so badly and people living in Baghdad would confirm that living standards did not change markedly. However, following the imposition of the total blockade in 1990, things changed dramatically. The economy collapsed, and the ability to feed a family in general evaporated. The very basic necessities of life started to disappear. Although the introduction of the Oil for Food Program enabled the Iraqi Government to implement a good rationing service which provided the minimum of survival requirements, the problem of malnutrition was not solved. The OFF Program only allowed Iraq to keep $4B dollars from oil sales which only allowed $160/person per year. The effects on children in Iraq may be summarized under the following sub-headings.

Psychological Problems

Half of Iraq's 30 million today are under the age of 20. This means that half of Iraqis today were born after the 1991 attack and grew up through the genocidal blockade, war, invasion, occupation and terror. Although physical impairment is visible and its results are easily observable, psychological illnesses are not. A Harvard research team, which visited Iraq following the 1991 massive attack, reported the children of Iraq "were the most traumatized children of war ever described" and that "a majority of the children would suffer from severe psychological problems throughout their lives."[113]

For twenty years the Iraqi population generally and children specifically have endured unprecedented conditions of military attacks, terror, torture, insecurity, and witnessed explosions and mutilated bodies on a daily basis, which made Medicines Sans Frontiers (MSF) conclude that many Iraqis have been pushed to their limit. A WHO report in 2005 concluded that "the fourth leading cause of morbidity among Iraqis older than five years is "mental disorders, which ranked higher than infectious diseases."[114] A 2007 survey by the Iraqi Government and the WHO found that more than one-third of respondents had significant psychological disorders.[115] There have been a few surveys carried out in Iraq to evaluate the scale of psychological disorders among children.[116] One notable study is that carried out by the Dean of the Psychological Research Center at Baghdad University, who concluded that as many as 28% of Iraqi children could be suffering from the effects of Post-Traumatic Stress Disorder (PTSD).[117] Such results mean that the number of Iraqi children suffering from PTSD could be as high as 3 million.[118]

Malnutrition

Levels of nutrition are directly linked to the general health of the nation. Poor nutrition has a lasting effect on the population as it affects children most and any physical or mental damage to a child is generally irreversible. A 1996 a WHO report states that the vast majority of the Iraqi population had been on a semi-starvation diet for years while a 1997 report stated that a third of Iraqi children under the age of five were chronically malnourished.[119] In its submission to The Iraqi Commission in 2007, Medact reported that the notional status of Iraqi children under 5 years of age were moving away from, rather than progressing towards The Millennium Development Goals (MDGs),[120] with malnutrition rates more than doubling since pre-sanction levels.[121] We have just seen that one third of Iraqi children have been psychologically affected and one third have been malnourished. It seems that the obvious question is:

what future is there for Iraq when in twenty years' time these children become the adult population of Iraq?

Child Labour

Since 1991 Iraqis started to witness children between the age of six and fifteen walking between cars selling small items or working in car repairs or blacksmith shops.[122] In most cases children had to drop out of school and go to work because their fathers had disappeared, either killed or imprisoned, and the family had no other source of income and no state support. Other children may have dropped out of school and gone to work to assist their fathers attempting to make ends meet. This situation started during the hard years of the blockade. But it was thought that following the invasion and occupation, the end of sanctions and restart of the flow of oil money, the trend would have been reversed and child labour would have dwindled. However, the facts indicate the opposite. In fact in 2012, nine years after the invasion, child labour is increasing rather than decreasing.[123] Estimates of child labour under the age of 14 in 2012 vary from 6%[124] to 15%.[125]

Drug Abuse

While both Iran and Egypt have been suffering from the spread of drugs for decades, Iraq had been virtually clean, partly because of cultural reasons and partly because of the stern Ba'ath treatment of drugs addiction and trafficking. But this situation changed after 2003 with the birth of 'democracy'. We have no way of knowing how drugs began to flow into Iraq and who was behind it, but we would not be surprised if it transpired that some US personnel were behind it. What concerns us here are the numerous reports about the spread of drug use among children. No one really knows the scope of the problem because no Government authority has troubled itself to look into this potentially destructive trend. But there have been some reports of a rapidly escalating situation with an increase of 30% in addiction between 2005 and 2008 alone.[126] It is not difficult to see how vulnerable orphans are when they are approached by drug dealers to get them to work carrying drugs in return for some money, which would eventually lead them to become addicts and prisoners of this vice ring themselves.

Education

We have already addressed the success of Iraq during the Ba'ath rule in education and eliminating illiteracy with the acknowledgment of the UNESCO.[127] In its report to Congress in 2012, the SIGIR had this to say:

> Until the 1980s, Iraq's education system was among the best in the Middle East, producing high literacy rates. But Saddam's despotism, a debilitating war, and consequent restrictive sanctions sunk the system.[128]

But what the SIGIR missed, and presumably the Congress too, is that it was precisely that so-called 'despotism' of Saddam which eliminated illiteracy in Iraq, and it was the birth of 'democracy' with the invasion which brought it back. This fact is manifested in the report's acknowledgment that, eight years after the invasion and occupation and the efforts by the US, which the report highlights, "the Education Committee of Iraq's Council of Representatives estimated in 2011 that 5 million Iraqis were illiterate."[129] But the Council of Representatives, which consists of mostly corrupt and inefficient people,[130] is not a body that could be trusted so easily and one is tempted to think that they would minimize any serious problem lest it exposes their failures. An independent US researcher advises us that "overall, 74.1% of the population is illiterate, which is the fifth worst in the Middle East and North Africa."[131] If we accept that both estimates are not accurate, we can still conclude that illiteracy in Iraq today applies to anywhere between 20% and 70% of the population.

So the undemocratic Iraq, which in 1982 was awarded a medal by UNESCO for eradicating illiteracy, ended up thirty years later with democracy and something between 20% and 70% of its people illiterate!

This most successful educational system in the Middle East, in fact, began to crumble with the imposition of the total blockade in 1991 when even pencils were not allowed into the country. Thus children started dropping out of schools. Lack of maintenance due to lack of funds meant that school buildings and teaching facilities were depleted as the blockade dragged on. It was expected by all Iraqis that with the promised 'democracy' and the abundance of funds, things would take a different turn after 2003. But that did not happen. What happened was the complete opposite: a process of continuous destruction.

Firstly, the de-Ba'athification Order meant that thousands of qualified teachers lost their jobs overnight, many of whom were killed, displaced or forced to leave Iraq permanently. Iraq had invested billions into training those qualified men and women and it was not possible to replace them with members of a Shi'ia militia, the majority of whom were army deserters with no education—notwithstanding that Bremer thought they ought to be rewarded for fighting the Ba'ath. The sectarian conflict that was instigated by the occupiers led to over two million Iraqis being displaced within Iraq and two millions forced out of the country. All

185

children in that mass displacement, second only to that of the Palestinians in 1948, were subject to deprivation and difficulties to adjust to new schools—where they existed. It is not difficult to realize that a delay or break in education may cause lasting effects in the development of a child.

Up to 1990 the Ba'ath success meant that almost 100% of Iraqi children attended primary school. That went down to 91% in 1990, 85% in 2007, before rebounding a bit since then. By 2010, 89% of youths in urban areas, and 77% in rural ones were in school. That covered 87% of boys, and 82% of girls.[132] A recent survey by the Tamuz Organization for Social Development done in the first half of 2011 reported that "more than 20% of primary students, around four million children, drop out each year, and that up to 65% of children in southern Iraq don't go to school."[133]

The unavoidable question must be: why does a country with abundant oil, whose income last year amounted to $100 billion (equivalent to 10 years of income during the Ba'ath rule, as in 1985 oil income was $B10.1 and in 1990 it was $B9.5), fail to achieve the 100% enrolment of primary school children which existed even during the Iraq-Iran war?

The SIGIR report's section on education repeatedly refers to the need to 'revise textbooks', 'initiate curriculum reform', and 'modernize the curriculum'. All such phrases indicate that the US embarked on modernizing the teaching curricula in Iraq because it was defective. In our view, there is nothing defective in the curriculum. A curriculum does not grow in a vacuum and cannot be imported from a distant, foreign land. It is part of the cultural and social development of a society and in that respect Iraq is no different to other nations. Iraqis who have gone through these curricula have excelled in post-graduate work all over the world. But it is possible to discern in the SIGIR's report a reflection of the purpose of the invasion and occupation of Iraq, namely to restructure Iraq on a new 'US' model for states in the Middle East. It was more important for the US to see that Iraqis are taught about free market and democracy than to worry about historical accuracy or how to address the fact that Iraq had been depleted of its teaching staff and intellectual capacity, or to ensure that more schools were built during the ten years since the invasion.

Thus the SIGIR advises us that '33,000 new teachers had been trained,'[134] but quoting such a number has no value in itself unless it is compared to the total number of teachers in Iraq or the number of teachers that used to qualify every year in Iraq before the invasion. Indeed we are advised by an independent US researcher that the Iraqi Minister of Education stated that "70% of teachers are not properly trained."[135]

Although the SIGIR report goes on to itemize how much money was spent on building and rehabilitating schools during the nine years after the invasion, the Iraqi Minister of Education is quoted in March 2012 as having said that "Iraq needed 12,000 new schools, and 600 added each year. Since 2003, only 2,600 new ones have been built, however, and last year, the Ministry said it could only build 200 that year. The major problem is the lack of funding. The annual budgets simply do not allot enough to build all of the schools that are needed."[136]

New schools are not being built, even though existing schools are overcrowded. In 2012 Ahmad Rashid, education adviser to Baghdad's Provincial Council, was quoted as saying that: "most Baghdad classrooms were designed for 25 to 30 students but now have more than 80. He says some classrooms have up to 120 students."[137]

As the UN and World Bank had indicated that Iraq requires an investment of nearly $5 billion to restore its education back to the 1980s level, then massive sums of money need to be allocated by the Government.[138] This is just to restore the level to the 1980s and not to improve on it. With the new information technology requirements, the need may be even greater than estimated. Again, half of Iraqis today are under 20 years of age. Any country needs to invest in educating its youngsters if it has any hope for a proper future. Iraq needs even more to invest in educating children per capita than does a developed Western state. Iraq should not be short of funds considering that it has not initiated any development plans as the Ba'ath did in their two five-year plans between 1970 and 1980. It has no army to waste money on as they claimed Saddam Hussein did. So why are they not investing in the future of Iraq by educating its children? Where is the money going? Is it truly possible that children in urban Karbala in 2012 were reported by Reuters to attend a school in a tent? [139]

Disability in Children

We have commented above on the deprivation and psychological disorders that have been inflicted on the children of Iraq. The physical destruction of Iraqi children is impossible to quantify because the Government has no record of how many Iraqi children have been killed through direct fire at the time of the invasion, during the sectarian conflict or through the daily bombings throughout Arab Iraq, let alone the number or scale of death caused by the lack of immunization, spread of infectious diseases or malnutrition.

But one example of physical damage that could be noticed and monitored is that of disabilities caused by wars. The main causes of war disabilities among children have been landmines and cluster bombs. It has been reported that "Casualties from failed cluster sub munitions rose between 1991 and 2007 from 5,500 to 80,000, 45.7% between the age of 15 and 29 years of age, and 23.9% were children under the age of 14. Both

UNICEF and UNDP believe these figures are an underestimation".[140] The link between these disabilities and wars is shown in the reported figure that in the "last decade the Al Munthanna and Basra provinces of Iraq have challenged Angola for the highest proportion to total population of children amputees."[141] Both provinces witnessed the biggest battles between the invading armies and the Iraqi resistance in 2003.

Child Mortality

There are no clear statistics on child mortality in Iraq post 2003, because the Iraqi authorities either do not supply them or do not carry out any studies. We are not able to conclusively give figures, but we can give examples.

In August 2002, and after 12 years of total blockade, there were 530 babies born in Fallujah General Hospital with only six deaths, and one deformity. In September 2009, the same hospital reported that, out of 170 babies born that month, 24 percent died within the first seven days, of which 75 percent were deformed. It is quite clear that the situation had worsened, and doctors in Falllujah were warning women not to have children.[142]

The situation elsewhere in Iraq is not much different. Most individuals reportedly killed by coalition forces were women and children. The risk of death from violence in the period after the invasion was 58 times higher than in the period before the war.[143] This was in 2004 before the escalating sectarian violence began. We can only speculate about the real number of children who died as a result of the invasion and the suffering it brought.

After having presented one leaf of the sad story of Iraqi children we cannot but agree with Bie Kentane's conclusion that:

> The Occupying powers bear full responsibility for the violations of these provisions and Conventions related to children. They should be held fully accountable for the harm they have inflicted upon the Iraqi children. They have deliberately changed the social fabric of the country, used ethnic cleansing to break up the unity of the country, destroyed water purification systems, health and educational facilities and indiscriminately bombed dense populated areas, leaving the children extremely vulnerable on all levels.[144]

Women

Women in Iraq have had a better life than women in many countries in the Middle East throughout the 20th century and up to the invasion. There is no way to make a comparison between women in Iraq and women in Arabia for example. While Iraqi women can study, work, travel and move as they please, they have no such luck in Arabia as they are still not allowed even to drive their cars. Yet we in the West seem to be adamant about changing liberal regimes like that of Iraq and Syria while acquiescing in the unjust regimes of despots like the one in Arabia. When Western politicians are asked about this they would respond that we have vital interests in Arabia. Does that not mean that had our interest in Iraq and Syria been protected then we would have been very happy with 'despotic Saddam' or 'despotic Bashar'?

In many ways women in Iraq have enjoyed better equality than women in some highly developed countries in Europe. They had the right to vote before women in Switzerland did, and they enjoyed automatic equal pay to men when executing the same jobs which women in Britain or Finland still do not enjoy. We are not trying to argue that women in Iraq have been enjoying perfect rights and privileges, but we are saying that compared to countries around them and within the historical and social context of developments, they have been liberated. In fact, women in Iraq got the right to vote in 1948, before Chile, India, Canada, Greece, Portugal and Switzerland. In 1959, Iraq had its first woman minister in Iraq's modern history, and the first woman cabinet minister in the Arab world, Naziha ad-Dulaimi, as minister of municipalities. All regimes since the 1920s up to 1968 have generally tried to improve life for women in Iraq. There were ups and downs which were in line with changing political climate. Thus when Qasim amended the Iraqi Personal Status Law so that women could share inheritance equally with men as opposed to having half the share of men, the 1963 coup reversed that under pressure from Islamic elements who took part in the coup.[145]

When the Ba'ath assumed power in 1968 and in line with their ambitious plans for developing modern Iraq, a few legislative Acts were passed in order to improve the status of women and achieve rapid economic development,[146] Article 19 of the Iraqi Provisional Constitution 1970 declares that "all citizens are equal before the law regardless of sex, blood, language, social origin, or religion." It may be argued that many constitutions have such a clause but not activated in reality. The Ba'ath went on to enact several other laws to enforce that equality. The Compulsory Education Law (118/1976) made it compulsory for children of both sexes to attend school between the ages of six to ten after which girls were allowed to leave school with the approval of their parents or guardians.[147] This legislation was indeed enforced and by the 1980s all children in Iraq in that age group were enrolled and attended school. At the same time the gap between the sexes in literacy shrank when a law, 'The Law of the National Comprehensive Campaign for the Compulsory Eradication of Illiteracy No 92/1978', was passed to eradicate illiteracy. It was a revolutionary legislation by any standard. It called on all illiterate Iraqi men and women between the age of fifteen and forty-five to attend classes at 'literacy centers' created throughout the country. It met with strong opposition, especially in conservative rural parts of the country, but 'despotism' exercised on behalf of the nation seems to have had the power to do good. By 1982 Iraq had achieved a success not paralleled by any developing country or even some developed countries in having eradicated illiteracy. The impact of this revolutionary measure in education should not be underestimated. It opened the horizons of people and raised the self-esteem of adults who had never before imagined their ability to read and write and share in their children's education.

In extending the equal treatment of women the Ba'ath Government promulgated Labour Law 151/1970 (later repealed by Law 81/1987)[148] which granted women equal pay with men and freedom from harassment in the workplace. The Maternal Leave Law of 1987 allowed women to have a fully paid six months maternity leave with another six months leave at half pay.[149]

It could of course be argued that the Ba'ath should have done more for women such as repealing the law enabling a husband to discipline his wife or equating women to men in inheritance rights. But there are several factors to be taken into account when assessing the possibilities of such expectations. Prevailing cultural values, which take a long time to change, were in action against such changes. But the most important element against such dramatic changes, we believe, is due to the cultural twisting of Islamic teaching, which has gone on for some fourteen centuries and would take more than just legislation to change.

But this trend of securing decent and equitable standards for women in what is in fact a patriarchal society was to be reversed soon after the invasion of 2003. In fact the promised democracy of Bremer led to a wave of assaults on Iraqi women. Soon after the invasion and the dismantling of the state without creating an alternative, women in Iraq generally and in Baghdad particularly faced a wave of kidnapping which was difficult to understand. Human Rights Watch (HRW) documented a wave of "sexual violence and abductions against women in Baghdad."[150] Another HRW report tells us that "after 2003, militias, insurgents, Iraqi security forces, multinational forces, and foreign private military contractors raped and killed women."[151] The report goes on to indicate that no Iraqi has yet been charged with rape although one example of one US soldier who raped a 14 year-old girl and killed her and her family is cited. Women and girls were kept out of schools and work as a matter of self-preservation.[152]

It is true that during the last years of the sanctions era women were beginning to be subjected to changes in their status when the Ba'ath fell under the influence of religious zealots who advocated and pioneered the so-called 'campaign of faith'.[153] But the collapse of the state in 2003 with no alternative mechanism to protect women unleashed new powers and authority. In Iraqi society, the culturally-based practice of 'honour killing' still exists. Tribal customs, religious fundamentalist practices and patriarchal family values prevailed and led to deleterious effect on women's rights. All in all this led to a state in which the women in Iraq whom Laura Bush promised to save ended up "with less rights and more violence" than they ever faced during the previous eighty years.[154] The usually conservative HRW, as a result of its survey, made the following statement on the status of women in Iraq in 2011:

> The deterioration of security since 2003, combined with a rise in tribal influence, religiously-inflected political extremism, and hardline conservative political parties, have all had a deleterious effect on women and girls.[155]

Zillah Eisenstein, an active feminist who has researched the status of Iraqi women since the invasion and occupation, observed that "It is hard to say which is worse: an almost secular state with a totalitarian ruler named Saddam Hussein, or right wing religious extremists vying for their patriarchal vision of life."[156] She advises us that neither Bush nor Obama have had the protection of women's rights at the center of their policies in Iraq, despite this forming one of the focal talking points justifying their policies. She also informs us of the activity of a group called "MADRE", which has been on the ground in Iraq for nearly a decade researching and cataloguing the rape and abuse of Iraqi women by US and Iraqi forces. We believe that most Iraqi women today would prefer the former over the latter if that is the only choice available to them.

One of the most serious changes that have befallen women in Iraq has been trafficking in women, which has lasting effects on the fabric of society. It is true that during the latest times of the sanctions era, when some families began to find it impossible to feed their children, some of them in desperation resorted to marrying their daughters off in arranged marriages to people outside Iraq, which enabled them to have one less mouth to feed plus a good dowry for the married young girl. But since the invasion this practice became even more sinister. We are not going to dwell on the reason as to why families would sell their children, be that out of greed, a real need of money, or effects of the promiscuous way of life brought into Iraq by the invaders. But whatever the reason, Iraq has unfortunately become one of the main exporters of prostitutes in the Middle East in the second decade of the twenty-first century.

The conservative Iraqi society, which up until the 1990s did not know much migration, has suddenly been shaken and transformed by war and its effect with dramatic changes in moral values not very different to those changes that took place in Europe between the two World Wars or to a larger degree following WWII. Wars seem to produce such results. In Iraq this has led to enslavement of women and girls who are forced into prostitution, which "follows market demand and, in post-conflict situations, that demand is often created by international peacekeepers."[157] Although it is accepted that sexual violence has accompanied warfare throughout history, nevertheless "what is happening in Iraq today reveals how far a once progressive country (relative to its neighbours) has regressed on the issue of women's rights and how ferociously the seams of a traditional Arab society, that values female virginity, have been ripped apart."[158] No one really knows how deep an impact this sex market will have on women's values, the family and Iraq in general.

Trafficking in women in Iraq has become big business. HRW tells us that demand for young girls between the ages 11 and 12 is very high where 'sick' old men from the Gulf are willing to pay up to $30,000 for each child.[160] Girls who are above 20 are considered by the market to be too old to fetch a good price—their price may be as low as $2,000.

It seems that many people have taken part in this new practice of exported prostitution. A trafficker would marry four girls and take them to Syria or Jordan. Once there he would divorce them into the slave market and come back to marry another four and so on. His repeated practice would naturally raise some questions among immigration officers on border control, but as corruption has become the norm in Iraq, they will keep quiet so long as they are well looked after. Another supporting element in the sex market has been a religious practice among both Sunni and Shi'ia clergy where both have acquiesced in accepting temporary marriage, known as *Misyar* for the former and *Mut'a* for the latter.[161] So Islam, which was meant to protect vulnerable women, has been twisted in democratic Iraq into a tool of torture, honour killing and sexual enslavement. HRW has recorded several cases where women, especially widows in need of help, had been harassed by clergies to enter into temporary marriage, in return for favours in securing work for them.[162]

It has been estimated that "4,000 Iraqi women, one-fifth of whom are under 18, have disappeared in broad daylight since the 2003 invasion; many are believed to have been trafficked."[163]

The Grab for Iraq's Oil

When the British imperialists occupied Iraq in 1918, they made sure that whatever the political outcome of that occupation was going to be, there would be no negotiation over their full ownership of the promising oil reserves of Iraq. They forced the puppet Government which they planted in Baghdad to grant them rights to explore all of Iraq for oil for close to 90 years.[164] The agreement was a very sinister one, centred on serving the interests of the giant international oil companies with total disregard for Iraq's interests. Thus prices were fixed by the oil companies, and level of production was determined by them with no role for Iraq in either.

This state of affairs dragged on until the 1958 coup led by General Qasim, who started negotiations with the oil companies to change the agreement leasing all of Iraq to them. The resistance of the oil companies to any such change was strong and manipulative; they reacted by supporting many political movements opposed to Qasim. When these negotiations failed, Qasim promulgated the most revolutionary law in the history of Iraq in the 20th century, opening the way to many political upheavals and changes and causing, among other things, the downfall of Qasim himself. Law 81 of 1961 took away oil companies' rights to all of Iraq that had not yet been exploited by them, which amounted to some 99% of Iraq's land. After the 1963 coup which toppled General Qasim, there was inaction on oil for some time, in part planned by the oil companies and implemented by their allies within Iraq's political elite of the 1960s and in part caused by infighting over political supremacy in Iraq.[165]

However, when the Ba'ath assumed total power over Iraq in 1968, a new approach to oil, which the Ba'ath considered to be the pivotal point in the development of Iraq, was put into motion. New serious negotiations were conducted between the oil companies and an ambitious and revolutionary Iraqi team led by the young Saddam Hussein. When the negotiations began to drag on again, the oil companies put pressure on Iraq by cutting production levels. The Ba'ath Government took the lead and embarked on a nationalization program that by 1975 put all of Iraq's oil in the hands of the Iraqis for the first time since it was discovered.

Between 1975 and 2003 Iraqis managed to exploit, produce, refine and export oil without the need for the giant international oil companies which had previously exercised control over Iraq's oil for over forty years. When the total blockade was imposed on Iraq in 1990, oil was an immediate casualty, as was indeed intended. In the years before the Oil for Food program was put into action, no spare parts were allowed into Iraq even for the vital oil industry, which forced Iraq to rely on the black market and smuggling to maintain the vital services for exploitation and pumping. But even after the introduction of the Oil for Food Program, the dictatorial Sanctions Committee, whose decisions did not need to be justified, could not be appealed and could be made by any of its fifteen members, prevented many orders for oil spare parts to be honoured despite demand for them by the experts appointed by Kofi Annan, the UN Secretary General. The effects were so dire that Annan advised the Security Council that Iraq's oil industry was on the verge of collapse.[166] In a statement to the same meeting, the SG stated:

> ...However, Iraq's oil industry is seriously hampered by lack of parts and equipment, and this threatens to undermine the Programme's income in the longer term.
>
> That is why I have repeatedly recommended a significant increase in the allocation of resources under the Programme for the purchase of spare parts for the oil industry. I understand that the Council is now ready to consider these recommendations favourably, and I would very much welcome that.
>
> But I should also mention that many of the "holds" on contract applications, imposed by members of the 661 Committee, do have a direct negative impact on the humanitarian programme, and on efforts to rehabilitate Iraq's infrastructure, most of which is in appalling disrepair. We need a mechanism to review these holds, in order to ensure the smooth functioning of the Programme.[167]

Why should it be thought that Iraq needs foreign oil companies to take over its oil industry today when it has successfully managed it alone for forty years up to 2003?

It is well understood that oil is a significant factor in the geopolitical map of the Middle East. Oil has been and will remain vital for the world's economy until an alternative cheap and abundant source of energy, like hydrogen, solar or wind power, becomes available. Predictably, the capitalist imperialists want to control not only the exploitation of oil but also its marketing. The control over oil is a very powerful tool to intimidate nations that have no sources of energy themselves. The clout which the US would have over Japan and Germany once it controls all the world sources of energy, its production and its distribution, should not be underestimated. As Iraq was estimated in the most recent study by the Center for Global Energy Studies and Petrolog & Associates to have a known reserve of 300 billion barrels (bbl), which means that at the current production rate of nearly 3 million barrels/day it will be pumping oil at this rate for the next 300 years, making it a leading candidate among states whose oil, so they felt, should be under the control of the current world imperialists.[168] There was another reason for the desire to control Iraq's oil. For the cost of as little as $1 per barrel for the production of Iraq's oil, inclusive of all exploration, oilfield development, production costs and a 15% return, Iraq's oil was the cheapest in the world to produce![169]

The revival of interest in securing Iraq's oil began early in the 1990s following the crippling sanctions of 1991.

> Earlier, in 1993, six giant oil companies, Royal Dutch Shell, British Petroleum, Conoco Phillips, Exxon Mobil, Halliburton and Chevron, sponsored the International Tax and Investment Center (ITIC) which eventually included 110 corporations. Documents obtained through the Freedom of Information Act reveal that in late 1990s Anglo-American representations were made on behalf of oil companies to secure Iraqi oil contracts. ITIC was advised to write a report emphasizing Production Sharing Agreements (PSA) to ensure the success of long-term control over oil.[170]

Thus it was clear from the early stages of the blockade that the oil giants were out to secure as big a share as possible in Iraq's oil when they were advised, as were individual Iraqis, that the US was not going to ease sanctions on Iraq until the regime either changes or collapses.

The Future of Iraq Project (FIP), referred to in Chapter 3, outlined US preparation for the invasion of Iraq, which was declared by Rumsfeld on 11 September 2001.[171] It gathered some 200 Zionist Iraqis and divided them into 17 working groups led and managed by US experts and intelligence servicemen in order to prepare the post-Ba'ath policies for Iraq. One of those working groups addressed 'Oil and Energy' as would have been expected. Not surprisingly, the group concluded that Iraq's oil industry should be opened to private investment and called for the establishment of Production Sharing Agreements (PSA) between Iraq and multinational oil companies,[172] which would enable the return of foreign control of Iraq's oil. The conclusion of the 'Oil and Energy' group was, again unsurprisingly, precisely what the ITIC had recommended for the future of Iraq's oil earlier in 1990s.[173] One of the members of the 'Oil and Energy' group was Ibrahim Bahr al-Uloum who, in September 2003, was appointed by Bremer as Iraq's new post-invasion Oil Minister.

It was natural for the US/UK while planning to invade and occupy Iraq to deny that it was even partly because of oil. But when in history has an invader ever declared his true reasons for aggression? However, it was unavoidable that some statements openly declared that oil indeed topped the list of reasons for invading Iraq. Here is a sample of these statements:

- In 1999 while acting as CEO of Halliburton, Dick Cheney said: "... While many regions of the world offer great oil opportunities, the Middle East with two thirds of the world's oil and the lowest cost, is still where the prize ultimately lies."[174]

- General John Abizaid, former Commander of CENTCOM, who was responsible for Iraq, said: "Of course it's about oil. We can't really deny that."[175]

- Chuck Hagel, the recently replaced US Secretary of Defense, said in 2007: *"People say we're not fighting for oil. Of course we are.* They talk about America's national interest. What the hell do you think they're talking about? We're not there for figs.[176]

- Former Federal Reserve Chairman Alan Greenspan wrote in 2007: "I am saddened that it is politically inconvenient to acknowledge what everyone knows: 'the Iraq war is largely about oil.' What other evidence do deniers need before accepting this obvious reality?"[177]

In the first week of Bush's first term in office and following up on his statement of 1999, Dick Cheney set up the National Energy Policy Development Group, bringing the administration and the oil companies together to plot the collective energy future. "In March, the task force reviewed lists and maps outlining Iraq's entire oil productive capacity."[178] This was further evidence that the invasion of Iraq was planned even before the 9/11 attack. Why else would the group chaired by Cheney be studying a map of Iraq's oil sites in March 2000? Paul O'Neill, Bush's first Treasury secretary, is quoted as having said that "already by February [2001], the talk was mostly about logistics, not the why [to invade Iraq], but the how and how quickly."[179]

In the UK the oil companies were just as active in pursuit of securing Iraq's oil. Agreements between British Petroleum (BP) and other transnational corporations to operate in Iraq existed before the invasion, demonstrating further that the invasion was planned not in search of WMDs as were alleged by USA/UK Governments. The UK based *Independent* newspaper, although arguing that oil was not the primary motivation for the war, commented on these agreements and their effects on the Iraq Enquiry as follows:

....they do make it clear that, contrary to ministerial

denials, oil was something that ministers were thinking about in those months prior to the invasion.

These documents were not, apparently, reviewed by the Chilcot inquiry, which has been tasked with investigating Britain's involvement in the Iraq invasion. That is manifestly unsatisfactory. No independent inquiry into the Iraq imbroglio can be complete without taking into account the influence of Big Oil. Unless Chilcot takes this important new evidence into consideration, it is hard to see how its conclusions can be credible.[180]

There was pressure from the oil companies for Bremer to pass a new oil law in Iraq enabling the seizure of Iraqi oil by these companies. But the administration decided to be more prudent as it would have been very difficult to pass such a law while still maintaining its argument that Iraq had not been invaded because of a desire to seize its oil. Towards that end, Ibrahim Bahr al-Uloum was appointed Oil Minister in September 2003, in the hope that he would implement such a law for them.

Between 2004 and 2008 the US tried, using all its influence, to get support for the proposed Iraq Hydrocarbon Law which would have ensured the success of the Cheney plan for Production Sharing Agreements (PSAs). But it faced strong resistance even among some of its Iraqi puppets like the Speaker of Parliament, Usama al-Nujeyfi. The main opposition, however, came from the general public spearheaded by the Iraqi Federation of Oil Unions representing half of oil workers in southern Iraq.[181]Upon failing to pass the proposed law through Iraq's Parliament, the US devised a new approach, designing new long term contracts between the Iraqi Oil Ministry and the oil companies which granted the companies almost all they demanded except the privatization of the oil industry and thus keeping the industry nominally under Government control. These contracts do not oblige the oil companies to keep produced oil in Iraq; to invest any of the returns in the country or employ a majority of Iraqis in the industry.[182] The details of the contracts signed between the Ministry of Oil and the oil companies are not publicly available; such information is pieced together from media reports and scattered statements made by some officials.

Dr Abdulhay Yahya Zalloum, an international oil consultant with forty years' experience, commented that western oil companies have successfully acquired the lions' share of Iraq's oil, but they gave a little piece of the cake for China and some of the other countries and companies to keep them silent[183]—and likely to obscure their dominant presence. The available information today gives the following map:

- BP and CNPC [China National Petroleum Corporation]

was awarded one of the largest oil fields in the country, the 17 billion barrel super giant Rumayla field.

• ExxonMobil, with junior partner Royal Dutch Shell, won the 8.7 billion barrel West Qurna Phase 1 project beating Russia's Lukoil.

• Italy's Eni SpA, with California's Occidental Petroleum and the Korea Gas Corp, was awarded Iraq's Zubair oil field with estimated reserves of 4.4 billion barrels.

• Shell was the lead partner with Malaysia's Petroliam Nasional Bhd., awarded a contract for the super-giant Majnoon field, one of the largest in the world, with estimated reserves of up to 25 billion.[184]

Thus although the US and other Western oil companies were not successful in securing the passage of a new Iraq Oil Law which would have secured privatization using Production Sharing Agreements (PSAs), they managed through separate contracts to get a foot in the door which would enable them to reap huge profits from a country whose reserve is estimated to be around 300bbl, with only around 2000 wells and only 10% of its land exploited so far.

Forty years after Iraq nationalized its oil industry and ran it successfully, foreign multinational oil companies were brought back by the invasion to control Iraq's oil under the disguise of Iraq's need for technical and financial support. The new contracts have been awarded to the same companies whose interests were nationalized in the 1970s. It is part of the continuous destruction of Iraq.

Utilities

In our modern world everything depends on electricity. In every aspect of life electricity is needed. Stop the supply of electricity and everything comes to a standstill—from operating your laptop to controlling air traffic. It provided the most devastating tool to cripple Iraq during the blockade years when Iraq was denied not only an opportunity to build new power stations but also access to spare parts to refurbish ageing generators, sub-stations and distribution networks.

During the Ba'ath rule, a full distribution grid was installed that covered the whole country and generation was ahead of demand so much that Iraq exported electricity to Turkey in 1987.[185] In his final report to Congress titled "Learning from Iraq", the Special Inspector General for Iraq Reconstruction (SIGIR) who was appointed by Congress to oversee

Iraq's reconstruction, started his section on electricity by confirming this fact with the following statement: "During the 1980s, average electricity production from Iraq's power plants increased from about 1,200 megawatts to 3,100 MW, generally keeping pace with rising demand."[186]

During the massive 1991 US attack on Iraq allegedly to drive Iraq out of Kuwait, all except two of Iraq's 20 power-generating stations were knocked out of service.[187] This is how the *New England Medical Journal* Special Report described it:

> In the first days of the war, 13 of Iraq's 20 power generating plants were incapacitated or destroyed. At the end of the bombing only two plants remained operational producing less than 4% of the pre-war output. By early May 1991, Iraq had regained only 23% of pre-war output. Many of the power plants were destroyed beyond repair and will have to be completely rebuilt. At the time of our visit, damaged facilities could only be repaired by cannibalizing parts from other plants.[188]

Indeed cannibalizing was the norm which restored part of the capacity for some time, while the Iraqi government held onto the naïve hope that sanctions were going to be eased on spare parts for electricity, if not completely lifted. When it was no longer possible to buy spare parts as before, Iraqis resorted to buying spare parts on the black markets and smuggling them into the country—the only available alternative before the Oil for Food Program at last allowed some spare parts in, albeit with some difficulties and delays. But the Program did not enable Iraq to build new generating plants as was required and had been planned before the Kuwait crisis. It followed naturally that as demand was increasing and the ailing plants failed to deliver their maximum output, a serious shortage resulted.

Thus on the eve of the 2003 invasion Iraq was only producing just over 4000 Megawatts when the estimated demand was at least double that figure. The looting and sabotage that resulted from the 'creative chaos' brought about by the invasion, with US/UK acquiescence, led to electricity production falling to a mere 711 Megawatts by June 2003.[189]Despite the fact that the importance of electricity in rebuilding Iraq could not be overestimated and although Bremer had the kind of authority no one had ever had in Iraq, had all the money he needed and the military to protect any plan to build new power generating plants, he left Iraq with only one single contract awarded to build one single station [190] Indeed, "by the time the Americans handed over power to an Iraqi interim government in June 2004, production had climbed back up to 3,621 megawatts per day."[191] But with all the US and international expertise at his disposal, Bremer could not even regain the pre-war output level which Saddam Hussein managed despite 12 years of total blockade. Had there been a genuine intention to rebuild Iraq as we have been repeatedly told, Bremer could have called upon US and international companies to make offers for some five new plants of 1000MW each in areas close to fuel sources and awarded them before his departure. Had he done so, Iraq would have had doubled its electrical generating capacity by 2006-2007 and Iraqis would have been given a glimpse of a decent life after nearly 20 years of deprivation, and all of that would have been paid for by half of the $20 *billion* that went missing under Bremer's watch.

There is more than one aspect to the supply of electricity. It is not sufficient to generate it. There should be enough substations to step down the voltage from generation to usage in addition to networks of overhead lines and cables to carry the electricity from the plants to the user and around the country in a grid. The looting referred to above was not of generating stations but rather of substations and the grid. Copper was sought after as an easy way of making money. Cables and transformers have plenty of copper which once melted could not be traced. Iraq was the first country in the Arab East to have had a fully integrated microwave network operating in the 1970s using coaxial cables and microwave relay stations covering the full country. Large sections of the valuable coaxial cable were dug out in the 1990s and sold by Kurdish fighters as copper in Iran. It was not surprising that such practice extended on a larger scale when Iraq was invaded and the US/UK either encouraged the looting or did nothing to stop it. This is how the SIGIR reported it:

> The pre-invasion bombing and subsequent combat damaged nearly 50 electrical transmission towers, and by mid-June 2003, 700 towers had been destroyed by looters who stripped them of valuable metals for sale in Iran and Kuwait.[192]

The immediate result of this was a real degradation of the 132kV system which has been in need of "extensive repairs, rehabilitation and expansion, as it is the cause of many of the power cuts, especially in and around Baghdad"[193] as reported by the UNDP in 2011. So even if the generating capacity had improved, which it had not, the supply of electricity would have still been interrupted because of the failure of the transmission system. However in the eight years after the invasion, neither Bremer, nor any of the slave Governments that followed thereafter, did much to rectify this imbalance. In ten years between 1970 and 1980 the Ba'ath Government not only generated a surplus of electricity but built and maintained a grid to cover all of Iraq.

The same UNDP report advises us that the prospects for the delivery of electricity is being portrayed as not possible by 2015-2016 because of the failure to rectify the shortcomings of the distribution system grid. This is how the report puts it:

> Iraq needs to conduct an inventory and assessment of the condition of the entire distribution network [only a sample was analyzed by consulting firm] as a necessary precondition to design the absolutely essential investment project in rehabilitation/replacement of individual feeders and secondary distribution networks. The investment required for the distribution systems (grids) averages $2.6 billion per year between 2011 and 2015, or a total of $13.2 billion over 2011-2015. But more than money, this very painstaking kind of work requires time and must be started in all areas that are to receive important increases in supply.[194]

But what is the true story on the generating side? We are advised that the "cumulative supply on Iraq's grid in 2012, drawn from all sources, averaged about 8,400 MW, which was 3,225 MW higher than the total output from government power plants."[195] Simple arithmetic leads us to conclude that Iraqi State plants were generating 5,175 MW in 2012. But we know that on the eve of the 2003 invasion and despite the blockade and devastation, Iraq was producing over 4000MW. It seems that nine years after the establishment of democracy and the massive sums of money allocated for electricity from both the US and Iraq, they managed to increase the production by a mere 1175MW. There are only two possible explanations for such a dismal performance: Either there was a determined will to prevent any real reconstruction, or the corruption was so massive that the real question that should again be asked is: Where did all the money go?

The difference between the output of the States' plants and the available output came from three other sources:[196]

> 1.   Private Power Plants in Kurdistan which produced nearly 2000MW by the summer of 2012. This venture was very much in line with Bremer's plan for privatization of all utilities in Iraq. Some attempts were made to encourage the Central Government in Baghdad to imitate the experiment but were faced with strong resistance because the Iraqi public would find it difficult to accept the concept of privatized electricity.

> 2.   Turkish Powerships [sic] in Basrah which supplied just over 200MW by 2012.

3.   Imports of electricity which reached about 1000MW and were mainly from Iran. However, this has not gone smoothly and may not be repeated. The reason has been the failure of the Iraqi Trading Bank to transfer to Iran the sums due because of the refusal of the corresponding US bank to carry out the transaction by virtue of the US economic sanctions against Iran.[197]

As the generation and distribution of electricity is highly technical, some parts of the jigsaw may neither be clear nor easily understood by the general public. One such matter is the misleading statement that the current generating capacity of some 8000MW in Iraq equals half of the current demand. The relationship between the existing capacity and the actual demand is rather more complex than that, which renders short sweeping statements about meeting the expected demand in a couple of years sound even more hollow. The 2011 UNDP Report puts it as follows:

> The Iraqi electric power system has limitations of both capacity (the number of MWs installed and/or needed) and energy (the number of MW hours generated and/ or needed), and therefore, the estimate that 50% of demand is not met is, most likely, a gross underestimate ...The 50% deficit would be accurate if both the peak demand and the peak generation capacity were correct AND the energy generated (in MWh) were exactly 50% of the energy demanded (in MWh). So, the deficit is much greater than 50% when calculated accurately.[198]

Despite this warning from UNDP, we have the SIGIR advising us that:

> As of September 2012, the GOI's Ministry of Electricity had 41 power plants under construction. These new plants could increase generating capacity to 22,000 MW by the end of 2015. Assuming no delays, the International Energy Agency estimated that Iraq's gridbased electricity generation would catch up to peak demand by 2015.[199]

It remains to be seen whether or not the Iraqis are at last going to have some decent electricity supply which they have not had since 1991 or is this going to be another failed promise like the one Bremer made as reported by the SIGIR:

In July 2003, the CPA established the goals of increasing
generating capacity to 4,000 MW by October 2003, to
5,000 MW by January 2004, to 7,000 MW by 2005,
and to 14,000 MW by 2009. That same month, the
CPA made a more ambitious prediction: electricity
supply would be back to prewar levels of 4,400 MW
by October 2003.[200]

This turned out to be a mirage like many of Bremer's promises!

Water

The supply of fresh drinking water did not fare any better since
the invasion although the matter has not been so severe because of the
simple fact that nature has been kind to Iraqis in providing them with
several sources of fresh water.

During the golden years of Iraq's prosperity under the Ba'ath
Government of the 1970s, the government embarked on a plan to provide
drinking water to remote parts of the country. Villages that were not
covered by a fresh water network were provided with compact units that
addressed the needs of the particular village. It is reported that by the
1980s more than 90% of all Iraqis had sustained access to clean drinking
water.[201] Water, like every other necessity of life, was affected by the
blockade—which was the purpose of imposing it. In the 1990s the service
deteriorated due to several factors including the blockade on importing
spare parts and even chlorine. It seems that the same evil people in the
Sanctions Committee, who decided that pencils should not be allowed
into Iraq because graphite in them could be used in Nuclear Reactors,
were also the decision makers concerning chlorine, and thought that
chlorine should be banned because it could be converted into chemical
weapons!

Thus by mid 1990s, the percentage of Iraqis having access
to fresh water dropped to 81%.[202] The situation deteriorated further
when according to the SIGIR "by 2003, this sector had experienced a
devastating decline. Water distribution lines deteriorated from age, and
the corroded system allowed contaminants in, causing a sharp rise in
disease rates."[203] But the SIGIR did not even attempt to explain why the
supply of water had reached such a state by 2003. UNICEF acknowledged
that by 2002 approximately 25% of all children's deaths in Iraq were
caused by waterborne bacteria which were due to the failing supply of
fresh water.[204] Much of the urban network was probably damaged by
bombs and tanks, and there was a lack of spare parts and water treatment
chemicals and facilities.

The SIGIR advises us that the US Government spent over $2.71 billion to rehabilitate and improve Iraq's water and sanitation sector.[205] Whatever actually happened to that money is not clear but the end results by 2012 do not have much to show. Let us consider one example. The Nasiriya water supply project was awarded in April 2004 and completed in September 2007 at a cost of $277 million.[206] It was designed to serve some 500,000 people in five surrounding cities. The SIGIR advises us that it was well executed and handed over to Iraqi control. But soon after that, the SIGIR visited the project, met with local people and officials, and concluded that the system was falling apart and suffering from regular breakdowns due to poor operation and maintenance.[207]

How is it possible that Iraqis had managed for decades to operate and maintain their water supply systems without any problem, only to find after 2003 that they could not maintain a small water treatment plant in Nasiriyah? Is it not because all the skilled people have been killed, imprisoned, or exiled as a result of the invasion?

So what is the current situation of fresh water supply in Iraq?

> In March 2011, the United Nations reported that, while Iraq had the second-highest amount of available water per capita in the Middle East, its water quality was poor, violating Iraq National Standards and World Health Organization guidelines.[208]

A survey of nearly 30,000 households conducted in 2011 by the Iraqi Ministry of Planning Statistics Organization, the Kurdistan Regional Statistics Office and the UN, and reported by the Iraq Knowledge Network (IKN) found that:

> ... more than one-quarter of the population had access to water from the general network for less than two hours a day, and nearly half the population rated the quality of water services in their area as bad or very bad.[209]

The SIGIR report advises Congress that the Nassiriya plant began to suffer breakdowns shortly after its transfer to Iraqi control.[210] We do not know whether or not Congress questioned the reasons for this failure considering that Iraq managed to run its water plants quite well for eighty years even during the difficult years of total blockade and shortages of spares. In fact the SIGIR's report goes further and states that:

> After the United States turned over the large water projects to Iraqi control, reconstruction officials

discovered that, in many cases, the Iraqis were not operating these projects properly. Shortfalls included equipment theft, badly trained staff, poor operations and maintenance practices, and inadequate supplies of electricity and treatment chemicals.[211]

While addressing all the failures of infrastructure in post-2003 Iraq would require a full book to do justice to the topic, we still feel compelled to refer to the matter of the Mosul Dam to highlight the failure in handling this dangerous state of affairs. In 1984, and during the Iran-Iraq war, Iraq completed the construction of the Mosul Dam on the Tigris River to supply drinking water, irrigation, flood control, and hydroelectric power to the region. The authorities in charge of the Dam noticed in the late 1980s that the soil under it was being eroded and there was a real fear of the Dam collapsing and creating a Biblical flood that could flood the Tigris valley from Mosul to north Baghdad.[212] The Iraqis tried to solve this problem by carrying grouting programs to fill the sub-surface cavities under the dam's structure to stop the danger of the erosion. The treatment failed and there was a real need for international experts to come to the rescue of Iraq. However, it was then the 1990s and the total blockade prevented that. Several applications were made by Iraq to the Sanctions Committee to invite international consultants to make an appraisal of the danger and recommend remedial solutions. But the US blocked the Iraqi request without giving reasons, as was the prevailing practice of the Sanctions Committee.[213] Needless to say, in addition to the serious danger of the collapse of the Mosul Dam, repairing the dam could not have enhanced Iraq's capacity to develop WMDs which was the alleged excuse for imposing the blockade.

It was not until 2005 that the US Government started a project consisting of awarding some 21 contracts worth $27 million to mitigate the dam's deficiencies. But this project went just like other projects post 2003. It was left without any monitoring body or accountability, so much so that the SIGIR inspectors reported in 2007 that: "The inspection concluded that approximately $19.4 million worth of equipment and materials for implementing improvements to the grouting operations was not being used." [214]

As we have shown in the short presentation in this section, there has been a general failure in supplying utilities and providing services in Iraq. The question that forces itself is why have the occupiers and their collaborating governments failed so dramatically compared to the previous regime despite the availability of money, international technical expertise and the massive international political and military backup?

We suggest that there are two reasons for these failures. Firstly, the de-Ba'athification policy, the assassinations, intimidations and threats, had depleted Iraq of its intelligentsia, including skilled engineers and technicians, which left many utilities to be run by semi-literate army deserters who had come back from Iran and elsewhere and were rewarded by Bremer for having served US interests in fighting Saddam Hussein.[215] Secondly, since 2003 corruption became the norm in Iraq. It has become standard that you must pay somebody for everything, even if you are applying to get a copy of a legitimate birth certificate. During the Ba'ath rule of Iraq, officials who were caught accepting bribes, especially from foreign companies, were tried and executed. Post 2003, newcomers who came with the invaders from the US, Europe, Iran, and Syria were running the government departments. Most of those new officials had been deprived for so long that big money was tempting. Power corrupts and corruption is an erosive process. Slowly it crept into every department until the accepted norm became that no project could be awarded without a bribe. This chaotic state of corruption was fuelled by the fact that many US officials and contractors were themselves involved in corruption and a few were caught by the SIGIR office.[216]

Only one service has flourished in Iraq since the invasion, that of mobile telephones. Prior to 2003, Iraq had no mobile phone service, but no sooner had the invaders landed than several companies sprang up offering such a developed communication service to the people of Iraq, some of whom had never had a telephone. The reason for this exception in offering Iraqis good service, unlike all other services, lay in two facts: who owns it and how much revenue it is producing!

The first mobile telecommunications company in Iraq, Asiacell, was established in the city of Suleimaniyah in northern Iraq in 1999. As one of the largest providers of telecommunication services, its network covers 99% of Iraq's population, enjoying about 43% of market share.[217] Asiacell's key shareholder is Qatar Telecom (Ooredoo) which owns 64.1% of the company. The net profit of Asiacell as of 19 November 2013 was ID 471.8 Billion (about $383 million).[218]

The second company is Korek Telecom, Iraq's third largest mobile operator, which was established in 2000 in Erbil in Northern Iraq and is therefore the second oldest telecom company in Iraq.[219] In March 2011, France Telecom Orange acquired 20% of the company's shares, while Agility, a Kuwaiti logistics company, holds a 24 per cent indirect stake. Korek has around 3 million mobile customers.[220] The company is alleged to be owned by the Kurdistan Democratic Party (KDP) and its leader, Massoud Barzani. Korek's managing director has denied these allegations.[221] There are no profit figures publicly available for the company.

Another leading operator is Zain Iraq, which was established in December 2003 and currently serves over 13.5 million customers, with a network that covers more than 98% of the population.[222] 76% of the shares are owned by the Zain Group, which was established in Kuwait in 1983 and is today a leading mobile and data services operator in the Middle East and North Africa. As of 30 September 2013, the Group provides mobile voice and data services to over 44.3 million individual and business customers.[223]. The Zain Iraq net income of the first nine months of 2013 is reported to be $261m.[224]

The last telecom company operating in Iraq is "Itisaluna Abr Al Iraq". It is the latest National Fixed Wireless Voice and Data Telecommunications Company in Iraq. Established in 2007, the company has succeeded in its work by mainstreaming a wireless local loop network through utilizing CDMA technology. The headquarters of the company is in Amman, Jordan. The company claims over 200,000 customers.[225] No official financial information is available on the company.

It is obvious that this industry has prospered because a few powerful Iraqis are making huge profits along with foreign investors. The state owned Iraqi Telecom has been kept out of the field through a political decision.

9

THE
RIGHT OF
REMEDY

For decades the Security Council (SC) has acted with impunity as a court of law passing judgment on nations: imposing sanctions on innocent people; depriving them of their basic human rights and even legitimizing unjust wars in the name of securing international peace and security. In Volume I of *Genocide in Iraq* we identified the crimes committed by the imperialists against the Iraqi people during the genocidal years of total blockade and the nefarious, complicit role the SC played in these crimes.[1] In this chapter we will identify the crimes committed since the invasion and consider what remedies are available to the people of Iraq. Both catalogues of crimes considered together constitute a serious condemnation of all those who took part in them; acquiesced; or kept silent when these crimes were being committed.

It is a blot on the Western conscience.

The Inviolability of Security Council Resolutions

As the victors of WWII have dominated the SC, it is not too surprising that none of the punitive measures available under the UN Charter were taken against those powers or their immediate allies and clients. The presumption that the SC was entitled to act as effectively a ruling world judiciary and executive was not only accepted by the judiciary in the West, but also indeed welcomed as it saved them from the embarrassment of having to find arguments for their refusals to hear blatant breaches of international law committed by their governments. This effectively meant that crimes were committed but went unpunished on the ground that these actions were committed under the authority of a SC resolution.

This was best summed up by Lord Hope in expressing his inability to hear a case of possible breach of law because he believed the authorities in Iraq were acting under the authority of the SC.[2]

Heretofore, the question of the legality of Security Council Resolutions and their implementation has not been open to wide discussion or argument in the UK. The predominant wisdom has been that as they deal with issues of international politics they remain outside the jurisdiction of courts. This is the law upheld in the UK and by the ICJ.

The prevailing view among the judiciary both in the UK and at the ICJ is that matters dealing with international politics,[3] national security, and defence[4] are acts of states and thus should not be reviewed even if they raise legal matters. On the enforceability of SC resolutions, the law in England has been that these resolutions are automatically enforced and not open to review by courts of law.[5] In the *Lockerbie* case, the ICJ ruled that the SC resolution, adopted after the ICJ had started considering a case, had overruled its authority to proceed with the consideration of the case.[6] This poses a serious problem in international law: it enables any permanent member of the SC, when in dispute with a smaller state, to resort to the SC to either secure a resolution or a declaration that the SC is seized of the matter, thus thwarting any possibility of judicial adjudication of the dispute. Such a scenario is prejudicial to the interests of smaller parties in disputes and may give rise to a miscarriage of justice. But more importantly, in our opinion, it puts the SC above the law.

However, it is refreshing to realize that this untenable state of affairs is about to change. The European Court has made a ruling unparalleled in international law since the creation of the UN and the ICJ.

The ECJ has reached views contrary to the above prevailing views. In the *Kadi* case, an opinion contrary to that prevailing in the UK on judicial review of political issues was expressed. The ECJ considered the issue of relationship between the international legal order under the UN and the Community legal order and concluded:

> In this connection it is to be borne in mind that the Community is based on the rule of law, inasmuch as neither its Member States nor its institutions can avoid review of the conformity of their acts with the basic constitutional charter, the EC Treaty, which established a complete system of legal remedies and procedures designed to enable the Court of Justice to review the legality of acts of the institutions (Case 294/83 *Les Verts v Parliament* [1986] ECR 1339, paragraph 23).[7]

The strongest opinion was expressed by Advocate General Poiares Maduro in the *Kadi* case, saying: "The implication that the present case concerns a 'political question', in respect of which even the most humble degree of judicial interference would be inappropriate, is, in my view, untenable. The claim that a measure is necessary for the maintenance of international peace and security cannot operate so as to silence the general principles of Community law and deprive individuals of their fundamental rights."[8] It is suggested here that this should be the principle under international law.

On the question of examining the conformity of SC resolutions to international law the Court of First Instance held that it is open to domestic courts to question the compatibility of the SC resolutions with *jus cogens*.[9]

Although it has never been suggested prior to our so doing in Volume I of *Genocide in Iraq*, we believe that the people of Iraq have a case in a court of law against the SC in that particular composition of individual states which voted for imposing the total blockade on Iraq and maintained it for twelve years as being a measure which breached the basic human rights of the people of Iraq, directly responsible for the deaths of innocents on a massive scale. Furthermore, we believe that the people of Iraq have a case that might rightfully be brought against members of the SC, which voted to approve what was (as subsequently admitted by the SC Secretary General) an illegal invasion of Iraq under international law, and granted the US/UK the authority to rule Iraq causing destruction, and the ongoing damage that is continuing even ten years after the invasion. Such actions may be brought by individuals or as a group action. Any national European Court of Law will be obliged to consider any such application in the light of the European Court ruling above.

The Crime of Aggression

It would only be natural for the policy makers in the US and UK to deny that they had intentionally launched a war of aggression. But when in history had an invader ever made such an admission? On 14 December 1974 the UN General Assembly adopted resolution 3314 which defined aggression and condemned it.[10] When the Statute of the International Criminal Court was being negotiated in the 1990s, there were disputes on adopting a definition for 'Aggression' so that it could be incorporated in the Statute. Thus when the Statute of Rome (as it came be known)[11] was adopted in 2002, it left the definition to be filled at a later stage. After further negotiations a resolution was adopted on 11 June 2010 which incorporated into the Statute a definition of a Crime of Aggression. [12]

It is true that the definition of the Crime of Aggression was adopted later than the invasion of Iraq. But that very definition has long been accepted by the world as constituting the meaning of aggression and was incorporated in the General Assembly Resolution 3314 which amounted to a principle under customary international law that prevailed even before the adoption of the Rome Statute. We submit that the definition of aggression as adopted and incorporated in the Rome Statute in 2010 was already a valid principle of law in 2003 and thus bound the action of the invaders of Iraq. It can be easily seen that the 'Crime of Aggression' was committed by the US/UK in invading Iraq as the following actions, as incorporated in the Statute, reflect the military actions of the US/UK:

> The invasion or attack by the armed forces of a State of the territory of another State, or any military occupation, however temporary, resulting from such invasion or attack, or any annexation by the use of force of the territory of another State or part thereof;......
>
> An attack by the armed forces of a State on the land, sea or air forces, or marine and air fleets of another State.

It follows that the people of Iraq had a case against the Governments of the US and the UK and against official individuals in both states who took the decision to invade Iraq. Such legal action may be brought by the Government of Iraq or directly by the ICC prosecutor. It is doubtful that any current government in Iraq would undertake such a measure because these governments owe their very existence to the invaders and still rely on the US for their political survival—as has been made evident by their 2014 appeal for US support in resisting the Islamic State. In short, every government in Iraq since 2004 has been a client of the US. Thus it would be unrealistic to expect any such action to be brought by an Iraqi Government.

However, there is no legal reason why individual Iraqis should not approach the prosecutor at the ICC seeking an investigation to initiate such criminal proceedings. Such action is equally available before domestic courts in such countries that assume jurisdiction in international criminal law. It should be emphasized that there is no defense in the crime of aggression that people had invited an invader to come to their rescue or that an elected Government that followed the invasion has later condoned the invasion. Murder is considered to have been committed even if the deceased had invited the killer to kill. The Crime of Aggression in Iraq will be sustained once it is established that the acts as cited above took place and that the perpetrators had a mental orientation toward committing these acts. The mental element is defined in Article 30 of the Rome Statute.[13] We believe that it will be easy to prove to a court of law that the mental element existed because both the US and UK meant to undertake the invasion of Iraq; it was a planned act and not an accident. Further, they intended the consequences of the invasion to occur, and were aware of their happening.

We would like to add one significant observation before proceeding to consider details of crimes which relate to the meaning of occupation. The US/UK were very keen to invite the SC to adopt resolutions declaring a sovereign government in Iraq in what was a clear attempt at obviating any legal liability for ruling Iraq. However, under international law a country is occupied so long as the foreign troops controlling it had not been thrown out or willingly withdrawn. Thus both the US and UK remain liable for crimes committed in Iraq until their last occupying soldier departed and no SC resolution could change that fact or eliminate legal liability.

Crimes in using WMD

In Chapter 8 we discussed the use of WMD, as defined there, and their possible effect on both general health and specific diseases. We must emphasize a very important issue that has been cleverly masked by the invaders and their scientific and legal supporters. This relates to the fundamental principle enshrined in Article 36 of the Protocol I 1977 to the Geneva Conventions 1949 which reads as follows:

> In the study, development, acquisition or adoption of a new weapon, means or method of warfare, a High Contracting Party is under an obligation to determine whether its employment would, in some or all circumstances, be prohibited by this Protocol or by any other rule of international law applicable to the High Contracting Party.[14]

It is evident from the text that its drafters appreciated the difficulty a civilian would have in showing that a new weapon had caused him/her injury or damage. But Protocol I, contrary to the normal principle under criminal law, shifted the burden of proof from the accuser to the accused. It is the duty of users of new weapons, such as depleted uranium and white phosphorous, to prove that their new weapons comply with principles of international law. We submit that the US/UK have not yet produced any scientific evidence, including their testing of these new weapons, to show that they do indeed comply with rules of international law. To simply claim, as they have been doing for the last twenty years, that there is no evidence to link any death or diseases to the use of these weapons is not sufficient to meet the criteria of Article 36. They need to provide evidence to support their claim.

The sudden rise in cancer, especially among children, and the alarming rise in birth deformities in areas that had witnessed intensive military activity during the 1991 attack and 2003 invasion and afterwards, and the discovery of heavy metals in the cells of parents of these children, are grounds for bringing legal action against the US/UK accusing them of the breach of Article 36. We believe that they will not be able to meet the requirement of Article 36 to show that these new weapons comply with rules of international law.

Assuming the remote possibility that US/UK scientists can come up with scientific evidence from their research and measurements that show no link between radioactivity of depleted uranium and the astronomical rise in cancers and other diseases, it would be impossible to show that uranium and phosphorous, for example, are not toxic. It is scientifically proven that they are. It is also legally established that the use of poisonous and toxic material in wars is forbidden. This is one of the earliest established principles of customary law of war principles. It dates back to 1675 when the Strasbourg Agreement[15] was signed banning the use of chemical weapons and which later formed the bases of the Geneva Protocol 1925.[16]

In short, individual Iraqis have a case to bring against the perpetrators of both 1991 attack and 2003 invasion for having used weapons prohibited by rules of international law by virtue of being either radioactive, toxic or both. Needless to say, any success of a legal action by any Iraqi in such a case will open the gates for US/UK personnel to sue their respective governments for having subjected them to such weapons, having worked in either transporting or delivering them.

Crimes against Humanity

The Rome Statute compiled within one paragraph what the world has accepted over the last two centuries as crimes. We shall consider two of these crimes as committed in Iraq. The first relates to paragraph (h) of Article 7 which reads:

Article 7, *'Crimes against humanity'*,

1. For the purpose of this Statute, "crime against humanity" means any of the following acts when committed as part of a widespread or systematic attack directed against any civilian population, with knowledge of the attack:

......

(h) Persecution against any identifiable group or collectivity on political, racial, national,

ethnic, cultural, religious, gender as defined in
paragraph 3, or other grounds that are universally
recognized as impermissible under international
law, in connection with any act referred to in this
paragraph or any crime within the jurisdiction of
the Court;

We have earlier addressed the passing of the de-Ba'athification
Order by the CPA.[17] We submit that the Order falls fully within paragraph
(h), having been a persecution of thousands of Iraqis simply on the
political ground of having adhered to an ideology, which is precisely what
the Rome Statute was set up to criminalize. Thousands of people lost their
jobs; families were left destitute and hundreds were arrested without
having committed any crime. This crime was incorporated in the Rome
Statute at the very time that the invaders passed the de-Ba'athification
Order and created the witch-hunt that followed.

We submit that any one of those who suffered from this crime
is entitled to remedy before a court of law. There is a strong current
public demand in Iraq to repeal the de-Ba'athification legislation and all
the measures that followed. But such demand has been resisted by the
present political leadership in Iraq because they feel it deprives them of
their legitimacy insofar as it was only due to the anti-Ba'athist policy that
they assumed power. It is inconceivable that any court of law properly
constituted and devoid of political influence will not find in favor of a
Ba'athist who suffered that persecution simply because he belonged
to the Ba'ath Party. In short such a court of law will find that the de-
Ba'athification Order was a Crime against Humanity!

In Chapter 8 we attended briefly to the torture and inhumane
treatment to which Iraqis were subjected following the 2003 invasion
at the hands of US/UK personnel. Such acts were not committed simply
at the hands of the military. Torture was committed by CIA members,
private security companies' personnel and Iraqi militias who all operated
under direct orders from the US/UK authorities or through their direct
supervision and control. As the US/UK asked the Security Council
for authority to rule Iraq and were granted such authority subject to
international law, according to which they became responsible for the
security of Iraqis and liable for any breach of law while their remit lasted.
It is no defense to argue that some acts of torture or inhuman treatments
were committed without their knowledge. The abuse in Abu Ghraib was
so well organized and so widespread that it is inconceivable that it was
committed without approval or sanction at the highest levels. It is equally
unbelievable that acts of torture committed by different militia groups,
especially between 2005 and 2007, were done without US sanction.
These militias were set up, armed and trained by the US. Are US officials

so naïve as to think that people will accept their denial of knowledge of these militias' activities? We submit that any Iraqi who had been tortured at any time during the years of occupation has a case to bring against the US/UK governments under Article 7 of the Rome Statute. Such legal action may be initiated in any country that accepts jurisdiction for crimes in the Rome Statute and need not be Iraq, the US or UK where it would be unlikely that a court of law will be sufficiently free of political influence to entertain such an application. The recent revelations about torture, though they come as no surprise to us, should enhance the argument of the Iraqis for a remedy to the damage caused.

Crimes that Breach Basic Human Rights

Denying the right to life and torturing people, which we have already attended to, are some but not all of the breaches of basic human rights that have been taking place in Iraq since and because of the invasion. We shall attempt to consider some of those other breaches here.

We believe that breaching the rights of the child tops the list. It must be a disgrace to the American nation that its government appears on the UN Treaty Collection website as second only to Somalia in declining so far to ratify the Convention on the Rights of the Child.[18] Such a refusal by a country, which claims to champion human rights protection, to ratify a Convention, which almost all the world has accepted, if for no other reason than its being a political attempt to protect the most vulnerable of the human species, seems quite indefensible to the rest of humanity. In the 23 years since its adoption in 1990, several presidents have assumed power and both main parties have had a majority in the Congress but still the refusal is maintained. We have yet to read any of those Presidents telling us in his elegantly edited memoirs his reasons for having declined to ratify such a Convention when he was willing to condemn the 'Saddams' and the 'Ayatollahs' for mistreating their peoples.

We believe that whether or not the US ratified the Convention, it remains bound by it because it is internationally accepted and has become part of customary international law. It may be accepted as defense for an American to plead not guilty for having breached the convention before a US Court but it will not be accepted before any other court in the world. No less significant is the fact that the UK, which had ratified the Convention, was and remained throughout the occupation of Iraq a full partner of the US and is thus complicit in any crimes committed by its partner. Some of the main breaches of the Convention of the Rights of the Child are as follows:

- The occupiers breached Article 20 of the Convection[19] when they failed to restore the orphanages that were ransacked following the invasion and set up shelters for children whose parents were arrested or murdered by their soldiers or the militias armed and trained by them. This led to tens of thousands of Iraqi children being forced into slave labor, prostitution and drugs.

- The occupiers failed to uphold Article 22 of the Convention[20] when they failed to provide protection and humanitarian assistance to the children of Iraq who were displaced by sectarian violence, which was initiated and triggered by the same occupiers' policies of arming different sectarian militias and setting them loose in the street of Iraq.

- The occupiers breached Article 27 of the Convention[21] when they deliberately deprived thousands of Iraqi children of a standard of living adequate for a child's physical, mental, spiritual, moral and social development, having expelled their parents from work following the de-Ba'athification Order.

- The occupiers failed to implement Article 28 of the Convention[22] when they failed to enforce the Ba'athist government law of compulsory primary school education and failed to build the new schools desperately needed after twelve years of the blockade. This deprivation led to thousands of children ending up on the streets.

- The occupiers failed to implement Article 33 of the Convention[23] when they did nothing to prevent children who were left uncared for on the street, from becoming drug addicts and carriers of drugs as we addressed briefly in Chapter 8.

- The occupiers failed to enforce Article 34 of the Convention.[24] In Chapter 8 we touched briefly on the plight of young Iraqi girls being sold into prostitution through organized trafficking and the backing of religious clergy. We submit that the occupiers found it expedient to let this religious bigotry operate in Iraq so long as these men were siding with them, which was clearly in breach of their obligation under international law and contrary to their claim of bringing democracy and human rights to Iraq.

- The occupiers failed to implement Article 37 of the Convention.[25] As a matter of common practice children were arrested by the occupying power and detained for indefinite lengths of time without any legal assistance and in clear breach of the Convention.

> More than 1,000 children were being held in Iraqi
> detention and reformatories at the end of 2008 and
> many of them may have been abused by security
> forces. Children are often held without proper care
> or legal representation. Because of the emphasis on
> confession in the Iraqi justice system, human rights
> groups are concerned about the level of intimidation
> or torture children are subjected to ... UNAMI has
> observed that children were frequently held in the
> same cells as adults, and where juvenile detention
> centres do exist, conditions were poor. During a visit to
> a juvenile detention facility in Kirkuk on 29 June, UNAMI
> noted that 22 children were crowded into two rooms,
> each with eight beds, without ventilation. None of the
> juvenile detainees had access to education. None of
> the prison staff had received training in dealing with
> juvenile offenders.[26]

Although we paid more attention to breaches of the human
rights of children in Iraq, we should not finish listing crimes without
making some comments on the general breaches of adults' human rights.
We have already commented on the murder, torture and inhumane
treatment of adults.

We earlier expressed our belief that many Americans must
feel uneasy about their government's preaching to the world on human
rights when their legislature finds it impossible to ratify basic human
rights treaties like the Convention on the Rights of the Child. Presumably
the same sentiment would apply in relation to the fact that thirty-four
years after its adoption, the US has still not ratified the Convention on
the Elimination of All Forms of Discrimination against Women, which
set out to prevent discrimination against women.[27] Nonetheless, the US
is still accountable under the Convention insofar as its principles have
become an integral part of international law. Accordingly, both the US
and the UK breached the Convention obligations when they allowed
religious fanaticism to take over and reverse the trend that was started
by the Ba'ath Government to achieve full equality between men and
women, part of which was explained in Chapter 8. One major failure by
the occupiers regarding the protection of women has been the breach of
Article 76 of Protocol 1 (1977), which was specifically drafted to protect
women against rape and forced prostitution which is understood to take
place following invasions and occupations.[28]

Other basic rights have been breached since the invasion through
its unleashing of primitive practices of tribal retribution and the settling

of feuds. Since the adoption by the UN of Universal Declaration of Human Rights in 1948 [29] the world has adopted a few conventions to protect basic human rights and restore lost dignity to human beings. The three main such conventions are: the International Covenant on Economic, Social and Cultural Rights 1966 (ICESCR), the International Covenant on Civil and Political Rights 1966 (ICCPR), and the Convention against Torture and Other Cruel, Inhuman or Degrading Treatment or Punishment 1984 (CAT)[30]. As we have already dealt with the crime of torture under the Rome Statute, we shall here outline the main breaches of both Conventions of 1966. These breaches are in addition to breaches of the Fourth Geneva Convention 1949 and its Protocol I 1977 for the protection of civilians in time of war and occupation.[31] As this is not meant to be a legal treatment we shall confine ourselves to outlining which rights were breached with minimum comment.

- Right to Life – Thousands of Iraqis were denied their basic right to life contrary to Article 75(2) of the Protocol I (1977) additional to the Fourth Geneva Convention 1949[32] and Art 6 ICCPR when they were unlawfully killed both during the invasion and the years of occupation.[33]

- Right to Political Life – Hundreds of thousands of people in Iraq were denied their right to political life contrary to Article 25 ICCPR when the de-Ba'athification Order set out to eradicate an Arab nationalist ideology that had existed for seventy years in the Arab world,[34] which was further enhanced with Order 62 related to Disqualification from Public Office, prohibiting a Ba'ath Party member from standing as a candidate in an election.

- Right to Protection from Arbitrary Arrest – Thousands of civilians in Iraq were arbitrarily arrested following the invasion contrary to Article 79 of the Fourth Geneva Convention[35] and Article 9 ICCPR.[36] Hundreds of people, who were arbitrarily arrested following the invasion, still remain in custody ten years after the invasion as their detention has passed from the occupier to the Iraqi Governments that assumed power since.

- Right to Protection from Retroactivity of a Criminal act – Thousands of civilians in Iraq were arrested for actions, which were not criminalized at the time of their commission, contrary to Article 70 of the Fourth Geneva Convention[37] and Article 15 ICCPR.[38] The conviction and execution of Saddam Hussein and other members of the Ba'ath leadership are examples.

- Right to protection from torture – We have already established that thousands of people in Iraq were subjected to torture, cruel and inhumane treatment while in the hands of the occupiers or in the hands of militias operating under their supervision. All such acts were committed contrary to Article 7 ICCPR[39] and Articles 27 of the Fourth Geneva Convention 1949 [40] and Article 75(2) of Protocol 1 1977.

- Right of Protection of Freedom of Belief and Expression – The de-Ba'athification order denied millions of people in Iraq their right to belief and expression when the simple belief in Arab Nationalism as represented by the Ba'ath ideology became a crime contrary to Article 19 ICCPR.[41]

- Rights to work, family, adequate standard of living – Many other rights were denied to the people of Iraq either deliberately or through the indifference and carelessness of the occupiers. Whether or not they intended to deny millions of Iraqis the right to work, keep a family and secure an adequate standard of living is irrelevant. What matters is that policies, like de-Ba'athification, resulted in millions of Iraqis being denied these rights. Expulsion from work, arbitrary arrest, detention for years, denied tens of thousands of Iraqis and millions of their dependents such rights contrary to Articles 6, 10 and 11 of ICESCR.[42]

The above brief summary of rights denied and rights for remedy shows that there is a catalogue of breaches and opportunities open to any future Iraqi Government that has the integrity to secure the interests of Iraqis, and to individual Iraqis today or in the future, to seek justice and damages. It is obvious that war reparations should be sought from the invaders who occupied Iraq and left it in ruins. Personal damages should be sought by every Iraqi who has suffered injustice whether in arrest, detention, expulsion from work or displacement as a result of the invasion and occupation and the 12-year blockade.

APPENDIX I

In 1902, the British Foreign Secretary, the Marquess of Lansdowne, summed up British policy towards the Sheikh of Kuwait and other Sheikhs in the Gulf in the following Memorandum:

> The situation at Koweit is becoming more and more embarrassing, and the time has come for looking it in the face.
>
> We have saddled ourselves with an impossible client in the person of the sheikh. He is apparently an untrustworthy savage, no one knows where his possessions begin and end, and our obligations towards him are as ill-defined as the boundaries of his Principality. We have distinctly announced that he does not enjoy British 'protection'; on the other hand, we once made him a present of 1,000l, and promised him our 'good offices', whatever that may mean. When we made this promise we were, I feel no doubt, thinking of Koweit proper, if there is such a thing, and not of Boobyan or other outskirts over which the Sheikh has rights of one sort or another. We have up to the present sheltered ourselves not unsuccessfully, during our discussion with the Turks on the one side and foreign Governments on the other, behind the plausible announcement that we desire to maintain the status quo in regard to Koweit. But I doubt whether any one really knows what the status quo is. We have, at any rate in my opinion, no right to tell the Turks that they may not move troops for the purpose of putting down a rebellion in the Nejd region, or that they must not look out for a suitable terminus of the Baghdad Railway for fear of disturbing the status quo.
>
> If matters are left as they are, we shall involve ourselves in a very unsatisfactory dispute. And we shall, as Admiral Bosanquet has lately pointed out, be obliged to keep the squadron on sentry go at the head of the Gulf in order to maintain the peace.
>
> We might, it seems to me, explain (1) to the Porte (2) to the Sheikh and (3) to the foreign Powers immediately interested the objects of our policy.

I should be inclined to say that our engagements to Koweit do not extend beyond the district adjoining or close to the bay of that name, and to endeavour to obtain the adhesion of the Porte and the Sheikh to an approximate definition of that district. It may be necessary to reconcile the Sheikh by the payment of another 1,000l, or of an even larger sum.

I would make it clear to the Turks that we do not want to stand in the way of an arrangement under which the terminus of the line might be placed at some spot other than Koweit to their advantage if they can make anything out of it.

As to the foreign Powers, I have already explained to most of them that we are not going to oppose the railway project, provided British capital receives a share at least equal to that of any other Power in respect of construction, management, and orders for materials; and I have added that while we do not grudge a debouche for international commerce in the Gulf, and have no wish to make it into a British lake, we shall resist to the utmost all attempts by other Powers to obtain a foothold on its shores for naval or military purposes.

This I take it, is the 'bed rock' of our policy in the Gulf, and we shall pursue that policy, not in virtue of ambiguous understanding with local Chiefs, but as the predominant Powers in Southern Persia and in the Gulf - the Power whose commercial interests in those regions far exceed those of other Powers, the Power to whose efforts in the past it is due that the waters of the Gulf are open to the trade of the world, and whose duty it will be in the future to protect the new trade route. If it is understood that we have to be reckoned with, whoever builds the railway, and wherever it finds a terminus, because we are that Power, we can regard with indifference the local intrigues of any number of Sheikhs and Emirs.

(Signed) Lansdowne
Foreign Office, March 21, 1902

APPENDIX II

United Nations

S/2003/538

 Security Council

Distr.: General
8 May 2003

Original: English

Letter dated 8 May 2003 from the Permanent Representatives of the United Kingdom of Great Britain and Northern Ireland and the United States of America to the United Nations addressed to the President of the Security Council

The United States of America, the United Kingdom of Great Britain and Northern Ireland and Coalition partners continue to act together to ensure the complete disarmament of Iraq of weapons of mass destruction and means of delivery in accordance with United Nations Security Council resolutions. The States participating in the Coalition will strictly abide by their obligations under international law, including those relating to the essential humanitarian needs of the people of Iraq. We will act to ensure that Iraq's oil is protected and used for the benefit of the Iraqi people.

In order to meet these objectives and obligations in the post-conflict period in Iraq, the United States, the United Kingdom and Coalition partners, acting under existing command and control arrangements through the Commander of Coalition Forces, have created the Coalition Provisional Authority, which includes the Office of Reconstruction and Humanitarian Assistance, to exercise powers of government temporarily, and, as necessary, especially to provide security, to allow the delivery of humanitarian aid, and to eliminate weapons of mass destruction.

The United States, the United Kingdom and Coalition partners, working through the Coalition Provisional Authority, shall inter alia, provide for security in and for the provisional administration of Iraq, including by: deterring hostilities; maintaining the territorial integrity of Iraq and securing Iraq's borders; securing, and removing, disabling, rendering harmless, eliminating or destroying (a) all of Iraq's weapons of mass destruction, ballistic missiles, unmanned aerial vehicles and all other chemical, biological and nuclear delivery systems and (b) all elements of Iraq's programme to research, develop, design, manufacture, produce, support, assemble and employ such weapons and delivery systems and subsystems and components thereof, including but not limited to stocks of chemical and biological agents, nuclear-weapon-usable material, and other related materials, technology, equipment, facilities and intellectual property that have been used in or can materially contribute to these programmes; in consultation with relevant international organizations, facilitating the orderly and voluntary return of refugees and displaced persons; maintaining civil law and order, including through encouraging international efforts to rebuild the capacity of the Iraqi civilian police force; eliminating all terrorist infrastructure and resources within Iraq and working to ensure that terrorists and terrorist groups are denied safe haven; supporting and

03-35319 (E)   080503
0335319

S/2003/538

coordinating demining and related activities; promoting acountability for crimes and atrocities committed by the previous Iraqi regime; and assuming immediate control of Iraqi institutions responsible for military and security matters and providing, as appropriate, for the demilitarization, demobilization, control, command, reformation, disestablishment, or reorganization of those institutions so that they no longer pose a threat to the Iraqi people or international peace and security but will be capable of defending Iraq's sovereignty and territorial integrity.

The United States, the United Kingdom and Coalition partners recognize the urgent need to create an environment in which the Iraqi people may freely determine their own political future. To this end, the United States, the United Kingdom and Coalition partners are facilitating the efforts of the Iraqi people to take the first steps towards forming a representative government, based on the rule of law, that affords fundamental freedoms and equal protection and justice under law to the people of Iraq without regard to ethnicity, religion or gender. The United States, the United Kingdom and Coalition partners are facilitating the establishment of representative institutions of government, and providing for the responsible administration of the Iraqi financial sector, for humanitarian relief, for economic reconstruction, for the transparent operation and repair of Iraq's infrastructure and natural resources, and for the progressive transfer of administrative responsibilities to such representative institutions of government, as appropriate. Our goal is to transfer responsibility for administration to representative Iraqi authorities as early as possible.

The United Nations has a vital role to play in providing humanitarian relief, in supporting the reconstruction of Iraq, and in helping in the formation of an Iraqi interim authority. The United States, the United Kingdom and Coalition partners are ready to work closely with representatives of the United Nations and its specialized agencies and look forward to the appointment of a special coordinator by the Secretary-General. We also welcome the support and contributions of Member States, international and regional organizations, and other entities, under appropriate coordination arrangements with the Coalition Provisional Authority.

We would be grateful if you could arrange for the present letter to be circulated as a document of the Security Council.

(Signed) Jeremy Greenstock
Permanent Representative of the United Kingdom

(Signed) John D. Negroponte
Permanent Representative of the United States

ENDNOTES

Chapter 1: The Imperialist Design for Iraq

1   'Western European' includes North America, Canada, Australia, S. Africa and several other colonial adherents

2   Riley-Smith, Jonathan, ed., (1999) *'The Oxford History of the Crusades'*, Oxford University Press, Oxford, pp. 1-2

3   *Ibid*, p. 37

4   *Ibid*, p. 111-114

5   Bessis, Sophie (2003) *'Western Supremacy: the triumph of an idea?'*, Zed Books, London, p. 5

6   For information on the background of The Knights of the Temple of Solomon of Jerusalem, see eg. Barber, Malcolm and Bate, Keith (2002) *'The Templars: Selected Sources'*, Manchester University Press, Manchester, England, , pp. 1-23

7   The Catholic Encyclopaedia, *'Freemasonry'*<http://www.newadvent.org/cathen/09771a.htm#II>

8   Esposito, John L. (1999) *'The Oxford History of Islam'*, Oxford University Press, New York, p. 374

9   Olson, James S. et al. (1991) *'Historical Dictionary of European Imperialism'*, Greenwood Press, New York, p. 472

10   Salih, Zaki (1995) *'Britain and Iraq: A Study in British Foreign Affairs'*, Books & Books, London, pp.14-15

11   *Ibid*, p. 18

12   Kheirallah, George (1952) *'Arabia Reborn'*, University of New Mexico Press, Albuquerque, pp. 56-57

13   Philby, H. St. John (1955) *'Saudi Arabia'*, Ernest Benn, London, p. 33

14   Dunwoodie, Peter (1998) *''Writing French Algeria'*, Clarendon Press, Oxford, p. 1

15   Entelis, John P. (1986), *'Algeria: The Revolution Institutionalized'*, Westview Press, Boulder, CO., p. 56

16   Longrigg, Stephen Hemsley (1958) *'Syria and Lebanon under French Mandate'*, Oxford University Press, London, p. 22

17   *Ibid*, pp. 123

18   Ryness, Shari (5 November 2012), *'France's Hollande: 'Lebanon must ensure its unity, stability and ingerity' on first Middle East trip'*, European Jewish Press<http://ejpress.org/article/62890>

19   Xinhua (4 February 2013), ' *Hollande holds phone talks with Lebanese president on Syrian refugees'*, http://english.cntv.cn/20130402/100439.shtml. Like Algeria, France continues to interfere in Lebanon's internal affairs, supporting certain factions over others.

20   The British captured the island of Hormuz on the Gulf from the Portuguese in 1622. See: Lawson, Philip (1993), *'The East India Company: A History'*, Longman, London, p. 28

21   Salih, op.cit., pp. ix-x
22   The story of the carving of Kuwait out of Iraq, and Iraq's desires and actions to reclaim it, has not been properly addressed by the Iraqis. Although the Kuwaitis and some of their paid agents have written on this matter in an attempt to give credence to a fictitious Kuwaiti entity, the Iraqis have done very poorly in arguing their case, despite Kuwait being a key to the start of the campaign to dismantle modern Iraq. See: Simons, Geoff (1996), *'Iraq: From Sumer to Saddam'*, Macmillan, Basingstoke, p. 3
23   Salih, op.cit., pp. xiv-xv
24   *Ibid*, pp. xi
25   *Ibid*, pp. xii-xiv
26   Simons, op.cit., p. 197
27   Karsh, Efraim & Inari (2001), *'Empires of the Sand: The Struggle for Mastery in the Middle East, 1789-1923'*, Harvard University Press, Cambridge, MA., p. 252
28   *Ibid*, p. 254
29   Melman,Yossi & Raviv, Dan (1989), *'Behind the Uprising: Israelis, Jordanians, and Palestinians'*, Greenwood Press, New York, p. 32
30   Herzl, Theodor, *'The Jewish State'* <http://www.gutenberg.org/files/25282/25282-h/25282-h.htm>
31   Aziz, Jean (17 April 2013),*'What Are Saudi Arabia's Intentions in Lebanon?'* <http://www.al-monitor.com/pulse/originals/2013/04/saudi-arabia-intentions-lebanon.html>
32   Beattie, Kirk J. (1949), *'Egypt during the Nasser Years: Ideology, Politics, and Civil Society'*, Westview Press, Boulder, CO., p. 1
33   St. John, Robert (1960), *'The Boss: The Story of Gamal Abdel Nasser'*, McGraw-Hill, New York, pp. 246- 247
34   Global Security, *'Suez Crisis / Sinai War / Tripartite Invasion / 1956 War'* <http://www.globalsecurity.org/military/world/war/egypt2.htm>
35   Khadduri, Majid (1960) *'Independent Iraq, 1932-1958:A Study in Iraqi Politics'*, 2nd. Ed., Oxford University Press, London, p. 348
36   Barnett,Michael N. (1998), *'Dialogues in Arab Politics: Negotiations in Regional Order'*, Columbia University Press, New York, p.121
37   Al-Eyd, Kadhim A. (1979), *'Oil Revenues and Accelerated Growth: Absorptive Capacity in Iraq'*, Praeger, New York, p. 19
38   Entelis, op.cit., p. 57
39   Langley, Jason (16 January 2013) *'Politics and Religion in Iraq and Syria: What is the Ba'ath Party?*, Global Research <http://www.globalresearch.ca/the-baath-party-as-the-west-doesnt-want-you-to-know-it/5319120>
40   US Department of State's Background Notes, (November 2005) *'Libya – History'*, U.S. Dept. of State. http://www.state.gov/r/pa/ei/bgn/5425.htm, Retrieved 20 April 2013
41   Melman, Raviv, op.cit., p. 63 . See also: O'Leary, Brendan; Lustick, Ian S. & Callaghy, Thomas (2001), *'Rightsizing the State: The Politics of Moving Borders'*, Oxford University Press, Oxford, p. 274, and: Minasian, Sergey (2007), *'The Israeli-Kurdish Relations'*, Noravank Foundation, "21st CENTURY" magazine, <http://www.noravank.am/upload/pdf/256_en.pdf>
42   Smith, Simon C. (2004), *'Britain's Revival and Fall in the Gulf: Kuwait, Bahrain, Qatar, and the Trucial States, 1950-71'*, Routledge Curzon, New York, pp.8-14
43   Caryn, Aviv & Shneer, David (2005), *'New Jews: The End of the Jewish Diaspora'*, New York University Press, New York, p. 10
44   Brockelmann, Carl, Perlmann, Moshe & Carmichael, Joel (1947), *'History of the Islamic Peoples: With a Review of Events, 1939-1947'*, G. P. Putnam's Sons, New York, p. 361
45   Powell, Sara (September 2004), *'51 Documents: Zionist Collaboration with the*

Nazis', Washington Report on Middle East Affairs, Volume: 23, Issue: 7, p. 86. See also: <http://www.ihr.org/jhr/v13/v13n4p29_Weber.html>

46   Gorny,Yosef (1987), *'Zionism and the Arabs, 1882-1948: A Study of Ideology'*, Oxford University Press, Oxford, England, pp.217-218

47   See for example: Guyénot, Laurent (27 May 2013), *'The machiavelian threefold game of the neoconservatives'*, Voltaire Network, http://www.voltairenet. org/article178638.html. See also: Smith, Grant (14 April 2014), *'Will the US Also Deny Visas to Israel's Spies?'*, Antiwar.com <http://original.antiwar.com/ smith-grant/2014/04/13/will-the-us-also-deny-visas-to-israels-spies/>

48   Salih, op.cit., pp xi

49   Stoddard, Philip H; Cuthell, David C. and Sullivan, Margaret W. [Eds.] (1981) *'Change and the Muslim World'*, Syracuse University Press, Syracuse, NY., p. 52

50   Beattie, Kirk J. (1994), *'Egypt during the Nasser Years: Ideology, Politics, and Civil Society'*, Westview Press, Boulder, CO., p.100

51   Stacher, Joshua, (2012), *'Adaptable Autocrats: Regime Power in Egypt and Syria'*, Stanford University Press, Stanford, CA., p. 75

52   Talhamy, Yvette (Spring 2012), *'The Muslim Brotherhood Reborn, The Syrian Uprising'*, Middle East Quarterly, pp. 33-40

53   Aranas, Paul F.J. (2012), *'Smokescreen: The US, NATO and the Illegitimate Use of Force'*, Algora, New York, pp. 36-37

54   BBC News (4 April 2005) *'Who's who in Iraq: Hajim al-Hassani'*<http://news. bbc.co.uk/2/hi/middle_east/4409619.stm>

55   Barnard, Anne (18 March 2013), *'Syrian Rebels Pick U.S. Citizen to Lead Interim Government'*, New York Times <http://www.nytimes.com/2013/03/19/world/ middleeast/syria-warplanes-hit-lebanon-for-first-time.html?pagewanted=all&_ r=0>

56   Cordesman, Anthony H. (1999) *'Iraq and the war of sanctions: conventional threats and weapons of mass destruction'*, Greenwood Publishing Group, p. 295

57   Chossudovsky, Michel (6 August 2006), *'Triple Alliance : The US, Turkey, Israel and the War on Lebanon'*, Global Research, <http://www.globalresearch.ca/ triple-alliance-the-us-turkey-israel-and-the-war-on-lebanon/2906>

58   *See:* Yinon, Oded (1982), *'A Strategy for Israel in the Nineteen Eighties'*, translation and foreword by Israel Shahak, <http://cosmos.ucc.ie/cs1064/jabowen/ IPSC/articles/article0005345.html>

59   Dawisha, Adeed (2009), *'Iraq: A Political History from Independence to Occupation'*, Princeton University Press, Princeton, NJ. , pp. 237-238

60   Ayalon, Ami (1995), *'Middle East Contemporary Survey: 1993,Volume: 17'*, Westview Press, Boulder, CO., pp. 392-393

61   Thring, James (2011) *'Peace with Libya'* monologue, Ministry of Peace, London.

62   Council on Foreign Relations (30 November 2011) *'Tunisia's Challenge: A Conversation with Rachid al-Ghannouchi'*, Washington D.C.<http://www.cfr.org/ tunisia/tunisias-challenge-conversation-rachid-al-ghannouchi/p26660>

63   Russia Today (1 March 2011) *'Airstrikes in Libya did not take place – Russian military'* <http://rt.com/news/airstrikes-libya-russian-military/>Nazemroaya, Mahdi Darius (17 October 2011), *'Libya: Human rights impostors used to spawn NATO's fraudulent war'*, Voltairenet.org <http://www.voltairenet.org/ Lybia-Human-rights-impostors-used>

64   Hargreaves, Steve (25 October 2011) *'Libya oil eyed by Western companies'*, CNNMoney, <http://money.cnn.com/2011/10/25/news/international/libya_oil/ index.htm>

65   Shams El-Din, Mai (13 June 2012) *'Hamdeen Sabahi's surprise rise'*, The Egypt Monocle <http://egyptmonocle.com/EMonocle/hamdeen-sabahis-surprise-rise/>

66   Miller, Elhanan (29 March 2012) *'Egyptian Muslim Brotherhood: We acknowl-*

edge peace with Israel', The Times of Israel <http://www.timesofisrael.com/muslim-brotherhood-official-we-are-the-only-egyptian-party-to-acknowledge-peace-with-israel/> Egypt Independent (1 October 2012) **'Brotherhood forms committee to support Syrian uprising'**, <http://www.egyptindependent.com/news/brotherhood-forms-committee-support-syrian-uprising>

Chapter 2: Iraq on the Eve of the 2003 Invasion:

1   Goode, James F., (2007) **'Negotiating for the Past: Archaeology, Nationalism, and Diplomacy in the Middle East, 1919-1941'**, University of Texas Press, Austin, TX., p. 198

2   For details of the McMahon-Hussein correspondence, see e.g: UNESCO Foundation For Palestine, **'Palestine: A Study of Jewish, Arab, and British Policies'.** *Volume: 2.* , Yale University Press, New Haven, CT., 1947, pp. 63 ff

3   Peretz, Don (1994) **'The Middle East Today'**, 6th. *Edition*, Praeger, Westport, CT., p. 107

4   *Ibid*

5   *Ibid* p. 108

6   *Ibid* p. 439

7   Falola, Toyin & Genova, Ann (2005) **'The Politics of the Global Oil Industry: An Introduction'**, Praeger, Westport, CT, p.184

8   Al-Eyd, Kadhim A. (1979) **'Oil Revenues and Accelerated Growth: Absorptive Capacity in Iraq'**, Praeger, New York, p. 4

9   Lukitz, Liora (1995) **'Iraq: The Search for National Identity'** F. Cass, London, pp. 95 ff

10   *Ibid*, pp. 100 ff

11   The Baghdad Pact began as the Turco-Iraq pact with Britian acceding to it. *See:* Yesilbursa, Behcet Kemal (2005) **'The Baghdad Pact: Anglo-American Defence Policies in the Middle East, 1950-1959'**, Frank Cass, London, p. 101

12   On 4 April 1955 in the House of Commons, Anthony Eden said: "The goal which we seek from the Baghdad Pact is very simple. By our adherence, we have consolidated our influence and raised our voice in the Middle East. Britain's adherence to the Baghdad Pact provides her with continued interference in the affairs of the Middle East." Eden added that "the object of the Baghdad Pact is to direct the attention of both sides to something other than Israel. And this pact would leave [Israel] in security and stability." At the same meeting, Anthony Nutting, Minister of State for Foreign Affairs, said that "we are working to have other countries in the Middle East join this agreement"(i.e. the Turco-Iraqi pact). He also said that the Baghdad Pact would achieve security for the Middle Eastern countries including Israel, and that the Baghdad Pact did not conflict with the interests of Israel. See Yesilbursa, op.cit., pp.101-102

13   Nuri As-Saeed<http://en.wikipedia.org/wiki/Nuri_al-Said>

14   Brockelmann, Carl; Perlmann, Moshe & Carmichael, Joel (1947) **'History of the Islamic Peoples: With a Review of Events, 1939-1947'**, G. P. Putnam's Sons, New York, pp. 361

15   Salvemini, Gaetano (1954) **'The French Revolution, 1788-1792'**, Jonathan Cape, London, p. 14

16   Williams, Albert Rhys (1921) **'Through the Russian Revolution'**, Boni and Liveright, New Yorkp. 30.

17   Fouskas, Vassilis K. & Gökay, Bülent (2005) **'The New American Imperialism: Bush's War on Terror and Blood for Oil'**, Praeger Security International, Westport, CT., p. 194

18   Anderson, Terry H. (2011) **'Bush's Wars'**, Oxford University Press, New York, p. 17

19   *Ibid*

20   K.Ali Alrubaie, Falah (2010) *'Analysis of changes: in the orientation of eco-nomic policy in Iraq'*, MPRA Paper No. 28371, 15 March, <http://mpra.ub.uni-muenchen.de/28371/1/MPRA_paper_28371.pdf> (in Arabic)

21   Yesilbursa, op.cit. p. 215

22   Frisch, Hillel (2008) *'The Palestinian Military: Between Militias and Armies'*, Routledge, New York, p. 42

23   *Cable from Abdul-Karim Qasim to the Sheikh of Kuwait (20 June 1961)*, in Arabic <http://www.moqatel.com/openshare/Behoth/IraqKwit/3/doc05.doc_cvt.htm>

24   *'Memorandum from the Government of Iraq to Arab and foreign Ambassadors in Baghdad (26 June 1961)'* in Arabic <http://www.moqatel.com/openshare/Behoth/IraqKwit/3/doc06.doc_cvt.htm>

25   Kearney, Milo (2003) *'The Indian Ocean in World History'*, Routledge, New York, p. 157

26   Al-Eyd, Kadhim A. (1979) *'Oil Revenues and Accelerated Growth: Absorptive Capacity in Iraq'*, Praeger, New York, pp. 19

27   Alnasrawi, Abbas (1994) *'The Economy of Iraq: Oil, Wars, Destruction of De-velopment and Prospects, 1950-2010'*, Greenwood Press, Westport, CT., p.12

28   Hurst, Steven (2009) *'The United States and Iraq since 1979: Hegemony, Oil and War'* , Edinburgh University Press, Edinburgh, p. 231

29   Al-Ani, Abdul-Haq (2008) *'The Trial of Saddam Hussein'*, Clarity Press, Atlanta,, pp. 40-41

30   *Ibid*, pp. 43-44

31   *Ibid*, p. 44

32   *Ibid*

33   See Al-Ani Abdul-Haq & Al-Ani, Tarik (2012) *'Genocide in Iraq: The Case against the UN Security Council and Member States'*, Clarity Press, Atlanta, GA., Chap-ters 3 and 4

34   Alnasrawi, Abbas, *Iraq: economic embargo and predatory rule*, 2000, p. 3-4 <http://www.casi.org.uk/info/alnasrawi9905.html>

35   Chapin Metz, Helen, *'A Country Study: Iraq'* p. 138 http://lcweb2.loc.gov/frd/cs/iqtoc.html

36   World Health Organization (March 1996) *'The Health Conditions of the Popula-tion in Iraq Since the Gulf Crisis'*, <http://www.who.int/disasters/repo/5249.html>

37   Al-Ani, *The Trial of Saddam Hussein,* op.cit. pp. 49-50

38   *Ibid*, p. 50

39   Al-Ani, *The Trial of Saddam Hussein,* op.cit. p. 43

40   Seale, Patrick (1990) *'Asad: The Struggle for the Middle East'*, University of California Press

41   "As it became increasingly clear that the dispute between Saddam and Khomeini could lead to war, Saddam also began looking for allies among his neighbours. ... The most important of these meetings was with Saudi Prince Fahd. As if con-tracting a mafia hit team, Fahd promised Saddam billions of dollars of support for any move to eliminate Khomeini. The United States followed all this with obvious approval. ... [T]he U.S. made certain that Saddam Hussein understood that an attack on Khomeini would be welcomed by Washington and supported by its allies in the Gulf. Indeed, when Iraqi forces swept into Iran on September 22, 1980, there were no indignant speeches from Western leaders or calls for a U.S. embargo, as there were when Saddam invaded Kuwait ten years later." Lando, Barry M. (2007) *Web Of Deceit*, Other Press. **Quoted in***: 'United States support for Iraq during the Iran–Iraq war'* <http://en.wikipedia.org/wiki/United_States_support_for_Iraq_during_the_Iran%E2%80%93Iraq_war> See also: Boyle, Francis A. (14-16 December 2002) *'US Policy During the Iran/Iraq War'*, Counterpunch<http://www.counterpunch.org/2002/12/14/us-policy-during-the-iran-iraq-war/>

42   Interview with *Al-Sharq* newspaper /Qatar, 10 January 2007 (in Arabic)<http://www.libyaforum.org/archive/index.php?option=com_content&task=view&id=3908&Itemid=1>

43   Russia Today (20 March 2013) *'TV interview with Salim Al-Jumaili'*<http://www.youtube.com/watch?v=XEm4dBnMw-Y>

44   Egypt, Lebanon, Jordan and Syria signed armistice agreements with Israel. Information on these is available at the Avalon Project of Yale Law School for Documents in Law History and Diplomacy. <http://avalon.law.yale.edu/default.asp> The agreements are: *'Egyptian-Israeli General Armistice Agreement'*, February 24, 1949, U.N. doc. S/1264/Rev. 1, Dec. 13, 1949; *'Lebanese-Israeli General Armistice Agreement'*, March 23, 1949, U.N. doc. S/1296/Rev. 1, Apr. 8, 1949; *'Jordanian-Israeli General Armistice Agreement'*, April 3, 1949, U.N doc. S/1302/Rev. 1, June 20, 1949; and *'Israeli-Syrian General Armistice Agreement'*, July 20, 1949, U.N. doc. S/1353/Rev. 1

45   Henry Kissinger is reported to have said: 'I hope they kill each other' and 'too bad they both can't lose' in Chubinl, Shahram, and Trip, Charles (1988) *'Iran and Iraq at War'*, Westview Press, Boulder, CO., P. 207 And when asked "Which side should America back?" he more cynically replied "Both sides; we want them both to win."

46   For sources on Iran-Iraq war see: Abu Ghazala, General Abdul-Halim (1993-94) *'The Iraq-Iran War'* (in Arabic <http://www.mediafire.com/?ghnitt2eqyj>; Al Saud, General Khalid bin Sultan, *'The Iran-Iraq War from an Arab Perspective'* (in Arabic), <http://www.moqatel.com/openshare/Behoth/Siasia2/IranIraqAr/index.htm>; Al-Hamdani, Staff General Raad (2007) *'Before History Leaves us'* (in Arabic) (Arabic Scientific Publishers, Beirut; Matar, Fouad et al (1994) *'Encyclopedia of the Gulf War'* (2 Vol.) (Arab Institute for Research and Publishing Beirut); As-Samarrae, General Wafiq (1997) *'The Ruins of the Eastern Gate'* (in Arabic) (Dar Al Qabas Publishing, Kuwait); Heikel, Muhammad Hasanein (1992) *'Illusions of Power and Victory'* (in Arabic) (Al-Ahram Centre); Willemse, Marijn (2006) *'The Most Powerful Partner in Crime; How the United States took Sides in the Iran-Iraq War 1980-1988'* (Master's Thesis, Rotterdam) <http://www.scribd.com/doc/50278236/Most-Powerful-Partner-in-Crime>; Huwaidi, Fahmi (1991) *'Arabs and Iran'* (in Arabic) (Dar Ash-Shuruq, Cairo); Hiro, Dilip (2001) *'Neighbors, Not Friends: Iraq and Iran after the Gulf Wars'* (Routledge, London); Workman, W. Thom (1994) *'The Social Origins of the Iran-Iraq War'* Lynne Rienner Publishers, Boulder CO); Rajaee, Farhang (Ed.) (1997) *'Iranian Perspectives on the Iran-Iraq War'* (University Press of Florida, Gainesville FL); Joyner, Christopher C. (Ed.) (1990) *'The Persian Gulf War: Lessons for Strategy, Law, Diplomacy'* (Greenwood Press, New York); and *'The United States and Iran-Iraq War 1980-1988'*, <http://www.irandefence.net/showthread.php?t=446>

47   See Britannica definition of containment as: "strategic foreign policy pursued by the United States in the late 1940s and the early 1950s in order to check the expansionist policy of the Soviet Union". In an anonymous article in the July 1947 issue of *Foreign Affairs*, George F. Kennan, diplomat and US State Department adviser on Soviet affairs, suggested a "long-term, patient but firm and vigilant containment of Russian expansive tendencies" in the hope that the regime would mellow or collapse. The Truman Doctrine of 1947, with its guarantee of immediate economic and military aid to Greece and Turkey, was an initial application of the policy of containment." <http://www.britannica.com/EBchecked/topic/134684/containment>

48   On the different treatment by the USA and its European and Arab allies of events in Syria and Bahrain *see*: DiNardo, Chris (September 2011) *'Yemen, Bahrain and Syria must not be handled with hypocrisy'* Washington Square News 22 <http://nyunews.com/opinion/2011/09/22/22dinardo/>; Murphy, Dan (18 February 2011) *'From Libya to Bahrain, Mideast autocracy under fire'*, Christian Science Monitor <http://www.csmonitor.com/World/Middle-East/2011/0218/From-Libya-to-Bahrain-Mideast-autocracy-under-fire>; Bowles, Willia (23 June 2011) *'Syria/*

Libya versus Bahrain: A BBC Factoid', Globalresearch <http://www.globalre-search.ca/index.php?context=va&aid=25373>; On views among some Arab writers *see*: Jabir, Mahmood (30 April 2011)*'AdDawr Al-Wahabi bain Suriya we Al Bahrain'* (In Arabic), An-Nafees, <http://www.elnafis.net/%D9%85%D9%82%D8%A7%D9%84%D8%A7%D8%AA/6823.html>; As-Salim, Saqir (7 August 2011) *'AlA'hil As Saudi Yed'u lewaqf AlQatl fi Suriya'* (In Arabic) Hiwar we Tajdeed, <http://www.hiwart.net/news-action-show-id-13587.htm>; Editorial (7 June 2011) *'AlFerq bain Tughian AlBahrain we Tughian Surriya'*, Alwaten AlJezairiya, <http://www.elwatandz.com/opnenword/1570.html>

49   Muhammad Hasanain Heikel, the prominent Egyptian journalist, reported his encounter with Khomeini as follows. Heikel asked him whether or not he was concerned about breaching international law. This is how Khomeini is reported to have responded. "What benefits has Iran got out of international law? Did international law prevent the Shah from appropriating Iranian wealth? Did it prevent the USA from toppling a constitutional Iranian Government and killing its leaders [in reference to the Government of Muhammad Mosadeg]. We see that International law has not been respected in its application to Iran. Consequently we see no reason that imposes on us the demand to respect it". Heikel, Muhammad H. *(*2002) *'Medafi' Aiyatullah'*, Dar AsSherook, Cario, 6th Edition, (Arabic), p. 250. [The writer's translation]

50   See eg. Salinger, Pierre & Laurent, Eric (1991) *'Secret Dossier: The hidden agenda behind the gulf war'*, Penguin Books, London,

51   Hardy, Roger (25 September 2005) *'The Iran-Iraq War: 25 Years On'*, BBC News, London <http://news.bbc.co.uk/2/hi/4260420.stm>; Black, Ian (23 September 2010) *'Iran and Iraq remember war that cost more than a million lives'*, The Guardian, London, <http://www.guardian.co.uk/world/2010/sep/23/iran-iraq-war-anniversary>; *Iran-Iraq War (1980-1988)*, <http://www.globalsecurity.org/military/world/war/iran-iraq.htm>; and Cordesman, Anthony and Wagner, Abraham, *'The Lessons of Modern War'* vol. 2, *'The Iran-Iraq War'*, <http://csis.org/files/media/csis/pubs/9005lessonsiraniraqii-toc.pdf >

52   Private conversation with a high ranking Ba'ath party member who requested to remain anonymous.

53   Al-Khalil, Samir (1989) *'Republic of Fear: The Inside Story of Saddam's Iraq'*, Hutchinson Radius, London

54   A good review of events that preceded the invasion of Kuwait and the 1991 attack on Iraq appeared in Clark, Ramsey, (1992) *'The Fire This Time, US War Crimes in the Gulf'*, Thunder's Mouth Press, New York, Chapter 1. On Kuwait's waging 'economic warfare' against Iraq in increasing its output of oil and slant –drilling in the Rumayla oil fields see: Hayes, Thomas, *'Big Oilfields Is at the Heart of Iraq-Kuwait Dispute' New York Times* (September 3, 1990); Schuler, G. Henry, *'Congress Must Take a Hard Look at Iraq's Charges Against Kuwait' Los Angeles Times* (December 2, 1990); and Salinger and Laurent, op.cit.

55   Gordon, Joy, *'When Intent Makes All the Difference in the World: Economic Sanctions on Iraq and the Accusation of Genocide'* (2002) vol 5 *Yale Human Rights & Development Law Journal*, p. 57. The above statement is the first sentence in Gordon's article. At no stage during the article does she elaborate or expand on that statement. The rest of the article is an attempt at showing that the SC sanctions imposed on Iraq were not genocide because they lack the element of 'specific intent.'

56   Summarized agreements reached at a meeting with CIA director William Webster at the CIA headquarters in Langley, Virginia, on Nov. 14 1989 were published. The document, unknown to Saddam at that time, showed collaboration between the Kuwaiti Security Department (KSD) and the US Central Intelligence Agency (CIA). Paragraph 5 of the memorandum stated: "We agreed with the American side that it was important to take advantage of the deteriorating economic situation in Iraq in order to put pressure on that country's government to delineate our common border." *See* Clark, op.cit, p. 16

57   See: *'The Glaspie Transcript: Saddam Meets the US Ambassador (25 July 1990)'*,

in Sifry, Micah and Cerf, Christopher (Eds.), (1991) *'The Gulf War Reader'*, Times Books, New York, p. 130

58   See Herring, Eric, *'Sanctions on Iraq Despite their Human Cost'* in Ismael, Tarek Y and Haddad, William W. (eds) (2004) *'Iraq The Human Cost Of History'*, Pluto Press, London, pp. 34-35; Also, Herzfeld, Michael (1992) *'The Social Production of Indifference: Exploring the Symbolic Roots of Western Bureaucracy'*, Berg, p. I

59   Charter of the United Nations, adopted on 26 June 1945, in force on 24 October 1945, 892 UNTS 119, (UN Charter) Preamble. For a greater articulation of the values referred to in that document, including a commentary on the relevant articles see Simma, Bruno [et al] (2002) *'Charter of the United Nations: A Commentary'*, 2nd ed, Oxford University Press, pp. 13-33

60   UN Charter art 33

61   UN Charter art 38

62   "There was an aggression by Iraq against Kuwait, of the sort that the Security Council has witnessed numerous times since its inception, sometimes taking action other than sanctions and sometime doing nothing at all." Gordon, op.cit. pp. 57, 76

63   Al-Ani & Al-Ani, op.cit.

64   Katzman, Kenneth (2003) *'Iraq: Oil-For-Food Program, International Sanctions, and Illicit Trade', Report for Congress'*, CRS, Updated 16 April, pp. 12-17<http://fpc.state.gov/documents/organization/19851.pdf>

65   Al-Ani & Al-Ani, op.cit. , p. 132

Chapter 3: Preparation for the Invasion

1   *H.R.4655 - Iraq Liberation Act of 1998* (Enrolled Bill [Final as Passed Both House and Senate] - ENR) <http://thomas.loc.gov/cgi-bin/query/z?c105:H.R.4655.ENR>

2   Human Rights Watch (1993) *'GENOCIDE IN IRAQ: The Anfal Campaign Against the Kurds'* , A Middle East Watch Report <http://www.hrw.org/reports/1993/iraqanfal/>

3   *H.R. 1828 (108th): Syria Accountability and Lebanese Sovereignty Restoration Act of 2003* <http://www.govtrack.us/congress/bills/108/hr1828>

4   These are eg. Sanctions Against the Commercial Bank of Syria (2006), and Executive Orders 13315, 13224, 13382, 13338, 13399, 13441, 13460, and the Executive Order signed on April 29, 2011, the President of the United States has imposed financial sanctions on Syrian individuals and entities for involvement in proliferation of weapons of mass destruction; association with al Qaida, the Taliban or Osama bin Laden; or destabilizing activities in Iraq and Lebanon; or benefiting from public corruption. <http://damascus.usembassy.gov/sanctions-syr.html>

5   See eg. Salinger, Pierre & Laurent, Eric (1991) *'Secret Dossier: The Hidden Agenda behind the Gulf War'*, Penguin Books, London

6   Gellman, Barton (23 June 1991) *'Allied Air War Struck Broadly in Iraq; Officials Acknowledge Strategy Went Beyond Military Targets'*, The Washington Post<http://www.envirosagainstwar.org/know/1991USHitCivilianTargets.pdf>

7   Speech by James Woolsey in the Americans For Victory Over Terrorism presentation at Columbia University in New York City (12 February 2003), *'Iraq and the War on Terrorism'* <http://www.c-spanvideo.org/program/Iraqandth>

8   Article 6 of SC Resolution 661 (1990) <http://daccess-dds-ny.un.org/doc/RESO-LUTION/GEN/NR0/575/11/IMG/NR057511.pdf?OpenElement>

9   See: Al-Ani Abdul-Haq & Al-Ani, Tarik (2012) *'Genocide in Iraq: The Case against the UN Security Council and Member States'*, Clarity Press, Atlanta, GA.

10   Statement of Principles, The Project for the New American Century, <http://www.newamericancentury.org/statementofprinciples.htm>

11   <http://www.newamericancentury.org/iraqletter1998.htm>
12   <http://www.newamericancentury.org/iraq-121597.htm> The website no longer exists.
13   <http://www.newamericancentury.org/iraqclintonletter.htm>
14   <http://www.newamericancentury.org/Editorial_Feb.2_98.pdf>
15   <http://www.newamericancentury.org/Editorial_Mar9_98.pdf>
16   <http://www.newamericancentury.org/AttackIraq-Nov16,98.pdf>
17   <http://www.newamericancentury.org/Editorial_Jan4-11_99.pdf>
18   The Bush administration agreed on 12 September 2001 that it should pursue a general 'war on terrorism' wider than just Afghanistan, and there was general agreement that Iraq would be a target eventually. See: Woodward, Bob (28 January 2002*) 'We Will Rally the World'*, Washington Post, <http://www.washingtonpost.com/wp-dyn/content/article/2006/07/18/AR2006071800686_5.html> (retrieved 1.5.2013)
19   Kagan, Robert (21 July 2002) *'Iraq: The Day After'*, Washington Post <http://www.resisttyranny.com/pnac/web.archive.org/web/20021005141259/www.newamericancentury.org/iraq-072102.htm>
20   Brenner, Lenni (1983), *'Zionism in the Age of the Dictators'*, Lawrence Hill & Co, Westpoint. Conn.
21   Fetzer, James H. (Ed.) (2007), *'The 9/11 Conspiracy, The Scamming of America'*, Catfeet Press, Illinois
22   Cambone Stephen, *'A Profile*, History Commons, <http://www.historycommons.org/entity.jsp?entity=stephen_a._cambone> (Retrieved 25 April 2013)
23   Moore James (2004) *'Bush's War For Reelection: Iraq, the White House, and the People'*, John Wiley & Sons, New Jersy, 2004, p. 18.
24   Borger, Julian, (24 February 2006) *'Blogger bares Rumsfeld's post 9/11 orders'*, The Guardian <http://www.theguardian.com/world/2006/feb/24/freedomofinformation.september11>
25   Borger, Julian, (23 March 2004) *'Interview: Richard Clarke'*, The Guardian <http://www.guardian.co.uk/world/2004/mar/23/usa.september111/print>
26   Baker, Russ, (27 October 2004) *'Bush Wanted To Invade Iraq If Elected in 2000'*, Guerrilla News Network <http://www.russbaker.com/archives/Guerrilla%20News%20Network%20-%20Bush.htm
27   De la Vega, Elizabeth (2006) *'United States v. G. W. Bush et al.'*, Seven Stories Press, New York, p. 78
28   *Ibid*, p. 79
29   PBS Newshour, (11 October 2000)*'The 2nd Presidential Debate Part 1: Governor Bush and Vice President Gore'* <http://www.pbs.org/newshour/bb/politics/july-dec00/2ndebate1.html>
30   Democracy Now, (23 March 2007) *'Video Interview with General Wesley Clark'* <http://www.globalresearch.ca/we-re-going-to-take-out-7-countries-in-5-years-iraq-syria-lebanon-libya-somalia-sudan-iran/5166>
31   The New York Times (9 September 2002) *'THREATS AND RESPONSES; With Few Variations, Top Bush Advisers Present Their Case Against Iraq'* <http://www.nytimes.com/2002/09/09/world/threats-responses-with-few-variations-top-bush-advisers-present-their-case.html>
32   *President Bush to Send Iraq Resolution to Congress Today*, 19 September 2002 <http://georgewbush-whitehouse.archives.gov/news/releases/2002/09/20020919-1.html>
33   *Joint Resolution to Authorize the Use of United States Armed Forces Against Iraq* <http://georgewbush-whitehouse.archives.gov/news/releases/2002/10/20021002-2.html>
34   *President Bush Outlines Iraqi Threat,* 7 October 2002 <http://georgewbush-whitehouse.archives.gov/news/releases/2002/10/20021007-8.html>
35   Borger, Julian *'Blogger bares Rumsfeld's post 9/11 orders'*, op.cit.

36   National Security Archive Electronic Briefing Book No. 198, *'New State Depart-ment Releases on the "Future of Iraq" Project'*, posted 1 September 2006 <http://www.gwu.edu/~nsarchiv/NSAEBB/NSAEBB198/index.htm>

37   *Ibid*

38   Chulov, Martin & Pidd, Helen (15 February 2011) *'Defector admits to WMDS lies that triggered Iraq war'*, The Guardian <http://www.guardian.co.uk/world/2011/feb/15/defector-admits-wmd-lies-iraq-war>

39   United States Department of State, The Future of Iraq Project, *'Education Woprking Group'*, p. 1 from: National Security Archive Electronic Briefing Book No. 198, op.cit.

40   See: Al-Ani Abdul-Haq & Al-Ani, Tarik (2012) *'Genocide in Iraq: The case against the UN Security Council and member states'*, Clarity Press, Atlanta, GA., Chapter 4

41   United States Department of State, The Future of Iraq Project, *'Water, Agricul-ture, and Environment Woprking Group'*, p. 7, from: National Security Archive Electronic Briefing Book No. 198, op.cit.

42   Perhaps a reliable account would be the Witness Statement of Count Hans-Christof von Sponeck to the Iraq Inquiry given on 23 September 2010 <http://www.quistlaw.com/file_download/16/First+Witness+Statement+of+Count+Hans-Christof+von+Sponeck.pdf>

43   Security Council, 4120th Meeting, 24 March 2000, S/PV.4120, p. 6. <http://daccess-dds-ny.un.org/doc/UNDOC/PRO/N00/359/07/PDF/N0035907.pdf?OpenElement>

44   General Tommy Franks later acknowledged that the dramatic increase in of-fensive sorties was an attempt to destroy the Iraqi defenses in much the same way as the air strikes at the beginning of the Gulf War had. See: Franks, Tommy (2004) 'American Soldier', Harper Collins, New York, p. 342

45   NBC News (25 April 2005), *'CIA's final report: No WMD found in Iraq'* <http://www.nbcnews.com/id/7634313/ns/world_news-mideast_n_africa/t/cias-final-report-no-wmd-found-iraq/>

46   Private statement by Maj Gen Michael Laurie CBE - Director General Intelligence Collection, 2002 to 2003 <http://www.iraqinquiry.org.uk/media/52048/Laurie-2010-06-03-S1.pdf>

47   Submission made via the Iraq Inquiry website by Major General Michael Lauri, 27 January 2010 <http://www.iraqinquiry.org.uk/media/52051/Laurie-statement-FINAL.pdf>

48   *Iraq's Weapons Of Mass Destruction: The Assessment of the British Govern-ment* <http://news.bbc.co.uk/nol/shared/spl/hi/middle_east/02/uk_dossier_on_iraq/pdf/iraqdossier.pdf>

49   *Ibid*, p. 3

50   *Ibid*, p. 4

51   *Ibid*

52   Taylor, Peter (18 March 2013) *'Iraq: The spies who fooled the world'*, BBC News, <http://www.bbc.co.uk/news/uk-21786506>

53   The Guardian (23 May 2003), *'Blix casts doubts on WMDs'* <http://www.guardian.co.uk/world/2003/may/23/iraq1>

54   Taylor, Peter (18 March 2013), *'Iraq War: the greatest intelligence failure in living memory'*, The Telegraph, <http://www.telegraph.co.uk/news/worldnews/middleeast/iraq/9937516/Iraq-war-the-greatest-intelligence-failure-in-living-memory.html>

55   See for example: Roston, Aram (2008) *'The man who pushed America to war : the extraordinary life, adventures and obsessions of Ahmad Chalabi'*, Nation Books, New York

56   Evans, Dominic (7 February 2003), *'Blair Under Fire For Plagiarized Iraq Dossier'*

<*http://rense.com/plag.htm*>

57   **President Bush's Remarks at the United Nations General Assembly,** 12
        September 2002 <http://georgewbush-whitehouse.archives.gov/news/re-
        leases/2002/09/20020912-1.html>

58   Full text of Colin Powell's speech at the United Nations security council 5 Febru-
        ary 2003 <http://www.guardian.co.uk/world/2003/feb/05/iraq.usa>

59   Roston, Aram **'The man who pushed America to war'**, op.cit. pp. 206-211

60   Warrick, Joby (12 April 2006), **'Lacking Biolabs, Trailers Carried Case for War;
        Administration Pushed Notion of Banned Iraqi Weapons Despite Evidence
        to Contrary'**, Washington Post <http://www.washingtonpost.com/wp-dyn/
        content/article/2006/04/11/AR2006041101888.html?sub=AR>

61   *Ibid*

62   Democracy Now (6 February 2013), **'Decade After Iraq WMD Speech at UN,
        Ex-Powell Aide Lawrence Wilkerson Debates Author Norman Solomon'** <http://
        www.democracynow.org/2013/2/6/decade_after_iraq_wmd_speech_at>

Chapter 4: The Shock and Awe Invasion

1   **Transcript: Colin Powell on Fox News Sunday**, 21 October 2002, *Fox News*
        <http://www.foxnews.com/story/0,2933,62291,00.html>

2   Associated Press (19 September 2002) **'Saddam Defiantly Addresses U.N.
        Through Aide'** <http://www.foxnews.com/story/2002/09/19/saddam-defiantly-
        addresses-un-through-aide/#ixzz2Xmmx1guR

3   United Nations Press Release, SG/SM/8378 – GA/10045(12 September 2002>)
        **'When Force Is Considered, There Is No Substitute For Legitimacy Provided By
        United Nations, Secretary-General Says In General Assembly Address** <http://
        www.un.org/News/Press/docs/2002/SGSM8378.doc.htm>

4   Associated Press (19 September 2002) op.cit.

5   Dixon, Norm (25 September 2002) **'Iraq: Washington demands war de-
        spite inspectors' return'**, Green Left Weekly <http://www.greenleft.org.au/
        node/26664>

6   SC Resolution 1441 (2002) <http://daccess-dds-ny.un.org/doc/UNDOC/GEN/
        N02/682/26/PDF/N0268226.pdf>

7   **Iraq's letter of acceptance addressed to the United Nations of 13 November
        2002** <http://www.foxnews.com/story/0,2933,70253,00.html>

8   Hafidh, Hassan (23 February 2003), **'U.S. Says It's Deadline Time For Iraq To
        Disarm'**, Reuters <http://www.freerepublic.com/focus/f-news/850104/posts>

9   BBC News (29 June 20109 **'Iraq inquiry told France saw invasion as 'dangerous''**
        <http://www.bbc.co.uk/news/10437254>

10   Farley, Maggie & Wright, Robin, (20 February 2003) **'U.S., Britain to Set Deadlines
        for U.N., Iraq'**, Los Angeles Times <http://articles.latimes.com/2003/feb/20/
        world/fg-iraq20>

11   British Ministry of Defence (July 2003) **'Operations in Iraq: First Reflections'**,
        Her Majesty's Stationery Office, London, p. 3

12   Lake, Eli J. (19 September 2002), **Security Industry: Powell takes Iraq cause
        to Congress**, UPI <http://www.upi.com/Business_News/Security-Indus-
        try/2002/09/19/Powell-takes-Iraq-cause-to-Congress/UPI-72111032476928/>

13   **Full text of Colin Powell's speech** <http://www.guardian.co.uk/world/2003/
        feb/05/iraq.usa>

14   BBC News (5 February 2003), **'Leaked report rejects Iraqi al-Qaeda link'** <http://
        news.bbc.co.uk/2/hi/uk_news/2727471.stm>

15   **State of the Union, President George W. Bush** (28 January 2003) <http://
        georgewbush-whitehouse.archives.gov/news/releases/2003/01/20030128-19.
        html>

16   *Ibid*

17   US Department of State (5 February 2003), *'Iraq: Failing to Disarm: Transcript of Iraqi Conversation – Ammunition'* <http://web.archive.org/web/20030404073844 /><http://www.state.gov/ r/pa/ei/pix/ events/secretary/2003/17399.htm>

18   *Transcript of part one of Correspondent Brent Sadler's exclusive interview with Hussein Kamel,* CNN, 21 September 1995 <http://edition.cnn.com/WORLD/9509/iraq_defector/kamel_transcript/index.html>

19   Miller, Judith & Preston, Julia, (31 January 2003) *'Blix Says He Saw Nothing to Prompt a War'*, The New York Times,<http://www.nytimes.com/2003/01/31/international/middleeast/31BLIX.html>

20   *Ibid*

21   See: *Colin Powell's UN Presentation on Iraq WMD pt. 3,* starting at 7:01 minutes <http://www.youtube.com/watch?v=s54jr7uKnM0 >

22   Phyllis Bennis and Dennis J. Halliday interviewed by David Barsamian (2002,) *'Iraq: The Impact of Sanctions and US Policy'* in : Arnove, Anthony (Ed.), *'Iraq Under Siege - the deadly impact of sanctions and war'* (updated edition), South End Press, Cambridge, Massachusetts, p. 57

23   Cirincione, Joseph et al., (January 2004) *'W.M.D. in Iraq: Evidence and Implications'*, Carnegie Endowment for International Peace <http://carnegieendowment.org/files/Iraq3FullText.pdf>

24   BBC News (26 February 2004) *'GCHQ translator cleared over leak'* <http://news.bbc.co.uk/2/hi/uk_news/3485072.stm>

25   BBC News (26 February 2004) *'Transcript of Clare Short interview'* <http://news.bbc.co.uk/2/hi/uk_news/politics/3489372.stm>

26   Guinness World Records, *'Largest Anti-War Rally'* <http://web.archive.org/web/20040904214302/<http://www.guinnessworldrecords.com/content_pages/record.asp?recordid=54365>

27   Callinicos, Alex (19 March 2005) *'Anti-war protests do make a difference'*, Socialist Worker <http://www.socialistworker.co.uk/art.php?id=6067>

28   Remarks by the President in Address to the Nation (17 March 2003), *'President Says Saddam Hussein Must Leave Iraq Within 48 Hours'* <http://georgewbush-whitehouse.archives.gov/news/releases/2003/03/20030317-7.html>

29   Cordesman, Anthony H., (2003) *'The Iraq War: Strategy, Tactics, and Military Lessons'*, Praeger, Westport, CT., p. 487

30   *Ibid*, p. 490

31   Tucker, Mike and Faddis, Charles S. (2008) *'Operation Hotel California: The Clandestine War Inside Iraq'*, Globe Pequot, Guilford, CT

32   Cordesman, op.cit., p. 59

33   Antill, P. (2001), *Rapid Deployment Force, United States*, <http://www.history-ofwar.org/articles/weapons_rdf.html>

34   Cordesman, op.cit. , p. 60

35   Loeb, Vernon, (30 April 2003) *'U.S. Military Will Leave Saudi Arabia This Year'*, Washington Post <http://www.someplacesomewhere.com/viewtopic.php?f=5&t=15184>

36   Dobbs, Michael, (1 December 2003) *'U.S.-Saudi Alliance Appears Strong'*, Washington Post <http://www.udel.edu/globalagenda/2004/student/readings/saudirelations.html>

37   Loeb, op.cit.

38   Cordesman, op.cit. p. 490

39   *Ibid*

40   British Ministry of Defence, op.cit., pp. 6-7

41   Cordesman, op.cit. , pp. 15-16

42   British Ministry of Defence, op.cit., Annex A, IRAQ: MILITARY CAMPAIGN OBJECTIVES, p. 39

43   *Ibid*

44   Kinkade, Mark (July 2003) *'The First Shot'*, Airman Magazine <http://web.archive.org/web/20080517050321/<http://www.af.mil/news/airman/0703/air.html>

45   Burns, John F., (22 March 2003) *'A Nation at War: Baghdad; A Staggering Blow Strike at the Heart of the Iraqi Capital'*, New York Times <http://www.nytimes.com/2003/03/22/world/nation-war-baghdad-staggering-blow-strikes-heart-iraqi-capital.html?pagewanted=all&src=pm>

46   Flounders, Sara, (19 March 2013) *'Iraq: 10th anniversary of U.S. crime against humanity'*, Workers World <http://www.workers.org/2013/03/19/iraq-10th-anniversary-of-u-s-crime-against-humanity/>

47   *President Bush Addresses the Nation*, 19 March 2003 <http://georgewbush-whitehouse.archives.gov/news/releases/2003/03/20030319-17.html>

48   *Ibid*

49   *Ibid*

50   Cobb, Kim (1 November 2004) *'Writer says Bush talked about war in 1999'*, Houston Chronicle <http://www.chron.com/news/houston-texas/article/Writer-says-Bush-talked-about-war-in-1999-1975031.php>

51   John Howard (20 March 2003) *Address to the Nation* <http://www.theage.com.au/articles/2003/03/20/1047749877481.html>

52   The major sources include (but not restricted to):
- Woods, Kevin M. et al (2006) *'Iraqi Perspectives Project: A view of operation Iraqi Freedom from Saddam's senior leadership'*, The Joint Center for Operational Analysys, US Joint Forces Command,
- Cordesman, Anthony H. (2003) *'The Iraq War: Strategy, Tactics, and Military Lessons'*, Praeger, Westport, CT.
- Fontenot, COL Gregory; Degen, LTC E.J. & Tohn, LTC David (2004) *'The United States Army in Operation Iraqi Freedom- On Point'*, Operation IRAQI FREEDOM Study Group, Office of the Chief of Staff US Army Washington, DC <http://usacac.army.mil/cac2/cgsc/carl/download/csipubs/OnPointI.pdf>

53   *Ibid*, p. 61

54   *Ibid*, p. 58

55   Nichols, Ben, and Lopez, Joe (29 May 2003) *'Another US war crime: the use of depleted uranium munitions in Iraq'*, World Socialist Web Site <http://www.wsws.org/en/articles/2003/05/depu-m29.html>

56   Rohr, Maj Karl C. (1 December 2008) *'Fighting Through the Fog of War '*, Marine Corps Gazette <http://web.archive.org/web/20081201131311/<http://www.mca-marines.org/Gazette/06rohr.asp>

57   Scholtz, Leopold (2004) *'Iraq 2003 (Part 2): The Road to Baghdad'*, Scientia Militaria, South African Journal of Military Studies, Vol 32, Nr 1, p. 13 <http://scientiamilitaria.journals.ac.za>

58   Cordesman, Anthony, op.cit., p. 68

59   The 19-year old Jessica Lynch was taken by Iraqi soldiers to Nassiriya hospital where she received treatment. The story of her 'heroic rescue' was one of the most stunning and disgraceful pieces of news management (reversal of the truth) in the best style of Hollywood producers.See: Kampfner, John (15 May 2003) *'The truth about Jessica'*, The Guardian <http://www.theguardian.com/world/2003/may/15/iraq.usa2>

60   As Samawah is a city 280 Kilometers southeast of Baghdad. Al Faysaliah is a quarter of As Samawah.

61   Steele, Jonathan (22 October 2010) *'Iraq war logs: Apache helicopters kill 14 civilians in hunt for insurgents'*, The Guardian <http://www.theguardian.com/world/2010/oct/22/apache-helicopters-kill-iraqi-civilians>

62   Um Qasr is a strategically important port city in southern Iraq about 51 kilometres southeast of Basrah, located where the mouth of the Shatt al Arab waterway enters the Gulf.

63   Abu al Khasib is an agricultural town in the east of Basrah Governorate in

southern Iraq on the Shatt al Arab waterway.

64   Najaf is the holiest city for Shi'ia Muslims, housing the tomb of Imam Ali bin Abi Talib. It is located about 160 kilometres south of Baghdad.

65   Russell, Alec (2 August 2004) *'American 'double agent' sold Baghdad false war plans'*, The Telegraph <http://www.telegraph.co.uk/news/worldnews/middleeast/iraq/1468478/American-double-agent-sold-Baghdad-false-war-plans.html>

66   Kerbala is among the holiest cities of Shi'ia Muslims. It is located about 100 kilometres southwest of Baghdad.

67   Frontline (26 February 2004) *'Interview - Lt. Gen. Raad Al-Hamdani'*<http://www.pbs.org/wgbh/pages/frontline/shows/invasion/interviews/raad.html>

68   *Ibid*, Al-Hamdani explains:
I gave the commander of the sabotage force, Maj. Rawkan Al-Ajeeley, clear written and verbal orders that, whenever you feel that the enemy is close to the bridge, you should blow it up. We prepared this bridge for blowing with enough explosives to make it useless for the enemy, and force them to depend on building their own bridges, which will cost them time. But the approval on destroying the bridge was not issued in time.

69   Stillwell, Alexander (2007) *'Special Forces in Action'*, Amber Books Ltd

70   Petersen, Kim and Sabri, B.J. (24 February 2010) *'Combating the Disinformation, Psyops, and Cover-ups of the US Military'*, Dissident Voice <http://dissidentvoice.org/2010/02/combating-the-disinformation-propaganda-and-cover-ups-of-the-military-industrial-complex/>

71   Al Jazeera (09 Apr 2007) *'US accused of using neutron bombs'* <http://www.aljazeera.com/news/middleeast/2007/04/200852514126899448.html

72   Smith, W. Leon (2 April 2007), *'Battle of Baghdad Cover-Up Four Years Later:Interview With Captain Eric May Ghost Troop Commander'*, The Lone Star Iconoclast <http://www.iconoclastnews.com/AbsoluteNM/anmviewer.asp?a=1294>

73   Escobar, Pepe (25 April 2003) *'The Roving Eye – The Baghdad Deal'*, Asia Times <http://www.atimes.com/atimes/Middle_East/ED25Ak04.html>

74   Buncombe, Andrew (24 May 2003*) 'US Army Chief Says Iraqi Troops Took Bribes to Surrender Dollar Notes Easier to Take Than Bullets; Iraq: The Aftermath'*, The Independent - London

75   Graham, Bradley (7 April 2003) *'U.S. Airlift Iraqi Exile Force For Duties Near Nisiriyah'*, Washington Post <http://www.washingtonpost.com/wp-dyn/articles/A42859-2003Apr6.html>

76   Cordesman, Anthony, op.cit., p. 238

77   British Casualties: Iraq, Casualty Monitor <http://www.zen111450.zen.co.uk/casualty_monitor/ukcasualties3b.htm>

78   The *Iraq War Coalition* Fatalities Project <http://www.obleek.com/iraq/>

79   US Department of Defense (23 October 2003) *'Secretary of Defence Interview with Bob Woodward'* <http://www.defense.gov/transcripts/transcript.aspx?transcriptid=2511>

80   Epstein, Edward (23 March 2002) *'Success in Afghanistan hard to gauge'*, The San Francisco Chronicle <http://www.sfgate.com/news/article/Success-in-Afghan-war-hard-to-gauge-U-S-2861604.php>

81   Cordesman, Anthony, op.cit., p. 256

82   Documented Coalition Losses in the III Persian Gulf War <http://www.orbat.com/site/agtwopen/iraq_equipment_losses.html>

Chapter 5: The Failure of the Security Council

1   Article 27 of the Charter deals with Voting. It reads: Each member of the Security Council shall have one vote. Decisions of the Security Council on procedural matters shall be made by an affirmative vote of nine members.Decisions of the Security Council on all other matters shall be made by an affirmative vote

of nine members including the concurring votes of the permanent members; provided that, in decisions under Chapter VI, and under paragraph 3 of Article 52, a party to a dispute shall abstain from voting.<http://www.un.org/en/documents/charter/chapter5.shtml>

2   Johns, Christina Jacqueline, & Johnson, P. Ward (1994) 'State Crime, the Media and the Invasion of Panama' Praeger Publishers, Westport, CT., pp. 13-42. See also: The Independent Commission of Inquiry on the U.S. Invasion of Panama (1999) 'The U.S. Invasion of Panama: The Truth Behind Operational 'Just Cause' ' South End Press, Cambridge MA

3   We have established in our previous book **'Genocide in Iraq'** that Israel is in fact in control of the SC through the US after Zionism had reached the highest state of imperialism.

4   The UN General Assembly passed resolution GA res. 37/123 declaring the massacres as an 'act of genocide'.

5   Article 25 reads: "The Members of the United Nations agree to accept and carry out the decisions of the Security Council in accordance with the present Charter."

6   Article 108 reads: "Amendments to the present Charter shall come into force for all Members of the United Nations when they have been adopted by a vote of two thirds of the members of the General Assembly and ratified in accordance with their respective constitutional processes by two thirds of the Members of the United Nations, including all the permanent members of the Security Council."

7   Article 103 reads: "In the event of a conflict between the obligations of the Members of the United Nations under the present Charter and their obligations under any other international agreement, their obligations under the present Charter shall prevail."

8   Dreher, Axel; Sturm, Jan-Egbert & Vreeland, James Raymond (2008) **'Global Horse Trading: IMF loans for votes in the United Nations Security Council'**, <http://www.sciencedirect.com/science/article/pii/S0014292109000312>; See also: New Statesman (23 September 2002) **'John Pilger reveals how the Bushes bribe the world'** <http://www.newstatesman.com/200209230006>

9   Eronen, Mikko (20 November 1990) **'Finland accepts the use of force in the Persian Gulf'** (in Finnish) Helsingin Sanomat

10   Elsner, Alan (3 January 2010) 'Flashback to 1990: Jim Baker's Quick Trip to Yemen', Huff Post World, <http://www.huffingtonpost.com/alan-elsner/flashback-to-1990jim-bake_b_409725.html>

11   Pilger, John, op.cit.

12   *Ibid*

13   On the spirit of the UN Charter see the preamble and articles 1 and 2. For the peaceful means see Articles 33-38

14   **A resolution "deeply deploring" the United States-led invasion of Grenada was vetoed by the US. See: Bernstein, Richard (28 October 1983)** 'U.S. vetoes U.N. resolution 'deploring' Grenada invasion', **New York Times <http://www.nytimes.com/1983/10/29/world/us-vetoes-un-resolution-deploring-grenada-invasion.html>**

15   The US, Britain and France vetoed a SC resolution criticizing the American invasion of Panama. See: Lewis, Paul (24 December 1989) 'Fighting in Panama: United Nations; Security Council Condemnation of Invasion Vetoed', New York Times <http://www.nytimes.com/1989/12/24/world/fighting-panama-united-nations-security-council-condemnation-invasion-vetoed.html>

16   **USA Today (26 February 2003)** 'Mexico shifts toward U.S. position on Iraq'<http://www.usatoday.com/news/world/iraq/2003-02-26-us-mexico-iraq_x.htm>

17   SC Resolution 1454 (2002)<http://www.uncc.ch/resolutio/res1454.pdf>

18   Gilligan, Andrew (21 July 2013) 'The betrayal of Dr David Kelly, 10 years on', The

Telegraph<http://www.telegraph.co.uk/news/politics/10192271/The-betrayal-of-Dr-David-Kelly-10-years-on.html>

19   <http://www.uncc.ch/resolutio/res1472.pdf> SC Resolution 1472 (2003)

20   Rome Statute of the ICC, *'Crime of Aggression'*, Article 8 *bis*, p. 9 <http://www.icc-cpi.int/NR/rdonlyres/ADD16852-AEE9-4757-ABE7-9CDC7CF02886/283503/RomeStatutEng1.pdf>

21   Definition of Aggression, UN General Assembly Resolution 3314, 2319th Plenary Meeting, 14 December 1974.<http://www1.umn.edu/humanrts/instree/GAres3314.html>

22   Harris, Whitney R. (1 October 2004) *'The Crime of Waging Aggressive War'*<http://www.roberthjackson.org/the-man/speeches-articles/speeches/speeches-related-to-robert-h-jackson/the-crime-of-waging-aggressive-war/>

23   SC Resolution 1472 (2003) <http://www.uncc.ch/resolutio/res1472.pdf>

24   See: Al-Ani, Abdul-Haq (2008) *'The Trial of Saddam Hussein'* Clarity Press, Atlanta, GA., pp. 122 ff

25   Letter from the Permanent Representatives of the UK and the US to the UN addressed to the President of the Security Council<http://www.securitycouncil-report.org/atf/cf/%7B65BFCF9B-6D27-4E9C-8CD3-CF6E4FF96FF9%7D/Iraq%20S2003538.pdf>

26   SC Resolution 1483 (2003) <http://www.uncc.ch/resolutio/res1483.pdf>

27   Press Release: CENTCOM (Wednesday, 16 April 2003, 9:59 am) *'Pool Report: U.S. Iraqi Meeting At An Nasiriyah'*, <http://www.scoop.co.nz/stories/WO0304/S00240.htm

28   US Department of State, *'Visions of Freedom: 100 Iraqis Meet in Nasiriyah and Create Basis for New Government'*, <http://2001-2009.state.gov/p/nea/rls/19714.htm

29   Article 43, Convention (IV) respecting the Laws and Customs of War on Land and its annex: Regulations concerning the Laws and Customs of War on Land. The Hague, 18 October 1907.<http://www.icrc.org/ihl/385ec082b509e76c41256739003e636d/1d1726425f6955aec125641e0038bfd6>

30   UN Founding Member States<http://www.un.org/depts/dhl/unms/founders.shtml>

31   SC Resolution1500 (2003)<http://daccess-dds-ny.un.org/doc/UNDOC/GEN/N03/467/78/PDF/N0346778.pdf?OpenElement>

32   SC Resolution 1511 (2003)<http://daccess-dds-ny.un.org/doc/UNDOC/GEN/N03/563/91/PDF/N0356391.pdf?OpenElement>

33   See e.g. Paxton, Robert (1972) *'Vichy France: Old Guard and New Order, 1940-1944'*, Knopf, New York

34   SC Resolution 1546 (2004) <http://www.uncc.ch/resolutio/res1546.pdf>

35   *See:* Occupation and international humanitarian law: questions and answers <http://www.icrc.org/eng/resources/documents/misc/634kfc.htm>

36   SC Resolution 1762 (2007) <http://www.un.org/ga/search/view_doc.asp?symbol=S/RES/1762%282007%29>

37   SC Resolution 1956 (2010) <http://www.un.org/ga/search/view_doc.asp?symbol=S/RES/1956%282010%29>

38   SC Resolution 1957 (2010) <http://www.un.org/ga/search/view_doc.asp?symbol=S/RES/1957%282010%29>

39   SC Resolution 1958 (2010) <http://www.un.org/ga/search/view_doc.asp?symbol=S/RES/1958%282010%29>

40   SC Resolutions 2001 (2011) and 2061 (2012) <http://www.securitycouncilreport.org/atf/cf/%7B65BFCF9B-6D27-4E9C-8CD3-CF6E4FF96FF9%7D/CAC%20S%20RES%201998.pdf> <http://www.un.org/ga/search/view_doc.asp?symbol=S/RES/2061%282012%29>

41   On 27 June 2013, the SC decided to remove Iraq from Chapter VII of the UN Charter, unanimously agreeing to lift the UN sanctions imposed on Iraq since

1990, agreeing also that the issue of missing Kuwaiti people, property and archives should be handled under Chapter 6, instead of Chapter VII. <http://www.un.org/en/ga/search/view_doc.asp?symbol=S/RES/2107%282013%29>

42   Gordon, Joy (2002) *'When intent makes all the difference in the world: economic sanctions on Iraq and the accusation of genocide'*, Yale Human Rights and Development Law Journal, Vol. 5, 2002, p. 58.

43   UN Charter chapter VII

44   The Sanctions Committee was created by SC Resolution 661 (1990) to monitor the implementation of sanctions on Iraq. The Sanctions Committee adopted its own rules which enabled any member of the SC to veto the import of any item to Iraq without an explanation, thereby extending the veto of five members to fifteen. This was abused so much that on the eve of the 2003 invasion the Committee reported that: 'As of 30 April 2002, 1,439 applications are still on hold, with a total value of US$ 4.36 billion.' (S/2002/1261, 18 November 2002). This figure may even be misleading in its effect because an item on hold may be a small percentage of the total cost but enough to render the primary item inoperative such as a spark plug for a truck or a cable for a generator.

45   In June 1991 the UK/US set up in Iraq, without international authority, a 'no-fly zone' north of the 36th parallel and on 26 August 1992 George Bush announced a 'no-fly zone' in Iraq below the 32nd parallel in Iraq. *See:* Al-Ani, Abdul-Haq (2008) *'The Trial of Saddam Hussein'*, op.cit, p. 370

46   'Our data show that United States and United Kingdom aircraft invaded Iraqi airspace nearly 20,000 times between December 1998 and mid-March 2000. We are particularly concerned about reports of strikes against facilities that are being used in the United Nations humanitarian operation, in particular against food distribution warehouses and against metering stations along oil pipelines. According to these analyses, 42 per cent of these air strikes have resulted in human casualties. Over the past year, 144 innocent civilians have died and 466 people have been wounded as a result of these air strikes. Our data show that 57 people have been killed and 133 wounded in southern Iraq, and that 87 people have been killed and 313 wounded in the north. Claims that these strikes were not directed against civilian targets do not hold water. Facts — including facts from international experts — attest to the contrary. Nor does the notion that these air strikes were in retaliation for actions by Iraqi anti-aircraft defences hold water: our data show that facilities unrelated to anti-aircraft defence systems are being hit.' (From the address of Russian Federation representative, Mr. Lavrov, to the SC 4120th meeting on 24 March 2000, Document S/PV.4120, p. 6) http<http://daccess-dds-ny.un.org/doc/UNDOC/PRO/N00/359/07/PDF/N0035907.pdf?OpenElement>

47   The UN had already defined aggression in UN Resolution 3314 of 14 December 1974 and it ought to have applied that definition to Iraq as a principle under customary international law. The definition has since been incorporated into the Statute of Rome and is the definition of the crime of Aggression. We thus believe that the occupation of Iraq was a clear crime of aggression and many other clear breaches of international law were involved. From that point of view, the Security Council can be arguably seen as violating international law when it co-operated in the consummation of the violations. Instead of speaking of 'bestowing legitimacy' we would speak about co-operation to commit violations.

48   For details of these breaches of international law by the CPA, *see:* Chapter 4, Al-Ani, Abdul-Haq, *'The Trial of Saddam Hussein'*, op.cit.

49   'My first example is about how to reconcile two apparently equal values. It is a case about a man who was arrested and detained in a detention centre operated by British forces in Iraq. His internment was thought to be necessary for imperative reasons of security in Iraq. He was suspected of being a member of a terrorist group involved in weapons smuggling and other terrorist activities. But

he was not charged with any offence, and no charge or trial was in prospect. He complained that his continued detention infringed his rights under article 5(1) of the Convention. Various issues were raised. The one that is relevant to this discussion turned on the relationship between article 5(1) of the Convention, which protects the right to liberty, and article 103 of the UN Charter which provides that, in the event of a conflict between obligations under the Charter and their obligations under an international agreement, obligations under the Charter must prevail. The coalition forces were in Iraq under the authority of a Security Council resolution. This gave them authority to take all necessary measures to contribute to the maintenance of security and stability.' Lord Hope of Craighead, 'The Judges' Dilemma' (2009) 58(4) I.C.L.Q. 753, 757

Chapter 6: Bremer Dismantles Iraq

1   Lortz, MG (2005) *'A History of Kurdish Military Forces'*, p. 9 <http://etd.lib.fsu.edu/theses/available/etd-11142005-144616/unrestricted/003Manuscript.pdf>>

2   Halchin, L. Elaine (21 September 2006) *'The Coalition Provisional Authority (CPA): Origin, Characteristics, and Institutional Authorities'*, CRS Report for Congress, p. 1 <http://digital.library.unt.edu/ark:/67531/metacrs10420/m1/1/high_res_d/RL32370_2006Sep21.pdf>>

3   Feith, Douglas (11 February 2003) *'Post-war planning'*, Statement by Douglas J. Feith, Under Secretary of Defense for Policy, Senate Committee on Foreign Relations <http://www.centerforsecuritypolicy.org/2003/02/11/post-war-planning-2/>

4   Young, Michael (19 March 2003) *'Iraq's New Rulers, Handicapping the postwar administrators'*, <http://www.reason.com/news/show/32667.html>

5   BBC Newsnight (22 March 2004), *'Interview: General Jay Garner'* <http://news.bbc.co.uk/2/hi/programmes/newsnight/3552737.stm>

6   Halchin, L. Elaine, op.cit., p. 3

7   Crimes against peace, Principle IV(a), Principles of International Law Recognized in the Charter of the Nüremberg Tribunal and in the Judgment of the Tribunal, 1950, International Humanitarian Law: Treaties & Documents. <<http://www.icrc.org/ihl.nsf/FULL/390?OpenDocument>

8   Rome Statute of the International Criminal Court, *'Crime of aggression'*, Article 8 bis,<http://www.icc-cpi.int/nr/rdonlyres/ea9aeff7-5752-4f84-be94-0a655eb30e16/0/rome_statute_english.pdf>>

9   Convention (IV) respecting the Laws and Customs of War on Land and its annex: Regulations concerning the Laws and Customs of War on Land. The Hague, 18 October 1907. <http://www.icrc.org/applic/ihl/ihl.nsf/Article.xsp?action=openDocument&documentId=FC793177CA9A6F37C12563CD00516650>

10 Convention (III) relative to the Treatment of Prisoners of War. Geneva, 12 August 1949. <http://www.icrc.org/ihl.nsf/7c4d08d9b287a42141256739003e63bb/6fef854a3517b75ac125641e004a9e68>

11 Convention (IV) relative to the Protection of Civilian Persons in Time of War. Geneva, 12 August 1949. <http://www.icrc.org/ihl.nsf/385ec082b509e76c-41256739003e636d/6756482d86146898c125641e004aa3c5>

12 *Ibid*

13 *Ibid*

14 Rome Statute of the International Criminal Court <http://www.icc-cpi.int/nr/rdonlyres/ea9aeff7-5752-4f84-be94-0a655eb30e16/0/rome_statute_english.pdf>

15 As defined on the CPA site <http://www.iraqcoalition.org/regulations/>

16 Regulation 1, CPA <http://www.iraqcoalition.org/regulations/20030516_CPAREG_1_The_Coalition_Provisional_Authority_.pdf>

17 Resolution 1483 (2003) <http://daccess-dds-ny.un.org/doc/UNDOC/GEN/

N03/368/53/PDF>/N0336853.pdf>?OpenElement>

18 Coalition Provisional Authority Order Number 1, De-Ba`athification Of Iraqi Society <http://www.iraqcoalition.org/regulations/20030516_CPAORD_1_De-Ba_athification_of_Iraqi_Society_.pdf>

19 Rome Statute of the International Criminal Court, op.cit.

20 Coalition Provisional Authority Order Number 5, Establishment of the Iraqi De-Ba'athification Council <http://www.iraqcoalition.org/regulations/CPAORD5.pdf>

21 Coalition Provisional Authority Memorandum Number 1, Implementation of De-Ba'athification Order No. 1 <http://www.iraqcoalition.org/regulations/20030603_CPAMEMO_1_Implementation_of_De-Ba_athification.pdf>

22 Coalition Provisional Authority Order Number 62, Disqualification from Public Office <http://www.iraqcoalition.org/regulations/20040301_CPAORD62.pdf>>

23 Coalition Provisional Authority Order Number 2, Dissolution of Entities <http://www.iraqcoalition.org/regulations/20030823_CPAORD_2_Dissolution_of_Entities_with_Annex_A.pdf>

24 Coalition Provisional Authority Order Number 22, Creation of A New Iraqi Army <http://www.iraqcoalition.org/regulations/20030818_CPAORD_22_Creation_of_a_New_Iraqi_Army.pdf>

25 Coalition Provisional Authority Order Number 23, Creation of a Code of Military Discipline for the New Iraqi Army <http://www.iraqcoalition.org/regulations/20030820_CPAORD_23_Creation_of_a_Code_with_Annex.pdf>

26 Coalition Provisional Authority Order Number 26, Creation of a Department of Border Enforcement <http://www.iraqcoalition.org/regulations/20030824_CPAORD_26_Creation_of_the_Dept_of_Border_Enforcement.pdf>

27 Coalition Provisional Authority Order Number 27, Establishment of the Facilities Protection Service <http://www.iraqcoalition.org/regulations/20030904_CPAORD_27_Establishment_of_the_Facilities_Protection_Svc.pdf>

28 Coalition Provisional Authority Order Number 28, Establishment of the Iraqi Civil Defense Corps <http://www.iraqcoalition.org/regulations/20030903_CPAORD_28_Est_of_the_Iraqi_Civil_Defense_Corps.pdf>

29 Coalition Provisional Authority Order Number 42, Creation of the Defense Support Agency <http://www.iraqcoalition.org/regulations/20030923_CPAORD42.pdf>

30 Coalition Provisional Authority Order Number 75, Realignment of Military Industrial Companies <http://www.iraqcoalition.org/regulations/20040420_CPAORD_75_Realignment_of_Military_Industrial_Companies__with_Annex_A.pdf>

31 Coalition Provisional Authority Order Number 91, Regulation of Armed Forces and Militais within Iraq <http://www.iraqcoalition.org/regulations/20040607_CPAORD91_Regulation_of_Armed_Forces_and_Militias_within_Iraq.pdf>

32 *Ibid*

33 Fainaru, Steve (2008) **'Big Boy Rules- America's Mercenaries Fighting in Iraq'**, Da Capo Press, US, p. 24

34 Coalition Provisional Authority Order Number 17 (Revised), Status Of The Coalition Provisional Authority, MNF - Iraq, Certain Missions And Personnel In Iraq <http://www.iraqcoalition.org/regulations/20040627_CPAORD_17_Status_of_Coalition__Rev__with_Annex_A.pdf>

35 Fainaru, Steve, op.cit., pp. 176-183

36 Coalition Provisional Authority Order Number 75, op.cit.

37 Coalition Provisional Authority Memorandum Number 8, Exportation of Scrap Metal…..<http://www.iraqcoalition.org/regulations/20040226_CPAMEMO_8_Scrap_Metal_.pdf>

38 Coalition Provisional Authority Order Number 64, Amendment to the Company Law No. 21 of 1997 <http://www.iraqcoalition.org/regulations/20040305_

CPAORD64_Amendment_to_the_Company_Law_No._21_of_1997_with_Annex_A.pdf>

39 Stone, J. (1959) *'Legal Controls of International Conflict'*, Stevens & Sons Ltd, London, pp. 698-699.

40 Coalition Provisional Authority Order Number 56, Central Bank Law<http://www.iraqcoalition.org/regulations/20040306_CPAORD_56_Central_Bank_Law_with_Annex.pdf>

41 Coalition Provisional Authority Order Number 94, Banking Law of 2004 <http://www.iraqcoalition.org/regulations/20040607_CPAORD94_Banking_Law_of_2004_with_Annex_A.pdf>

42 Coalition Provisional Authority Order Number 76, Consolidations of State-Owned Enterprises <http://www.iraqcoalition.org/regulations/20040528_CPAORD_76_Consolidations_of_State-Owned_Enterprises_with_Annex_A.pdf>

43 Coalition Provisional Authority Order Number 39, Foreign Investment <http://www.iraqcoalition.org/regulations/20031220_CPAORD_39_Foreign_Investment_.pdf> was amended by: Coalition Provisional Authority Order Number 46 <http://www.iraqcoalition.org/regulations/20031221_CPAORD46-39Amend.pdf>

44 Coalition Provisional Authority Order Number 64, op.cit.

45 Coalition Provisional Authority Order Number 80, Amendment to the Trademarks and Descriptions law no. 21 of 1957 <http://www.iraqcoalition.org/regulations/20040426_CPAORD_80_Amendment_to_the_Trademarks_and_Descriptions_Law_No._21_of_1957.pdf>

46 Coalition Provisional Authority Order Number 81, Patent, Industrial Design, Undisclosed Information, Integrated Circuits and Plant Variety Law <http://www.iraqcoalition.org/regulations/20040426_CPAORD_81_Patents_Law.pdf>

47 Coalition Provisional Authority Order Number 83, Amendment to The Copyright Law <http://www.iraqcoalition.org/regulations/20040428_CPAORD82_Remembrance_Foundation.pdf>

48 Smith, Jeremy (27 August 2005) *'ORDER 81: Re-engineering Iraqi agriculture/ The ultimate war crime: breaking the agricultural cycle'*, The Ecologist, Vol. 35, No. 1 <http://www.globalresearch.ca/order-81-re-engineering-iraqi-agriculture/870, accessed 20 August 2013

49 Working Group on Transitional Justice, The Future of Iraq Project <http://www2.gwu.edu/~nsarchiv/NSAEBB/NSAEBB198/FOI%20Transitional%20Justice.pdf>

50 Coalition Provisional Authority Order Number 7, Penal Code <http://www.iraqcoalition.org/regulations/20030610_CPAORD_7_Penal_Code.pdf>

51 Coalition Provisional Authority Order Number 31, Modification of Penal Code and Criminal Proceedings Law <http://www.iraqcoalition.org/regulations/20030921_CPAORD31.pdf>

52 Coalition Provisional Authority Order Number 13 (Revised) (Amended), The Central Criminal Court of Iraq <http://www.iraqcoalition.org/regulations/20040422_CPAORD_13_Revised_Amended.pdf>

53 Coalition Provisional Authority Order Number 15, Establishment of the Judicial Review Committee <http://govinfo.library.unt.edu/cpa-iraq/regulations/20030623_CPAORD_15_ Establishment_of_the_ Judicial_Reveiw_Committee.pdf>

54 Coalition Provisional Authority Order Number 35, Re-Establishment of Council of Judges <http://www.iraqcoalition.org/regulations/20030921_CPAORD35.pdf>

55 Coalition Provisional Authority Order Number 17, op.cit.

56 Coalition Provisional Authority Memorandum Number 3 (Revised), Criminal Procedures <http://www.iraqcoalition.org/regulations/20040627_CPAMEMO_3_Criminal_Procedures__Rev_.pdf>

57   For a list of articles on Tariq Aziz, see:<http://www.theguardian.com/world/tariq-aziz>

58   Coalition Provisional Authority Order Number 92, The Independent Electoral Commission of Iraq <http://www.iraqcoalition.org/regulations/20040531_CPAORD_92_Independent_Electoral_commission_of_Iraq.pdf>

59   Coalition Provisional Authority Order Number 96, The Electoral Law <http://www.iraqcoalition.org/regulations/20040615_CPAORD_96_The_Electoral_Law.pdf>

60   Coalition Provisional Authority Order Number 97, Political Parties and Entities Law <http://www.iraqcoalition.org/regulations/20040615_CPAORD_97_Political_Parties_and_Entities_Law.pdf>

61   Coalition Provisional Authority, Law Of Administration For The State Of Iraq For The Transitional Period <http://www.iraqcoalition.org/government/TAL.html>

62   The Development Fund for Iraq <http://www.iraqcoalition.org/budget/DFI_intro1.html>

63   International Advisory and Monitoring Board (IAMB), Terms of Reference <http://www.iamb.info/tor.htm>

64   Global Policy Forum, *'Development Fund for Iraq'* <http://www.globalpolicy.org/humanitarian-issues-in-iraq/development-fund-for-iraq.html

65   KPMG Bahrain (June 2004), *'Development Fund for Iraq-Appendix/ Matters noted involving internal controls and other operations issues during the audit of the fund'* <http://www.iamb.info/auditrep/r123103.pdf>

66   KPMG Bahrain (June 2004), *'Development Fund for Iraq Agreed-Upon Procedures Report For the period from 22 May 2003 to 31 December 2003'* <http://www.iamb.info/auditrep/r052203b.pdf>

67   CPA Program Review Board was created by Bremer under Regulation 2 entrusted with reviewing all identified requirements for the resources and integrating these requirements into a funding plan that would forecast available resources; recommending allocation of these resources; and setting forth the justification for the proposed expenditure. It is rather difficult to figure out why when such task requires some deep knowledge of Iraq and its needs that out of the 22 members of the board there was only one Iraqi member!

68   Report of the International Advisory and Monitoring Board of the Development Fund for Iraq <http://www.iamb.info/pdf>/iamb_12142004.pdf>

69   *'Rebuilding Iraq U.S. Mismanagement Of Iraqi Funds'* (June 2005), United States House Of Representatives Committee On Government Reform — Minority Staff Special Investigations Division <http://oversight-archive.waxman.house.gov/documents/20050621114229-22109.pdf>

70   *'Statement of Rep. Henry A. Waxman'* (21 June 2005) Ranking Minority Member, Committee on Government Reform, Subcommittee on National Security, Emerging Threats, and International Relations Hearing on the Development Fund for Iraq: U.S. Management of Iraq Oil Proceeds and Compliance with U.N. Security Council <http://oversight-archive.waxman.house.gov/documents/20050629132455-23867.pdf>

71   Harriman, Ed (7 July 2005) *'So, Mr Bremer, where did all the money go?'*, The Guardian <http://www.theguardian.com/world/2005/jul/07/iraq.features11>

Chapter 7: Instituting Federalism

1   Bensahel, Nora et al (2008) *'After Saddam- Prewar Planning and the Occupation of Iraq'*, Prepared for the United States Army, Rand Arroyo Center, P. 53<http://www.rand.org/content/dam/rand/pubs/monographs/2008/RAND_MG642.pdf>

2   *Ibid*, p. 58

3   *Ibid*, pp. 58-59

4   *Ibid*

5   *Ibid*, p. 67

6   Bensahel, Nora, op.cit., p. 24

7   Chandrasekaran, Rajiv (2009) *'Imperial Life In The Emerald City- Inside Bagh-dad's Green Zone',* Bloomsbury, p. 36 (electronic edition)

8   See: *' Gen. Garner Arrives in Baghdad to Oversee Iraq's Reconstruction'*, Fox News, 21 April 2003 <http://www.foxnews.com/story/2003/04/21/gen-garner-arrives-in-baghdad-to-oversee-iraq-reconstruction/>

9   Ibid

10   Feith, Douglas J. (2008) *'War and Decision: Inside the Pentagon at the Dawn of the War on Terrorism',* Harper, New York, p. 369

11   *Ibid*, p.408

12   Dao, James & Schmitt, Eric (7 May 2003) *'After effects: Postwar Planning; President Picks A Special Envoy To Rebuild Iraq'*, The New York Times <http://www.nytimes.com/2003/05/07/world/aftereffects-postwar-planning-president-picks-a-special-envoy-to-rebuild-iraq.html>

13   *Ibid*

14   U.S. Office of Management and Budget (2 June 2003) *'Report to Congress: Pursu-ant to Section 1506 of the Emergency Wartime Supplemental Appropriations Act, 2003 (Public Law 108-11)'*, p. 2

15   The White House, President George W. Bush (6 May 2003) *'President Names En-voy to Iraq',* Statement by the Press Secretary <http://georgewbush-whitehouse.archives.gov/news/releases/2003/05/20030506-5.html>

16   Bremer, L. Paul & Malcolm McConnell (2006) *'My Year in Iraq – the struggle to build a future of hope'*, Simon & Schuster, New York, p. 51 (electronic edition). One can not escape noticing the clear mispresentation of facts in the book. Bremer blames everything in Iraq on the Ba'ath rule, without once mentioning the effects of the destruction of the attacks of 1991, the genocidal 12-year sanc-tions that followed them and the new destruction of the invasion. He describes women as "downtrodden under Saddam" which everyone who knows Iraq would know that was not true. He attributes the destruction of the infrastructure in schools, hospitals and elsewhere to the Ba'ath rule, while not mentioning the promise of his country's Secretary of State in 1991 to return Iraq to the Stone Age!

17   *Ibid*, p. 52

18   Coalition Provisional Authority Order Number 1, De-Ba`Athification Of Iraqi Society <http://www.iraqcoalition.org/regulations/20030516_CPAORD_1_De-Ba_athification_of_Iraqi_Society_.pdf>

19   Pavel, Ryan (April 2012) *'The De-Ba'athification of Iraq- The The development and implementation of an ostensibly necessary vetting policy that turned into a tool of sectarianism'*, University of Michigan, pp. 24-28<https://ictj.org/sites/default/files/ICTJ-Report-Iraq-De-Ba'athification-2013-ENG.pdf>

20   Roston, Aram (2008), *'The man who pushed America to war : the extraordinary life, adventures and obsessions of Ahmadal-Chalabi'*, Nation Books, New York, P. 238

21   Sanger, David E. (12 October 2002) *'Bush Says U.S. Won't Force Its Ways on a Beaten Iraq'* <http://www.nytimes.com/2002/10/12/international/middleeast/12REBU.html>

22   Chalabi, Ahmad (19 February 2003) *'Iraq for the Iraqis'*, The Wall Street Journal<http://www.mail-archive.com/sam11@erols.com/msg00060.html>

23   Chandrasekaranop.cit., pp. 78-79

24   Feith, op.cit., p. 427

25   Bremer, Paul L. (13 May 2007) *'What We Got Right in Iraq'*, The Washington Post <http://www.washingtonpost.com/wp-dyn/content/article/2007/05/11/AR2007051102054.html>

26   Coalition Provisional Authority Order Number 5, Establishment of the Iraqi De-Ba`Athification Council <http://www.iraqcoalition.org/regulations/CPAORD5.pdf>

27   Coalition Provisional Authority Order Number 62, Disqualification from Public Office <http://www.iraqcoalition.org/regulations/20040301_CPAORD62.pdf>

28   The Economist (27 November 2003) *'Iraq: Dangers of the inquisition – How de-Ba'athification is helping the rebels'* <http://www.economist.com/node/2256201>

29   See: paragraph (h) of Article 7 of the Rome Statute of the International Criminal Court <http://legal.un.org/icc/statute/romefra.htm>

30   Feith, op.cit., p. 361

31   Coalition Provisional Authority Order Number 2, Dissolution of Entities <http://www.iraqcoalition.org/regulations/20030823_CPAORD_2_Dissolution_of_Entities_with_Annex_A.pdf>

32   International Crisis Group (23 December 2003) *' Iraq: Building a New Security Structure'*, Middle East Report No. 20 <http://www.crisisgroup.org/en/regions/middle-east-north-africa/iraq-iran-gulf/iraq/020-iraq-building-a-new-security-structure.aspx>

33   William Luti, <http://rightweb.irc-online.org/profile/Luti_William>

34   Feith, op.cit., p. 366

35   Bensahel, op.cit., p. 122

36   Feith, op.cit., p. 434

37   Coalition Provisional Authority Order Number 22, Creation of A New Iraqi Army <http://www.iraqcoalition.org/regulations/20030818_CPAORD_22_Creation_of_a_New_Iraqi_Army.pdf>

38   *Ibid*

39   Coalition Provisional Authority Order Number 91, Regulation Of Armed Forces And Militias Within Iraq <http://www.iraqcoalition.org/regulations/20040607_CPAORD91_Regulation_of_Armed_Forces_and_Militias_within_Iraq.pdf>

40   Daniszewski, John (16 September 2003) *'New Iraqi Army Makes Its Debut'*, Los Angeles Times <http://articles.latimes.com/2003/sep/16/world/fg-army16>

41   Office of the Secretary of Defence, Department Of Defense Budget Fiscal Year (Fy) 2015 Budget Amendment (November 2014*) 'Justification for FY 2015 Overseas Contingency Operations Iraq Train and Equip Fund (ITEF)'*, p. 11 <http://1.usa.gov/11nsTuN>

42   Daily Times Report (20 October 2002) *'Training of Iraqi exiles authorised'* <http://www.dailytimes.com.pk/default.asp?page=story_20-10-2002_pg7_28>

43   Bensahel, op.cit., p. 160

44   Schmitt, Eric and Weisman, Steven R. (11 April 2003) *'A Nation At War: New Leadership; US to Recruit Iraqi Civilians to Interim Posts'*, The New York Times <http://www.nytimes.com/2003/04/11/world/a-nation-at-war-new-leadership-us-to-recruit-iraqi-civilians-to-interim-posts.html>

45   *Ibid*

46   Morello, Carol (6 May 2003) *'Nucleus of Iraqi Leaders Emerges- Occupation Chief Outlines Plan for Interim Authority'*, The Washington Post (repost by The Iraqi Foundation) <http://www.iraqfoundation.org/news/2003/emay/6_nucleus.html>

47   *Bremer, op.cit., p. 47*

48   Security Council Resolution 1483 (2003) <http://daccess-dds-ny.un.org/doc/UNDOC/GEN/N03/368/53/PDF/N0336853.pdf?OpenElement>

49   Transcript of press conference by Secretary-General Kofi Annan and Special Representative for Iraq, Sergio Vieira de Mello, 27 May 2003<http://www.un.org/apps/news/infocus/iraq/infocusnews.asp?NewsID=524&sID=12>

50   *Ibid*

51   Bremer, op.cit., p. 86

52   *Ibid*, p. 91

53   *Ibid*, p. 94

54   *Ibid*, p. 99

55   *Ibid*, p. 101

56   *Ibid*

57   Katzman, Kenneth, op.cit., p. 17

58   Bremer, op.cit., p. 123

59   *Ibid*, p. 124. We are not certain whether Bremer was referring to the salary per month or per year, as per year is not an excessive sum, considering how much other expenses they were getting.

60   United Nations Security Council Resolution 1500 <http://daccess-dds-ny.un.org/doc/UNDOC/GEN/N03/467/78/PDF/N0346778.pdf?OpenElement>

61   Security Council Resolution 1551 (16 October 2003) <http://daccess-dds-ny.un.org/doc/UNDOC/GEN/N03/563/91/PDF/N0356391.pdf?OpenElement>

62   Khammas, E.A. (11 August 2003) *'A Closed Circle of Collaborators'*, Occupation Watch Center <http://www.countercurrents.org/iraq-khammas110803.htm>

63   Allawi, Ali A. (2007) *'The Occupation of Iraq- Winning the War, Losing the Peace'*, Yale University Press, New Haven, P. 195

64   *Ibid*

65   Hess, Pamela (17 November 2003) *'Iraqi sovereignty on ambitious schedule'*, UPI <http://www.upi.com/Business_News/Security-Industry/2003/11/17/Iraqi-sovereignty-on-ambitious-schedule/UPI-90261069111918/>

66   Katzman, op.cit., p. 17

67   Diamond, Larry (2006) *'Squandered Victory: the American occupation and the bungled effort to bring democracy to Iraq'* (electronic copy), First Owl Books Edition, p. 44

68   *Ibid*, p. 46

69   *Ibid*, p. 89

70   The UN Security Council (23 February 2004) *'The Political Transition in Iraq: Report of the Fact-Finding Mission'* <http://www.un.org/News/dh/iraq/rpt-fact-finding-mission.pdf>

71   *'Statement from the Office of Grand Ayatollah on the Report of the Fact-Finding Mission '* (24 February 2004)

72   Coalition Provisional Authority Order Number 92, The Independent Electoral Commission of Iraq <http://www.iraqcoalition.org/regulations/20040531_CPAORD_92_Independent_Electoral_commission_of_Iraq.pdf>

73   Al-Ani, Abdul-Haq, (2008)*'The Trial of Saddam Hussein'*, Clarity Press Inc., Atlanta, GA, pp. 143-144

74   Otterman, op.cit.

75   *'Reply to Mr. Lakhdar Brahimi containg the opinion from Transitional Administrative Law for Iraq'* (19 March 2004) <http://www.sistani.org/arabic/statement/1476/>

76   See: Article 61 of the Transitional Administrative Law <http://web.archive.org/web/20090423064920/<http://www.cpa-iraq.org/government/TAL.html

77   The UN Security Council, *'Report of the Fact-Finding Mission'*, op.cit., p. 7

78   White, Josh & Weisman, Jonathan (22 April 2004) *'Limited Iraqi Sovereignty Planned'*, The Washington Post (reproduced by Information Clearing House) <http://www.informationclearinghouse.info/article6079.htm

79   Chandrasekaran, Rajiv (29 May 2004) *'Former Exile Is Selected AS Interim Iraqi Leader'*, The Washington Post <http://www.washingtonpost.com/wp-dyn/articles/A62691-2004May28.html

80   Hoge, Warren & Weisman, Steven. R. (29 May 2004) *'Surprising Choice for Premier of Iraq Reflects U.S. Influence'*, The New York Times <http://www.

nytimes.com/2004/05/29/politics/29ASSE.html>

81   Filkins, Dexter (3 June 2004) *'U.N. Envoy New Iraq Government to Court Foes of Occupation'*, The New York Times<http://www.nytimes.com/2004/06/03/ international/middleeast/03IRAQ.html>

82   Katzman, Kenneth, op.cit. pp. 17-18

83   Diamond, Larry, op.cit., p. 165

84   UN Security Council resolution 1546(2004)<http://daccess-dds-ny.un.org/doc/ UNDOC/GEN/N04/381/16/PDF/N0438116.pdf?OpenElement>

85   All of Bremers Regulations, Orders and Memoranda are available at:<http:// www.iraqcoalition.org/regulations/index.html>

86   Coalition Provisional Authority Order Number 92, The Independent Electoral Commission of Iraq<http://www.iraqcoalition.org/regulations/20040531_ CPAORD_92_Independent_Electoral_commission_of_Iraq.pdf>

87   Coalition Provisional Authority Order Number 96, The Electoral Law<http://www. iraqcoalition.org/regulations/20040615_CPAORD_96_The_Electoral_Law.pdf>

88   Allawi, Ali, op.cit., p. 335

89   *Ibid*, p. 340

90   Ghazi, Mazen (18 November 2004) *'Forty-Seven Bodies Boycott Iraq Elections'*, Quoted by: Democratic Underground <http://www.democraticunderground. com/discuss/duboard.php?az=view_all&address=102x1002839>

91   Katzman, Kenneth, op.cit., p. 21

92   *Ibid*

93   *Ibid*

94   Diamond, Larry, *'Consensus and Iraq's Constitution'*, Los Angeles Times, 15 October 2005.

95   Morrow, Jonathan, *'Iraq's Constitutional Process II- an opportunity lost'*, United States Institute of Peace, p. 14<http://www.usip.org/sites/default/files/sr155. pdf>

96   Jawad, Saad N., *'The Iraqi Constitution: Structural Flaws and Political Implications'*, LSE Middle East Centre Paper Series/01, November 2013, p. 5 <http:// www.lse.ac.uk/middleEastCentre/publications/Paper-Series/SaadJawad.pdf>

97   'The visible involvement of a foreign power in something so uniquely sovereign as the writing of a constitution is probably always regrettable. Especially with Iraq, even moderate Sunni Arab nationalsts would frequently express the fear that the Iraq constitution would be written in Washington, D.C.' in Morrow, Jonathan, op.cit.

98   Ibid, p. 2

99   'From the time the Leadership Council was formed, U.S. Ambassador Zalmay Khalilzad attended meetings regularly, and U.S. Embassy officials were engaged in less-than-subtle efforts to accelerate a final constitution. Several of the early meetings of the Leadership Council took place at the U.S. Embassy.'in Morrow, Jonathan, op.cit. pp. 14-15

100   'The U.S. Embassy circulated its own draft constitution in English' Morrow, Jonathan, op.cit. p. 15

101   Article 115, Iraqi Constitution <http://www.iraqinationality.gov.iq/attach/ iraqi_constitution.pdf>

102   Article 119: One or more governorates shall have the right to organize into a region based on a requestto be voted on in a referendum submitted in one of the following two methods: First: A request by one-third of the council members of each governorate intending to form a region. Second: A request by one-tenth of the voters in each of the governorates intending to form a region.

103   Bruno, Greg (22 October 2007), *'Plans for Iraq's Future: Federalism, Separatism, and Partition'*, Council for Foreign Relations <http://www.cfr.org/iraq/ plans-iraqs-future-federalism-separatism-partition/p14547#p2

104   Ibid

105   Ibid

106   Article 58, TAL

(A)   The Iraqi Transitional Government, and especially the Iraqi Property Claims Commission and other relevant bodies, shall act expeditiously to take measures to remedy the injustice caused by the previous regime's practices in altering the demographic character of certain regions, including Kirkuk, by deporting and expelling individuals from their places of residence, forcing migration in and out of the region, settling individuals alien to the region, depriving the inhabitants of work, and correcting nationality. To remedy this injustice, the Iraqi Transitional Government shall take the following steps:

(1)   With regard to residents who were deported, expelled, or who emigrated; it shall, in accordance with the statute of the Iraqi Property Claims Commission and other measures within the law, within a reasonable period of time, restore the residents to their homes and property, or, where this is unfeasible, shall provide just compensation.

(2)   With regard to the individuals newly introduced to specific regions and territories, it shall act in accordance with Article 10 of the Iraqi Property Claims Commission statute to ensure that such individuals may be resettled, may receive compensation from the state, may receive new land from the state near their residence in the governorate from which they came, or may receive compensation for the cost of moving to such areas.

(3)   With regard to persons deprived of employment or other means of support in order to force migration out of their regions and territories, it shall promote new employment opportunities in the regions and territories.

(4)   With regard to nationality correction, it shall repeal all relevant decrees and shall permit affected persons the right to determine their own national identity and ethnic affiliation free from coercion and duress.

(B)   The previous regime also manipulated and changed administrative boundaries for political ends. The Presidency Council of the Iraqi Transitional Government shall make recommendations to the National Assembly on remedying these unjust changes in the permanent constitution. In the event the Presidency Council is unable to agree unanimously on a set of recommendations, it shall unanimously appoint a neutral arbitrator to examine the issue and make recommendations. In the event the Presidency Council is unable to agree on an arbitrator, it shall request the Secretary General of the United Nations to appoint a distinguished international person to be the arbitrator.

(C)   The permanent resolution of disputed territories, including Kirkuk, shall be deferred until after these measures are completed, a fair and transparent census has been conducted and the permanent constitution has been ratified This resolution shall be consistent with the principle of justice, taking into account the will of the people of those territories.

107   Article 140: First: The executive authority shall undertake the necessary steps to complete the implementation of the requirements of all subparagraphs of Article 58 of the Transitional Administrative Law. Second: The responsibility placed upon the executive branch of the Iraqi Transitional Government stipulated in Article 58 of the Transitional Administrative Law shall extend and continue to the executive authority elected in accordance with this Constitution, provided that it accomplishes completely (normalization and census and concludes with a referendum in Kirkuk and other disputed territories to determine the will of their citizens), by a date not to exceed the 31st of December 2007.

108   See for example: Mahmoud, Nawazad, *'Talks on New Iraqi Government Snag over Disputed Kurdish Territories'*, 7 September 2014<http://rudaw.net/english/middleeast/iraq/070920141>

109	Article 141: Legislation enacted in the region of Kurdistan since 1992 shall remain in force, and decisions issued by the government of the region of Kurdistan, including court decisions and contracts, shall be considered valid unless they are amended or annulled pursuant to the laws of the region of Kurdistan by the competent entity in the region, provided that they do not contradict with the Constitution.
110	Article 20: Iraqi citizens, men and women, shall have the right to participate in public affairs and to enjoy political rights including the right to vote, elect, and run for office.
111	Article 39: First: The freedom to form and join associations and political parties shall be guaranteed, and this shall be regulated by law. Second: It is not permissible to force any person to join any party, society, or political entity, or force him to continue his membership in it.
112	Article 42: Each individual shall have the freedom of thought, conscience, and belief.
113	Article 7: First: Any entity or program that adopts, incites, facilitates, glorifies, promotes, or justifies racism or terrorism or accusations of being an infidel (takfir) or ethnic cleansing, especially the Saddamist Ba'ath in Iraq and its symbols, under any name whatsoever, shall be prohibited. Such entities may not be part of political pluralism in Iraq. This shall be regulated by law. Second: The State shall undertake to combat terrorism in all its forms, and shall work to protect its territories from being a base, pathway, or field for terrorist activities.
114	Article 135: First: The High Commission for De-Ba'athification shall continue its functions as an independent commission, in coordination with the judicial authority and the executive institutions within the framework of the laws regulating its functions. The Commission shall be attached to the Council of Representatives. Second: The Council of Representatives shall have the right to dissolve this Commission by an absolute majority after the completion of its function. Third: A nominee to the positions of the President of the Republic, the Prime Minister, the members of the Council of Ministers, the Speaker, the members of the Council of Representatives, the President, members of the Federation Council, their counterparts in the regions, or members of the judicial commissions and other positions covered by de-Ba'athification statutes pursuant to the law may not be subject to the provisions of de-Ba'athification. Fourth: The conditions stated in clause "Third" of this Article shall remain in force unless the Commission stated in item "First" of this Article is dissolved. Fifth: Mere membership in the dissolved Ba'ath party shall not be considered a sufficient basis for referral to court, and a member shall enjoy equality before the law and protection unless covered by the provisions of De-Ba'athification and the directives issued according to it. Sixth: The Council of Representatives shall form a parliamentary committee from among its members to monitor and review the executive procedures of the Higher Commission for De-Ba'athification and state institutions to guarantee justice, objectivity, and transparency and to examine their consistency with the laws. The committee's decisions shall be subject to the approval of the Council of Representatives.
115	Article 126: First: The President of the Republic and the Council of the Ministers collectively, or one-fifth of the Council of Representatives members, may propose to amend the Constitution. Second: The fundamental principles mentioned in Section One and the rights and liberties mentioned in Section Two of the Constitution may not be amended except after two successive electoral terms, with the approval of two-thirds of the members of the Council of Representatives, the approval of the people in a general referendum, and the ratification by the President of the Republic within seven days. Third: Other articles not stipulated in clause "Second" of this Article may not be amended, except with the approval

of two-thirds of the members of the Council of Representatives, the approval of the people in a general referendum, and the ratification by the President of the Republic within seven days. Fourth: Articles of the Constitution may not be amended if such amendment takes away from the powers of the regions that are not within the exclusive powers of the federal authorities, except by the approval of the legislative authority of the concerned region and the approval of the majority of its citizens in a general referendum. Fifth: A- An amendment is considered ratified by the President of the Republic after the expiration of the period stipulated in clauses "Second" and "Third" of this Article, in case he does not ratify it. B- An amendment shall enter into force on the date of its publication in the Official Gazette.

Chapter 8: The Destruction Continujes

1   Nagy, Thomas J.(2004) *'Safeguarding Our American Children by Saving Their Iraqi Children'*, in Ismael, Tareq Y. and Haddad, William W., *'Iraq The Human Cost Of History'*, Pluto Press, pp. 150-151.

2   For an overview of *'The Future Of Iraq Project"* see <http://www2.gwu.edu/~nsarchiv/NSAEBB/NSAEBB198/FOI%20Overview.pdf>

3   Donald Rumsfeld wrote in a Memorandum in March 2001: America must be "willing and prepared to act decisively to use the force necessary to prevail, plus some,''. See: Shanker, Thom (14 October 2002), *'Rumsfeld Favors Forceful Actions To Foil An Attack',* New York Times.

4   What has been termed *"The 1992 Los Angeles Riots"* lasted for several days, with widespread looting, assault, arson and murder, causing the death of 55 people, injuring almost 2,000, leading to 7,000 arrests, and causing nearly $1 billion in property damage, including the burnings of more than 3,000 buildings. See: <http://www.laweekly.com/microsites/la-riots/>

5   Rajiv, Chandrasekharan (2006) *'Imperial Life in the Emerald City: Inside Iraq's Green Zone'*, New York: Vintage Books, p. 179.

6   From 1989 to 2000, Agresto served as President of St. John's College in Santa Fe. In 2002-03 he was Lily Senior Research Fellow at Wabash College

7   *Ibid*, p. 180.

8   Bahrani, Zainab, *'Archaeology And The Strategies Of War'* in Baker, Raymond W.; Ismael, Shereen T. and Ismael, Tareq Y. (Eds.), (2010) *'Cultural Cleansing In Iraq'*, Pluto Press, p. 69.

9   *Bahrani, Zainab (9 April 2008) "Desecrating History", The Guardian https://www.theguardian.com/commentisfree/2008/apr/09/plunderingiraq*

10   *Bahrani, Zainab, 'Archaeology And The Strategies Of War' Op. Cit. p. 69.*

11   Klein, Naomi (2007)*'The Shock Doctrine: The Rise of Disaster Capitalism',* Metropolitan Books, New York, p. 259 (electronic copy)

12   Transparency International, Corruption by Country, Iraq, Corruption Perceptions Index <http://www.transparency.org/country#IRQ>

13   Interview with Haider Al-Mulla, As-Sumariya Channel <https://www.youtube.com/watch?v=ZdGeNMVFGmg>

14   Ferris, Elizabeth G. (August 2008) *'The Looming Crisis: Displacement and Security in Iraq'*, Foreign Policy at Brookings, Policy Paper No. 5, pp. 3-4. <http://www.brookings.edu/~/media/research/files/papers/2008/8/iraq%20ferris/08_iraq_ferris>

15   HRW (February 2011) *'At a Crossroads - Human Rights in Iraq Eight Years after the US-Led Invasion'*, p. 17 <http://www.hrw.org/sites/default/files/reports/iraq0211W.pdf>

16   Al-Ani, Abdul-Haq and Al-Ani, Tarik (2012) *'Genocide in Iraq: The Case Against the UN Security Council and Member States'*, Clarity Press, Atlanta, GA.

17   Iraq Body Count records the violent civilian deaths that have resulted from the

2003 military intervention in Iraq. Its public database includes deaths caused by US-led coalition forces and paramilitary or criminal attacks by others. IBC's documentary evidence is drawn from crosschecked media reports of violent events leading to the death of civilians, or of bodies being found. The BRussells Tribunal is an activist think tank and peace organisation with a special focus on Iraq, and is one of the few organizations worldwide which continue to monitor Iraq.

18   Adriaensens, Dirk (27 March 2013) *'The scandalous underestimation of Iraqi civilian casualties'*<http://www.brussellstribunal.org/article_view.asp?id=803#. UVP_hhk-4Xc>

19   Iraq Body Count, *'Documented civilian deaths from violence'*<http://www. iraqbodycount.org/database/>

20   Adriaensens, op.cit.

21   Burnham, et al (12 October 2006) *'Mortality after the 2003 invasion of Iraq: a cross-sectional cluster sample survey'*, The Lancet, Volume 368, Issue 9545, <http://www.thelancet.com/journals/lancet/article/PIIS0140-6736(06)69491-9/ abstract>

22   Adriaensens, op.cit.

23   ORB Survey (16 September 2007) *'More than 1,000,000 Iraqis murdered since 2003 invasion'* <http://www.zcommunications.org/more-than-1-000-000-iraqis-murdered-since-2003-invasion-by-orb.html>

24   Hagopian, Amy et al (15 October 2013) *'Mortality in Iraq Associated with the 2003–2011 War and Occupation: Findings from a National Cluster Sample Survey by the University Collaborative Iraq Mortality Study'*, POLS Medicine <http://www.plosmedicine.org/article/info%3Adoi%2F10.1371%2Fjournal. pmed.1001533>

25   Global research TV (22 February 2011) *'4.5 Million Orphans in Iraq: Protests Over Food and Shelter'* <http://tv.globalresearch.ca/2011/02/45-million-orphans-iraq-protests-over-food-and-shelter>

26   AIN Statistics (In Arabic) (2 November 2013) *'Average Casualties of 100 Every Day'*, All Iraq News <http://www.alliraqnews.com/2011-04-18-02-59-24/105516--------101---.html>

27   Roman (1 October 2004) *'Killed to wounded ratio'*, Armed Forces of the World Discussion Board <http://www.strategypage.com/militaryforums/30-30582. aspx#startofcomments>

28   Adriaensens, op.cit.

29   Singh, Amrit (2013) *'Globalizing Torture: Cia Secret Detention And Extraordinary Rendition'*, Open Society Justice Initiative, p. 16-17 <http://www.opensociety-foundations.org/sites/default/files/globalizing-torture-20120205.pdf> see also: Boardman, William (7 April 2013) *'America's Hired Death Squads and Torture Teams Are Still Operating in Iraq'*<http://www.brussellstribunal.org/article_view. asp?id=930>

30   Horowitz, Jonathan and Cammarano, Stacy (5 February 2013) *'20 Extraordinary Facts about CIA Extraordinary Rendition and Secret Detention'*, Open Society Foundation, Open Society Justice Initiative <http://www.opensocie-tyfoundations.org/voices/20-extraordinary-facts-about-cia-extraordinary-ren-dition-and-secret-detention>

31   Singh, Amrit, op.cit.

32   Human Rights Watch (July 2006) *'No Blood, No Foul: Soldiers' Accounts of Detainee Abuse in Iraq'*, Volume 18, No. 3(G), p. 4 <http://www.hrw.org/sites/ default/files/reports/us0706web.pdf>

33   Boardman, William, op.cit.

34   Jamail, Dahr (11 January 2007) *' Negroponte and the escalation of death'*, Asia Times <http://www.atimes.com/atimes/Middle_East/IA11Ak03.html>

35   Hirsh, Michael and Barry, John (9 January 2005) *'The Salvador Option'*,

Newsweek<http://www.commondreams.org/headlines05/0109-06.htm>

36   Jamail, Dahr ' *Negroponte and the escalation of death'*, op.cit.

37   The Guardian (6 March 2013) *'James Steele: America's Mystery Man in Iraq'*-Video <http://www.theguardian.com/world/video/2013/mar/06/james-steele-america-iraq-video>

38   Mahmood, Mona et al (6 March 2013) *'Revealed: Pentagon's link to Iraqi torture centres'* Video, The Guardian.<http://www.theguardian.com/world/2013/mar/06/pentagon-iraqi-torture-centres-link>

39   *Ibid*

40   *Ibid*

41   *Ibid*

42   *Ibid*

43   Served from September 2001 as Vice Chairman of the Joint Chiefs of Staff until August 2005 when he was appointed Chairman of the Joint Chiefs of Staff.

44   Boardman, William, op.cit.

45   Fisk, Robert (26 May 2004) *'The Things Bush Didn't Say in His Speech'*, The Independent (reposted by Counterpunch <http://www.counterpunch.org/2004/05/26/the-things-bush-didn-t-say-in-his-speech/>

46   Jamail, Dahr, *'Death, Displacement, Or Flight'*, in Chapter 8, *'Cultural Cleansing In Iraq'*, op.cit. p. 207

47   Ferris, Elizabeth G. (August 2008) *'The Looming Crisis: Displacement and Security in Iraq'*, Foreign Policy at Brookings, Policy Paper No. 5, p. 1

48   HRW (February 2011) *'At a Crossroads - Human Rights in Iraq Eight Years after the US-Led Invasion'*, <http://www.hrw.org/sites/default/files/reports/iraq0211W.pdf>

49   Jamail, Dahr, op.cit., p. 207

50   UN Office for the Coordination of Humanitarian Affairs (8 April 2008) *'Opening remarks by Sir John Holmes, USG for Humanitarian Affairs and ERC at the DIHAD 2008 Conference'* <http://reliefweb.int/report/world/opening-remarks-sir-john-holmes-usg-humanitarian-affairs-and-erc-dihad-2008-conference>

51   Up until he left Iraq in 1967, Kanaan was never involved in politics nor did he show any interest in it. But sometime during his architecture studies at MIT, Kanaan became a Trotskyist, difficult as that may be to believe. His father, Dr. Muhammad Makiya, was a former head of the department of architecture at the University of Baghdad and a pioneer of Iraqi architecture. He was imprisoned by the Ba'ath government accused of being a member of a defunct Free Mason lodge, but was released later and appointed by Saddam Hussein to develop certain areas of Baghdad. In 1989, Kanaan wrote *'Republic of Fear'* using the pseudonym Samir al-Khalil. There are reasons to believe that Kanaan did not write the book himself, simply because he had not lived a day under Ba'ath rule, and some of the information in the book could have only come from a well-equipped intelligence agency, such as the CIA. It was only in 1991, after the Kuwait crisis that Kanaan came out openly to become an opposition figure.

52   Al-Tikriti, Nabil *'Negligent Mnemocide And The Shattering Of Iraqi Collective Memory'*, in Chapter 5, *'Cultural Cleansing In Iraq'* op.cit., p. 105. See also: Eakin, Hugh (1 July 2008) *'Iraqi Files in U.S.: Plunder or Rescue?'* The New York Times <http://www.nytimes.com/2008/07/01/books/01hoov.html>

53   Al-Ani, Abdul-Haq (2008) 'The Trial of Saddam Hussein', Clarity Press, Atlanta, GA, p. 261.

54   Bahrani, Zainab, *'Archaeology And The Strategies Of War'*, op.cit., p. 79.

55   Al-Hussainy, Abbas *'The Current Status Of The Archaeological Heritage Of Iraq'*, in Chapter 7, *'Cultural Cleansing In Iraq'*, op.cit., pp. 84, 88.

56   Stone, Elizabeth C. (2008) *'Patterns of Looting in Southern Iraq'*, Antiquity, No. 82, pp. 136.<http://antiquity.ac.uk/Ant/082/0125/ant0820125.pdf>

57   Al-Hussainy, Abbas, op.cit., p. 70.

58   Abbas al-Hussainy was Director-General of the State Board of Antiquities and Heritage of Iraq. He was also a member of the Department of Archaeology at Al-Qadissiyah University in Iraq, specializing in Islamic archaeology. Hussainy has guest lectured in numerous American and European universities on the state of affairs of Iraqi antiquities following the Anglo-American occupation. He is the author of numerous publications on the archaeology and antiquities of Iraq. In 2007–08 Hussainy was a visiting scholar in the department of Archaeology, University College, London. See also: Al-Hussainy, Abbas, op.cit., p. 84.

59   *Ibid*, 72.

60   Buckley, Cara (12 December 2007) *'Rare Look Inside Baghdad Museum'*, The New York Times <http://www.nytimes.com/2007/12/12/world/middleeast/12iraq.html?em&ex=1197522000&en=30bbb59d472df2fb&ei≈5087%0A>

61   Crain, Charles (17 January 2005) *'Approximately 300 Academics Have Been Killed'* USA Today <http://usatoday30.usatoday.com/news/world/iraq/2005-01-16-academics-assassinations_x.htm>

62   Adriaensens, Dirk *'Killing The Intellectual Class: Academics As Targets'* in *'Cultural Cleansing In Iraq'*, op.cit.,,p. 123.

63   Laurance, Jeremy (20 October 2006) *'Medics Beg for Help as Iraqis Die Needlessly'* The Independent <http://www.independent.co.uk/news/world/middle-east/medics-beg-for-helpas-iraqis-die-needlessly-420850.html>

64   Zoepf, Katherine (7 July 2006) *'Iraqi Academics are Marked for Death, Human-Rights Groups Say'* Chronicle of Higher Education, Vol. 52, No. 44. <http://chronicle.com/article/Iraqi-Academics-Are-Marked-for/23022>

65   Baker, Luke (16 January 2008) *'Iraq Healthcare in Disarray, report says'*, Reuters (reposted) <http://ns.bdnews24.com/details.php?id=88682&cid=1>

66   Naji, Zaineb (18 January 2008) *'Iraq's Scholars Reluctant to Return'*, Iraq Crisis Report No. 243 <http://www.iwpr.net/?p=icr&s=f&o=342062&apc_state=heniicr2008>

67   Rubin, Andrew (4 September 2004) *'The Slaughter of Iraq's Intellectuals'*, New Statesman <http://www.newstatesman.com/node/148771>

68   Hodges, Lucy (7 December 2006) 'Iraq's Universities are in Meltdown', The Independent <http://www.independent.co.uk/news/education/higher/iraqs-universities-are-in-meltdown-427316.html>

69   Beckett, Francis (12 December 2006) *'Professors in Penury'*, The Guardian. <http://www.theguardian.com/education/2006/dec/12/internationaleduca-tionnews.highereducation

70   Peterson, Scott (22 June 2006) *'Why Many of Iraq's Elite Don't Flee'*, The Christian Science Monitor <http://www.csmonitor.com/2006/0622/p01s02-woiq.html>

71   Greene, Ralph (20 April 2007) *'Horrible Tragedies Occur Virtually Every Day in Iraq'*, GwinnettForum.com <http://www.gwinnettforum.com/issue/07.0420.htm>

72   BRussells Tribunal, *'List of Killed, Threatened or Kidnapped Iraqi Academics'*, continuously updated, <http://www.brusselstribunal.org/academicsList.htm>

73   Ferris, Elizabeth, *'The Looming Crisis'*, op.cit., p.78.

74   Jalili, Ismail(15 June 2007) *'Iraq's Lost Generation: Impact and Implications'*, Report to Cross-Party Commission on Iraq, p. 14 <http://www.brusselstribunal.org/pdf/alJalili170607.pdf>

75   Fuller, Max and Adriaensens, Dirk, *'Wiping The Slate Clean'*, in Chapter 7, *'Cultural Cleansing In Iraq'* op.cit., p.164.

76   Rubin, Andrew (6 September 2003) *'The Slaughter of Iraq's Intellectuals'*, The New Statesman <http://www.newstatesman.com/node/148771>

77   Wolfsthal, Jon B. (13 June 2003) *'Stop Hunting Iraqi Scientists and Start Recruiting Them'*, Los Angeles Times <http://articles.latimes.com/2003/jun/13/opinion/oe-wolfsthal13>

78	Marquez, Humberto (17 February 2005) *'The plunder of Iraq's treasures'*, Asia Times <http://www.atimes.com/atimes/Middle_East/GB17Ak01.html>
79	Robinson, Nehemiah (1960) *'The Genocide Convention'*, Institute of Jewish Affairs, World Jewish Congress, NY, p. 19.
80	SIGIR (March 2003) *'Learning from Iraq'*, A Final Report From The Special Inspector General For Iraq Reconstruction, Washington DC, p. 110.
81	See: Chapter 4 in, Al-Ani, Abdul-Haq and Al-Ani, Tarik *'Genocide in Iraq'*, op.cit.
82	Aziz, Christine (18 October 2003) *'Struggling to Rebuild Iraq's Health-care System'*, The Lancet, Vol. 362, Issue 9391, pp. 1288-1289.
83	Garfield, Richard, Zaidi and Lennock (29 November 1997) *'Medical Care in Iraq After Six Years of Sanctions'*, BMJ, 315 (7120), pp. 1474-1475. <http://www.bmj.com/content/315/7120/1474>
84	Skelton, Mac, *'Health and Care Decline in Iraq: The Example of Cancer & Oncology'*, p. 1 <http://costsofwar.org/sites/default/files/Health_and_HealthCare1.pdf
85	HRW (February 2011) *'At a Crossroads'*, op.cit., p. 75
86	Ferris, Elizabeth, *'The Looming Crisis'*, op.cit., p. 16
87	*Ibid*
88	Integrated Regional Information Networks /IRIN (2 May 2013) *'War leaves lasting impact on healthcare'* <http://www.irinnews.org/Report/97964/War-leaves-lasting-impact-on-healthcare>
89	SIGIR *'Learning from Iraq'*, op.cit., p. 110.
90	*Ibid*, p.112.
91	IRIN, *'War leaves lasting impact on healthcare'*, op.cit.
92	*Ibid.*
93	See: MICS (2006) *'Multiple Indicator Cluster Survey, Volume 1: Final Report'*, Childinfo, UNICEF, p. 27 <http://www.childinfo.org/files/MICS3_Iraq_Final-Report_2006_eng.pdf> and: MICS (April 2011) *'Iraq Multiple Indicator Cluster Survey, Preliminary Report'*, Childinfo, UNICEF, p. 38 <http://www.childinfo.org/files/MICS4_Iraq_PreliminaryReport_Eng.pdf>
94	*Ibid*
95	Al-Ani, Abdul-Haq & Baker, Joanne (June 2009) *'Uranium in Iraq: The Poisonous Legacy of the Iraq Wars'*, Vanderplas Publishing, Fl., USA.
96	Jamail, Dahr (18 March 2013) *'Iraq: War's Legacy of Cancer'* <http://truth-out.org/news/item/15166-iraq-wars-legacy-of-cancer
97	Al-Ani & Baker *'Uranium in Iraq'*, op.cit.
98	See eg.: Al-Sabbak, Sadik Ali, Savabi, Savabi, Dastigri & Savabieasfahani (November 2012) 'Metal Contamination and the Epidemic of Congenital Birth Defects in Iraqi Cities', Bulletin of Environmental Contamination and Toxicology, Volume 89, Issue 5, pp. 937-944 <http://link.springer.com/article/10.1007%2Fs00128-012-0817-2>
99	*Ibid*
100	Lupkin, Sydney (25 March 2013) *'Birth Defects Plague Iraq, But Cause Unknown'*, ABC News <http://abcnews.go.com/Health/birth-defects-plague-iraq-10-years-us-invasion/story?id=18793428#.UVBy6Rk-4Xe>
101	The Cancer and Birth Defects Foundation (4 September 2010) *'Genetic damage and health in Fallujah Iraq worse than Hiroshima'*, International Journal of Environmental Studies and Public Health (IJERPH), Switzerland, Press Release <http://www.thecbdf.org/ar/cbdf-reaserch-papers/61-international-journal-of-environmental-studies-and-public-health-ijerph-switzerland-genetic-damage-and-health-in-fallujah-iraq-worse-than-hiroshima->
102	A visiting Professor in the University of Ulster and Scientific Director of Green Audit, an independent environmental research organization.
103	The Cancer and Birth Defects Foundation *'Genetic damage and health in Fallujah*

Iraq worse than Hiroshima', op.cit.

104 See: Al-Ani & Baker *'Uranium in Iraq'*, op.cit., pp. 42-43, 112-113.

105 Busby, Christopher (28 September 2013) *'Why the WHO report on congenital anomalies in Iraq is a disgrace'*, Russia Today <http://rt.com/op-edge/who-iraq-report-disgrace-461/>

106 Kirby, Alex (14 April 2003) *'US rejects Iraq DU clean-up'*, BBC News: "... there've been a number of studies - by the UK's Royal Society and the World Health Organisation, for example - into the health risks of DU, or the lack of them.... One thing we've found in these various studies is that there are no long-term effects from DU". <http://news.bbc.co.uk/2/hi/sci/tech/2946715.stm>

107 The Royal Society (22 May 2001) *'The health hazards of depleted uranium munitions Part I'* <http://royalsociety.org/policy/publications/2001/health-uranium-munitions-i/>

108 Skelton, Mac, *'Health and Care Decline in Iraq'*, op.cit., p. 5.

109 Busby, Christopher *'Why the WHO report on congenital anomalies in Iraq is a disgrace'*, op.cit.

110 *Ibid*

111 Article 36, Protocol Additional to the Geneva Conventions of 12 August 1949, and relating to the Protection of Victims of International Armed Conflicts (Protocol I), 8 June 1977.<http://www.icrc.org/applic/ihl/ihl.nsf/Treaty.xsp?action=openDocument&documentId=D9E6B6264D7723C3C12563CD002D6CE4>

112 Kentane, Bie (12 March 2013) *'Iraqi Children: Deprived Rights, Stolen future'*, The BRussells Tribunal, Presentation UN Geneva. <http://www.brussellstribunal.org/article_view.asp?id=824#.UqRNY42gfnA>

113 Lando, B. (*18* March 2007) *'4 Years Later: Dump Those Ungrateful, Vicious Iraqis'*, *The Huffington Post*, <http://www.huffingtonpost.com/barry-lando/4-years-later-dump-those-_b_43718.html>

114 Kentane, Bie, *'Iraqi Children'* op.cit.

115 IRIN, *'War leaves lasting impact on healthcare'*, op.cit.

116 *Ibid*

117 Chelala, César (21 March 2009) *'Iraqi Children: Bearing the Scars of War-What psychological damage is being done to the children of Iraq?'*, The Globalist <http://www.theglobalist.com/iraqi-children-bearing-the-scars-of-war/>

118 Kentane, Bie, *'Iraqi Children'* op.cit.

119 Skelton, Mac, *'Health and Care Decline in Iraq'*, op.cit., p. 1.

120 The United Nations Millennium Development Goals (MDGs) are eight goals that UN Member States have agreed to try to achieve by the year 2015.

121 Submission from Medact to the Iraqi Commission, June 2007, p. 6.

122 Kentane, Bie, *'Iraqi Children'* op.cit.

123 *Ibid*

124 MICS *'Iraq Multiple Indicator Cluster Survey, Preliminary Report'*, op.cit.

125 Child victims of war, (25 July 2012), Iraq. <http://childvictimsofwar.org.uk/get-informed/iraq/>

126 Kentane, Bie, *'Iraqi Children'* op.cit.

127 See: Chapter 4 in, Al-Ani, Abdul-Haq and Al-Ani, Tarik *'Genocide in Iraq'*, op.cit.

128 SIGIR *'Learning from Iraq'*, op.cit., p. 112.

129 *Ibid*, p.113.

130 Al-Ali, Zaid (22 March 2013) *'Iraq: ten years of hubris and incompetence'*, Open Democracy <http://www.opendemocracy.net/zaid-al-ali/iraq-ten-years-of-hubris-and-incompetence> International Crisis Group (26 September 2011) *'Failing Oversight: Iraq's Unchecked Government'*, Middle East Report No. 113.<http://www.crisisgroup.org/en/regions/middle-east-north-africa/iraq-iran-gulf/iraq/113-failing-oversight-iraqs-unchecked-government.aspx>

131 Wing, Joel (4 April 2012) *'Iraq's Struggling Education System'*, Musings on Iraq

<http://musingsoniraq.blogspot.com/2012/04/iraqs-struggling-education-system.html>

132   *Ibid*

133   *Ibid*

134   SIGIR *'Learning from Iraq'*, op.cit., p. 113.

135   Wing, Joel *'Iraq's Struggling Education System'*, op.cit.

136   *Ibid*

137   Synovitz, Ron (29 October 2012) *'Iraqi Schools More Crowded Than Ever After Reconstruction Blunder'* <http://www.brussellstribunal.org/article_view.asp?id=489#>

138   UN/World Bank (October 2003) 'Joint Iraq Needs Assessment', pp. 14–16 <http://siteresources.worldbank.org/INTIRAQ/Overview/20147568/Joint%20Needs%20Assessment.pdf>

139   Wing, Joel *'Iraq's Struggling Education System'*, op.cit.

140   UN General Assembly (28 February 2012), *'Iraqi children health situation'*, Human Rights Council, Nineteenth Session, A/HRC/19/NGO/147, Report on the violations by the occupying forces and the Iraqi authorities of the Convention (IV) relative to the Protection of Civilian Persons in Time of War, Geneva, 12 August 1949 and the UN Convention on the Rights of the Child.<http://www.iraqsolidaridad.org/2012/docs/G1210959.pdf>

141   Ariabi, Dr. Intisar (30 October 2011) *'Remember Fallujah'*, The Justice for Fallujah Project <http://thefallujahproject.org/home/node/76>

142   Indymedia Australia. (4 December 2011) *'IRAQ – landmines, bombs, depleted uranium – devastation – children amputees. How can you help'* <http://www.indymedia.org.au/2011/12/04/iraq-%E2%80%93-landmines-bombs-depleted-uranium-%E2%80%93-devastation-%E2%80%93-children-amputees-how-you-can-help>

143   Roberts; Lafta; Garfield; Khudairi and Burnham (29 October 2004) *'Mortality before and after the 2003 invasion of Iraq: cluster sample survey'*, The Lancet <http://web.mit.edu/humancostiraq/reports/lancet04.pdf>

144   Kentane, Bie, *'Iraqi Children'* op.cit.

145   Law No. 188 of the year 1959, *'Personal Status Law and amendments'* <http://apps.americanbar.org/rol/publications/iraq_personal_status_law_1959_english_translation.pdf>

146   Joseph, Suad *'Elite Strategies for State-Building: Women, Family, Religion and State in Iraq and Lebanon'* in Kandiyoti, Deniz , ed. (1992) 'Women, Islam and the State', Leiden, The Netherlands: E.J. Brill, p. 178-79.

147   *'The Compulsory Education Law 118/1976, Article 1/First'*, Iraqi Local Governance Law Library (Arabic) <http://www.iraq-lg-law.org/en/node/368> See also: UN Committee on the Elimination of Discrimination Against Women (19 October 1998) *'Second and Third Periodic Reports of State Parties: Republic of Iraq'*, CEDAW/C/IRQ/2-3, pp. 11-12. <http://daccess-dds-ny.un.org/doc/UNDOC/GEN/N00/223/84/IMG/N0022384.pdf?OpenElement>

148   *Labour Law No. 151/1970* (in Arabic) <http://www.legislations.gov.iq/LoadLawBook.aspx?SC=120120013397975> and: *Labour Law No. 71/1987* (in Arabic) <http://www.legislations.gov.iq/LoadLawBook.aspx?SC=291220051353154>

149   *'Maternity Leave Law No. 882/1987'* (in Arabic) <http://www.legislations.gov.iq/LoadLawBook.aspx?SP=REF&SC=301220054849199&Year=1987&PageNum=1>

150   Human Rights Watch (July 2003) *'Climate of Fear: Sexual Violence and Abduction of Women and Girls in Baghdad'*, Vol. 15, no. 7 (E <http://www.hrw.org/sites/default/files/reports/iraq0703.pdf>

151   HRW, 'At a Crossroads', op.cit., p. 8.

152   Honour killing is the homicide of a member of a family or social group by other members, which occurs in various cultures. This crime is especially targeted

against women, and the use of the term 'honour' comes from a belief held by the perpetrator(s) that the victim has brought dishonor or shame upon the family or community. Perpetrators committing these murders rationalize their actions, blaming victims for refusing to enter an arranged marriage, being in a relationship that is disapproved by their relatives, having sex outside marriage, dressing in ways which are deemed inappropriate, or engaging in homosexual relations.

153   Al-Ani, Abdul-Haq and Al-Ani, Tarik *'Genocide in Iraq'*, op.cit., pp. 55-56.See also: Smock, David R. (23 December 2003) *'The Role of Religion in Iraqi Politics'*, United States Institute of Peace<http://www.usip.org/publications/the-role-of-religion-in-iraqi-politics>

154   *Eisenstein, Zillah (23 Mar 2013) '"Leaning in" in Iraq: Women's rights and war?'*<http://www.aljazeera.com/indepth/opinion/2013/03/2013323141149557391.html>

155   HRW, *'At a Crossroads'*, op.cit., p. HAVE YOU THIS?

156   *Ibid*

157   Lavender, Linda (May 2012) *'Human Trafficking in Iraq- 2003 and beyond'*, Civil-Military Fusion Centre, Mediterranean Basin Team<https://www.cimicweb.org/cmo/medbasin/Holder/Documents/r015%20CFC%20Monthly%20Thematic%20Report%20%2814-May-12%29.pdf#page=1&zoom=auto,0,792>

158   Abouzeid, Rania (7 March 2009) *'Iraq's Unspeakable Crime: Mothers Pimping Daughters'*, Time world <http://www.time.com/time/world/article/0,8599,1883696,00.html>

159   HRW, *'At a Crossroads'*, op.cit., P. 12.

160   Abouzeid, Rania, *'Iraq's Unspeakable Crime'*, op.cit.

161   A *Misyar* marriage can be defined as an official marriage contract between a man and a woman, with the condition that the spouses give up one, two or several of their rights. These include: living together, equal division of nights between wives in cases of polygamy, the wife's right to housing and financial support. The bottom line in such arrangements is that the couple agree to live separately from each other, as before their *Nikah* contract, and see each other to fulfil their needs in a lawful manner when they so desire. At times, a *Misyar* marriage is contracted on a temporary basis which ends in divorce on the expiration date of the contract. *Mut'a* is a fixed-term or short-term marriage in Shi'ia Islam, where the duration and compensation are both agreed upon in advance. It is a private and verbal marriage contract between a man and an unmarried woman and there must be declaration and acceptance as in the case of *Nikah*. The length of the contract and the amount of consideration must be specified. Although there is no minimum or maximum duration for the contract, it is reported that the minimum duration of the contract should be at least three days. The wife must be unmarried, chaste and should not be addicted to fornication or a virgin without father.

162   HRW, *'At a Crossroads'*, op.cit., p. 25.

163   Kentane, Bie, *'Iraqi Children'* op.cit.

164   In 1925 the Turkish Petroleum Company received a seventy-five-year concession from the Iraqi government to operate throughout Iraq. In 1928 the TPC and the Near east Development Corporation (a consortium of U.S. oil companies: SONJ, SONY, Atlantic Refining Company, Gulf Oil Corporation, and Pan American Petrolum and Transport Company) agreed to act as one company, the Iraqi Petroleum Company (IPC). Mosul Petroleum Company was awarded a seventy-five-year concession in 1932 and Basra Petroleum Company was awarded a seventy-five-year concession in 1938.

165   In Volume I of *Genocide in Iraq* we treated oil and its relation to development and war. See Chapters 3 and 4. We have only presented a short summary in the previous paragraphs of that treatment.

166   United Nations Security Council (10 March 2000) *'Report Of The Secretary-General Pursuant To Paragraphs 28 And 30 Of Resolution 1284 (1999) And Paragraph 5 Of Resolution 1281 (1999)- S/2000/208'* <http://www.un.org/en/ga/search/view_doc.asp?symbol=S/2000/208> The report stated on page 5 the following: *"It is apparent that the decline in the condition of all sectors of the industry continues, and is accelerating in some cases. This trend will continue, and the ability of the Iraqi oil industry to sustain the current reduced production levels will be seriously compromised unless effective action is taken immediately to reverse the situation."*

167   Office of the Iraq Programme, Oil-for-Food, *'The Secretary-General Statement To The Security Council On The Humanitarian Situation In Iraq'* <http://www.un.org/depts/oip/background/reports/sg000324.html>

168   Luft, Gal (12 May 2003) *'How Much Oil Does Iraq Have?'* Brookings Institute <http://www.brookings.edu/papers/2003/0512globalenvironment_luft.aspx>

169   Baker, Raymond W.; Ismael, Shereen T. and Ismael, Tareq Y. (Eds.) (2010) *'Ending The Iraqi State'*, Chapter 1 in *'Cultural Cleansing In Iraq'*, op.cit., p. 19.

170   *Ibid*, pp. 18-19.

171   History Commons, *'Profile: Stephen Cambone'* <http://www.historycommons.org/entity.jsp?entity=stephen_a._cambone> (Retrieved 11 December 2013)

172   United States Department of State (20 April 2003) *'Summary Paper'*, Future of Iraq Project, Oil and Energy Working Group, subcommittee on Oil Policy <http://www.gwu.edu/~nsarchiv/NSAEBB/NSAEBB198/FOI%20Oil.pdf>

173   Baker, Raymond W.; Ismael, Shereen T. and Ismael, Tareq Y. *'Ending The Iraqi State'*, op.cit., pp. 18-19.

174   London Institute of Petroleum (8 June 2004) *'Full text of Dick Cheney's speech at the Institute of Petroleum Autumn lunch 1999'* <http://www.energybulletin.net/559.html>

175   Greenwald, Glenn (18 March 2013) *'David Frum, the Iraq war and oil'*, The Guardian <http://www.guardian.co.uk/commentisfree/2013/mar/18/david-frum-iraq-war-oil>

176   *Ibid*

177   *Ibid*

178   Juhasz, Antonia (15 April 2013) *'Why the war in Iraq was fought for Big Oil'*, CNN <http://edition.cnn.com/2013/03/19/opinion/iraq-war-oil-juhasz/>

179   *Ibid*

180   Leading Article (20 April 2011) *'How the Wheels of this Misadventure Were Oiled'*, The Independent <http://www.independent.co.uk/opinion/leading-articles/leading-article-how-the-wheels-of-this-misadventure-were-oiled-2269992.html>

181   Baker, Raymond W.; Ismael, Shereen T. and Ismael, Tareq Y. *'Ending The Iraqi State'*, op.cit., p.20.

182   Juhasz, Antonia *'Why the war in Iraq was fought for Big Oil'*, op.cit.

183   Jamail, Dahr (7 January 2012) *'Western oil firms remain as US exits Iraq'* <http://www.aljazeera.com/indepth/features/2011/12/2011122813134071641.html>

184   Ibid

185   Iraq Index (Data as of May 1988), *'Iraq-ELECTRICITY'* <http://www.mongabay.com/history/iraq/iraq-electricity.html>

186   SIGIR *'Learning from Iraq'*, op.cit., p. 75

187   Although no link existed between the presence of Iraqi troops in Kuwait and an electricity generating station in Mosul, the purpose of the attack was clearly emphasized by an officer involved in planning the air campaign stating that the purpose of the attack was to accelerate the effects of sanctions which were mainly to cripple Iraq by way of punishment. See: Gellman, Barton (23 June 1991) *'Allied Air War Struck Broadly in Iraq; Officials Acknowledge Strategy Went*

Beyond Purely Military Targets', Washington Post <http://www.envirosagainst-war.org/know/1991USHitCivilianTargets.pdf>

188   The Harvard Study Team (26 September 1991)*'Special Report – The Effect of the Gulf Crisis on the Children of Iraq'*, The New England Journal of Medicine, vol. 325, No. 13. <http://www.nejm.org/doi/full/10.1056/NEJM199109263251330>

189   SIGIR *'Learning from Iraq'*, op.cit.., p. 76.

190   *Ibid*, p. 77.

191   IRIN (22 April 2013) *'Iraq 10 years on: Blistering black-outs'* <http://www.irin-news.org/report/97896/blistering-black-outs>

192   SIGIR (2 February 2009) *'Hard Lessons: The Iraq Reconstruction Experience'*, Office of the Special Inspector General for Iraq Reconstruction, Washington DC, p. 147

193   IAU (May 2011) *'Electric Power Subsector: Current Situation and Prospects'*, UNDP <http://www.jauiraq.org/documents/1725/Electric%20Power%20subsector.pdf>

194   *Ibid*

195   SIGIR *'Learning from Iraq'*, op.cit., p. 77.

196   *Ibid*, pp. 77-78.

197   Khalil, Sa'ib (15 August 2011) *'What Does Electricity Tell Us About Iraq's Future?'* (in Arabic), Voice of Iraq's Left <http://saotaliassar.org/Writer/Saaieb%20Kalil/StrumMinester02.htm>

198   IAU *'Electric Power Subsector: Current Situation and Prospects'*, op.cit.

199   SIGIR *'Learning from Iraq'*, op.cit., p. 79.

200   *Ibid*, p.76.

201   IRIN (22 April 2013) *'Are the Taps flowing?'* <http://www.irinnews.org/Report/97894/Iraq-10-years-on-Are-the-taps-flowing>

202   *Ibid*

203   SIGIR *'Learning from Iraq'*, op.cit., p. 79.

204   Doyle, Brendan (July 2003) *'Iraq Watching Briefs: Water and Environmental Sanitation'*, UNICEF, Executive Summary <http://www.google.fi/url?sa=t&rct=j&q=&esrc=s&source=web&cd=2&ved=0CDQQFjAB&url=http%3A%2F%2Firaq.undg.org%2Fuploads%2Fdoc%2FWatching%2520Brief%2520WES%2520%252028.08.03.doc&ei=o9OqUvKjE8ap4ATy_oDgBw&usg=AFQjCNH78UoyJQosY0zgFuECzf5ZstimQg&bvm=bv.57967247,d.bGE&cad=rja

205   SIGIR *'Learning from Iraq'*, op.cit., p. 80.

206   Office Of The Special Inspector General For Iraq Reconstruction (28 October 2010) *'Review of Major U.S. Government Infrastructure Projects in Iraq: Nas-siriya and Ifraz Water Treatment Plants'*, SIGIR EV-10-002, What SIGIR found and Audit 12-007? <http://www.sigir.mil/files/evaluations/EV-10-002.pdf>

207   SIGIR *'Learning from Iraq'*, op.cit., p.79.

208   *Ibid*, p. 81.

209   IRIN, *'Are the Taps flowing?'*, op.cit.

210   SIGIR *'Learning from Iraq'*, op.cit., p. 79.

211   *Ibid*, p. 81.

212   We have discussed this issue in our book *"Genocide in Iraq"*, op.cit., p. 159. See also: Paley, Amit R. (30 October 2007) *'Iraqi Dam Seen In Danger of Deadly Collapse'*, The Washington Post <http://www.washingtonpost.com/wp-dyn/content/article/2007/10/29/AR2007102902193.html> and: Cockburn, Patrick (8 August 2007) *'Disaster Looms as Saddam-Era Tigris River Dam Verges on Collapse'*, The Independent <http://www.alternet.org/story/59166/disaster_looms_as_saddam-era_tigris_river_dam_verges_on_collapse>

213   See Chapter 6 in our book *"Genocide in Iraq"*, for further details of SC actions.

214   SIGIR *'Learning from Iraq'*, op.cit., p. 80.

215   Coalition Provisional Authority Order Number 91, Regulation Of Armed Forces

	And Militias Within Iraq <http://www.iraqcoalition.org/regulations/20040607_ CPAORD91_Regulation_of_Armed_Forces_and_Militias_within_Iraq.pdf>
216	SIGIR *'Learning from Iraq'*, op.cit., p. 11, 13-18, 23, 46, 84, 99, 103-104, 120 and 130
217	Asiacell home page <http://www.asiacell.com/pages.php?lang=&pid=47>
218	Asiacell Earnings Releaase <http://asiacell.com/images/pdf/Asiacell-9M-2013-Earnings-Release-EA.pdf>
219	Korek web page <http://www.korektel.com/top-links/about-us/introduction>
220	Goldstein, Phil (16 March 2011) *'France Telecom invests €175m in Iraqi operator Korek'*, Fierce Wirless Europe <http://www.fiercewireless.com/europe/story/france-telecom-invests-175m-iraqi-operator-korek/2011-03-16
221	Izzat, Benaw (5 April 2012) *' France Telecom/Agility mysterious joint venture in Korek'*, Kurd Net <http://www.ekurd.net/mismas/articles/misc2012/4/state6069.htm>
222	Zain Iraq web page <http://www.iq.zain.com/>
223	Zain Group's web page <http://www.zain.com/about-zain/>
224	Zain Group Earnings Release, 9 Months-2013, p. 8 <http://www.itisaluna.com/_page.php?page_id=20#body_cntnr>
225	Itisaluna web page <http://www.itisaluna.com/_page.php?page_id=20#body_cntnr>

Chapter 9: The Right of Remedy

1	Al-Ani, Abdul-Haq and Al-Ani, Tarik (2012) *'Genocide in Iraq: The Case Against the UN Security Council and Member States'*, Clarity Press, Atlanta, GA
2	'My first example is about how to reconcile two apparently equal values. It is a case about a man who was arrested and detained in a detention centre operated by British forces in Iraq. His internment was thought to be necessary for imperative reasons of security in Iraq. He was suspected of being a member of a terrorist group involved in weapons smuggling and other terrorist activities. But he was not charged with any offence, and no charge or trial was in prospect. He complained that his continued detention infringed his rights under article 5(1) of the Convention. Various issues were raised. The one that is relevant to this discussion turned on the relationship between article 5(1) of the Convention, which protects the right to liberty, and article 103 of the UN Charter which provides that, in the event of a conflict between obligations under the Charter and their obligations under an international agreement, obligations under the Charter must prevail. The coalition forces were in Iraq under the authority of a Security Council resolution. This gave them authority to take all necessary measures to contribute to the maintenance of security and stability.' Lord Hope of Craighead, 'The Judges' Dilemma' (2009) 58(4) I.C.L.Q. 753, 757
3	The ICJ held in the *Lockerbie* case that it could not proceed with a disputed case before it on the application of an international convention once the SC adopted a resolution in the matter. Questions of Interpretation and Application of the 1971 Montreal Convention arising from the Aerial Incident at Lockerbie (*Libyan Arab Jamahiriya v. United Kingdom*), Preliminary Objections, Judgment, I. C.J. Reports 1998, 9 (Lockerbie Case) paras 39-40
4	In the UK the 'courts will decline to embark upon the determination of an issue if to do so would be damaging to the public interest in the field of defence or national security.' Dominic McGoldrick, 'The Boundaries of Justiciability' (2010) 59(4) I.C.L.Q. 98 1, 1006
5	Lord Hope of Craighead, 'The Judges' Dilemma' (2009) 58(4) I.C.L.Q. 753, 757
6	*See : Lockerbie* Case
7	Joined Cases C-402/05 P and C-415/05 P, *Yassin Abdullah Kadi and Al Barakaat*

International Foundation v Council of the European Union and Commission of the European Communities, Judgment of 3 September 2008, *Kadi* case, para 281

8 Opinion of the Advocate General Maduro in case C-402/05 P, delivered on 16 January 2008, para 34.

9 The Court of First Instance found that it was, nonetheless, empowered to check, indirectly, the lawfulness of the resolutions of the Security Council in question with regard to jus cogens. *Kadi* case, para 87

10 Definition of Aggression General Assembly resolution 3314 (XXIX), 14 December 1974 http://legal.un.org/avl/ha/da/da.html

11 Rome Statute of the International Criminal Court
http://www.icc-cpi.int/nr/rdonlyres/ea9aeff7-5752-4f84-be94-0a655eb30e16/0/rome_statute_english.pdf

12 Article 8 *bis*, 'Crime of aggression', Rome Statute of the International Criminal Court, p. 9

   1.   For the purpose of this Statute, "crime of aggression" means the planning, preparation, initiation or execution, by a person in a position effectively to exercise control over or to direct the political or military action of a State, of an act of aggression which, by its character, gravity and scale, constitutes a manifest violation of the Charter of the United Nations.

   2.   For the purpose of paragraph 1, "act of aggression" means the use of armed force by a State against the sovereignty, territorial integrity or political independence of another State, or in any other manner inconsistent with the Charter of the United Nations.

Any of the following acts, regardless of a declaration of war, shall, in accordance with United Nations General Assembly resolution 3314 (XXIX) of 14 December 1974, qualify as an act of aggression:

   (a)   The invasion or attack by the armed forces of a State of the territory of another State, or any military occupation, however temporary, resulting from such invasion or attack, or any annexation by the use of force of the territory of another State or part thereof;

   (b)   Bombardment by the armed forces of a State against the territory of another State or the use of any weapons by a State against the territory of another State;

   (c)   The blockade of the ports or coasts of a State by the armed forces of another State;

   (d)   An attack by the armed forces of a State on the land, sea or air forces, or marine and air fleets of another State;

   (e)   The use of armed forces of one State which are within the territory of another State with the agreement of the receiving State, in contravention of the conditions provided for in the agreement or any extension of their presence in such territory beyond the termination of the agreement;

   (f)   The action of a State in allowing its territory, which it has placed at the disposal of another State, to be used by that other State for perpetrating an act of aggression against a third State;

   (g)   The sending by or on behalf of a State of armed bands, groups, irregulars or mercenaries, which carry out acts of armed force against another State of such gravity as to amount to the acts listed above, or its substantial involvement therein

http://www.icc-cpi.int/NR/rdonlyres/ADD16852-AEE9-4757-ABE7-9CDC-7CF02886/283503/RomeStatutEng1.pdf

13 Article 30 '*Mental element*', Rome Statute , Ibid, p. 20

1. Unless otherwise provided, a person shall be criminally responsible and liable for punishment for a crime within the jurisdiction of the Court only if the material elements are committed with intent and knowledge.
2. For the purposes of this article, a person has intent where:
   (a) In relation to conduct, that person means to engage in the conduct;
   (b) In relation to a consequence, that person means to cause that consequence or is aware that it will occur in the ordinary course of events.
3. For the purposes of this article, "knowledge" means awareness that a circumstance exists or a consequence will occur in the ordinary course of events. "Know" and "knowingly" shall be construed accordingly.

14 Article 36, '*New Weapons*', Protocol Additional to the Geneva Conventions of 12 August 1949, and relating to the Protection of Victims of International Armed Conflicts (Protocol I), 8 June 1977. http://www.icrc.org/applic/ihl/ihl.nsf/Article. xsp?action=openDocument&documentId=FEB84E9C01DDC926C12563CD-0051DAF7

15 Strasbourg Agreement 1675
http://en.wikipedia.org/wiki/Strasbourg_Agreement_%281675%29

16 Protocol for the Prohibition of the Use of Asphyxiating, Poisonous or Other Gases, and of Bacteriological Methods of Warfare. Geneva, 17 June 1925
http://www.icrc.org/ihl/INTRO/280?OpenDocument

17 See Chapters 7 & 8 of this book.

18 Office of the High Commissioner for Human Rights, 'Convention on the Rights of the Child' http://www.ohchr.org/en/professionalinterest/pages/crc.aspx

19 *Ibid*, Article 20
1. A child temporarily or permanently deprived of his or her family environment, or in whose own best interests cannot be allowed to remain in that environment, shall be entitled to special protection and assistance provided by the State.
2. States Parties shall in accordance with their national laws ensure alternative care for such a child.
3. Such care could include, inter alia, foster placement, kafalah of Islamic law, adoption or if necessary placement in suitable institutions for the care of children. When considering solutions, due regard shall be paid to the desirability of continuity in a child's upbringing and to the child's ethnic, religious, cultural and linguistic background.

20 *Ibid*, Article 22
1. States Parties shall take appropriate measures to ensure that a child who is seeking refugee status or who is considered a refugee in accordance with applicable international or domestic law and procedures shall, whether unaccompanied or accompanied by his or her parents or by any other person, receive appropriate protection and humanitarian assistance in the enjoyment of applicable rights set forth in the present Convention and in other international human rights or humanitarian instruments to which the said States are Parties.

21 *Ibid*, Article 27
1. S tates Parties recognize the right of every child to a standard of living adequate for the child's physical, mental, spiritual, moral and social development.

22   *Ibid*, Article 28

>   1.   States Parties recognize the right of the child to education, and with a view to achieving this right progressively and on the basis of equal opportunity....

23   *Ibid*, Article 33

>   States Parties shall take all appropriate measures, including legislative, administrative, social and educational measures, to protect children from the illicit use of narcotic drugs and psychotropic substances as defined in the relevant international treaties, and to prevent the use of children in the illicit production and trafficking of such substances.

24   *Ibid*, Article 34

>   States Parties undertake to protect the child from all forms of sexual exploitation and sexual abuse. For these purposes, States Parties shall in particular take all appropriate national, bilateral and multilateral measures to prevent:
>   (a) The inducement or coercion of a child to engage in any unlawful sexual activity;
>   (b) The exploitative use of children in prostitution or other unlawful sexual practices;
>   (c) The exploitative use of children in pornographic performances and materials.

25   *Ibid*, Article 37

>   States Parties shall ensure that:
>   (a) No child shall be subjected to torture or other cruel, inhuman or degrading treatment or punishment. Neither capital punishment nor life imprisonment without possibility of release shall be imposed for offences committed by persons below eighteen years of age;
>   (b) No child shall be deprived of his or her liberty unlawfully or arbitrarily. The arrest, detention or imprisonment of a child shall be in conformity with the law and shall be used only as a measure of last resort and for the shortest appropriate period of time;

26   Kentane, Bie (13 Mrch 2013) '*Iraqi Children: Deprived Rights, Stolen Future*', Global Research http://www.globalresearch.ca/iraqi-children-deprived-rights-stolen-future/5326552

27   Convention on the Elimination of All Forms of Discrimination against Women, Adopted and opened for signature, ratification and accession by General Assembly resolution 34/180 of 18 December 1979, http://www.ohchr.org/Documents/ProfessionalInterest/cedaw.pdf

28   Protocol I 1977, 'Article 76 — Protection of women'

>   1. Women shall be the object of special respect and shall be protected in particular against rape, forced prostitution and any other form of indecent assault. http://www.icrc.org/applic/ihl/ihl.nsf/Article.xsp?action=openDocument&documentId=5FB5CC7AD1C3AAF7C12563CD0051E08C

29   Office of the High Commissioner for Human Rights, 'Universal Declaration of Human Rights' http://www.ohchr.org/en/udhr/pages/introduction.aspx

30   Office of the High Commissioner for Human Rights, 'Convention against Torture and Other Cruel, Inhuman or Degrading Treatment or Punishment' http://www.ohchr.org/EN/ProfessionalInterest/Pages/CAT.aspx http://treaties.un.org/Pages/Treaties.aspx?id=4&subid=A&lang=en

31   Geneva Conventions 1949 and Protocol I 1977

32   Protocol I 1977, 'Article 75 – Fundamental guarantees'

>   2.   The following acts are and shall remain prohibited at any time and in any place whatsoever, whether committed by civilian or by military agents:

a) violence to the life, health, or physical or mental well-being of persons, in particular:

    i) murder;

    ii) torture of all kinds, whether physical or mental;

    iii) corporal punishment; and

    iv) mutilation;

b) outrages upon personal dignity, in particular humiliating and degrading treatment, enforced prostitution and any form of indecent assault;

c) the taking of hostages;

d) collective punishments; and

e) threats to commit any of the foregoing acts.

Protocol Additional to the Geneva Conventions of 12 August 1949, and relating to the Protection of Victims of International Armed Conflicts (Protocol I), 8 June 1977 http://www.icrc.org/applic/ihl/ihl.nsf/Article.xsp?action=openDocument&documentId=086F4B-B140C53655C12563CD0051E027

33   Office of the High Commissioner for Human Rights, 'International Covenant on Civil and Political Rights' http://www.ohchr.org/en/professionalinterest/pages/ccpr.aspx

Article 6

1. Every human being has the inherent right to life. This right shall be protected by law. No one shall be arbitrarily deprived of his life.

34   ICCPR', op.cit.,

Article 25

Every citizen shall have the right and the opportunity, without any of the distinctions mentioned in article 2 and without unreasonable restrictions: (b) To vote and to be elected at genuine periodic elections which shall be by universal and equal suffrage and shall be held by secret ballot, guaranteeing the free expression of the will of the electors;

35   Convention (IV) relative to the Protection of Civilian Persons in Time of War. Geneva, 12 August 1949, 'Article 79- Cases of internment and applicable provisions'

The Parties to the conflict shall not intern protected persons, except in accordance with the provisions of Articles 41, 42, 43, 68 and 78

http://www.icrc.org/applic/ihl/ihl.nsf/Article.xsp?action=openDocument&documentId=A6A40E7C0ABD0571C12563CD0051C043

36   ICCPR, op.cit.,

Article 9

1. Everyone has the right to liberty and security of person. No one shall be subjected to arbitrary arrest or detention. No one shall be deprived of his liberty except on such grounds and in accordance with such procedure as are established by law.

37   Convention (IV) , op.cit.

Article 70

Protected persons shall not be arrested, prosecuted or convicted by the Occupying Power for acts committed or for opinions expressed before the occupation, or during a temporary interruption thereof, with the exception of breaches of the laws and customs of war.

38   ICCPR, op.cit.,

Article 15

1. No one shall be held guilty of any criminal offence on account of any act or omission which did not constitute a criminal offence, under national or international law, at the time when it was committed.

39   ICCPR, op.cit.,
Article 7
>No one shall be subjected to torture or to cruel, inhuman or degrading treatment or punishment. In particular, no one shall be subjected without his free consent to medical or scientific experimentation.

40   Convention (IV), op.cit.
Article 27
>Protected persons are entitled, in all circumstances, to respect for their persons, their honour, their family rights, their religious convictions and practices, and their manners and customs. They shall at all times be humanely treated, and shall be protected especially against all acts of violence or threats thereof and against insults and public curiosity.

41   ICCPR, op.cit.,
Article 19
>1. Everyone shall have the right to hold opinions without interference.
>2. Everyone shall have the right to freedom of expression; this right shall include freedom to seek, receive and impart information and ideas of all kinds, regardless of frontiers, either orally, in writing or in print, in the form of art, or through any other media of his choice.

42   Office of the High Commissioner for Human Rights, 'International Covenant on Economic, Social and Cultural Rights'
Article 6
>1. The States Parties to the present Covenant recognize the right to work, which includes the right of everyone to the opportunity to gain his living by work which he freely chooses or accepts, and will take appropriate steps to safeguard this right.

Article 10
The States Parties to the present Covenant recognize that:
>1. The widest possible protection and assistance should be accorded to the family, which is the natural and fundamental group unit of society, particularly for its establishment and while it is responsible for the care and education of dependent children. Marriage must be entered into with the free consent of the intending spouses.

Article 11
>1. The States Parties to the present Covenant recognize the right of everyone to an adequate standard of living for himself and his family, including adequate food, clothing and housing, and to the continuous improvement of living conditions. The States Parties will take appropriate steps to ensure the realization of this right, recognizing to this effect the essential importance of international co-operation based on free consent.

INDEX

A

A-bombs 179
Abbasid 169
ABC News 178, 260
Abdel Abdel, Mohsen 19
Abdul Mahdi, Adel 144
Abdul-Nassir, Gemal 15
Abdul-Wahhab, Ibn 11, 12
Abizaid, General John 196
Abraham 168
Abrams 81
Abu Ghraib 159, 163, 164, 166, 214
academia 162
academic 37, 54, 58, 137, 168, 170, 171, 172
Ad-dulaimi, Naziha 189
Adab 168
addiction 184
addicts 184, 216
administrator 103, 104, 105, 124, 128, 132
Adriaensens, Dirk 160, 162
aerial 7, 55, 56, 227
Afghanistan 175
Africa 11, 16, 17, 18, 19, 39, 110, 130, 182, 185, 207
agencies 65, 101, 102, 108, 202, 228, 235
aggression 9, 41, 52, 55, 61, 67, 83, 84, 86, 87, 88, 89, 90, 93, 99, 103, 159, 166, 173, 195, 210, 211
Agresto, John 154
Ahmadenijad 34
airbases 69
airspace 55, 56, 69, 78, 245
airstrikes 73
Al-Askari, Ja'afar 24
Al-Assad, Hafidh 32, 35
Al-Assads 34
Al-Bakr, Ahmad Hasan 29
Al-Bakr, The Mina' export facility 75

Al-Chalabi, Ahmad 130, 131, 134, 136
Al-Faw peninsula 73, 74
Al-Ghaddafi, Mua'mmar 16, 18, 19, 21, 34
Al-Ghanouchi, Rashid 21, 32
Al-Hafid, Mahmood 100
Al-Hakim, Abdul-Aziz 134, 136
Al-Hamdani, Lt. Gen. Raad 77
Al-Hashimi, Yasin 24
Al-Hassani, Hajim 19, 144
Al-Ja'fari, Ibrahim 18, 143, 144
Al-Jumaili, Salim 33
Al-Maliki, Nuri 27
Al-Marashi, Ibrahim 58
Al-Mulla, Haider 157
Al-Musayib 77
Al-Nujeyfi, Usama 197
Al-Pachachi, Adnan 139
Al-Qaeda 49, 51, 55, 63, 78, 156
Al-Qaida 50
Al-Yawer, Ghazi 136, 144
Albania 163
Algeria 12, 18
Algiers Treaty 32
Ali, Muhammad 17, 26
Allawi, Iyad 96, 134, 136, 142, 144
Amman 54, 207
Anfal 41
Anglo-American 34, 82, 195
Anglo-Iraqi 25
Annan, Kofi 46, 67, 135, 139, 194
Ansar-ul-islam 78
anthrax 66
anti-Ba'athist 107, 118, 131, 214
anti-capitalists 19
anti-imperialists 19
anti-Saddam 136
Ar-Rawi, Fulayh Hassan Taha 78
Arif 29
artefacts 155, 168, 169

artillery 73, 76, 78, 111
As-Sadr, Muqtada 157
As-Saeed, Nuri 24, 26
As-Sahhaf, Mohammad Sa'eed 78
As-Sistani, Grand Ayatollah Ali 137, 138, 139, 141
Australia 11, 67, 68, 70, 73, 89, 110, 163
Austria 163
Awacs 69
Aziz, Tariq 121

B
Babylonian 147
bacteriological 267
Baez, Fernando 173
Baghdad 15, 26, 27, 28, 37, 46, 50, 65, 71, 74, 76, 77, 78, 79, 80, 81, 91, 95, 100, 123, 128, 129, 130, 134, 145, 150, 154, 155, 156, 159, 164, 165, 166, 167, 171, 173, 182, 183, 187, 190, 193, 200, 201, 205, 222
Balfour 14
Barzani, Massoud 134, 136, 206
Bases 15, 16, 25, 68, 69, 78, 133, 148, 149, 151, 156, 168, 213
Basrah 12, 13, 28, 73, 74, 76, 128, 169, 171, 175, 176, 177, 178, 188, 201
Ba'ath 16, 18, 19, 22, 29, 32, 33, 38, 39, 53, 54, 63, 75, 80, 104, 105, 106, 107, 109, 110, 113, 115, 118, 129, 130, 132, 133, 134, 136, 145, 149, 150, 151, 156, 157, 163, 168, 171, 174, 177, 178, 185, 186, 187, 189, 190, 193, 198, 200, 203, 214, 217, 219
Ba'athist 18, 19, 27, 28, 54, 109, 112, 120, 130, 131, 132, 146, 146, 163, 166, 171, 214, 216
Belgium 163
Bin Laden, Osama 49, 63
biological 46, 47, 52, 57, 58, 59, 62, 64, 65, 66, 67, 72, 227
Blair, Tony 19, 52, 57, 58, 63, 153
blockade 37, 38, 39, 42, 55, 158, 159, 174, 175, 176, 177, 178, 180, 182, 183, 184, 185, 188,

193, 195, 198, 200, 201, 203, 204, 205, 208, 210, 216
Bosnia-Herzegovina 163
Brahimi, Lakhdar 139, 141, 142
Bremer, Paul 94, 95, 100, 101, 103-107, 109-140, 142-144, 151, 154, 155, 156, 158, 164, 168, 185, 190, 195, 197, 199, 200, 202, 206
Brzezinski, Zbigniew 21
Busby, Chris 179, 181
Bush, George W. 19, 45, 48-52, 57, 59, 61-65, 67, 70, 72, 79, 80, 85, 101, 128, 134, 173, 191

C
Cairo 25
Cambone, Stephen 48, 49
Campbell, Alistair 58
Canada 70, 163, 189
cancer 177, 178, 179, 180, 181, 213
Chalabi, Ahmad 80, 250
Chile 189
China 22, 62, 66, 85, 146, 197
Churchill, Winston 25
Clinton, Bill 46, 50, 134
Coffman, Colonel James 165
colonialist 14, 37, 101, 147
Commander-in-chief 50, 68, 132
Croatia 163
Crocker, Ryan 91, 92
Cuba 85, 86
Cyprus 58, 163
Czech Republic 163

D
Damascus 23, 25, 35, 157
Da'wa Party 18, 136, 144, 157
De-Ba'athification 105, 106, 107, 113, 118, 128, 129, 130, 131, 170, 185, 205, 214, 216, 218, 219
democracy 15, 17, 18, 21, 34, 51, 89, 107, 137, 151, 153, 163, 174, 184, 185, 186, 190, 201, 216
Denmark 163
depleted uranium 73, 177, 181, 212, 213
Diyala 150
Djibouti 175

E
Egypt 15, 16, 17, 18, 21, 23, 26, 34,
   36, 43, 69, 85, 111, 163, 184
Eisenstein, Zillah 191
El-salvador 171
Elbaradei, Muhammad 58
Erbil 78, 160, 169, 206
Euphrates 75, 77

F
Faisal 25
Fallujah 144, 174, 178, 179, 188
fatwa 137
Fedayeen 75, 76, 78, 132
Feith, Douglas J. 101, 128, 130, 131,
   132
Fisk, Robert 166
France 12, 13, 14, 15, 24, 33, 55, 62,
   66, 93, 94, 206, 266

G
Garner, Lieutenant General Jay 102,
   103, 127, 128, 134
Geneva Convention 89, 92, 103, 104,
   119, 120, 181, 212, 213, 218, 219
Genocidal 38, 39, 42, 46, 72, 159,
   174, 176, 183, 208
Genocide 10, 29, 37, 83, 153, 159,
   167, 170, 173, 174, 208, 210
Georges-Picot, François 13
Georgia 163
Germany 66, 129, 130, 163, 194
Ghadban, Thamir 143
Gordon, Joy 37
graphite 45, 203
Greenstock, Jeremy 63, 103, 139,
   228
Gulf, Persian 12, 13, 14, 16, 18, 22,
   23, 32, 35, 36, 64, 68, 69, 70, 77,
   81, 85, 177, 192, 222, 223

H
Halabjah 78
Halliburton 196
Hamas 35
Hamdan, Malak 179
Herskowitz, Micky 50, 72
Hiltermann, Joost 149

Hiroshima 179
Hizbullah 35
Hollande, Francois 12
Honduras 164
Hussein, Saddam 20, 27, 29, 31, 32,
   33, 34, 36, 37, 41, 42, 46, 48-55,
   61, 63, 64, 68, 71, 72, 73, 86,
   105, 132,133, 134, 156, 163, 173,
   187, 191, 193, 200, 206, 219

I
ICCPR/ the International Covenant
   on Civil and Political Rights 1966
   218, 219
Iceland 163
ICESCR/ the International Covenant
   on Economic, Social and Cultural
   Rights 1966 218, 219
ICJ/ the International Court of
   Justice 85, 209
IEC/ Independent Electoral
   Commission 144
IIA/ Iraqi Interim Authority 128
IKN/ Iraqi Knowledge Network 176,
   204
ILC/ Iraqi Leadership Counci 134
imperialism 11, 12, 15, 16, 17, 18,
   19, 20, 21, 22, 26, 27, 28, 32, 33,
   34, 36, 42, 39, 40, 42, 44, 46, 48,
   53, 55, 56, 61, 71, 82, 86, 94, 97,
   100, 101, 155, 168, 172, 193,
   194, 195, 208
IPC/ Iraqi Petroleum Company 16,
   25
Iran 15, 22, 26, 31, 32, 33, 34, 35,
   36, 48, 51, 66, 85, 133, 146, 148,
   157, 164, 165, 182, 184, 200,
   202, 206
Iran-Iraq War 30, 31, 36, 205
Israel 15, 16, 19, 20, 22, 26, 33, 34,
   35, 36, 40, 47, 69, 74, 86, 100,
   101, 103, 111

J
Jackson, Robert H. 89
Japan 129, 173, 194
Jordan 14, 22, 36, 39, 48, 65, 68, 69,
   77, 111, 166, 175, 192, 207

K

Kagan, Robert 46, 47
Karbala 77, 160, 187
KDP/ Kurdistan Democratic Party 68,
    78, 134, 143, 145, 206
Kentane, Bie 188
Khalilzad, Zalmay 91, 92
Khamanei, Ali 138, 148
Khomeini, Ayatollah 31, 32, 34, 36,
    157
Kirkuk 73, 78, 150, 169, 217, 254
Kissinger, Henry 34, 36, 103
Koivisto, Mauno 85
Kurds 16, 32, 41, 63, 68, 78, 100,
    128,133-135, 141, 144-150, 156,
    170, 200; Kurdistan 147, 150,
    152, 157, 201, 204, 206
Kuwait 13, 14, 27, 28, 32, 36, 37, 42,
    50, 65, 68, 69, 74, 77, 83, 85, 86,
    87, 88, 96, 97, 98, 100, 127, 159,
    199, 200, 207, 222

L

Laurie, Major General Michael 57,
    88
Lebanon 12, 13, 14, 15, 34, 35, 85,
    100, 175
Libya 18, 19, 21, 22, 43, 83
Lord Goldsmith 67
Lord Hope 99, 209
Luti, William 132

M

Macedonia 163
Makiya, Kanan 36, 168
Marji'yah 141
Mehdi Army 164
militia 108, 109, 110, 132, 133, 134,
    143, 149, 156, 159, 163, 164,
    165, 166, 172, 185, 190, 214,
    215, 216, 219
Morocco 175
Mubarak, Hosni 22, 43

N

Nagasaki 179
Nahdha 21, 32

Najaf 74, 76, 77
Nasiriyah 74,75, 76, 80, 91, 92, 204
Neocon 34, 45, 46, 48, 154, 173
Nicaragua 164
NSC/ National Security Council 128,
    130
nuclear weao20, 35, 45, 52, 57, 58,
    62, 66, 67, 79, 203, 227
Nüremberg Tribunal 89, 103

O

OHRA/ Office of Reconstruction and
    Humanitarian Assistance 102,
    127, 128
oil 53, 74, 96, 122, 124, 125, 141,
    150, 154, 158; barrels, 75, 194,
    195, 198; exports, 69, export
    facilities, 75; fields, 57, 197;
    pipelines, 56; revenue, 93, 124,
    182
Oil-for-Food Programme 46, 97,
    122, 126, 182, 193, 194, 199
Ottoman Empire 10, 11, 12, 13, 14,
    1519, 24, 25, 100

P

Pakistan 15, 26
Palestine 11, 14, 15, 16, 17, 20, 35,
    39, 86, 166; Palestinians 14, 21,
    27, 33, 38, 83, 102, 166, 175,186
Panama 83, 86, 88
Petraeus, General David 165, 166
PNAC/ Project for the New
    American Century 45, 46, 47, 48
Portugal 163, 189
post-Saddam 53, 55
Powell, Colin 51, 52, 59, 61, 62, 63,
    64, 65, 66
propaganda 10, 27, 62, 75, 76, 89,
    90, 163
Pétain, Marshal Philippe 94, 96

Q

Qasim, General Abdul-Karim 13, 26,
    27, 28, 146, 189, 193
Qatar 68, 69, 168, 206

R
Radioactivity 180, 213
Rangwala, Glen 58
Republican Guard 76, 77, 78, 80, 108, 132
Ritter, Scott 46, 47
Romania 163
Rumaylah 75, 198
Rumsfeld, Donald 48, 49, 51, 52,128, 129, 131, 133, 155, 166, 195
Russia 22, 33, 62, 66, 146, 173, 198

S
Sabra and Shatila 83
Sabri, Naji 61
Saleh, Ali Abdullah 85
Sanctions 18, 29, 31, 38, 39, 42, 44, 45, 46, 50, 53, 55, 56, 61, 72, 74, 75, 81, 86, 89, 98, 107, 114, 122, 159, 175, 177, 182, 184, 185, 191, 194, 195, 199, 202, 203, 205, 208
Saudi Arabia 15, 33, 39, 48, 68, 69, 85, 86, 148, 161, 162
SCIRI/ Supreme Council for islamic Revolution in Iraq 136
Shah of Iran 31, 32, 157, 235
Shawys, Rozh 143, 145
Sheikh 13, 27, 222, 223
Sheriff of Mecca 13, 25
Shi'ia 18, 20, 133, 138, 144, 148, 149, 156, 157, 164, 165, 166, 185, 192
shock and awe 7, 61, 63, 65, 67, 69, 71, 72, 73, 75, 77, 79, 81, 154, 166
SIGIR/ Special Inspector General for Iraq Reconstruction 174, 175, 176, 184, 185, 186, 198, 200, 202, 203, 204, 205, 206
SPC/ Special Police Commandos 156, 165
Steele, James 164, 166
Sunni 18, 20, 133, 135, 138, 143, 144, 145, 148, 149, 156, 164, 165, 170, 166, 192
Sweden 163

Switzerland 189
Sykes-Picot Agreement 13, 24
Syria 10, 12, 14, 15, 16, 17, 18, 22, 23, 25, 26, 32, 34, 35, 36, 39, 40, 42, 43, 44, 48, 65, 83, 85, 101, 111, 136, 146, 157, 163, 166, 175, 189, 192, 206

T
tanks 65, 76, 78, 80, 81, 83, 111, 203
Thabit, General Adnan 165
Thatcher, Margaret 85
The Lancet 160
The Transitional Administrative Law (TAL) 121, 138, 139
Thring, James 6, 21
Tigris River 80, 205
Tikrit 73, 77, 78
torture 162, 163, 164, 165, 166, 183, 192, 214, 215, 217, 218, 219
Turkey 15, 19, 20, 22, 26, 39, 48, 68, 77, 78, 146, 198

U
UIA/ The United Iraqi Alliance 144, 145
Ukraine 83, 173
umma 32, 36
UNAMI/ United Nations Assistance Mission for Iraq 96, 97, 162, 217
UNDP 158, 188, 200, 201, 202
UNESCO 184, 185
UNHCR 171
UNICEF 177, 188, 203
UNMOVIC/ The United Nations Monitoring, Verification and Inspection Commission 58, 65, 96
UNSCOM/ The United Nations Special Commission 72, 88
Uranium 73, 177, 178, 179, 181, 212, 213
USA 33, 34, 35, 36, 37, 55, 67, 83, 85, 87, 99, 146, 147, 153, 170, 196

V

Vichy Government 94, 136
Vietnam 67, 78, 164

W

Wahhabis 20
Wallace, Lt. General William 73
Waxman, Representative Henry 126
Wikileaks 162, 164
WMDs 23, 41, 48, 52, 55, 57, 58, 59,
    62, 66, 71, 72, 79, 86, 88, 96, 98,
    101, 109, 173, 174, 177, 196,
    205, 212
Wolfowitz, Paul D. 51, 134, 142
Woolsey, James 42, 43
WWI 12, 13, 15, 40, 43, 145, 146,
    148
WWII 15, 26, 27, 33, 40, 42, 43, 82,
    83, 86, 87, 90, 99, 100, 147, 192,
    208

Y

Yemen 86, 175

Z

Zaire 85
Zalloum, Dr Abdulhay Yahya 197
Zionism 16, 17, 20, 36, 40, 43, 48,
    105, 147
Zionists 11, 14, 16, 17, 21, 34, 40,
    43, 44, 45, 46, 47, 102, 103, 105,
    138, 145, 147, 150, 166, 195
Zubayr 75

Made in the USA
Monee, IL
24 April 2022

95323513R00154